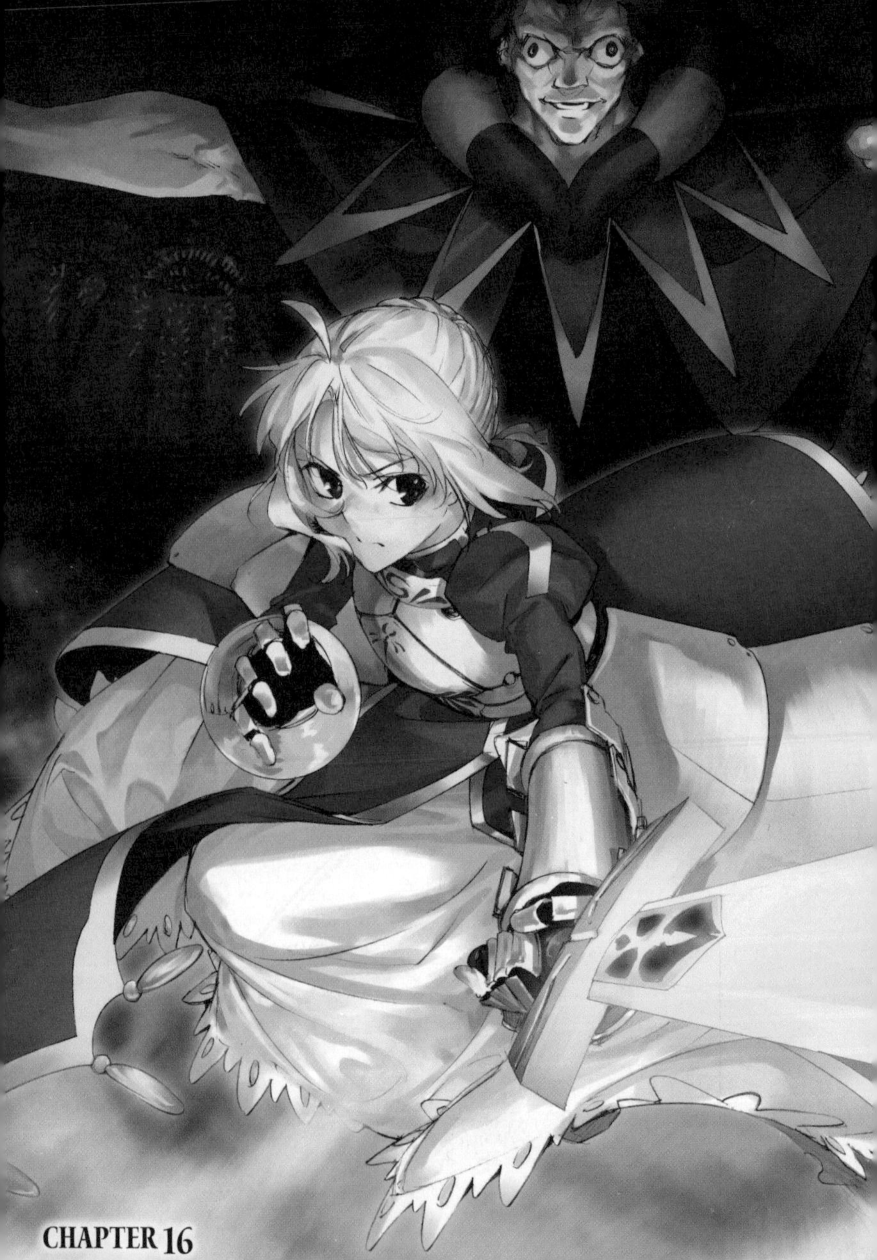

CHAPTER 16

Fate/Zero

フェイト／ゼロ

4

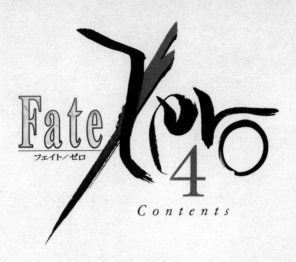

Contents

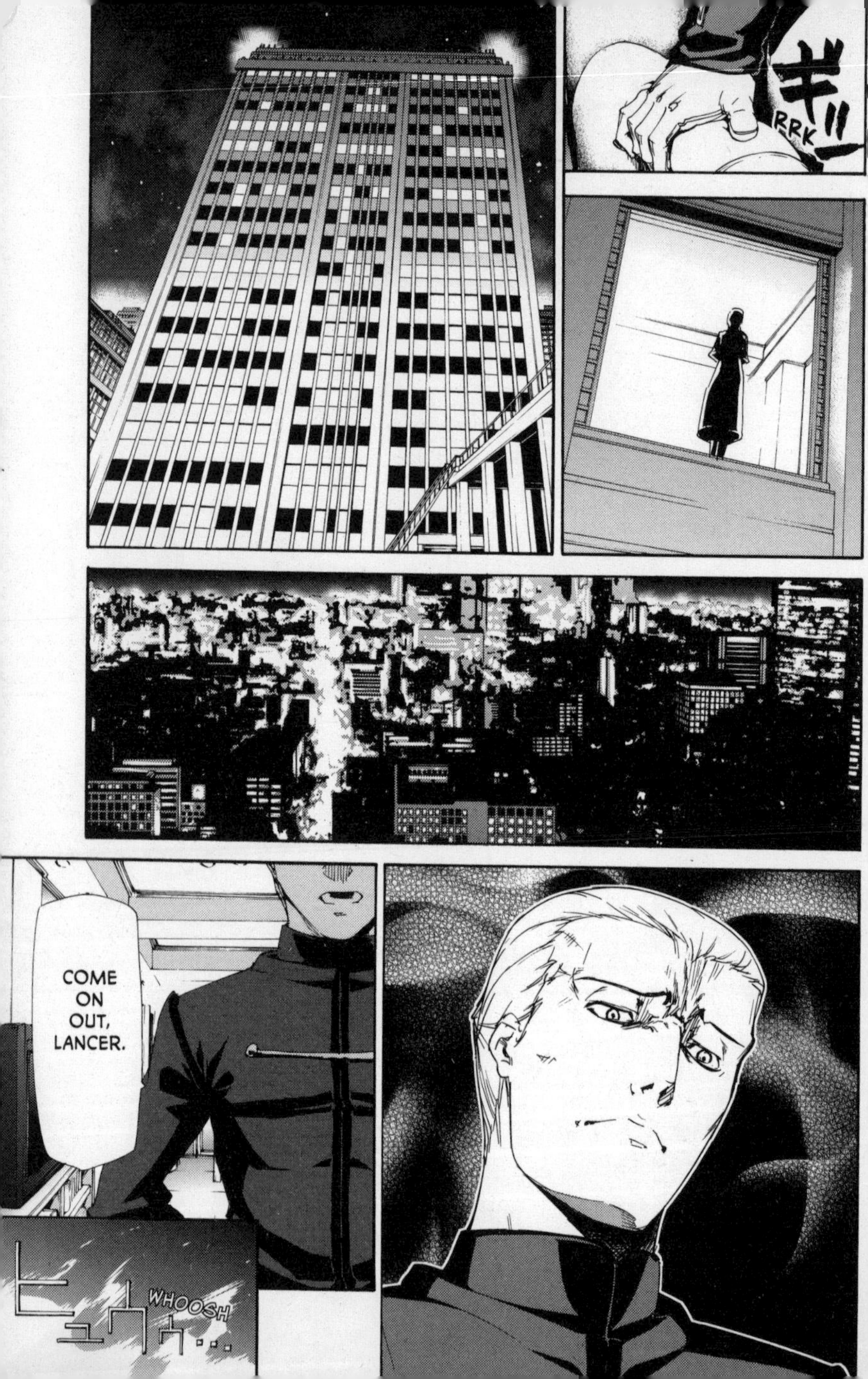
ギリ
RRK
COME ON OUT, LANCER.
ヒュウゥ…
WHOOSH

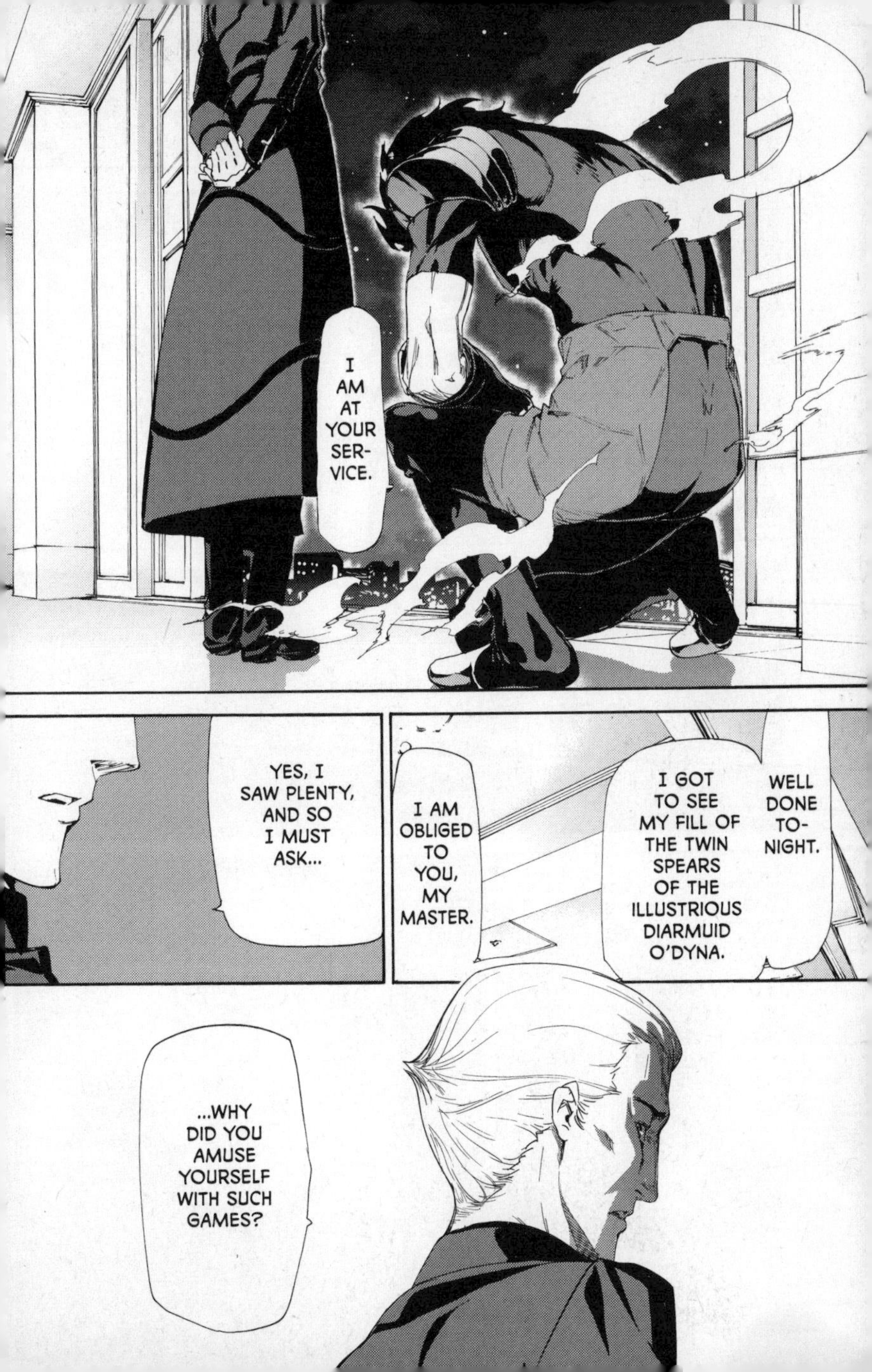
I AM AT YOUR SERVICE.
WELL DONE TONIGHT.
I GOT TO SEE MY FILL OF THE TWIN SPEARS OF THE ILLUSTRIOUS DIARMUID O'DYNA.
I AM OBLIGED TO YOU, MY MASTER.
YES, I SAW PLENTY, AND SO I MUST ASK...
...WHY DID YOU AMUSE YOURSELF WITH SUCH GAMES?

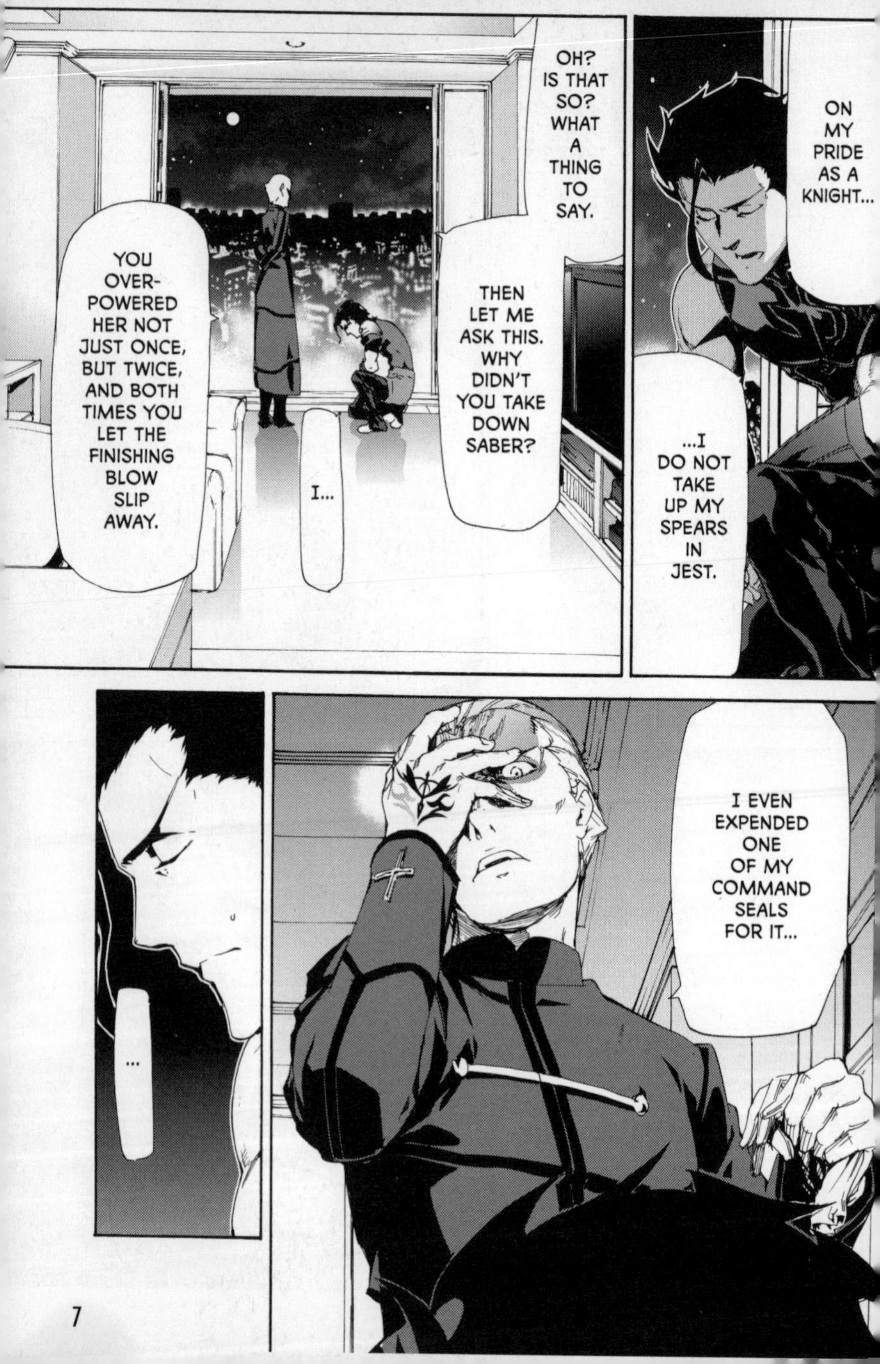
ON MY PRIDE AS A KNIGHT...
...I DO NOT TAKE UP MY SPEARS IN JEST.
OH? IS THAT SO? WHAT A THING TO SAY.
THEN LET ME ASK THIS. WHY DIDN'T YOU TAKE DOWN SABER?
YOU OVER-POWERED HER NOT JUST ONCE, BUT TWICE, AND BOTH TIMES YOU LET THE FINISHING BLOW SLIP AWAY.
I...
I EVEN EXPENDED ONE OF MY COMMAND SEALS FOR IT...
...

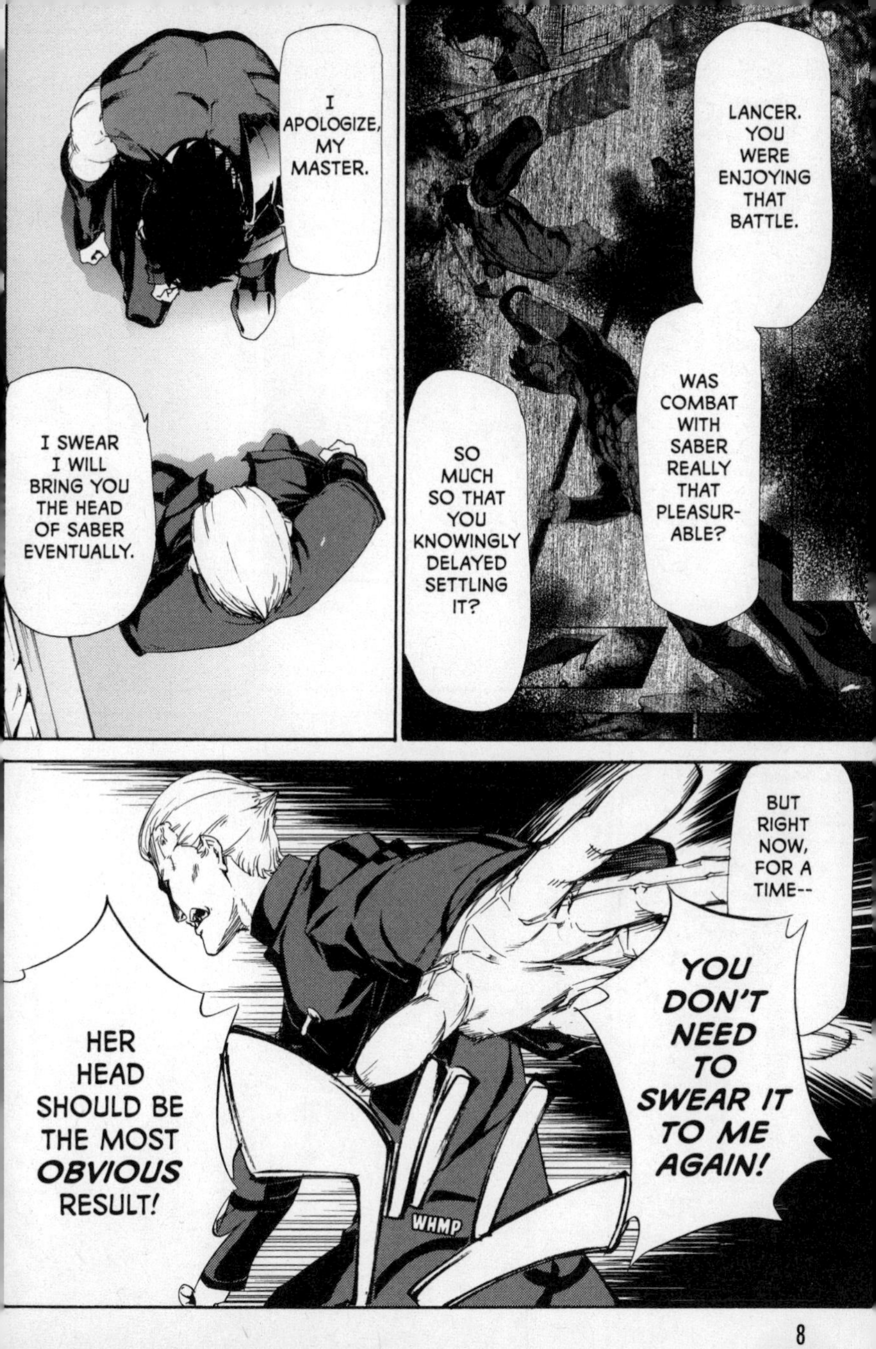
LANCER. YOU WERE ENJOYING THAT BATTLE.
WAS COMBAT WITH SABER REALLY THAT PLEASUR-ABLE?
SO MUCH SO THAT YOU KNOWINGLY DELAYED SETTLING IT?
I APOLOGIZE, MY MASTER.
I SWEAR I WILL BRING YOU THE HEAD OF SABER EVENTUALLY.
BUT RIGHT NOW, FOR A TIME--
YOU DON'T NEED TO SWEAR IT TO ME AGAIN!
HER HEAD SHOULD BE THE MOST OBVIOUS RESULT!
WHMP

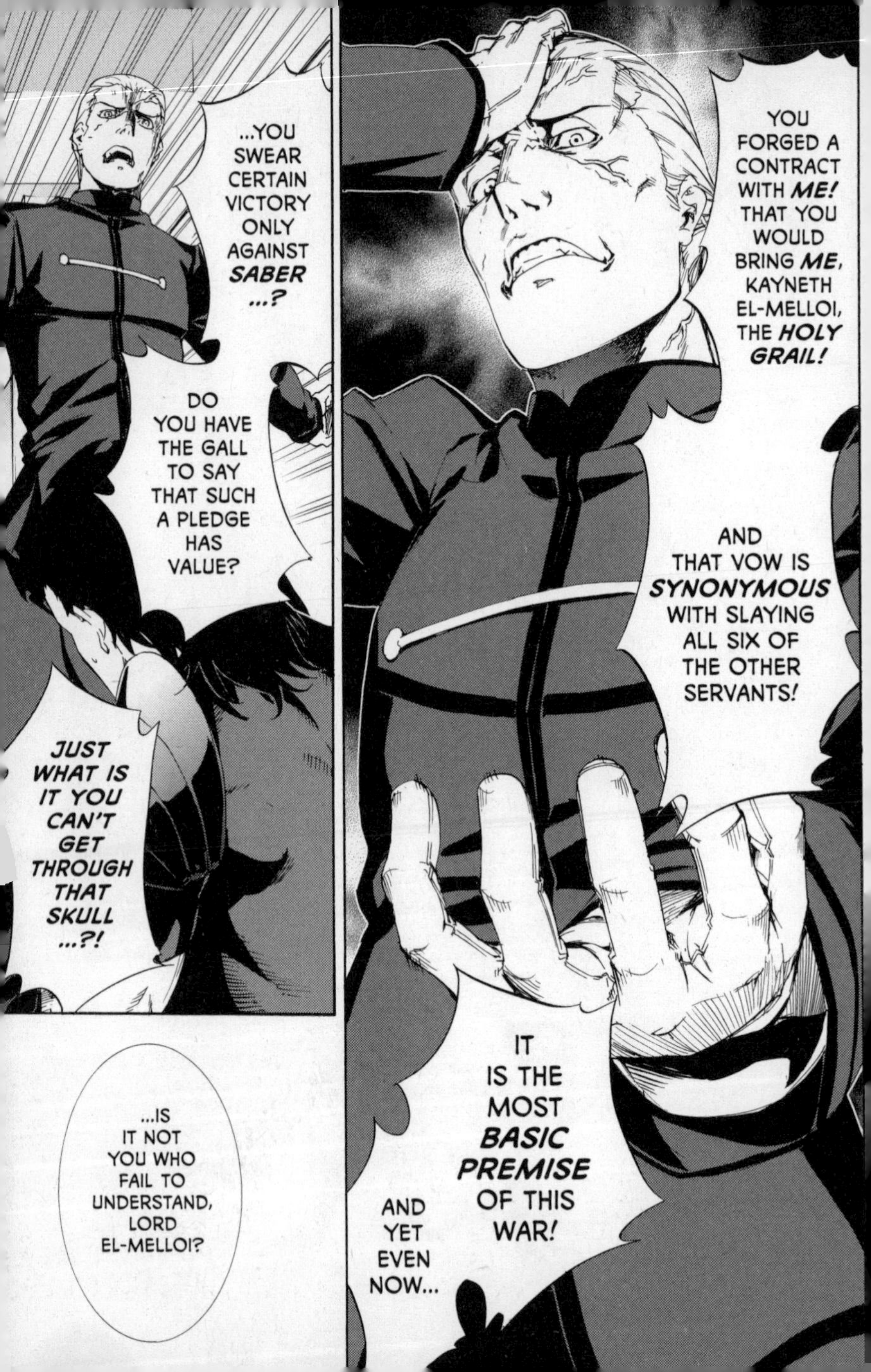
YOU FORGED A CONTRACT WITH ME! THAT YOU WOULD BRING ME, KAYNETH EL-MELLOI, THE HOLY GRAIL!
AND THAT VOW IS SYNONYMOUS WITH SLAYING ALL SIX OF THE OTHER SERVANTS!
IT IS THE MOST BASIC PREMISE OF THIS WAR!
AND YET EVEN NOW...
...YOU SWEAR CERTAIN VICTORY ONLY AGAINST SABER ...?
DO YOU HAVE THE GALL TO SAY THAT SUCH A PLEDGE HAS VALUE?
JUST WHAT IS IT YOU CAN'T GET THROUGH THAT SKULL ...?!
...IS IT NOT YOU WHO FAIL TO UNDERSTAND, LORD EL-MELLOI?

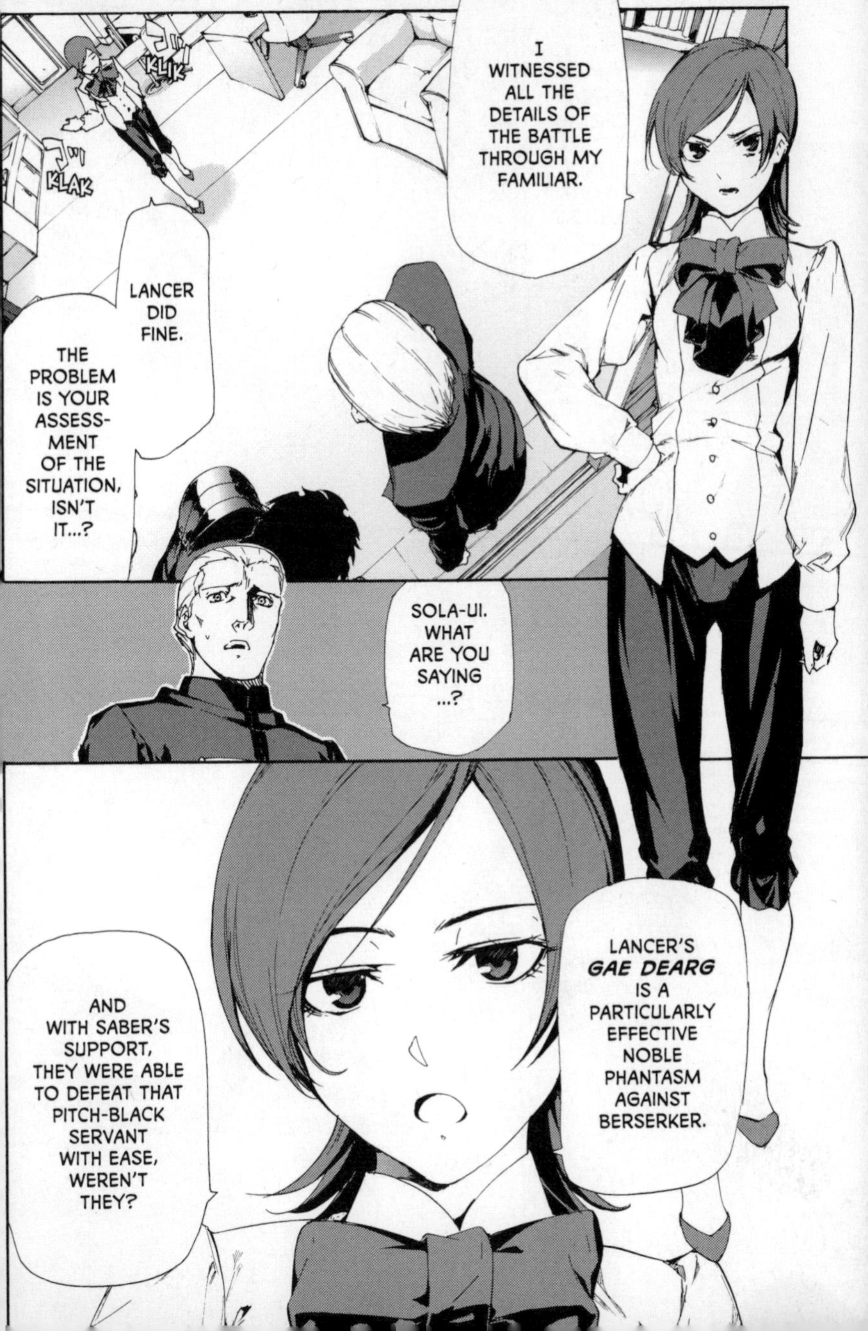
I WITNESSED ALL THE DETAILS OF THE BATTLE THROUGH MY FAMILIAR.
KLIK
KLAK
LANCER DID FINE.
THE PROBLEM IS YOUR ASSESS-MENT OF THE SITUATION, ISN'T IT...?
SOLA-UI. WHAT ARE YOU SAYING ...?
LANCER'S *GAE DEARG* IS A PARTICULARLY EFFECTIVE NOBLE PHANTASM AGAINST BERSERKER.
AND WITH SABER'S SUPPORT, THEY WERE ABLE TO DEFEAT THAT PITCH-BLACK SERVANT WITH EASE, WEREN'T THEY?

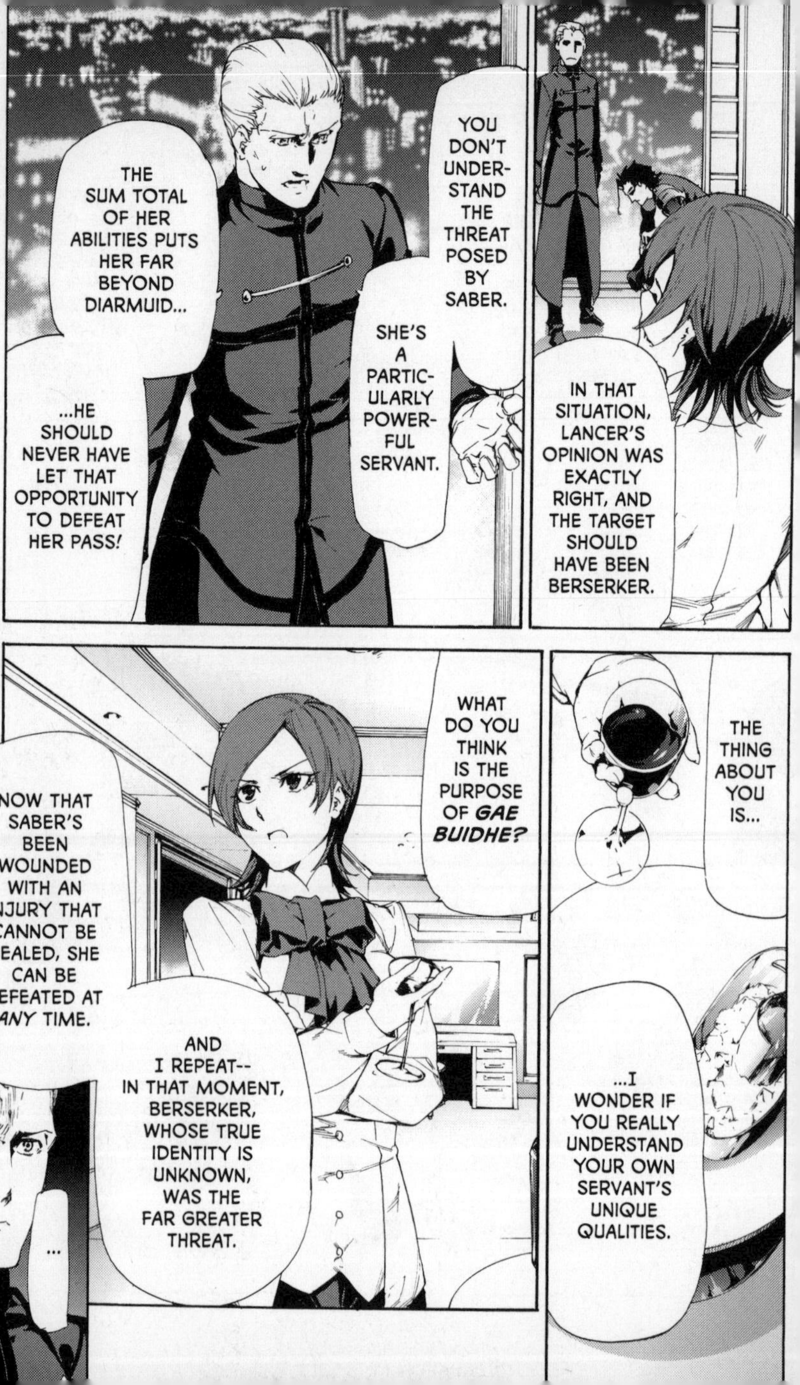
IN THAT SITUATION, LANCER'S OPINION WAS EXACTLY RIGHT, AND THE TARGET SHOULD HAVE BEEN BERSERKER.
YOU DON'T UNDER-STAND THE THREAT POSED BY SABER.
SHE'S A PARTIC-ULARLY POWER-FUL SERVANT.
THE SUM TOTAL OF HER ABILITIES PUTS HER FAR BEYOND DIARMUID...
...HE SHOULD NEVER HAVE LET THAT OPPORTUNITY TO DEFEAT HER PASS!
THE THING ABOUT YOU IS...
...I WONDER IF YOU REALLY UNDERSTAND YOUR OWN SERVANT'S UNIQUE QUALITIES.
WHAT DO YOU THINK IS THE PURPOSE OF *GAE BUIDHE?*
NOW THAT SABER'S BEEN WOUNDED WITH AN INJURY THAT CANNOT BE HEALED, SHE CAN BE DEFEATED AT *ANY* TIME.
AND I REPEAT-- IN THAT MOMENT, BERSERKER, WHOSE TRUE IDENTITY IS UNKNOWN, WAS THE FAR GREATER THREAT.
...

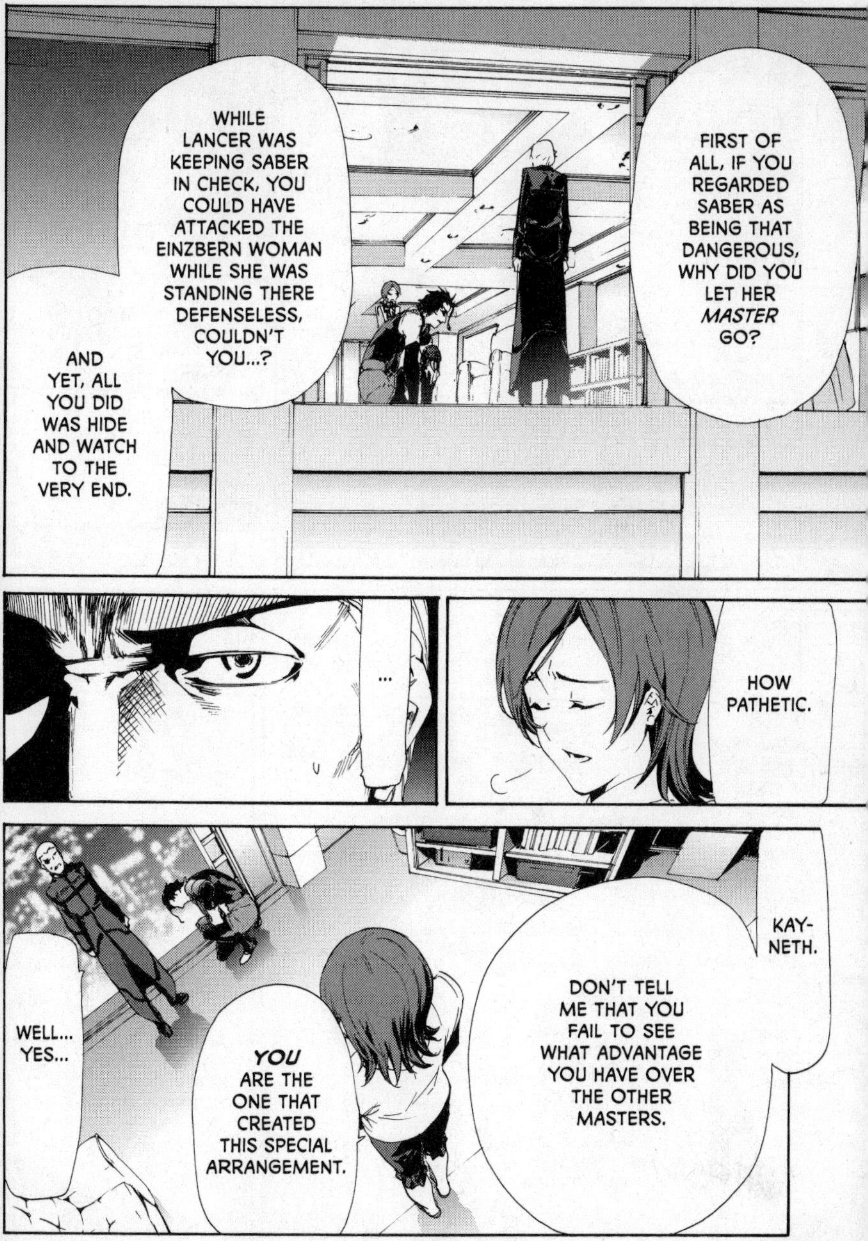
FIRST OF ALL, IF YOU REGARDED SABER AS BEING THAT DANGEROUS, WHY DID YOU LET HER *MASTER* GO?
WHILE LANCER WAS KEEPING SABER IN CHECK, YOU COULD HAVE ATTACKED THE EINZBERN WOMAN WHILE SHE WAS STANDING THERE DEFENSELESS, COULDN'T YOU...?
AND YET, ALL YOU DID WAS HIDE AND WATCH TO THE VERY END.
HOW PATHETIC.
...
KAY-NETH.
DON'T TELL ME THAT YOU FAIL TO SEE WHAT ADVANTAGE YOU HAVE OVER THE OTHER MASTERS.
YOU ARE THE ONE THAT CREATED THIS SPECIAL ARRANGEMENT.
WELL... YES...

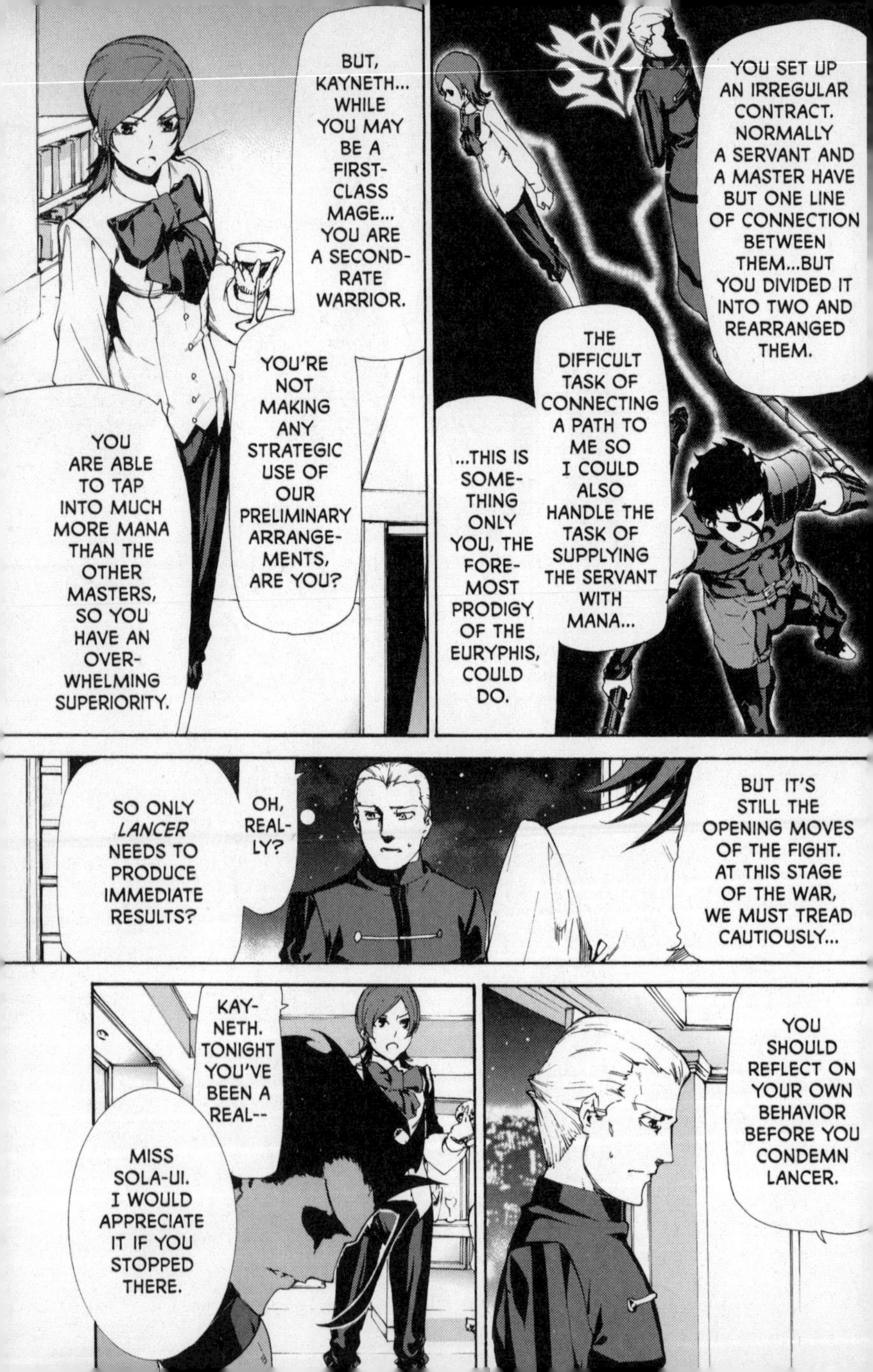
BUT, KAYNETH... WHILE YOU MAY BE A FIRST-CLASS MAGE... YOU ARE A SECOND-RATE WARRIOR.
YOU'RE NOT MAKING ANY STRATEGIC USE OF OUR PRELIMINARY ARRANGE-MENTS, ARE YOU?
YOU ARE ABLE TO TAP INTO MUCH MORE MANA THAN THE OTHER MASTERS, SO YOU HAVE AN OVER-WHELMING SUPERIORITY.
YOU SET UP AN IRREGULAR CONTRACT. NORMALLY A SERVANT AND A MASTER HAVE BUT ONE LINE OF CONNECTION BETWEEN THEM...BUT YOU DIVIDED IT INTO TWO AND REARRANGED THEM.
THE DIFFICULT TASK OF CONNECTING A PATH TO ME SO I COULD ALSO HANDLE THE TASK OF SUPPLYING THE SERVANT WITH MANA...
...THIS IS SOME-THING ONLY YOU, THE FORE-MOST PRODIGY OF THE EURYPHIS, COULD DO.
SO ONLY *LANCER* NEEDS TO PRODUCE IMMEDIATE RESULTS?
OH, REAL-LY?
BUT IT'S STILL THE OPENING MOVES OF THE FIGHT. AT THIS STAGE OF THE WAR, WE MUST TREAD CAUTIOUSLY...
KAY-NETH. TONIGHT YOU'VE BEEN A REAL--
MISS SOLA-UI. I WOULD APPRECIATE IT IF YOU STOPPED THERE.
YOU SHOULD REFLECT ON YOUR OWN BEHAVIOR BEFORE YOU CONDEMN LANCER.

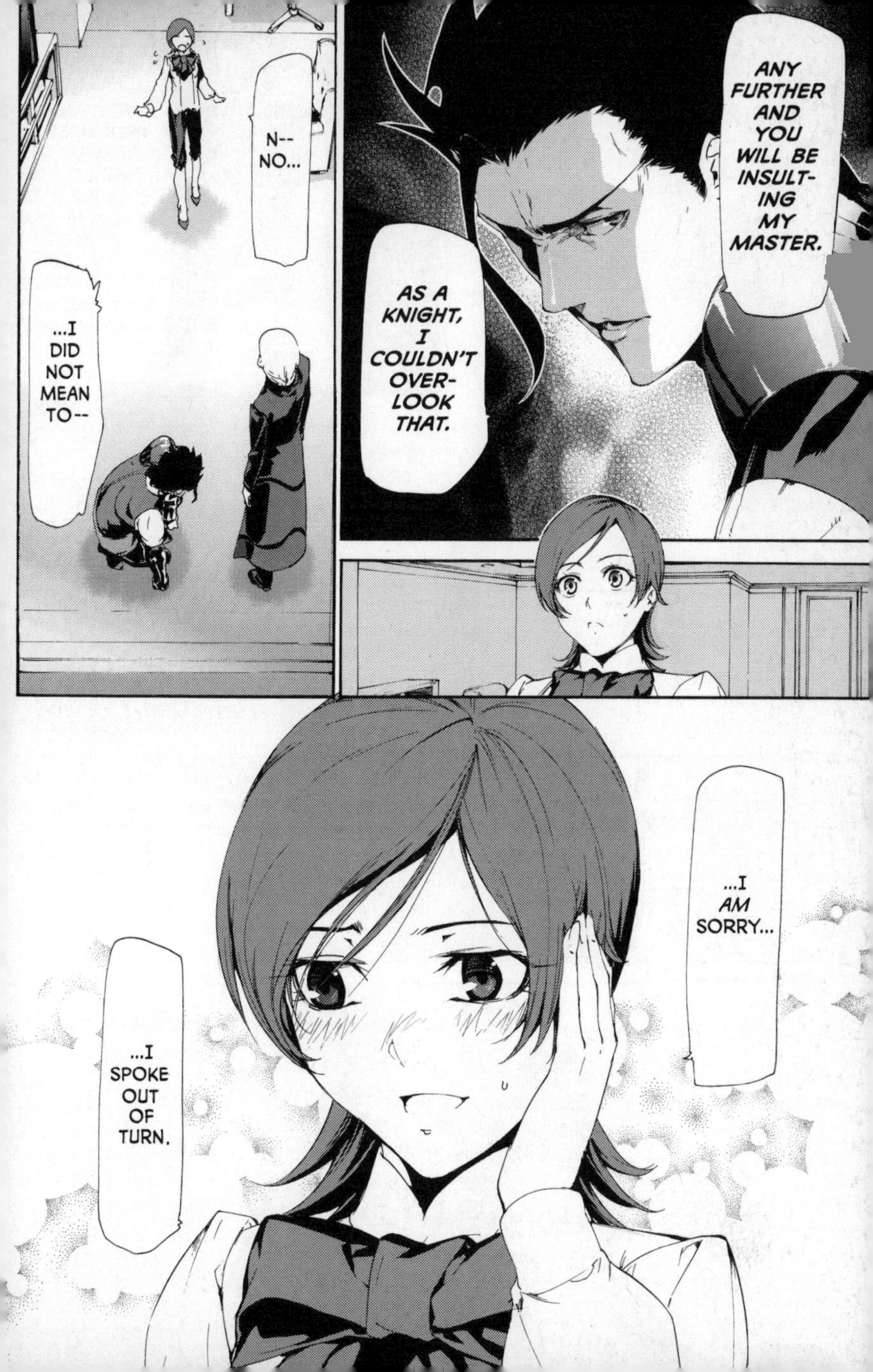
ANY FURTHER AND YOU WILL BE INSULT-ING MY MASTER.
AS A KNIGHT, I COULDN'T OVER-LOOK THAT.
N-- NO...
...I DID NOT MEAN TO--
...I AM SORRY...
...I SPOKE OUT OF TURN.

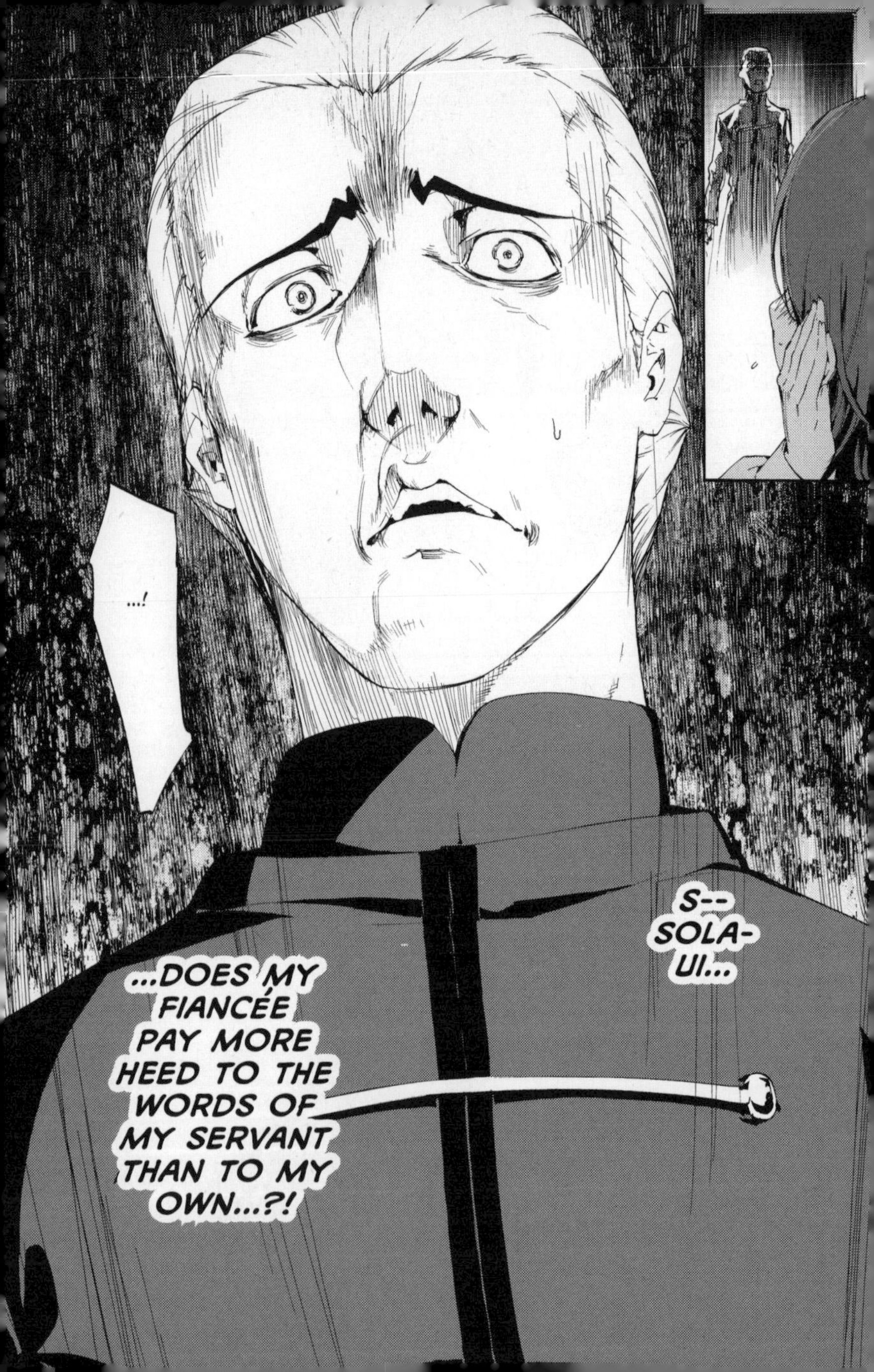
...!
S-- SOLA-UI...
...DOES MY FIANCÉE PAY MORE HEED TO THE WORDS OF MY SERVANT THAN TO MY OWN...?!

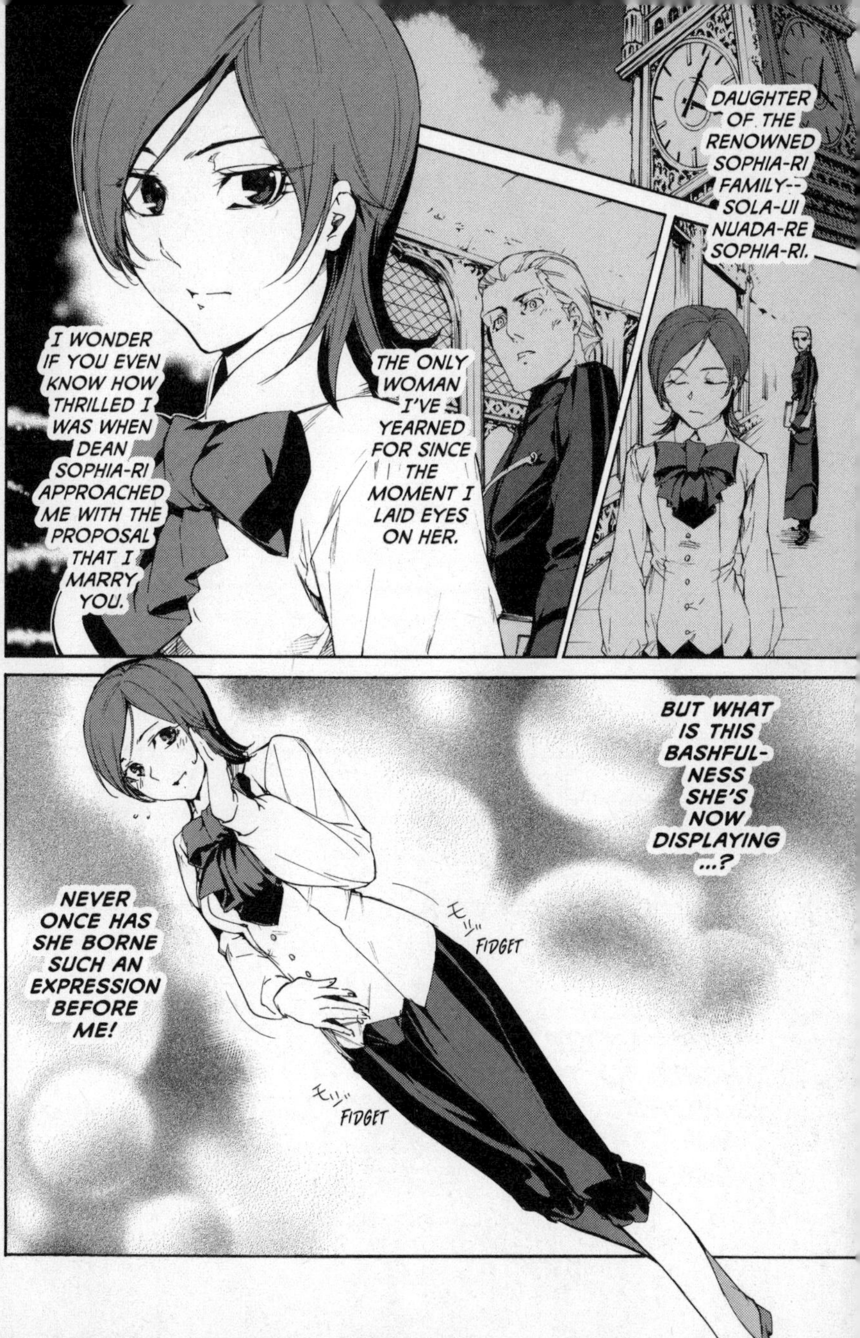
DAUGHTER OF THE RENOWNED SOPHIA-RI FAMILY-- SOLA-UI NUADA-RE SOPHIA-RI.
THE ONLY WOMAN I'VE YEARNED FOR SINCE THE MOMENT I LAID EYES ON HER.
I WONDER IF YOU EVEN KNOW HOW THRILLED I WAS WHEN DEAN SOPHIA-RI APPROACHED ME WITH THE PROPOSAL THAT I MARRY YOU.
BUT WHAT IS THIS BASHFUL-NESS SHE'S NOW DISPLAYING ...?
NEVER ONCE HAS SHE BORNE SUCH AN EXPRESSION BEFORE ME!
モジ FIDGET
モジ FIDGET

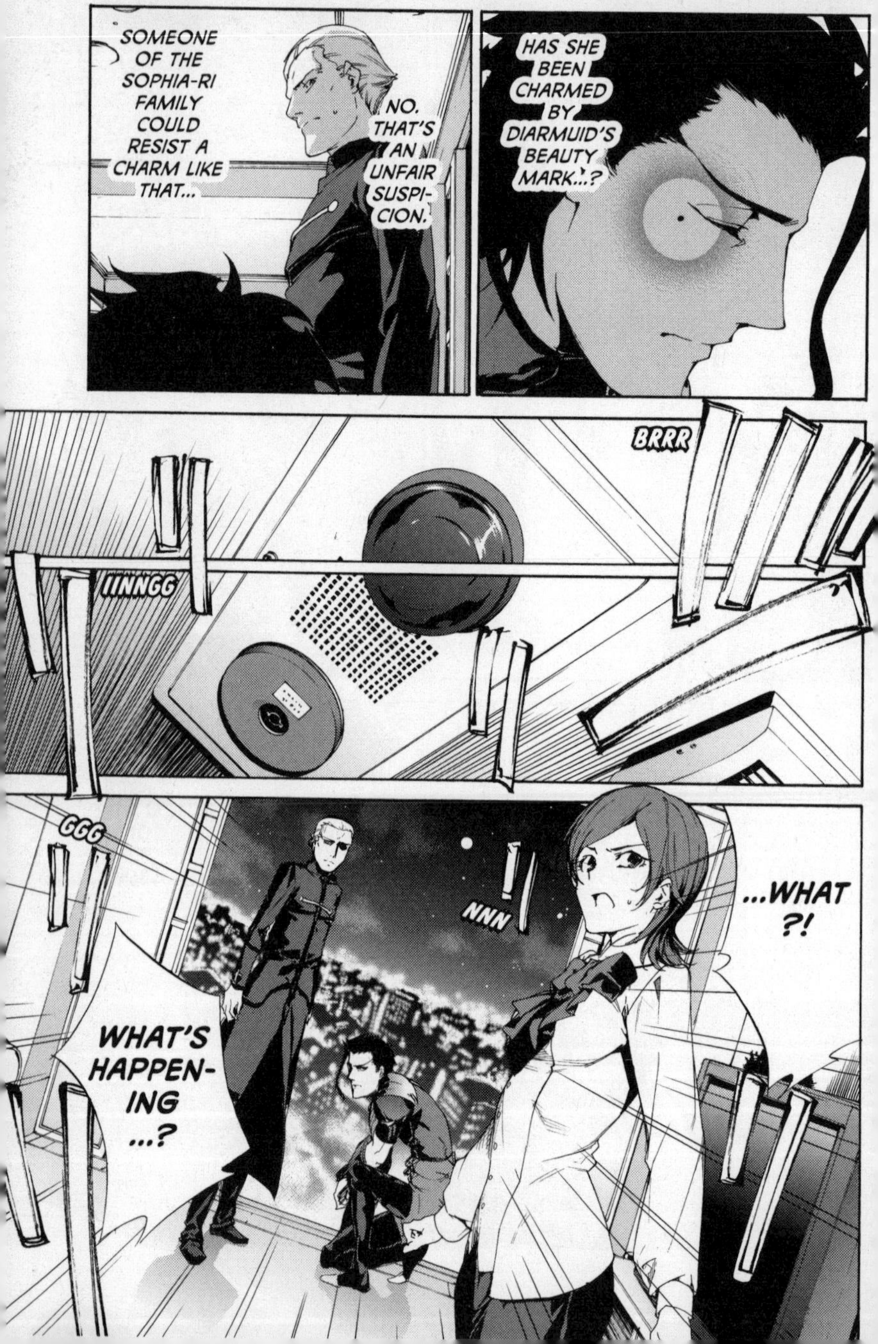
HAS SHE BEEN CHARMED BY DIARMUID'S BEAUTY MARK...?
SOMEONE OF THE SOPHIA-RI FAMILY COULD RESIST A CHARM LIKE THAT...
NO. THAT'S AN UNFAIR SUSPICION.
BRRR
IINNGG
...WHAT ?!
NNN
GGG
WHAT'S HAPPENING ...?

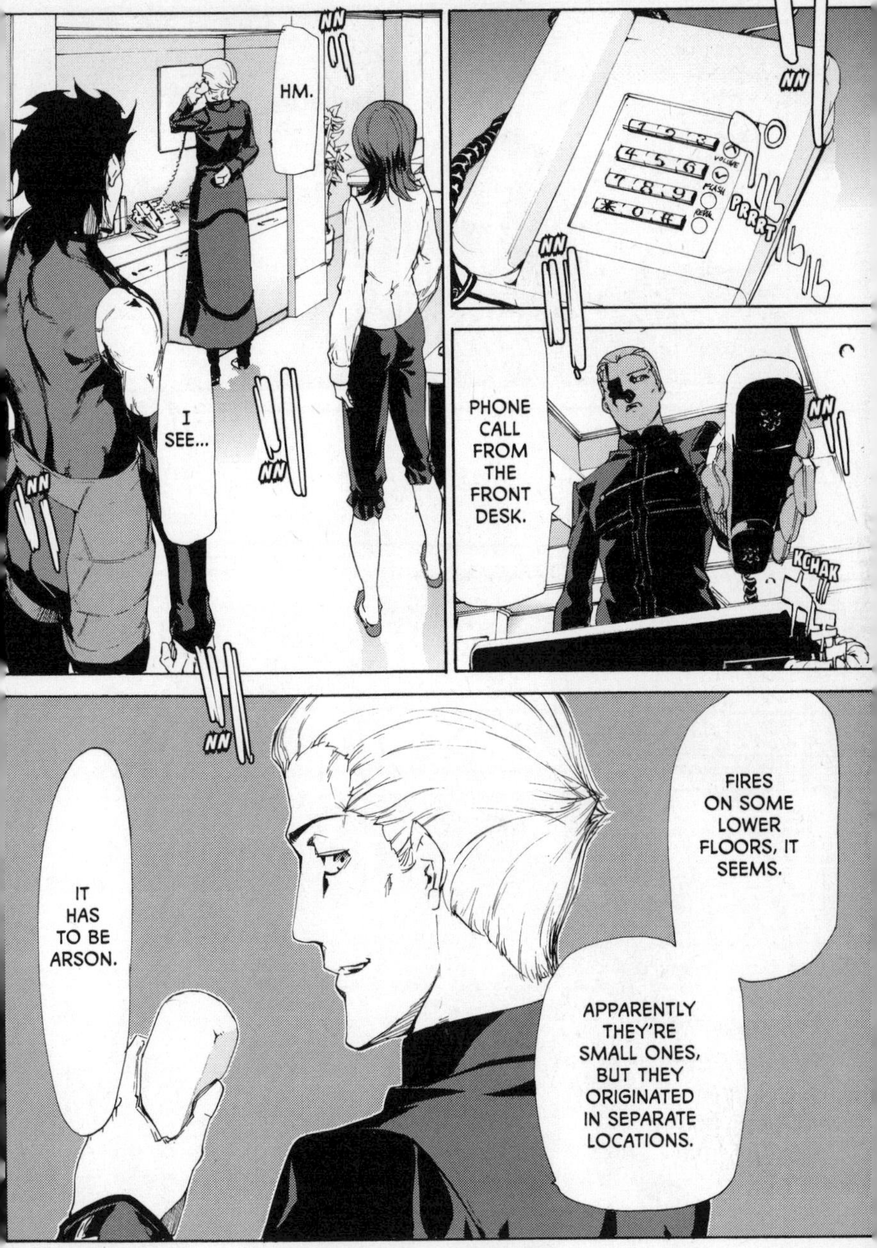
NN
PRRRT
NN
NN
PHONE CALL FROM THE FRONT DESK.
KCHAK
NN
HM.
I SEE...
NN
NN
NN
FIRES ON SOME LOWER FLOORS, IT SEEMS.
APPARENTLY THEY'RE SMALL ONES, BUT THEY ORIGINATED IN SEPARATE LOCATIONS.
IT HAS TO BE ARSON.

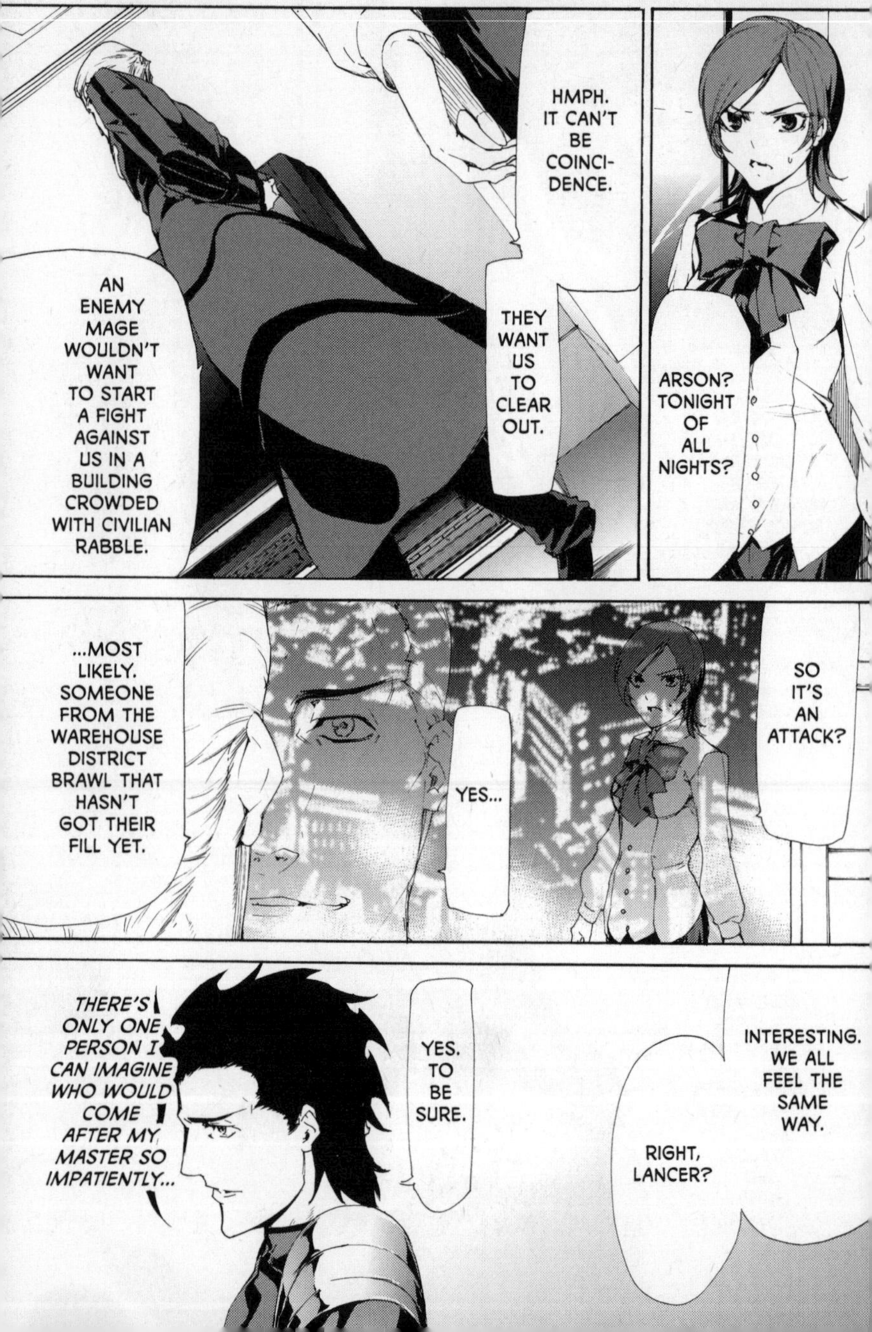
ARSON? TONIGHT OF ALL NIGHTS?
HMPH. IT CAN'T BE COINCIDENCE.
THEY WANT US TO CLEAR OUT.
AN ENEMY MAGE WOULDN'T WANT TO START A FIGHT AGAINST US IN A BUILDING CROWDED WITH CIVILIAN RABBLE.
SO IT'S AN ATTACK?
YES...
...MOST LIKELY. SOMEONE FROM THE WAREHOUSE DISTRICT BRAWL THAT HASN'T GOT THEIR FILL YET.
INTERESTING. WE ALL FEEL THE SAME WAY.
RIGHT, LANCER?
YES. TO BE SURE.
THERE'S ONLY ONE PERSON I CAN IMAGINE WHO WOULD COME AFTER MY MASTER SO IMPATIENTLY...

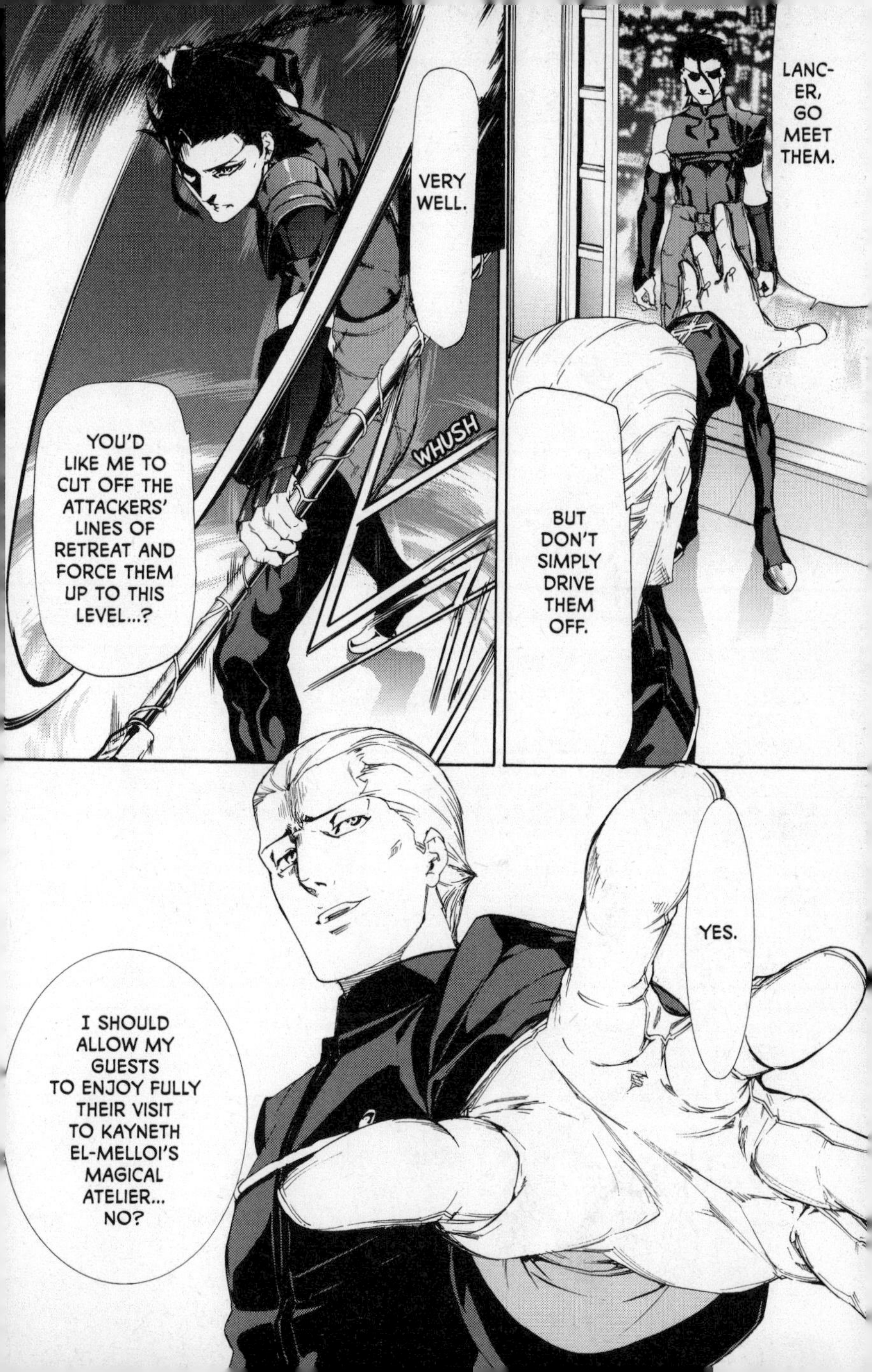
LANCER, GO MEET THEM.
BUT DON'T SIMPLY DRIVE THEM OFF.
VERY WELL.
YOU'D LIKE ME TO CUT OFF THE ATTACKERS' LINES OF RETREAT AND FORCE THEM UP TO THIS LEVEL...?
WHUSH
YES.
I SHOULD ALLOW MY GUESTS TO ENJOY FULLY THEIR VISIT TO KAYNETH EL-MELLOI'S MAGICAL ATELIER... NO?

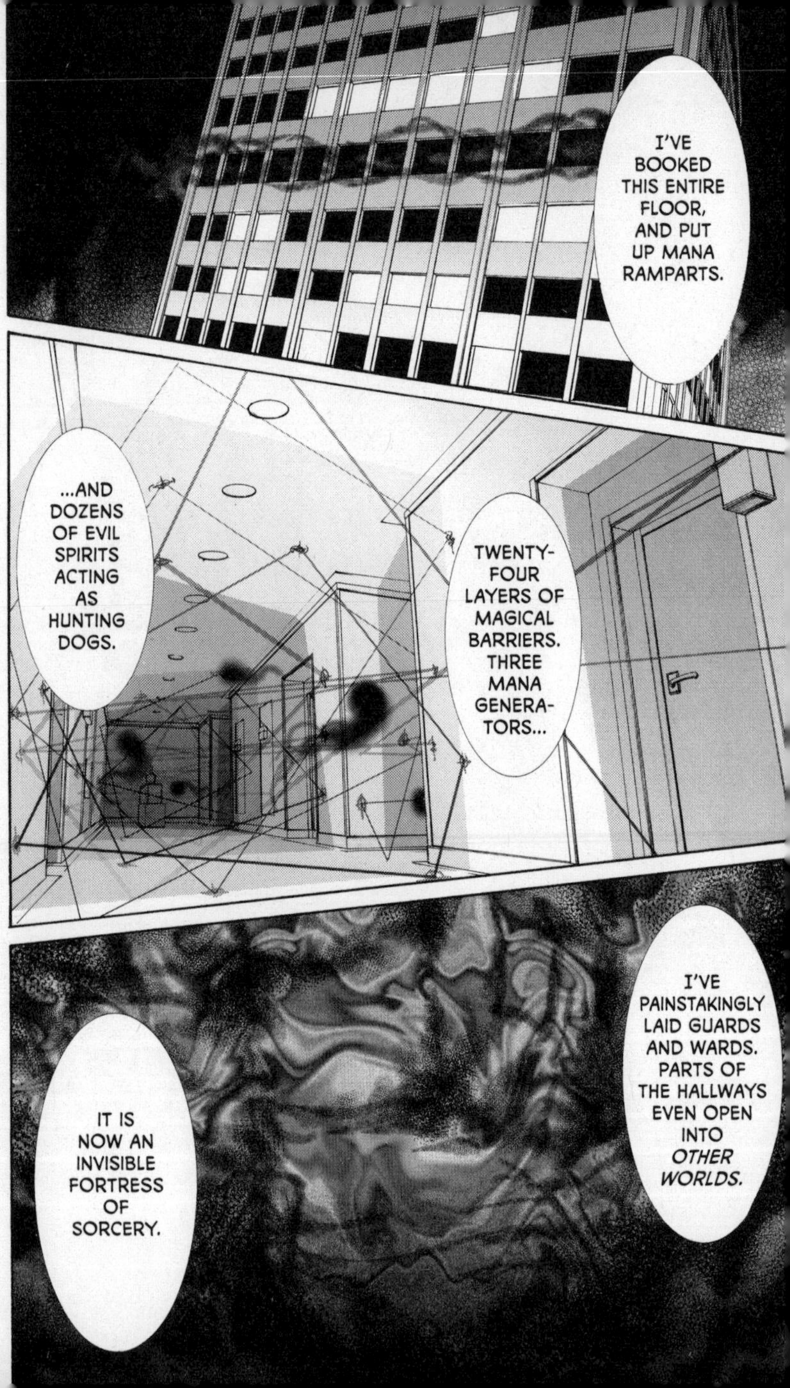
I'VE BOOKED THIS ENTIRE FLOOR, AND PUT UP MANA RAMPARTS.
TWENTY-FOUR LAYERS OF MAGICAL BARRIERS. THREE MANA GENERA-TORS...
...AND DOZENS OF EVIL SPIRITS ACTING AS HUNTING DOGS.
I'VE PAINSTAKINGLY LAID GUARDS AND WARDS. PARTS OF THE HALLWAYS EVEN OPEN INTO *OTHER WORLDS.*
IT IS NOW AN INVISIBLE FORTRESS OF SORCERY.

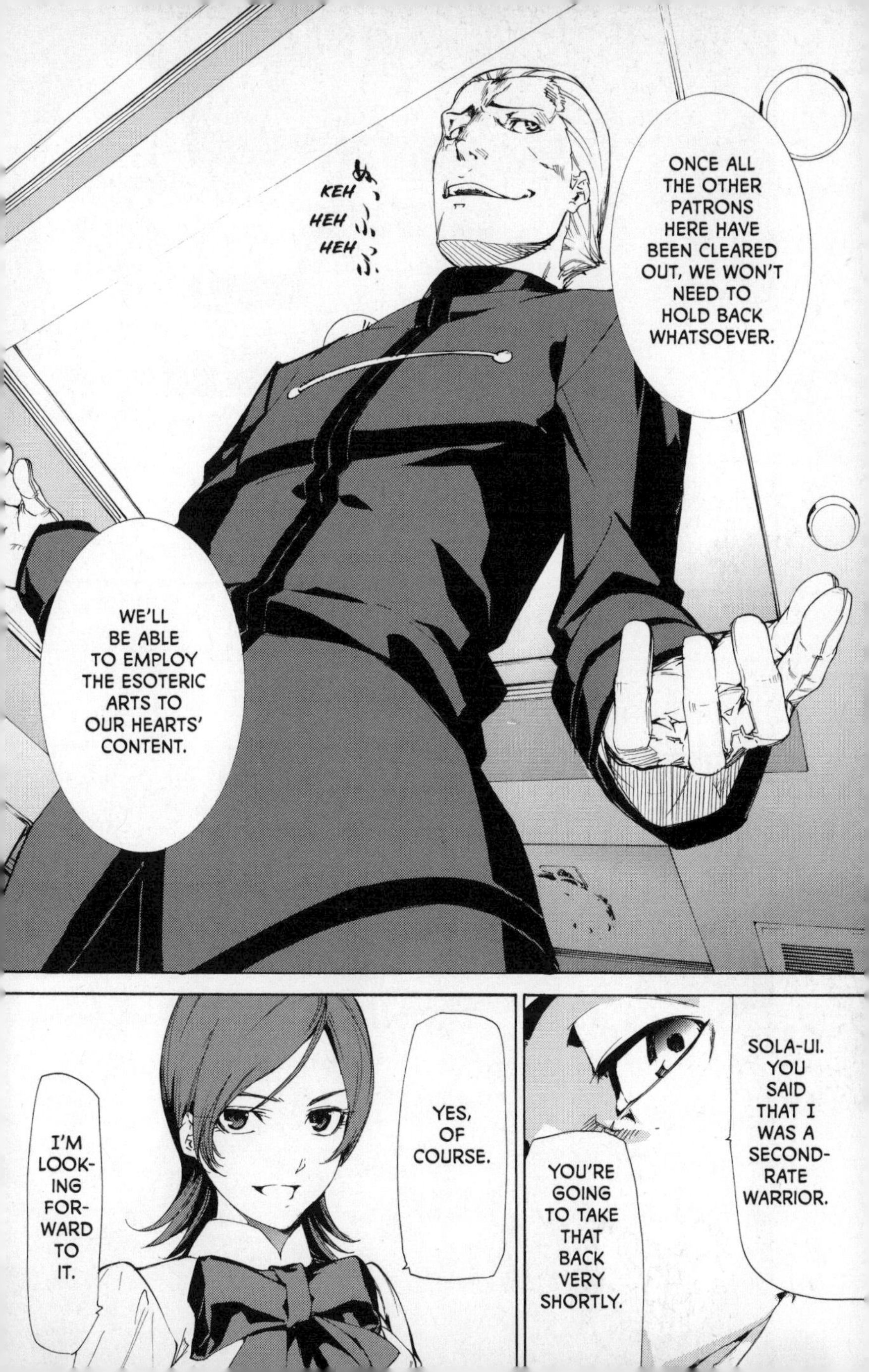
ONCE ALL THE OTHER PATRONS HERE HAVE BEEN CLEARED OUT, WE WON'T NEED TO HOLD BACK WHATSOEVER.
KEH HEH HEH
WE'LL BE ABLE TO EMPLOY THE ESOTERIC ARTS TO OUR HEARTS' CONTENT.
SOLA-UI. YOU SAID THAT I WAS A SECOND-RATE WARRIOR.
YOU'RE GOING TO TAKE THAT BACK VERY SHORTLY.
YES, OF COURSE.
I'M LOOKING-ING FOR-WARD TO IT.

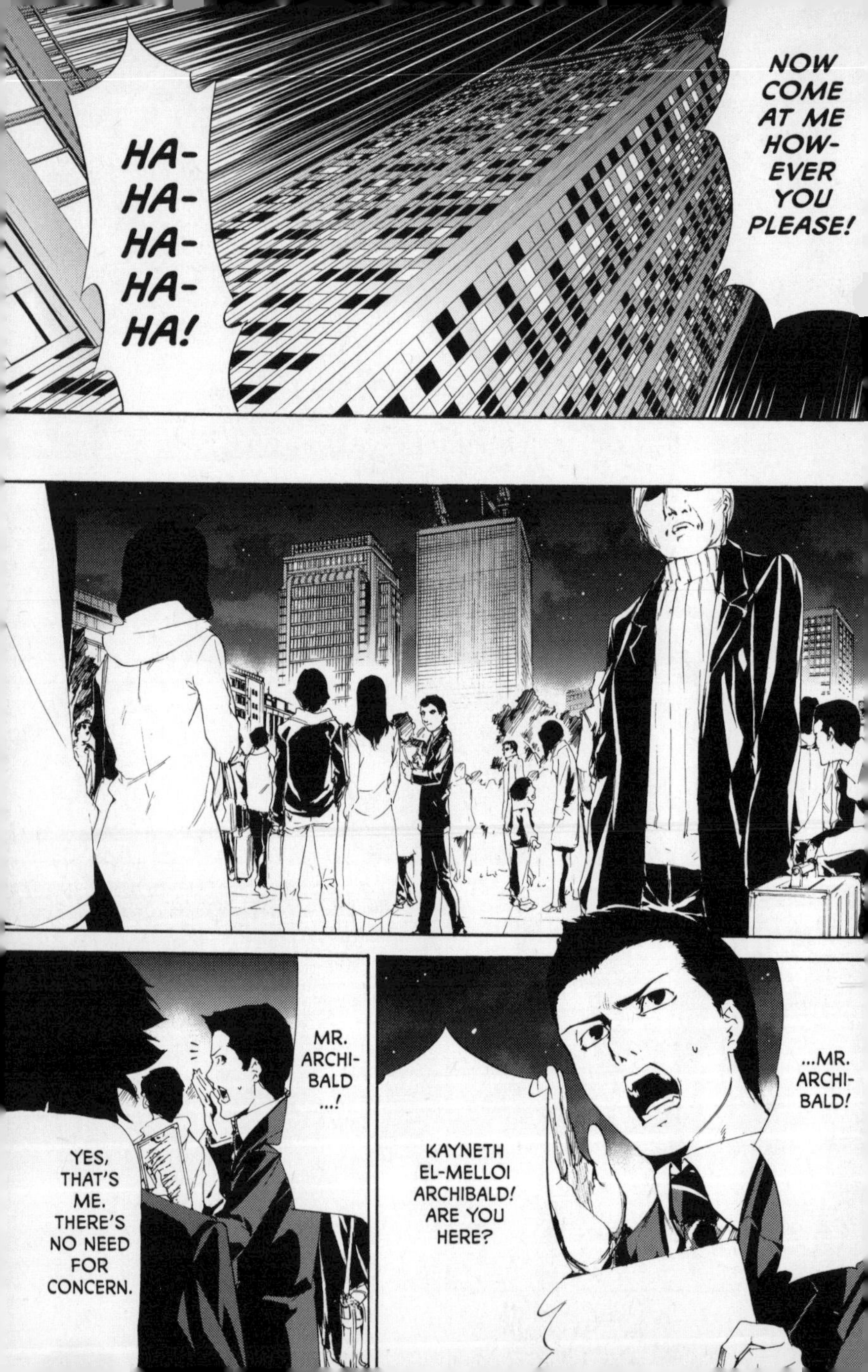
NOW COME AT ME HOW-EVER YOU PLEASE!
HA-HA-HA-HA-HA!
...MR. ARCHI-BALD!
KAYNETH EL-MELLOI ARCHIBALD! ARE YOU HERE?
MR. ARCHI-BALD ...!
YES, THAT'S ME. THERE'S NO NEED FOR CONCERN.

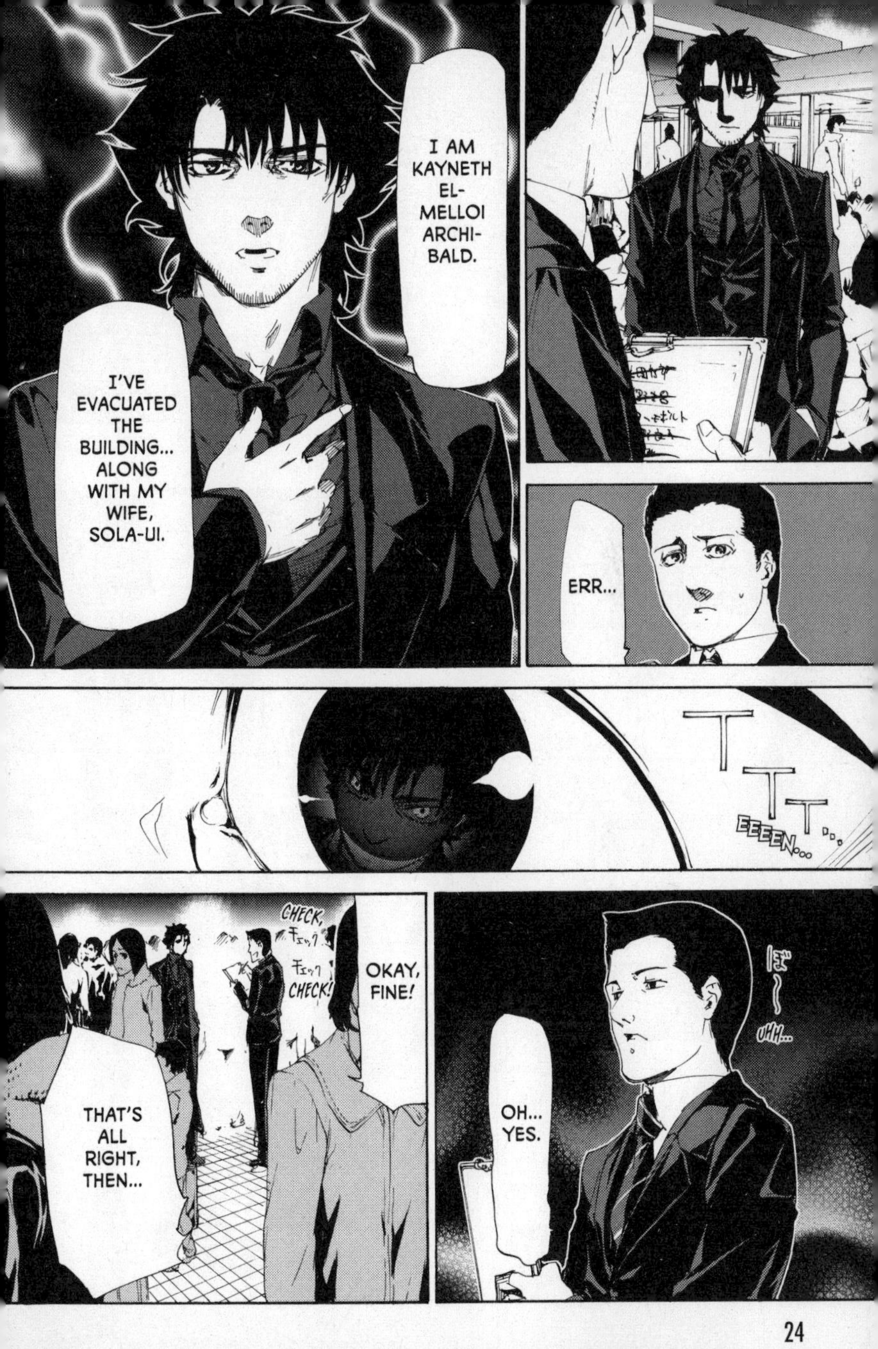
ERR...
I AM KAYNETH EL-MELLOI ARCHIBALD.
I'VE EVACUATED THE BUILDING... ALONG WITH MY WIFE, SOLA-UI.
TTTEEEEN...
ぼ~
UHH...
OH... YES.
OKAY, FINE!
CHECK, チェック
チェック CHECK!
THAT'S ALL RIGHT, THEN...

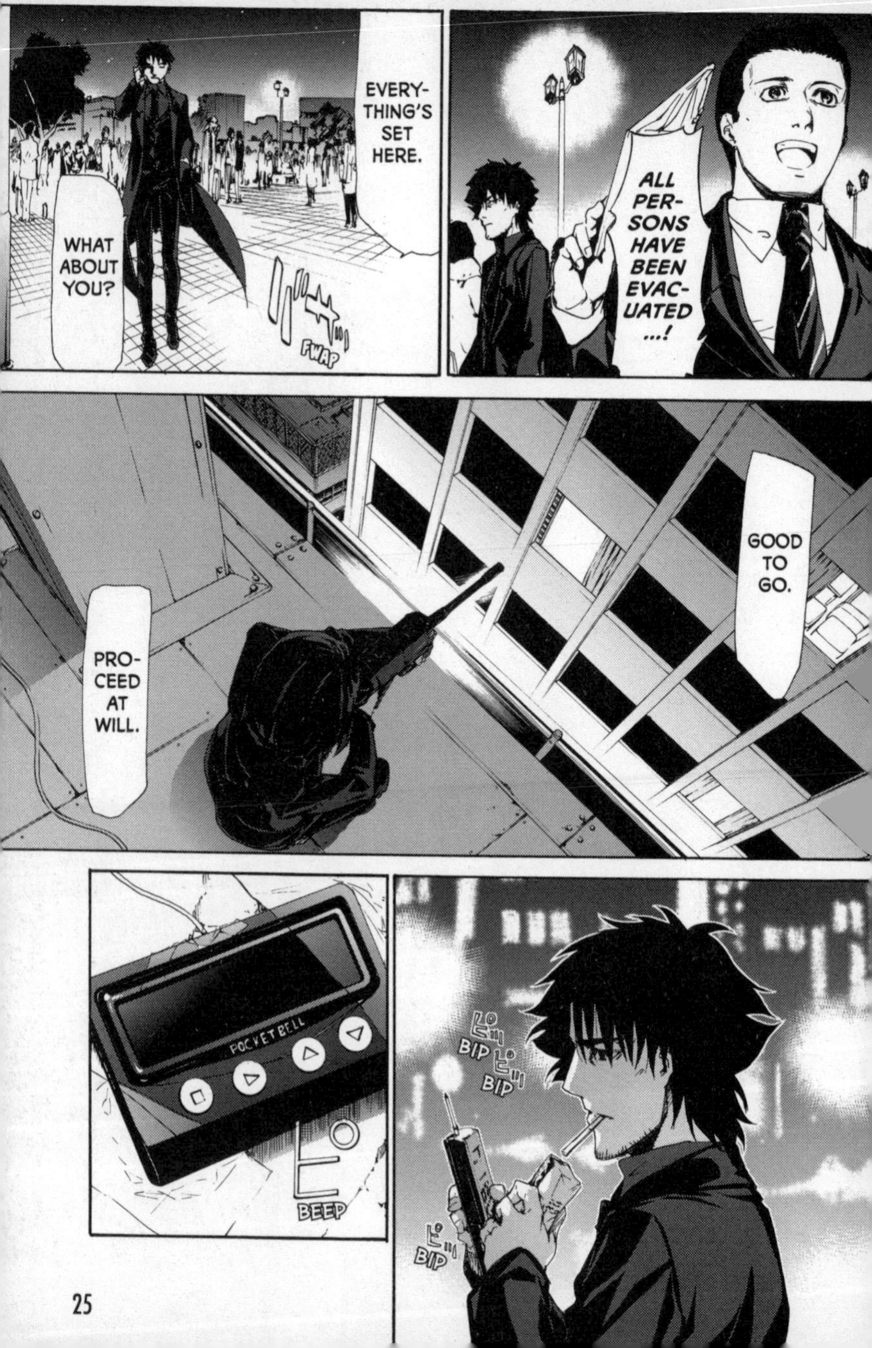
ALL PERSONS HAVE BEEN EVACUATED ...!
EVERYTHING'S SET HERE.
WHAT ABOUT YOU?
FWAP
GOOD TO GO.
PROCEED AT WILL.
BIP
BIP
BIP
BEEP
POCKET BELL

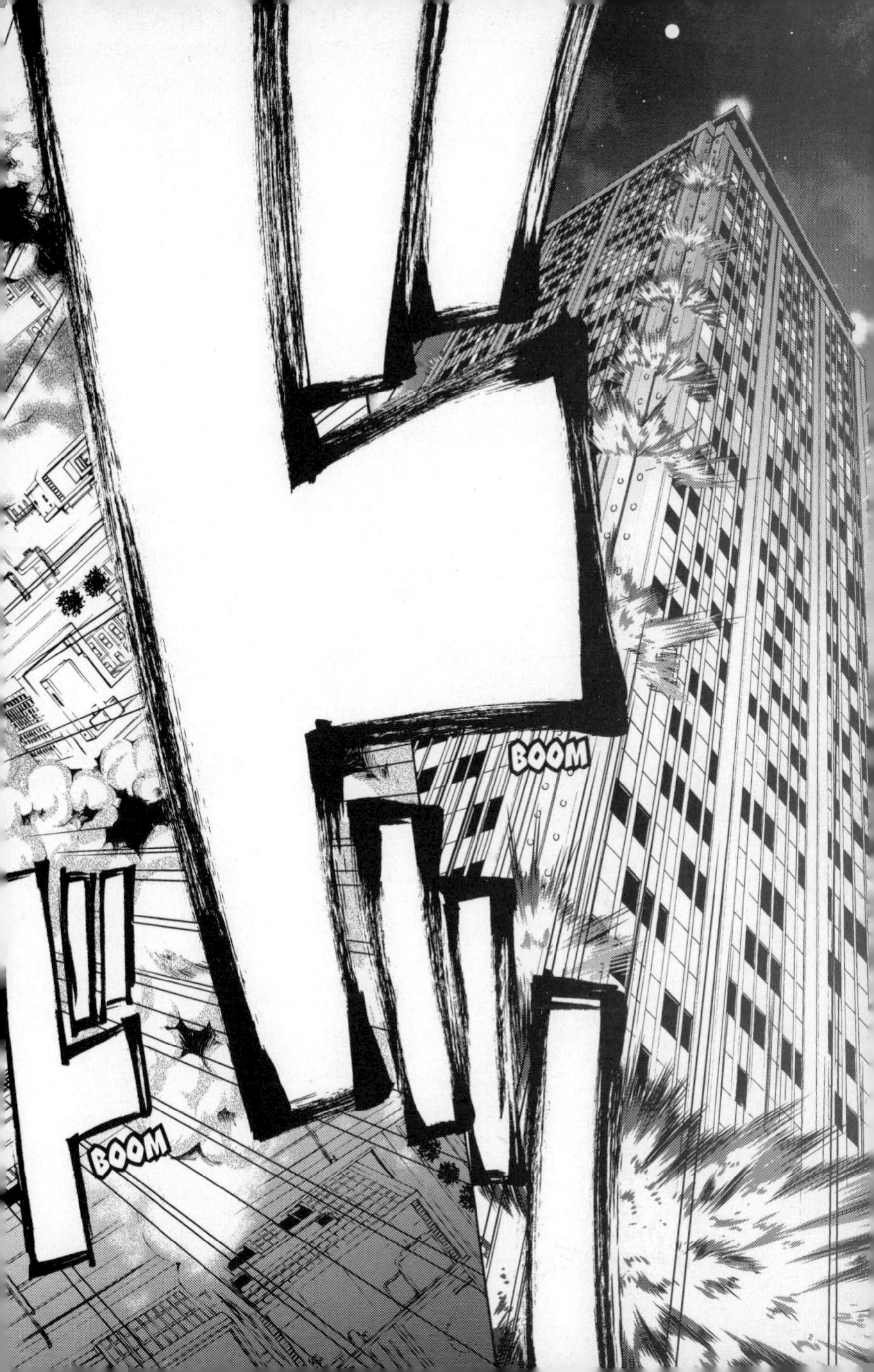
BOOM
BOOM

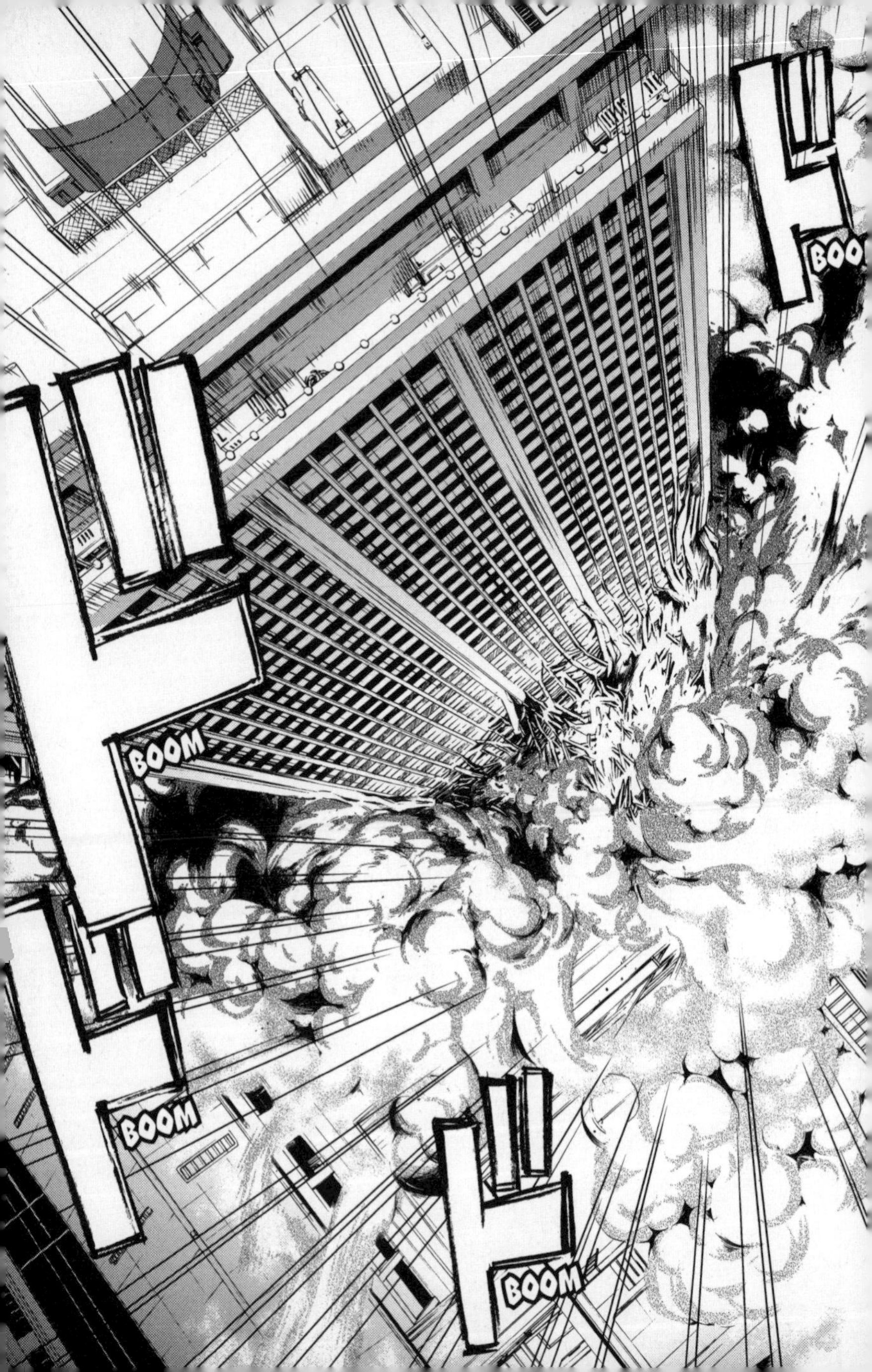
BOOM
BOOM
BOOM

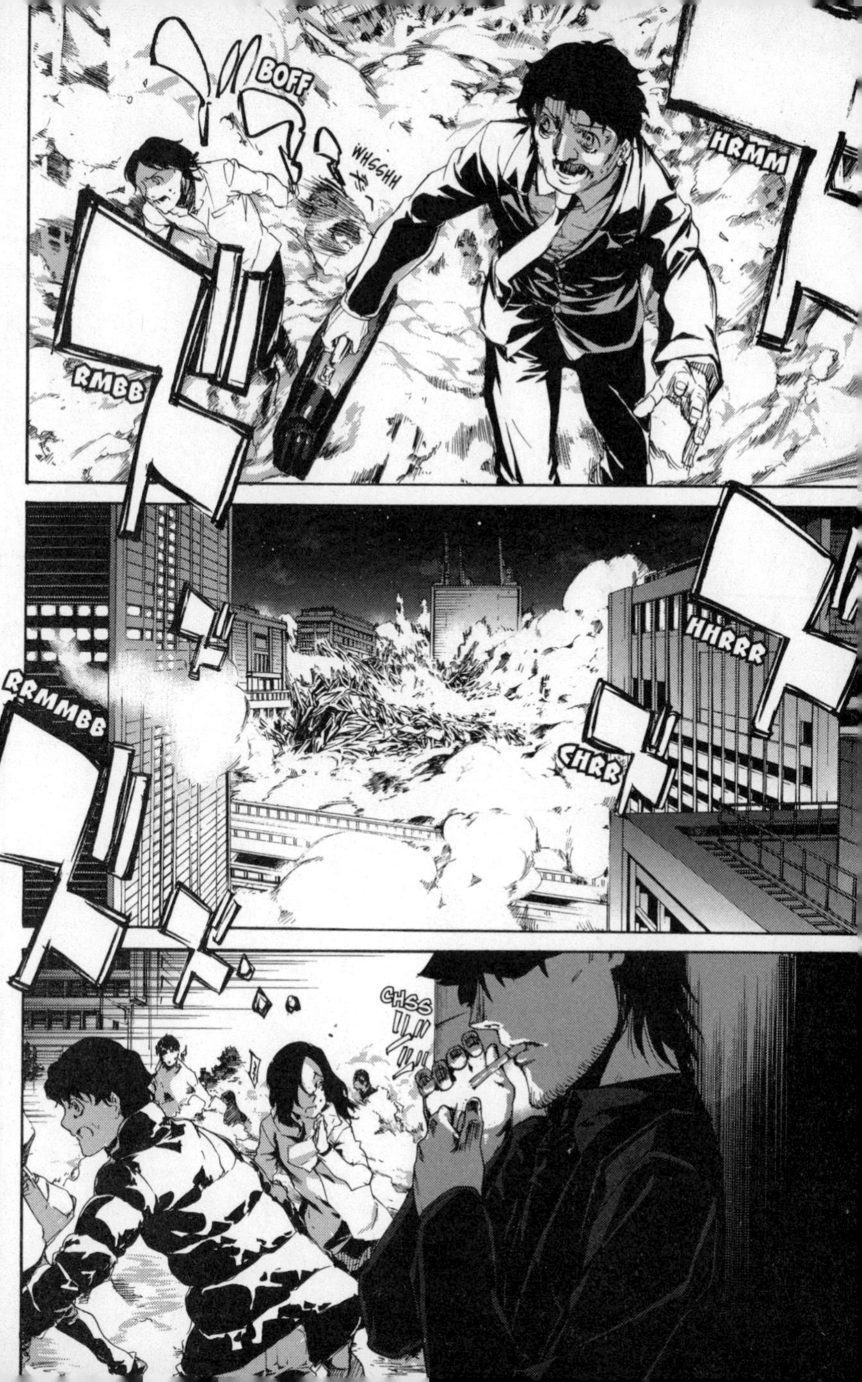
HRMM
BOFF
WHSSHH
RMBB
HHRRR
CHRR
RRMMBB
CHSS

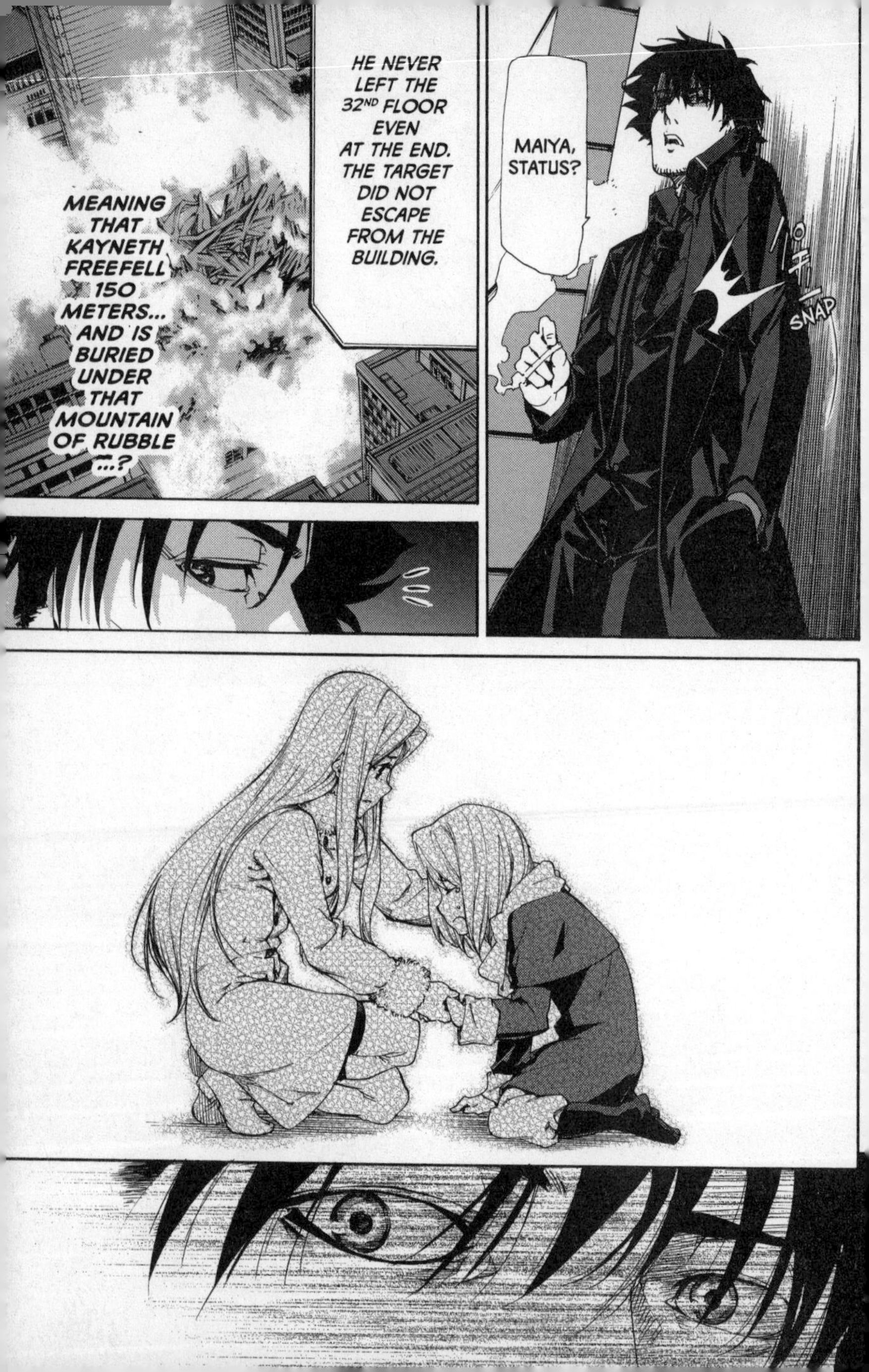
MAIYA, STATUS?
SNAP
HE NEVER LEFT THE 32ND FLOOR EVEN AT THE END. THE TARGET DID NOT ESCAPE FROM THE BUILDING.
MEANING THAT KAYNETH FREEFELL 150 METERS... AND IS BURIED UNDER THAT MOUNTAIN OF RUBBLE ...?

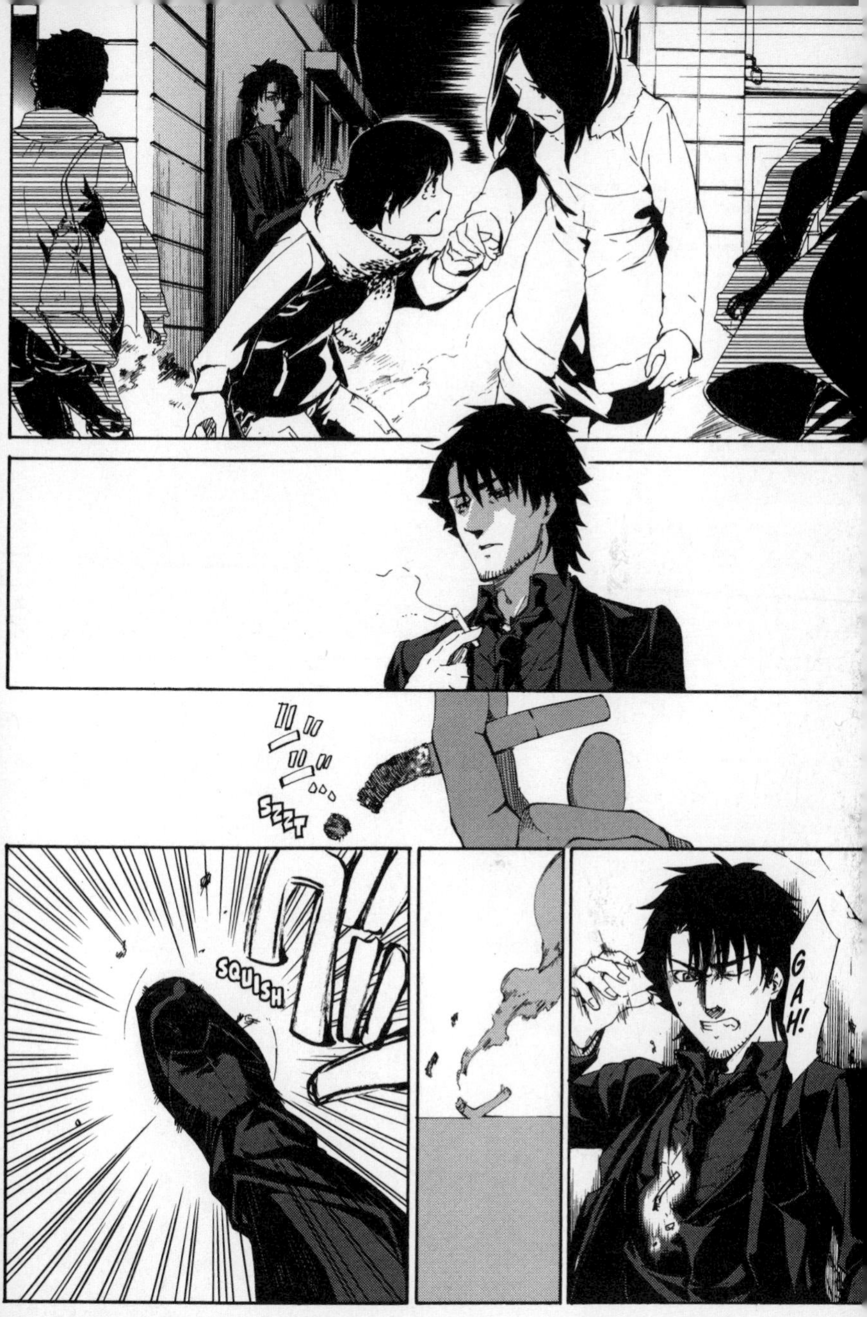
SZZT
SQUISH
GAH!

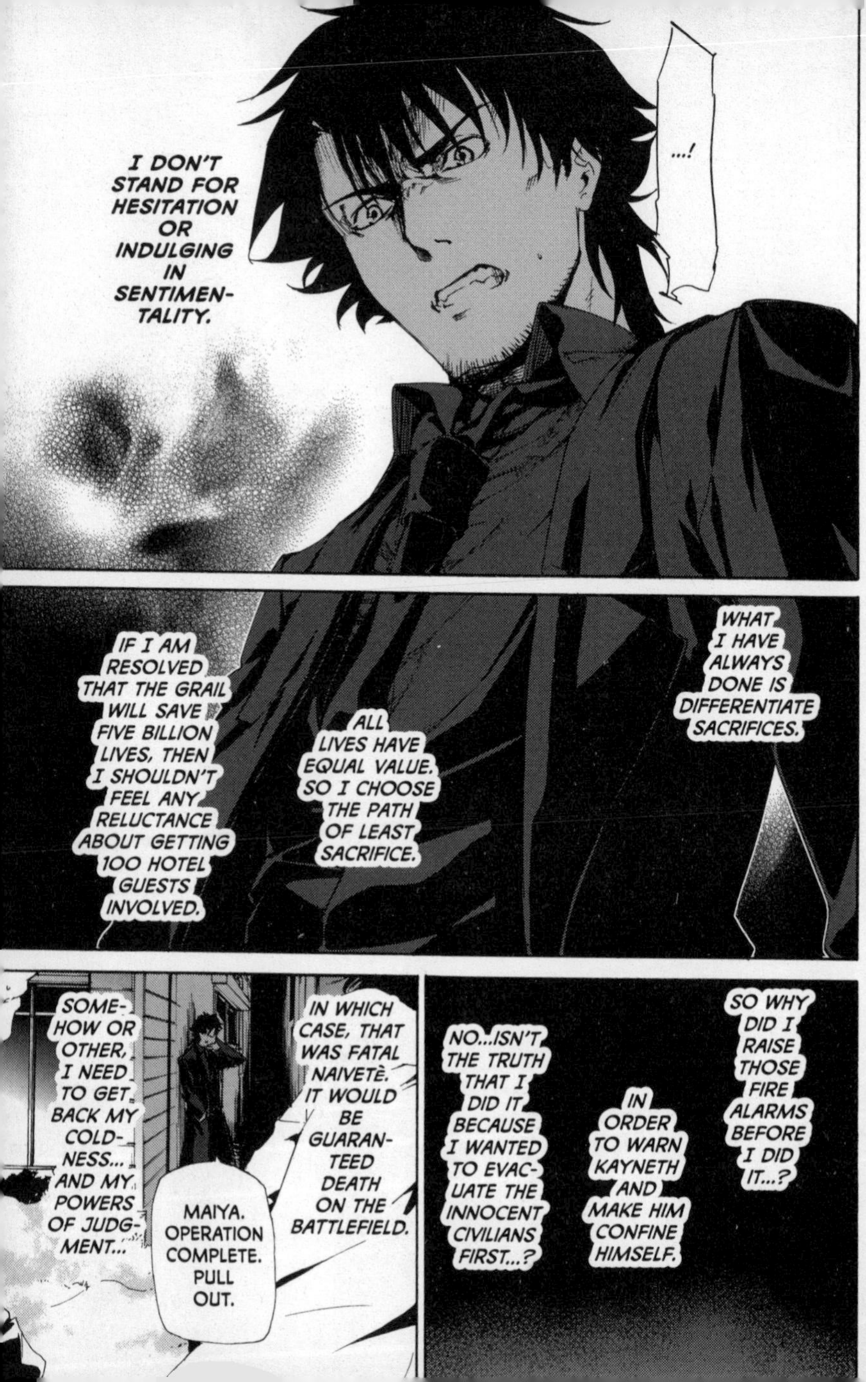
...!
I DON'T STAND FOR HESITATION OR INDULGING IN SENTIMEN-TALITY.
WHAT I HAVE ALWAYS DONE IS DIFFERENTIATE SACRIFICES.
ALL LIVES HAVE EQUAL VALUE. SO I CHOOSE THE PATH OF LEAST SACRIFICE.
IF I AM RESOLVED THAT THE GRAIL WILL SAVE FIVE BILLION LIVES, THEN I SHOULDN'T FEEL ANY RELUCTANCE ABOUT GETTING 100 HOTEL GUESTS INVOLVED.
SO WHY DID I RAISE THOSE FIRE ALARMS BEFORE I DID IT...?
IN ORDER TO WARN KAYNETH AND MAKE HIM CONFINE HIMSELF.
NO...ISN'T THE TRUTH THAT I DID IT BECAUSE I WANTED TO EVAC-UATE THE INNOCENT CIVILIANS FIRST...?
IN WHICH CASE, THAT WAS FATAL NAIVETÈ. IT WOULD BE GUARAN-TEED DEATH ON THE BATTLEFIELD.
SOME-HOW OR OTHER, I NEED TO GET BACK MY COLD-NESS... AND MY POWERS OF JUDG-MENT...
MAIYA. OPERATION COMPLETE. PULL OUT.

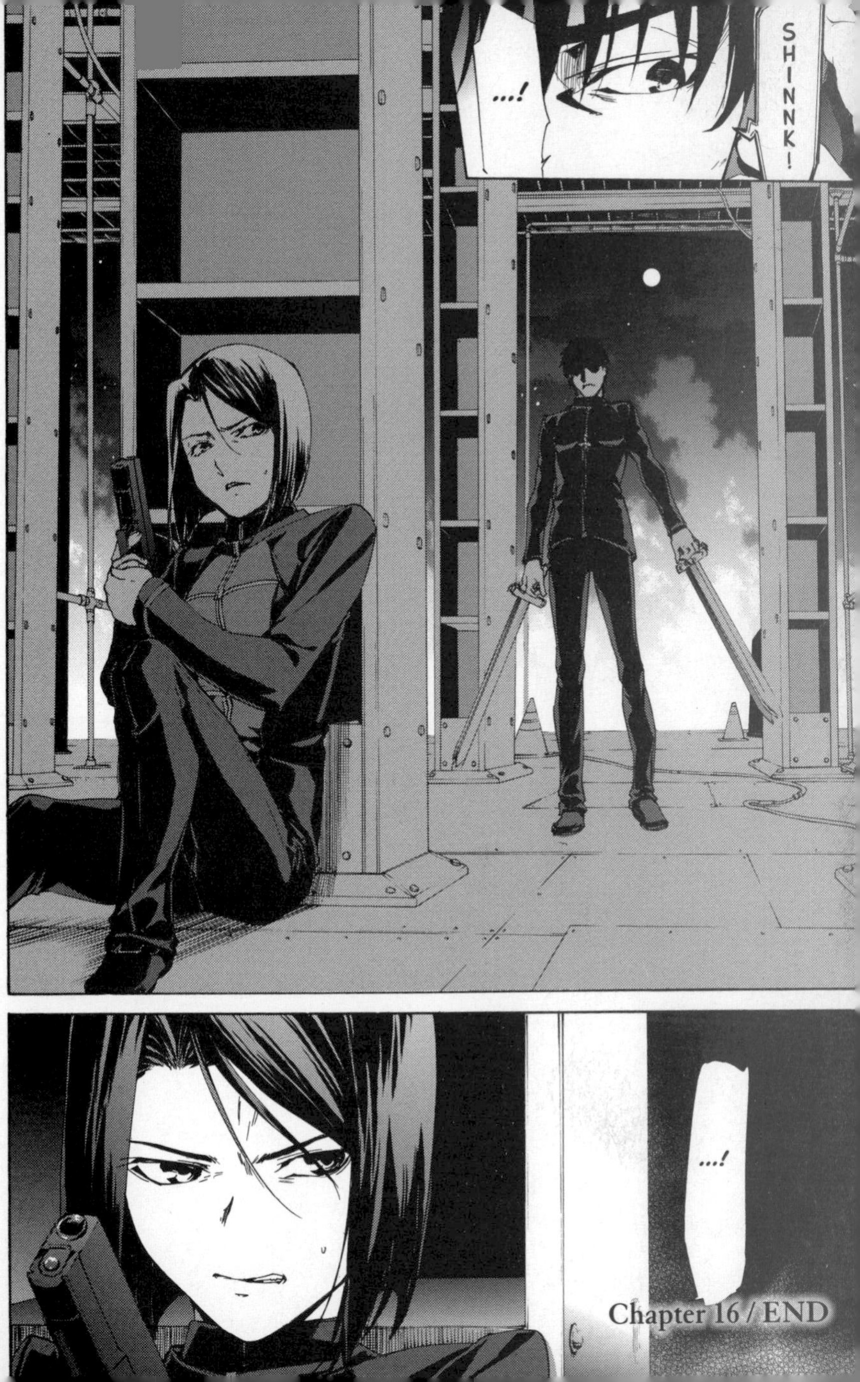
SHINNK!
...!
...!
Chapter 16 / END

CHAPTER 17

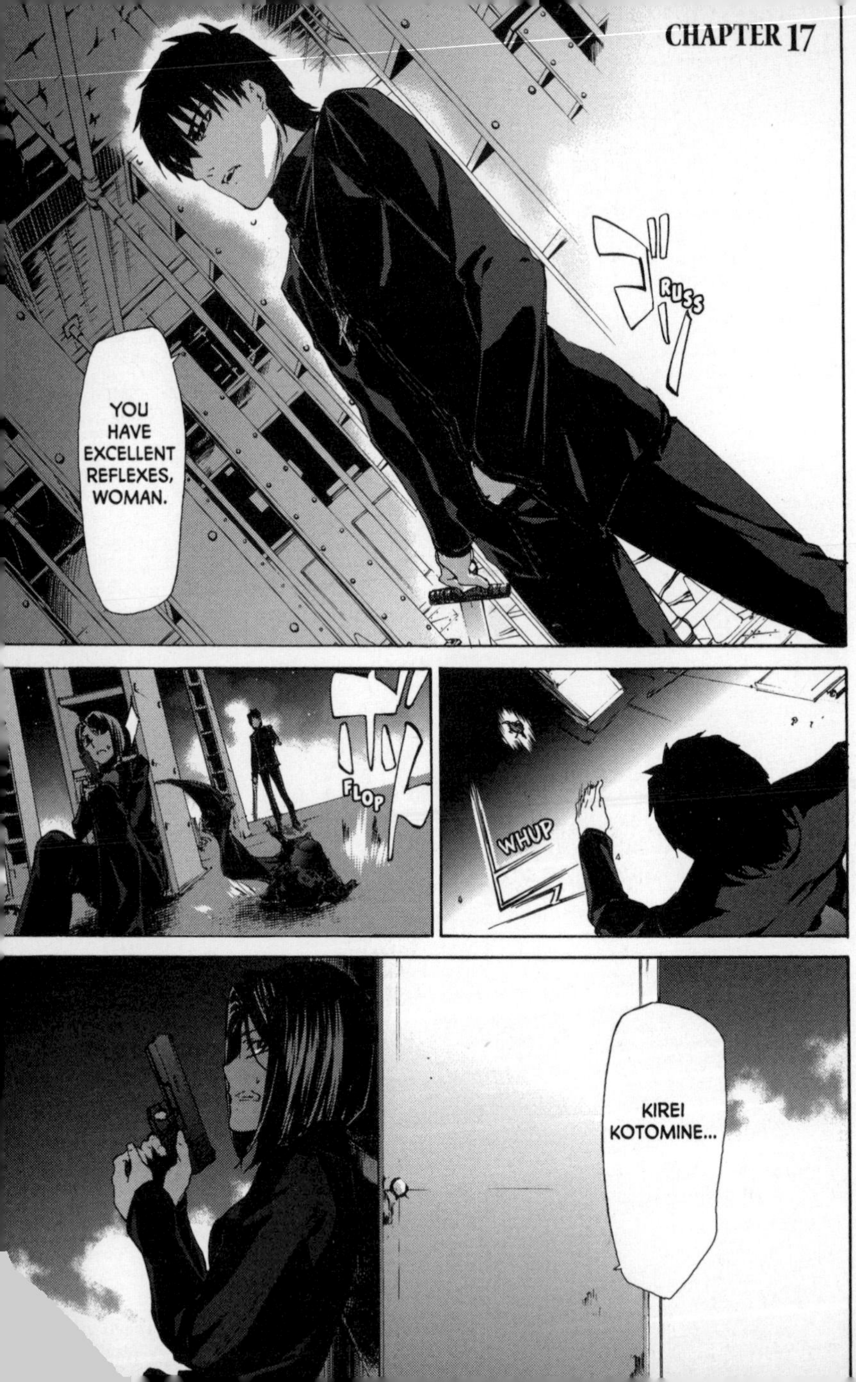
RUSS
YOU HAVE EXCELLENT REFLEXES, WOMAN.
WHUP
FLOP
KIREI KOTOMINE...

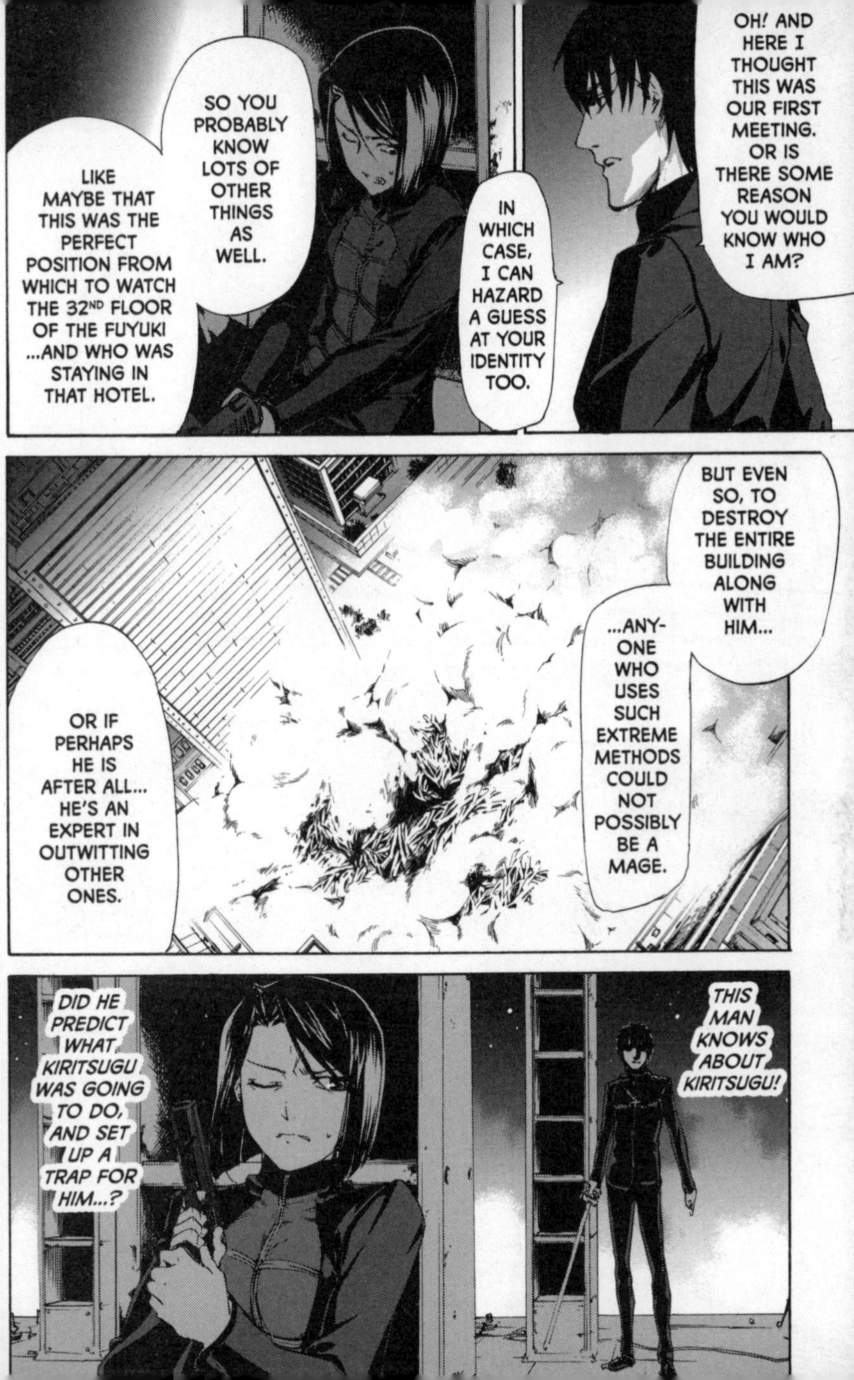
OH! AND HERE I THOUGHT THIS WAS OUR FIRST MEETING. OR IS THERE SOME REASON YOU WOULD KNOW WHO I AM?
IN WHICH CASE, I CAN HAZARD A GUESS AT YOUR IDENTITY TOO.
SO YOU PROBABLY KNOW LOTS OF OTHER THINGS AS WELL.
LIKE MAYBE THAT THIS WAS THE PERFECT POSITION FROM WHICH TO WATCH THE 32ND FLOOR OF THE FUYUKI ...AND WHO WAS STAYING IN THAT HOTEL.
BUT EVEN SO, TO DESTROY THE ENTIRE BUILDING ALONG WITH HIM...
...ANY-ONE WHO USES SUCH EXTREME METHODS COULD NOT POSSIBLY BE A MAGE.
OR IF PERHAPS HE IS AFTER ALL... HE'S AN EXPERT IN OUTWITTING OTHER ONES.
THIS MAN KNOWS ABOUT KIRITSUGU!
DID HE PREDICT WHAT KIRITSUGU WAS GOING TO DO, AND SET UP A TRAP FOR HIM...?

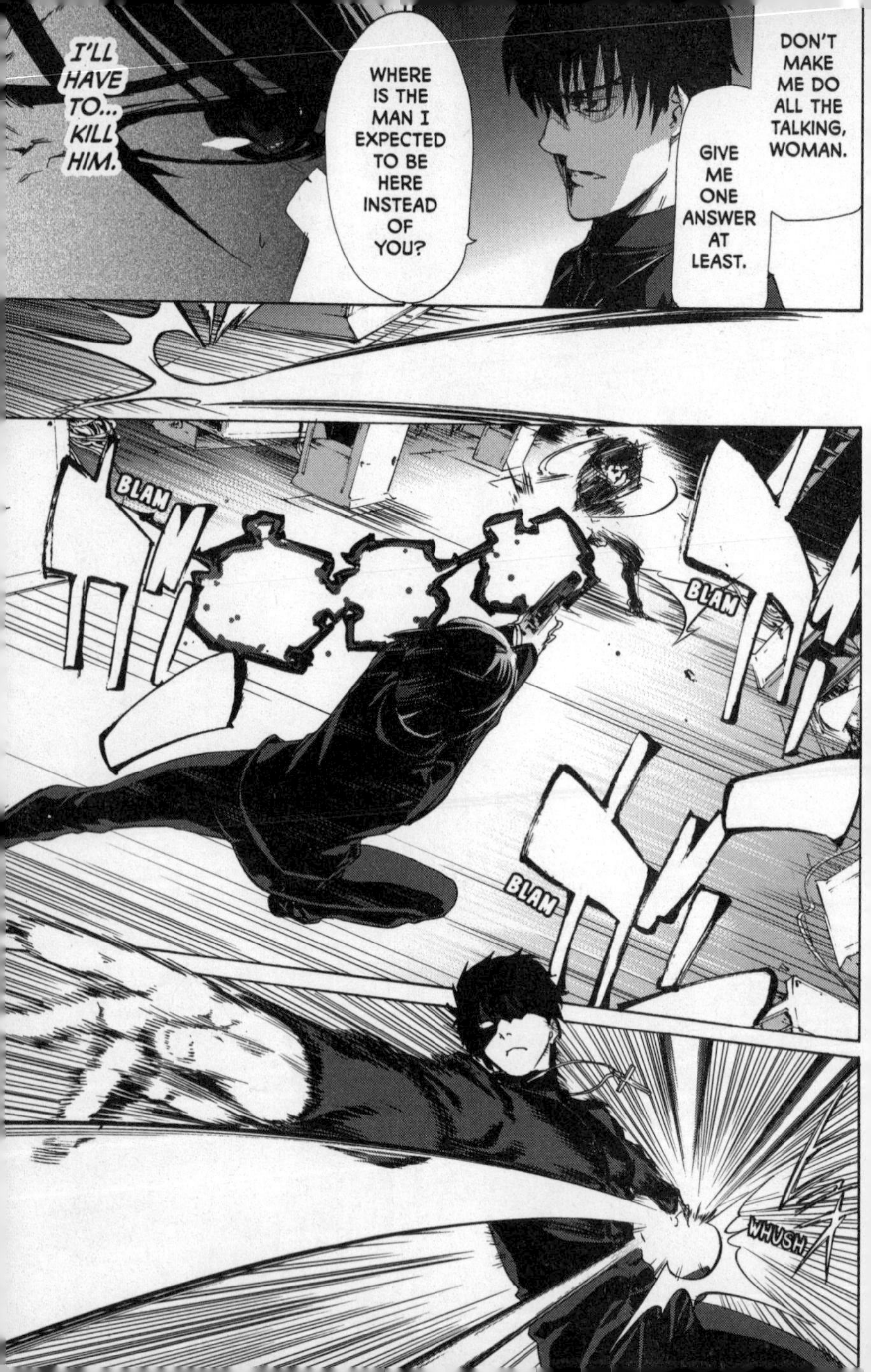
DON'T MAKE ME DO ALL THE TALKING, WOMAN.
GIVE ME ONE ANSWER AT LEAST.
WHERE IS THE MAN I EXPECTED TO BE HERE INSTEAD OF YOU?
I'LL HAVE TO... KILL HIM.
BLAM
BLAM
BLAM
WHUSH

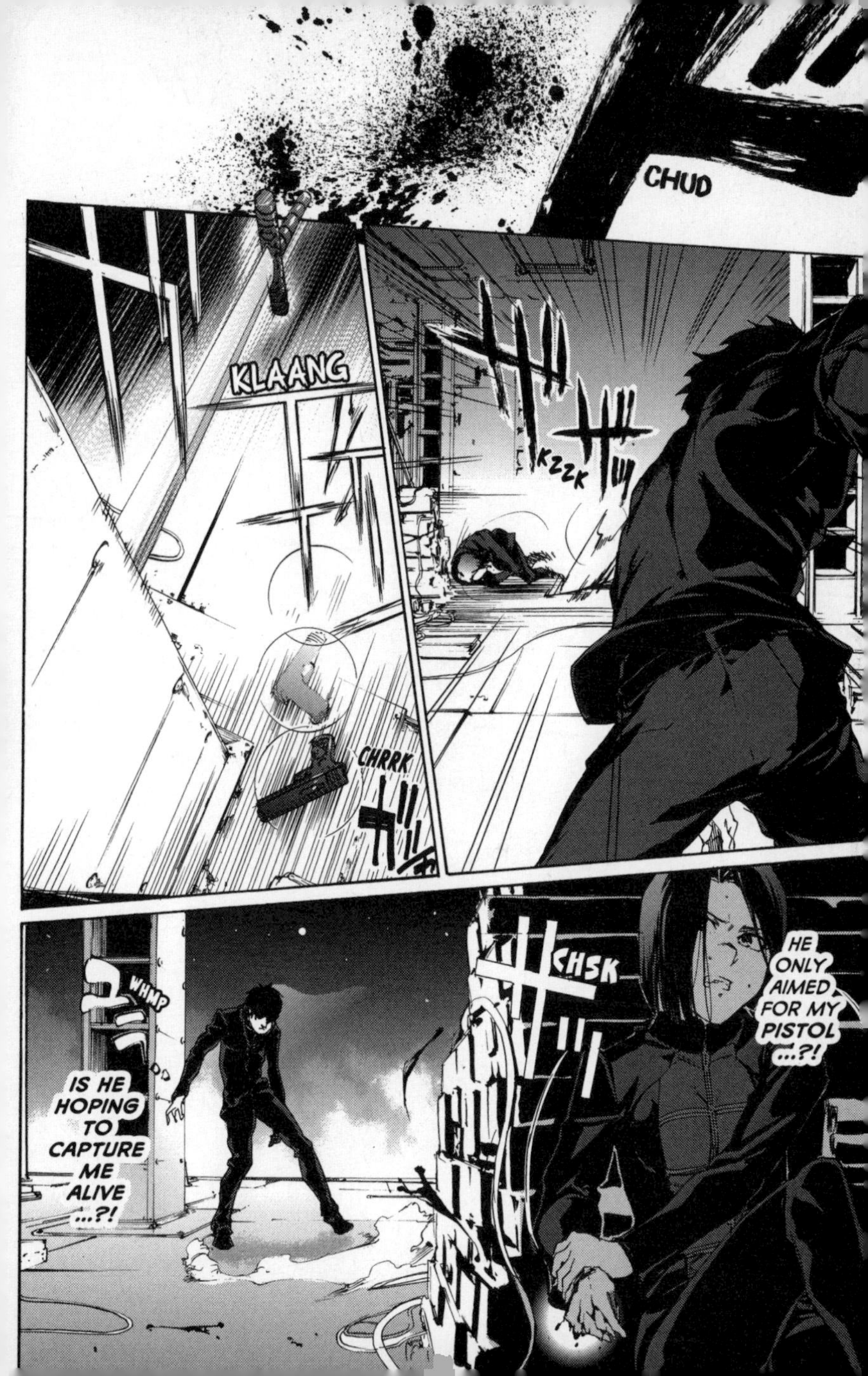
CHUD
KZZK
KLAANG
CHRRK
CHSK
HE ONLY AIMED FOR MY PISTOL ...?!
WHMP
IS HE HOPING TO CAPTURE ME ALIVE ...?!

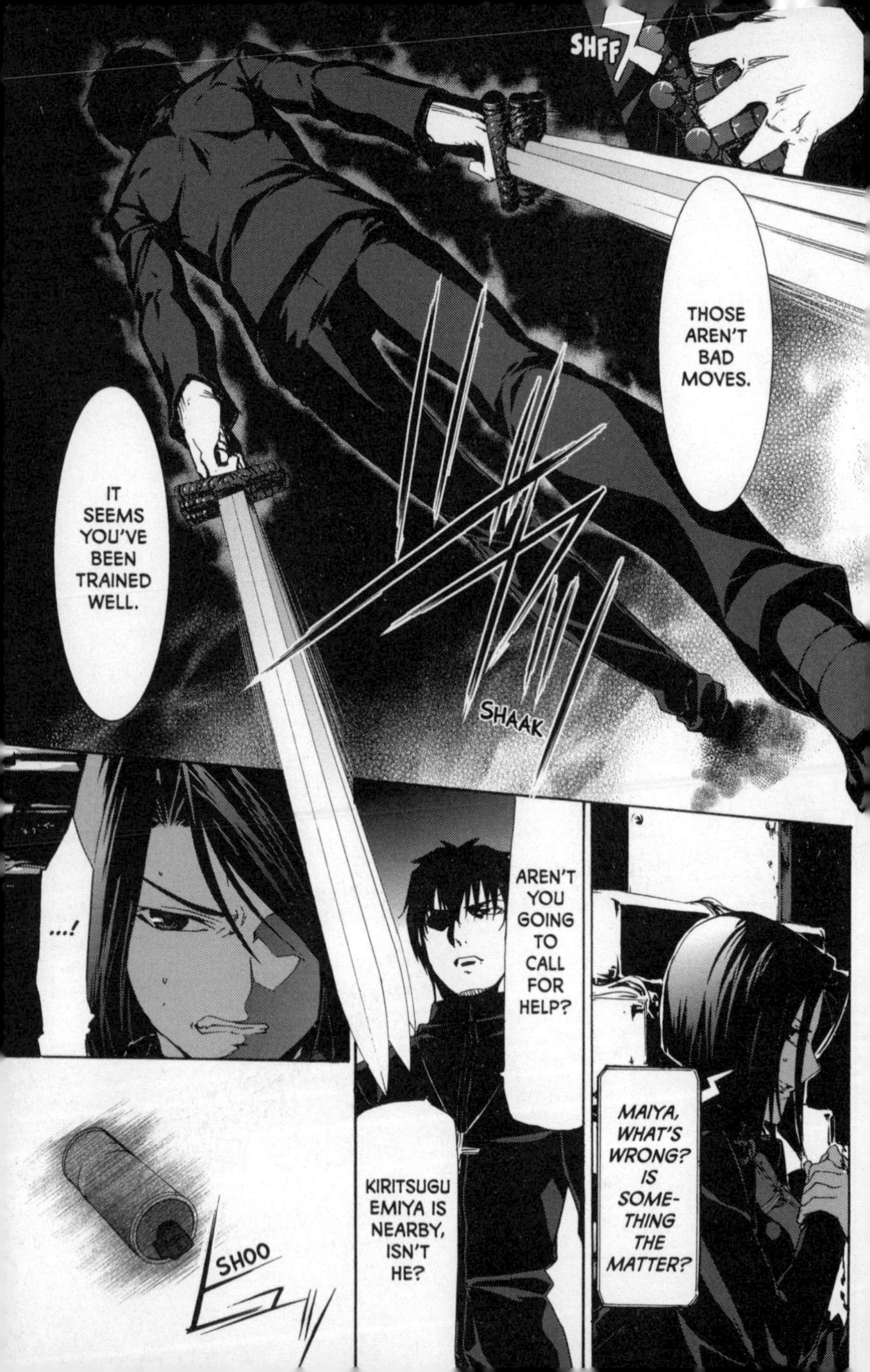
SHFF
THOSE AREN'T BAD MOVES.
IT SEEMS YOU'VE BEEN TRAINED WELL.
SHAAK
MAIYA, WHAT'S WRONG? IS SOME-THING THE MATTER?
AREN'T YOU GOING TO CALL FOR HELP?
KIRITSUGU EMIYA IS NEARBY, ISN'T HE?
...!
SHOO

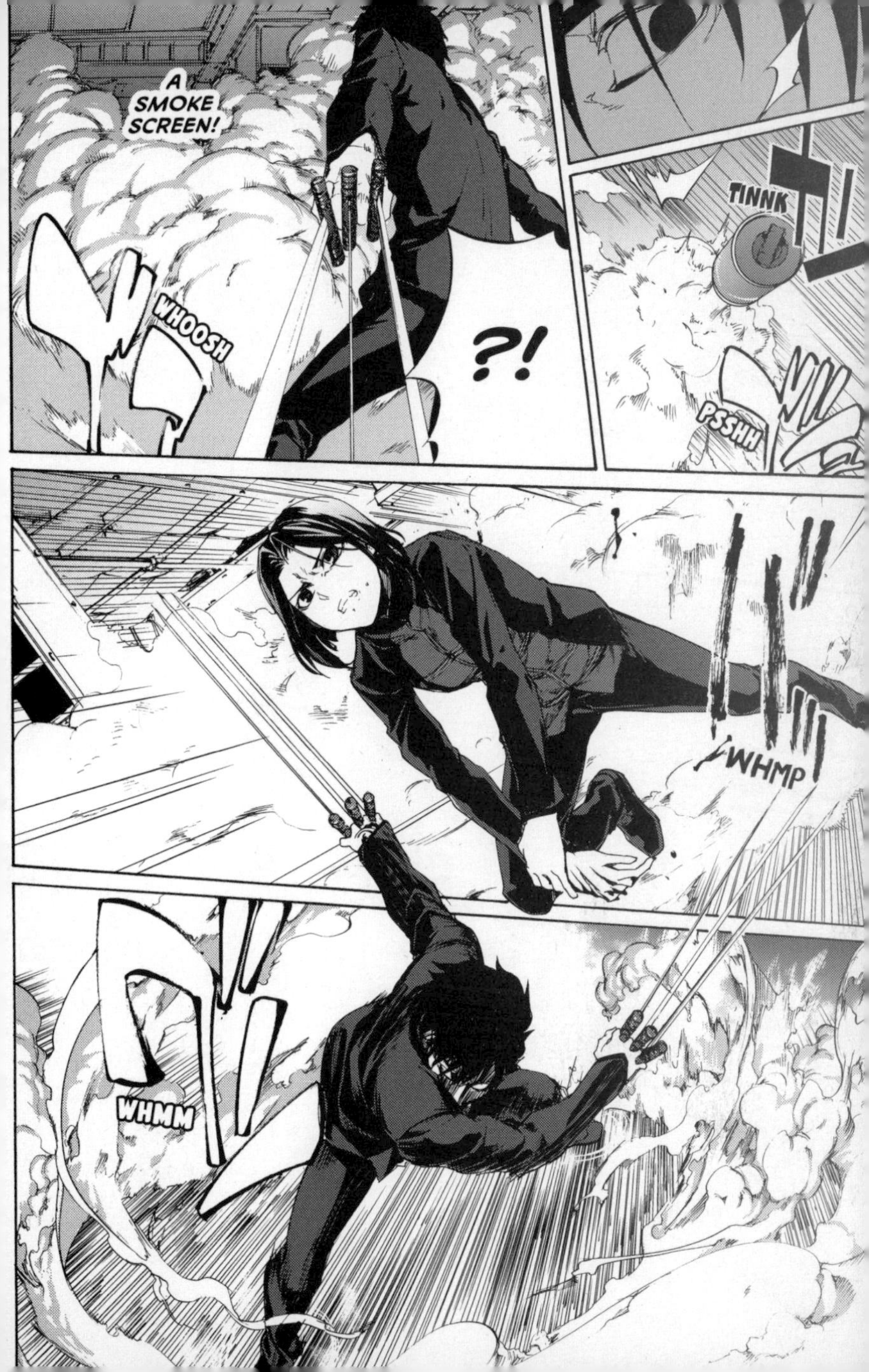
TINNK
PSSHH
A SMOKE SCREEN!
?!
WHOOSH
WHMP
WHMM

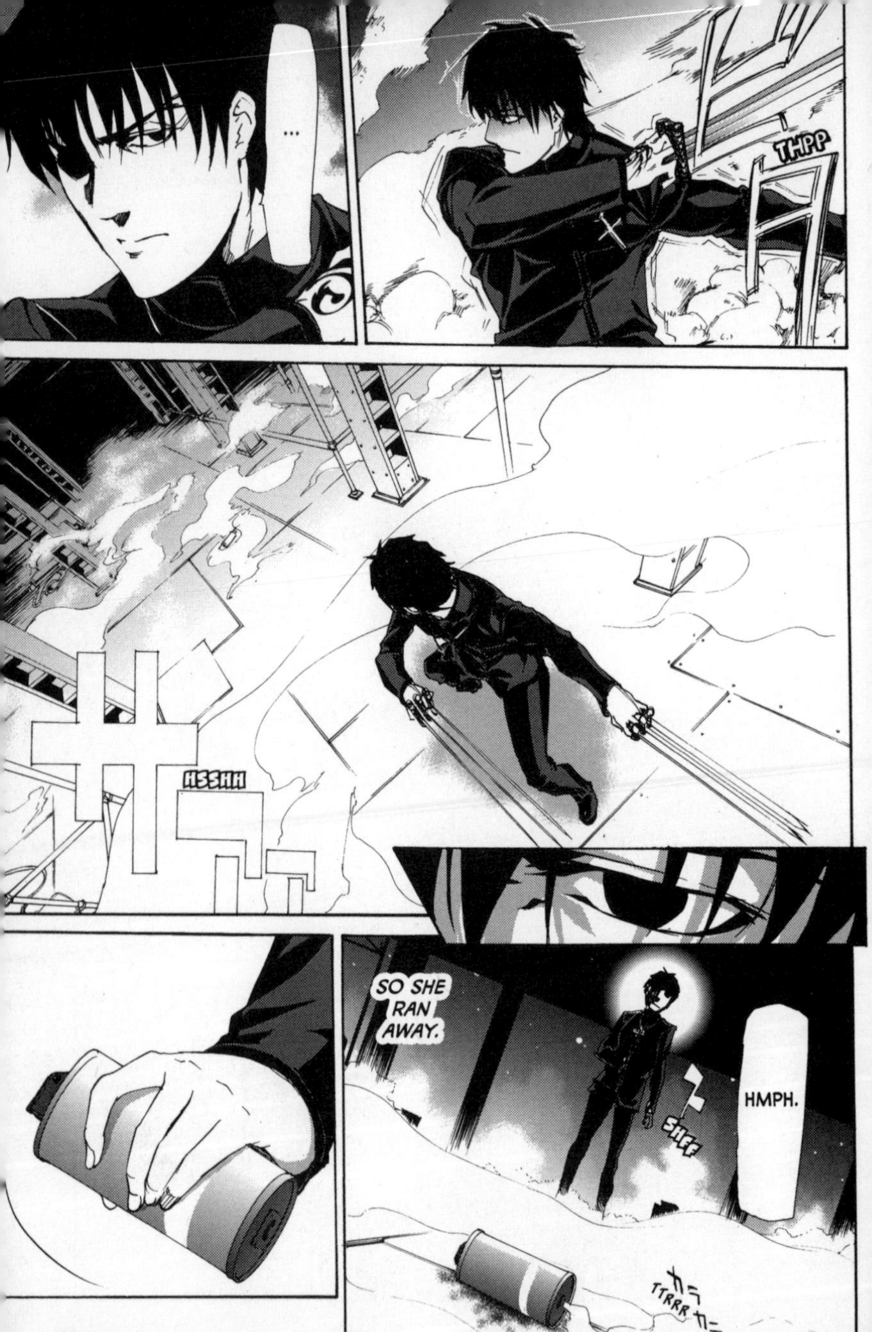
THPP
...
HSSHH
SO SHE RAN AWAY.
SHFF
HMPH.
TTRRR

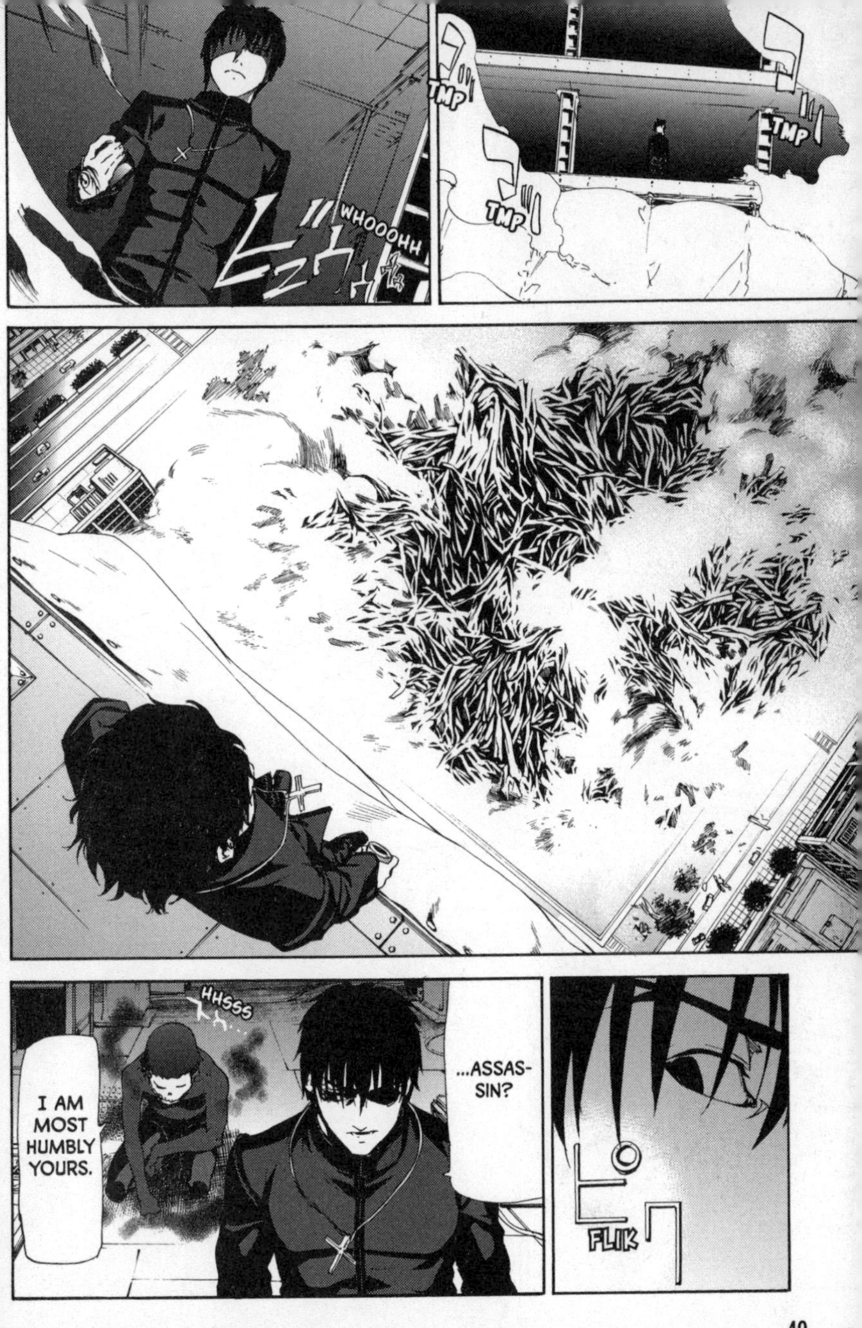
TMP
TMP
TMP
WHOOOHH
FLIK
HHSSS
...ASSAS-
SIN?
I AM
MOST
HUMBLY
YOURS.

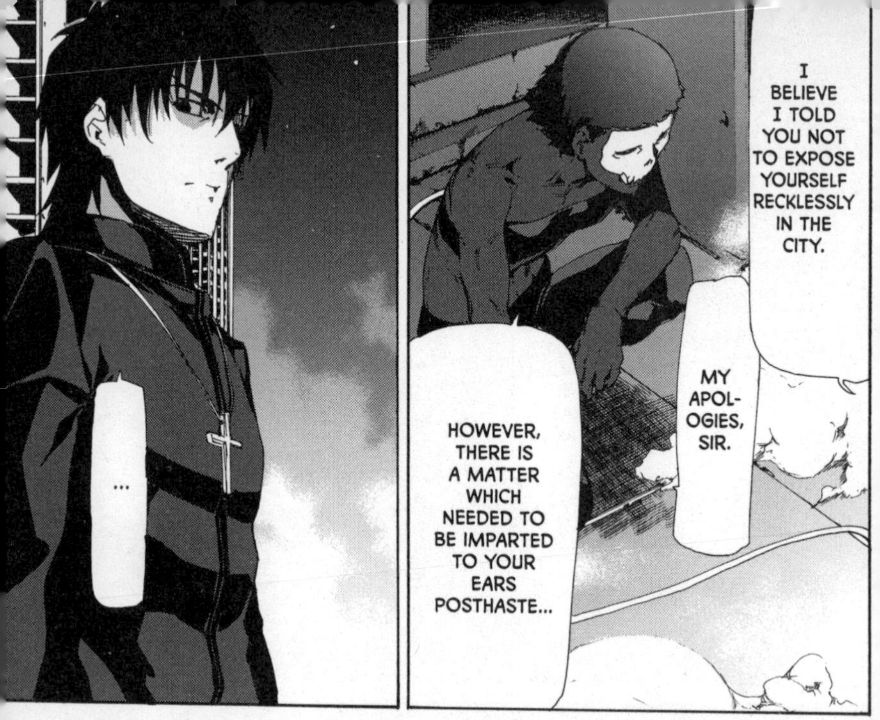
I BELIEVE I TOLD YOU NOT TO EXPOSE YOURSELF RECKLESSLY IN THE CITY.
MY APOLOGIES, SIR.
HOWEVER, THERE IS A MATTER WHICH NEEDED TO BE IMPARTED TO YOUR EARS POSTHASTE...
...

—144:09:25

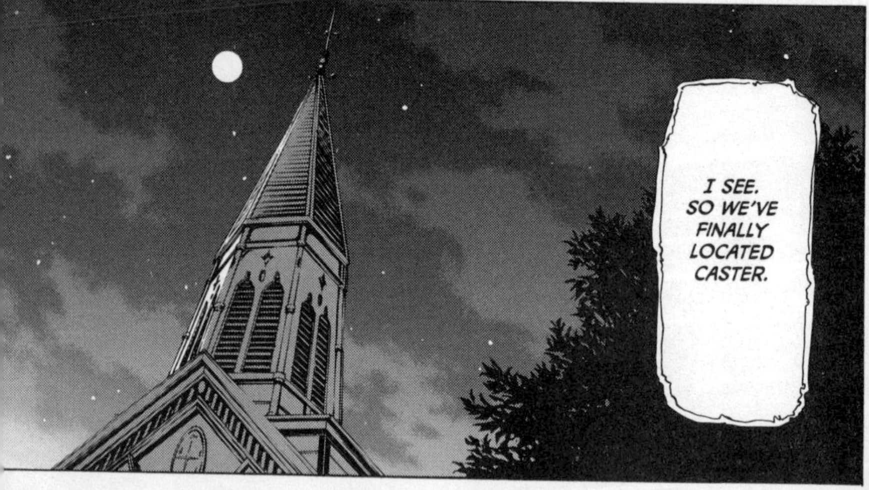
I SEE. SO WE'VE FINALLY LOCATED CASTER.

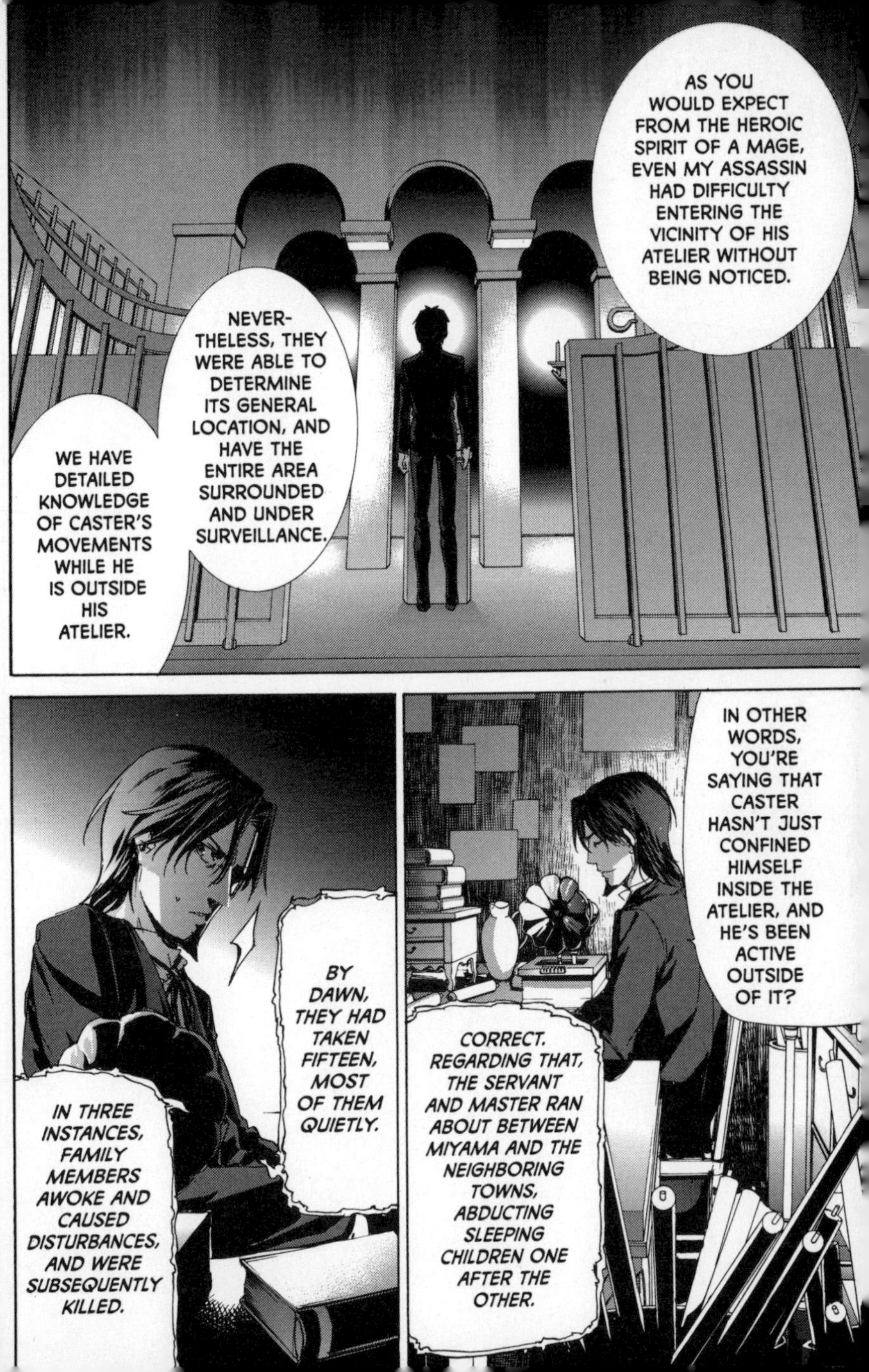
AS YOU WOULD EXPECT FROM THE HEROIC SPIRIT OF A MAGE, EVEN MY ASSASSIN HAD DIFFICULTY ENTERING THE VICINITY OF HIS ATELIER WITHOUT BEING NOTICED.
NEVER-THELESS, THEY WERE ABLE TO DETERMINE ITS GENERAL LOCATION, AND HAVE THE ENTIRE AREA SURROUNDED AND UNDER SURVEILLANCE.
WE HAVE DETAILED KNOWLEDGE OF CASTER'S MOVEMENTS WHILE HE IS OUTSIDE HIS ATELIER.
IN OTHER WORDS, YOU'RE SAYING THAT CASTER HASN'T JUST CONFINED HIMSELF INSIDE THE ATELIER, AND HE'S BEEN ACTIVE OUTSIDE OF IT?
CORRECT. REGARDING THAT, THE SERVANT AND MASTER RAN ABOUT BETWEEN MIYAMA AND THE NEIGHBORING TOWNS, ABDUCTING SLEEPING CHILDREN ONE AFTER THE OTHER.
BY DAWN, THEY HAD TAKEN FIFTEEN, MOST OF THEM QUIETLY.
IN THREE INSTANCES, FAMILY MEMBERS AWOKE AND CAUSED DISTURBANCES, AND WERE SUBSEQUENTLY KILLED.

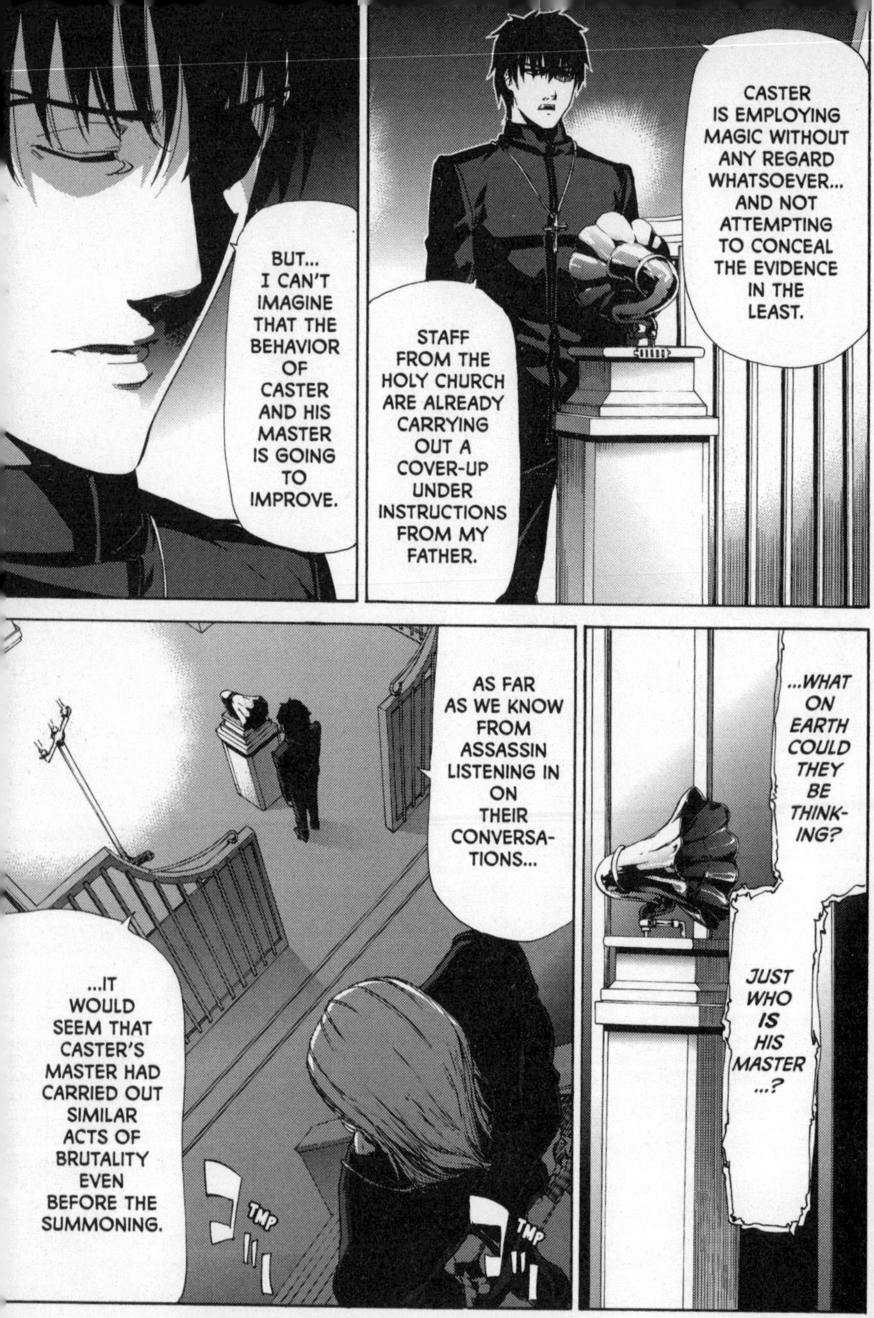
CASTER IS EMPLOYING MAGIC WITHOUT ANY REGARD WHATSOEVER... AND NOT ATTEMPTING TO CONCEAL THE EVIDENCE IN THE LEAST.
STAFF FROM THE HOLY CHURCH ARE ALREADY CARRYING OUT A COVER-UP UNDER INSTRUCTIONS FROM MY FATHER.
BUT... I CAN'T IMAGINE THAT THE BEHAVIOR OF CASTER AND HIS MASTER IS GOING TO IMPROVE.
...WHAT ON EARTH COULD THEY BE THINKING?
JUST WHO IS HIS MASTER ...?
AS FAR AS WE KNOW FROM ASSASSIN LISTENING IN ON THEIR CONVERSATIONS...
...IT WOULD SEEM THAT CASTER'S MASTER HAD CARRIED OUT SIMILAR ACTS OF BRUTALITY EVEN BEFORE THE SUMMONING.
TMP
TMP

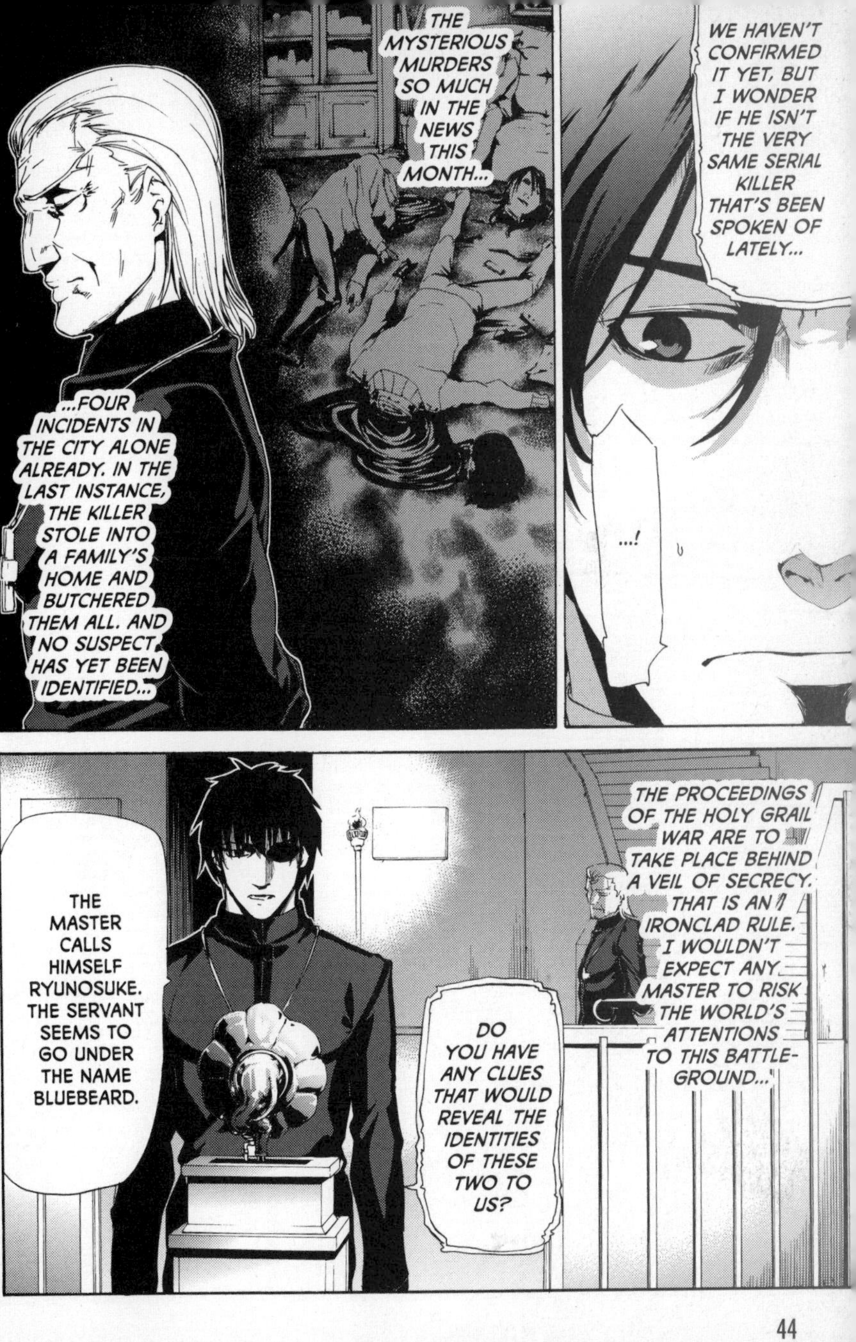
WE HAVEN'T CONFIRMED IT YET, BUT I WONDER IF HE ISN'T THE VERY SAME SERIAL KILLER THAT'S BEEN SPOKEN OF LATELY...
...!
THE MYSTERIOUS MURDERS SO MUCH IN THE NEWS THIS MONTH...
...FOUR INCIDENTS IN THE CITY ALONE ALREADY. IN THE LAST INSTANCE, THE KILLER STOLE INTO A FAMILY'S HOME AND BUTCHERED THEM ALL. AND NO SUSPECT HAS YET BEEN IDENTIFIED...
THE PROCEEDINGS OF THE HOLY GRAIL WAR ARE TO TAKE PLACE BEHIND A VEIL OF SECRECY. THAT IS AN IRONCLAD RULE. I WOULDN'T EXPECT ANY MASTER TO RISK THE WORLD'S ATTENTIONS TO THIS BATTLE-GROUND...
DO YOU HAVE ANY CLUES THAT WOULD REVEAL THE IDENTITIES OF THESE TWO TO US?
THE MASTER CALLS HIMSELF RYUNOSUKE. THE SERVANT SEEMS TO GO UNDER THE NAME BLUEBEARD.

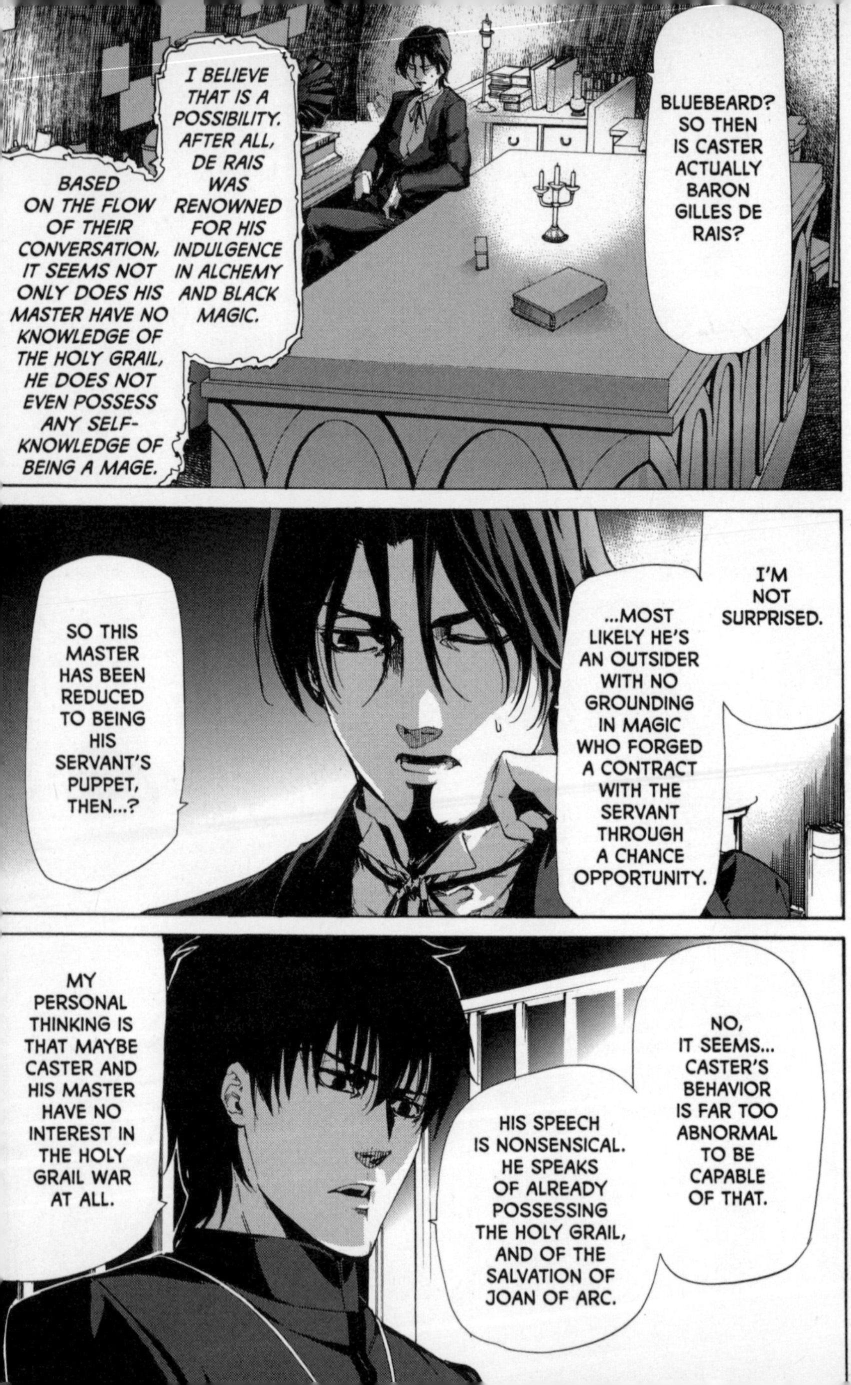
BLUEBEARD? SO THEN IS CASTER ACTUALLY BARON GILLES DE RAIS?
I BELIEVE THAT IS A POSSIBILITY. AFTER ALL, DE RAIS WAS RENOWNED FOR HIS INDULGENCE IN ALCHEMY AND BLACK MAGIC.
BASED ON THE FLOW OF THEIR CONVERSATION, IT SEEMS NOT ONLY DOES HIS MASTER HAVE NO KNOWLEDGE OF THE HOLY GRAIL, HE DOES NOT EVEN POSSESS ANY SELF-KNOWLEDGE OF BEING A MAGE.
I'M NOT SURPRISED.
...MOST LIKELY HE'S AN OUTSIDER WITH NO GROUNDING IN MAGIC WHO FORGED A CONTRACT WITH THE SERVANT THROUGH A CHANCE OPPORTUNITY.
SO THIS MASTER HAS BEEN REDUCED TO BEING HIS SERVANT'S PUPPET, THEN...?
NO, IT SEEMS... CASTER'S BEHAVIOR IS FAR TOO ABNORMAL TO BE CAPABLE OF THAT.
HIS SPEECH IS NONSENSICAL. HE SPEAKS OF ALREADY POSSESSING THE HOLY GRAIL, AND OF THE SALVATION OF JOAN OF ARC.
MY PERSONAL THINKING IS THAT MAYBE CASTER AND HIS MASTER HAVE NO INTEREST IN THE HOLY GRAIL WAR AT ALL.

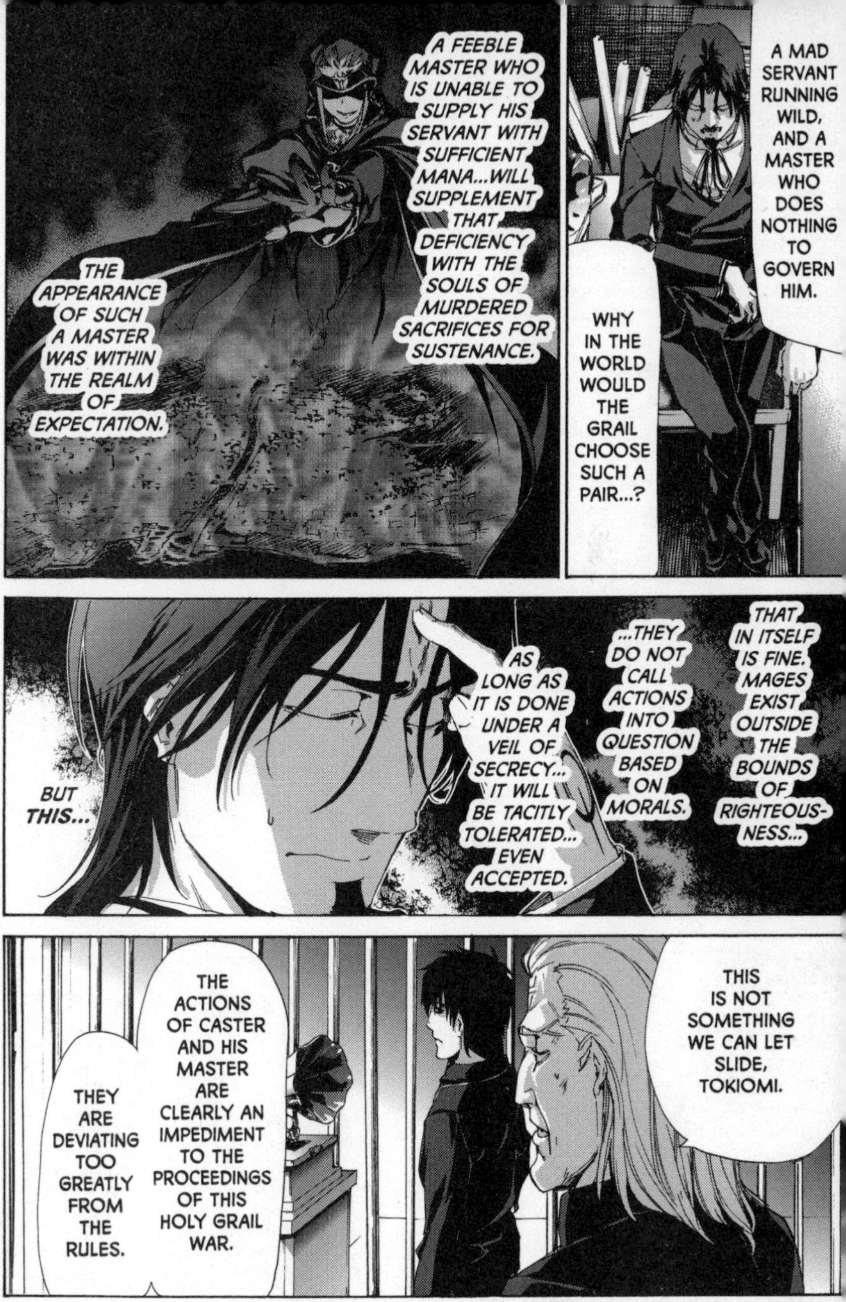
A MAD SERVANT RUNNING WILD, AND A MASTER WHO DOES NOTHING TO GOVERN HIM.
WHY IN THE WORLD WOULD THE GRAIL CHOOSE SUCH A PAIR...?
A FEEBLE MASTER WHO IS UNABLE TO SUPPLY HIS SERVANT WITH SUFFICIENT MANA...WILL SUPPLEMENT THAT DEFICIENCY WITH THE SOULS OF MURDERED SACRIFICES FOR SUSTENANCE.
THE APPEARANCE OF SUCH A MASTER WAS WITHIN THE REALM OF EXPECTATION.
THAT IN ITSELF IS FINE. MAGES EXIST OUTSIDE THE BOUNDS OF RIGHTEOUSNESS...
...THEY DO NOT CALL ACTIONS INTO QUESTION BASED ON MORALS.
AS LONG AS IT IS DONE UNDER A VEIL OF SECRECY... IT WILL BE TACITLY TOLERATED... EVEN ACCEPTED.
BUT THIS...
THIS IS NOT SOMETHING WE CAN LET SLIDE, TOKIOMI.
THE ACTIONS OF CASTER AND HIS MASTER ARE CLEARLY AN IMPEDIMENT TO THE PROCEEDINGS OF THIS HOLY GRAIL WAR.
THEY ARE DEVIATING TOO GREATLY FROM THE RULES.

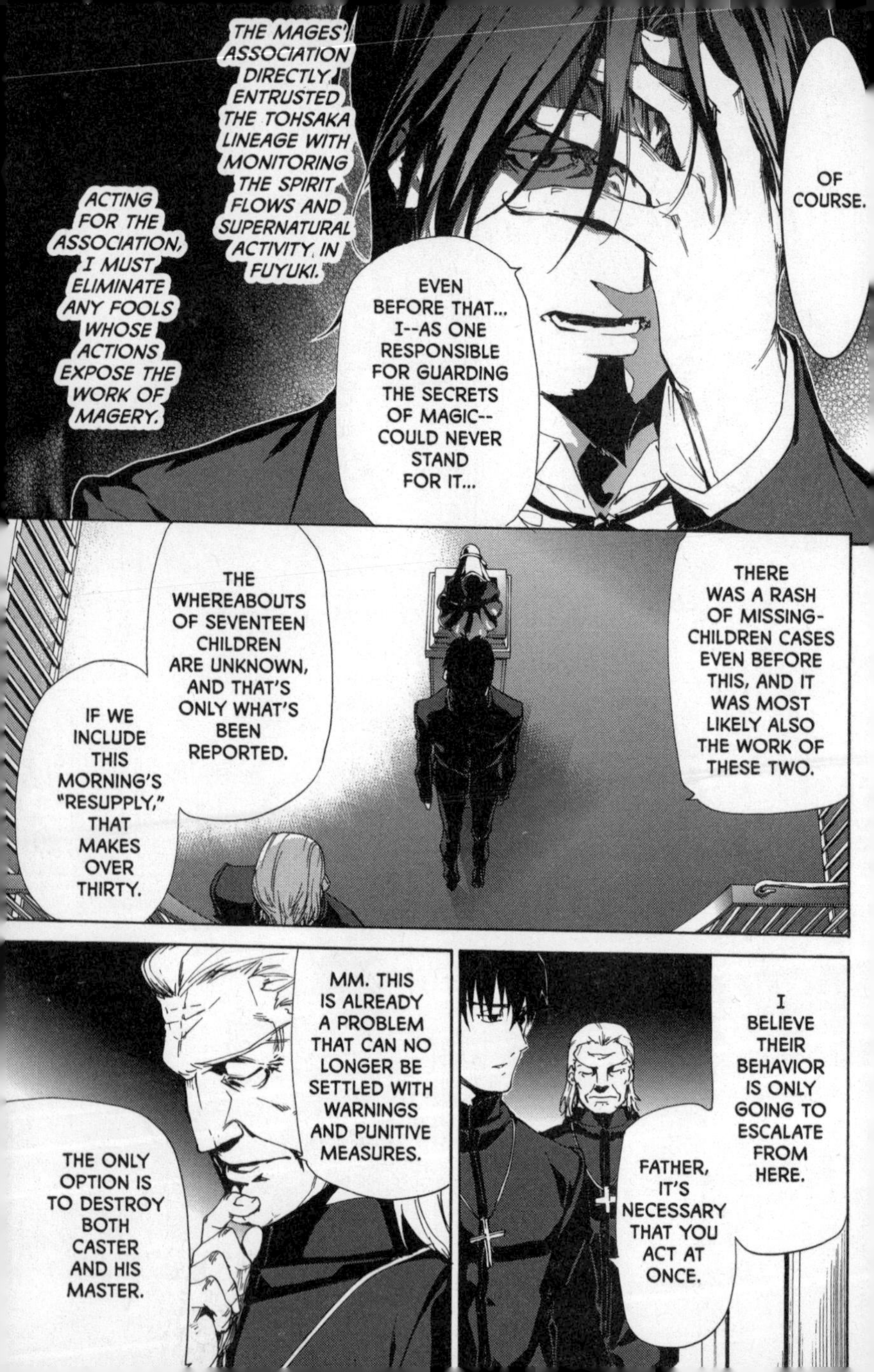
OF COURSE.
THE MAGES' ASSOCIATION DIRECTLY ENTRUSTED THE TOHSAKA LINEAGE WITH MONITORING THE SPIRIT FLOWS AND SUPERNATURAL ACTIVITY IN FUYUKI.
EVEN BEFORE THAT... I--AS ONE RESPONSIBLE FOR GUARDING THE SECRETS OF MAGIC--COULD NEVER STAND FOR IT...
ACTING FOR THE ASSOCIATION, I MUST ELIMINATE ANY FOOLS WHOSE ACTIONS EXPOSE THE WORK OF MAGERY.
THERE WAS A RASH OF MISSING-CHILDREN CASES EVEN BEFORE THIS, AND IT WAS MOST LIKELY ALSO THE WORK OF THESE TWO.
THE WHEREABOUTS OF SEVENTEEN CHILDREN ARE UNKNOWN, AND THAT'S ONLY WHAT'S BEEN REPORTED.
IF WE INCLUDE THIS MORNING'S "RESUPPLY," THAT MAKES OVER THIRTY.
I BELIEVE THEIR BEHAVIOR IS ONLY GOING TO ESCALATE FROM HERE.
FATHER, IT'S NECESSARY THAT YOU ACT AT ONCE.
MM. THIS IS ALREADY A PROBLEM THAT CAN NO LONGER BE SETTLED WITH WARNINGS AND PUNITIVE MEASURES.
THE ONLY OPTION IS TO DESTROY BOTH CASTER AND HIS MASTER.

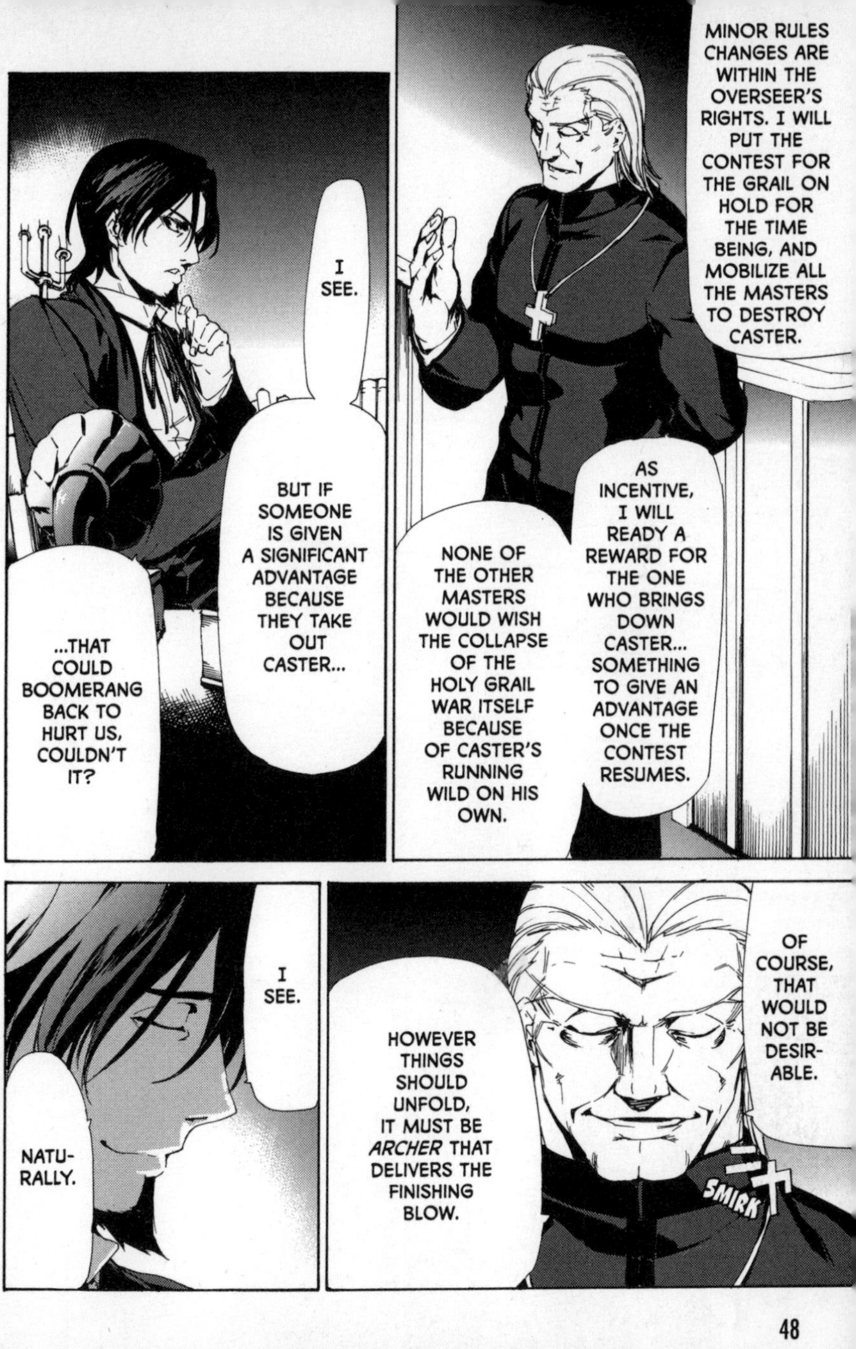
MINOR RULES CHANGES ARE WITHIN THE OVERSEER'S RIGHTS. I WILL PUT THE CONTEST FOR THE GRAIL ON HOLD FOR THE TIME BEING, AND MOBILIZE ALL THE MASTERS TO DESTROY CASTER.
AS INCENTIVE, I WILL READY A REWARD FOR THE ONE WHO BRINGS DOWN CASTER... SOMETHING TO GIVE AN ADVANTAGE ONCE THE CONTEST RESUMES.
NONE OF THE OTHER MASTERS WOULD WISH THE COLLAPSE OF THE HOLY GRAIL WAR ITSELF BECAUSE OF CASTER'S RUNNING WILD ON HIS OWN.
I SEE.
BUT IF SOMEONE IS GIVEN A SIGNIFICANT ADVANTAGE BECAUSE THEY TAKE OUT CASTER...
...THAT COULD BOOMERANG BACK TO HURT US, COULDN'T IT?
OF COURSE, THAT WOULD NOT BE DESIR-ABLE.
SMIRK
HOWEVER THINGS SHOULD UNFOLD, IT MUST BE *ARCHER* THAT DELIVERS THE FINISHING BLOW.
I SEE.
NATU-RALLY.

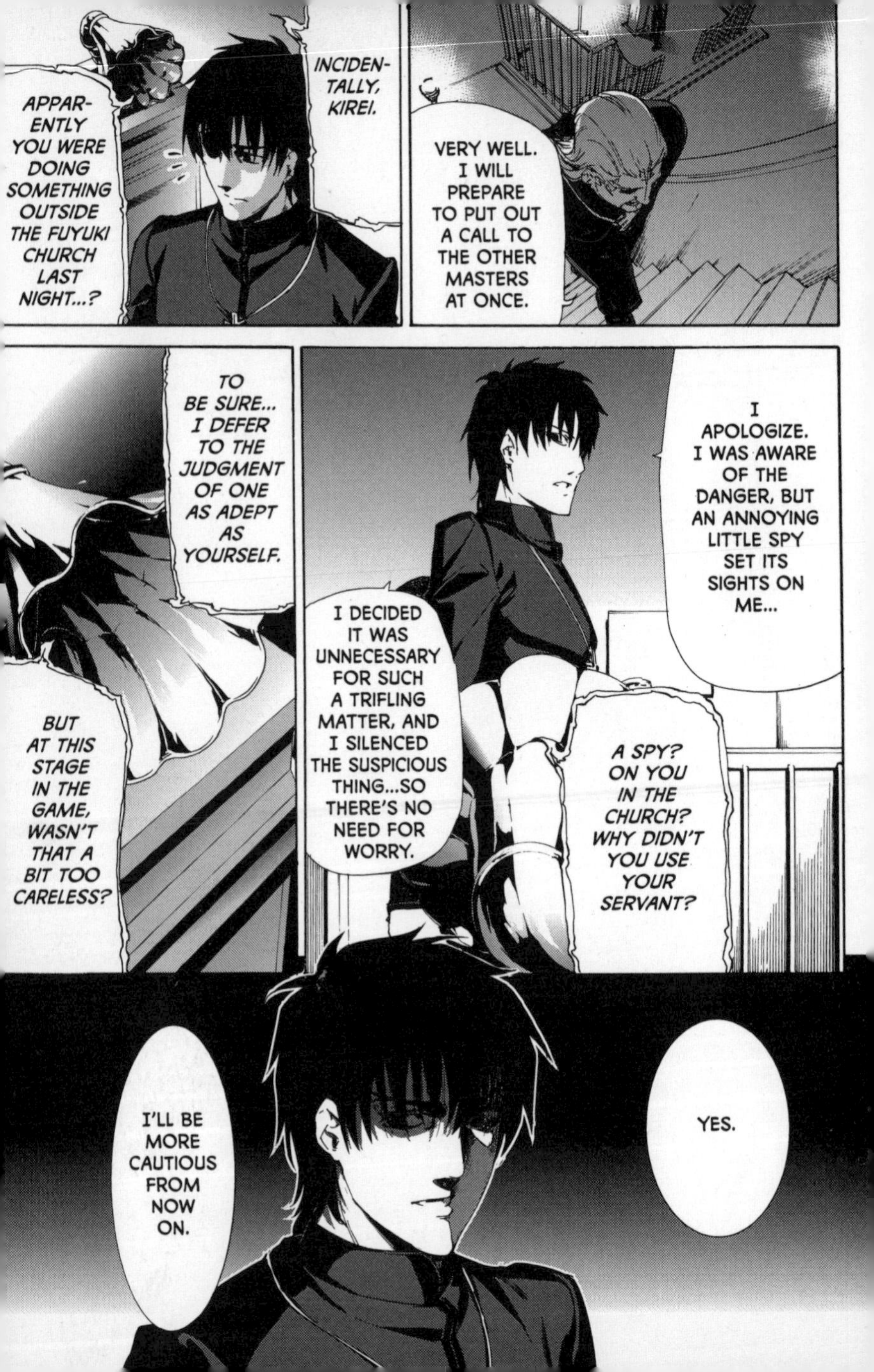
VERY WELL. I WILL PREPARE TO PUT OUT A CALL TO THE OTHER MASTERS AT ONCE.
INCIDENTALLY, KIREI.
APPARENTLY YOU WERE DOING SOMETHING OUTSIDE THE FUYUKI CHURCH LAST NIGHT...?
I APOLOGIZE. I WAS AWARE OF THE DANGER, BUT AN ANNOYING LITTLE SPY SET ITS SIGHTS ON ME...
A SPY? ON YOU IN THE CHURCH? WHY DIDN'T YOU USE YOUR SERVANT?
I DECIDED IT WAS UNNECESSARY FOR SUCH A TRIFLING MATTER, AND I SILENCED THE SUSPICIOUS THING...SO THERE'S NO NEED FOR WORRY.
TO BE SURE... I DEFER TO THE JUDGMENT OF ONE AS ADEPT AS YOURSELF.
BUT AT THIS STAGE IN THE GAME, WASN'T THAT A BIT TOO CARELESS?
YES.
I'LL BE MORE CAUTIOUS FROM NOW ON.

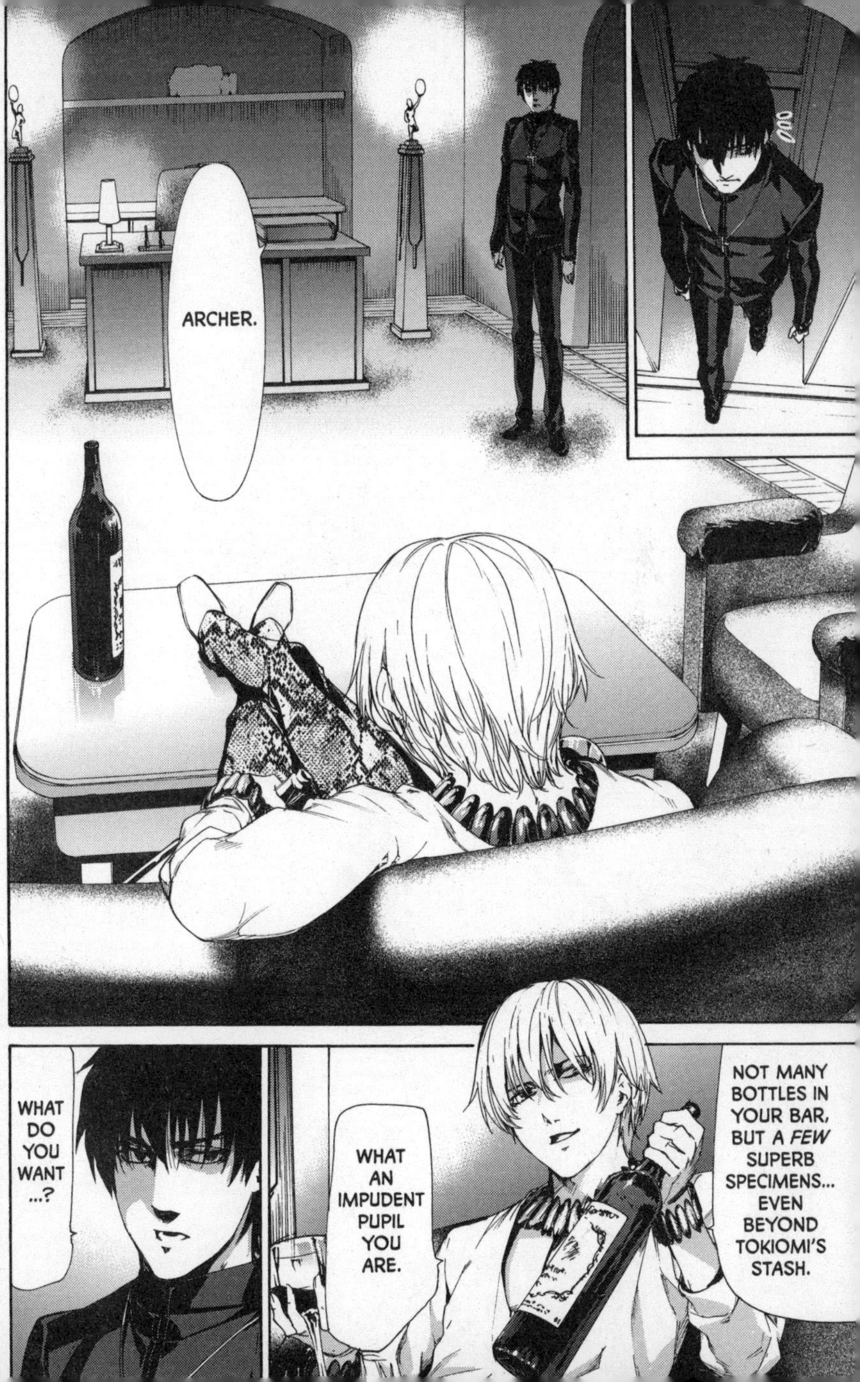
ARCHER.
NOT MANY BOTTLES IN YOUR BAR, BUT A *FEW* SUPERB SPECIMENS... EVEN BEYOND TOKIOMI'S STASH.
WHAT AN IMPUDENT PUPIL YOU ARE.
WHAT DO YOU WANT ...?

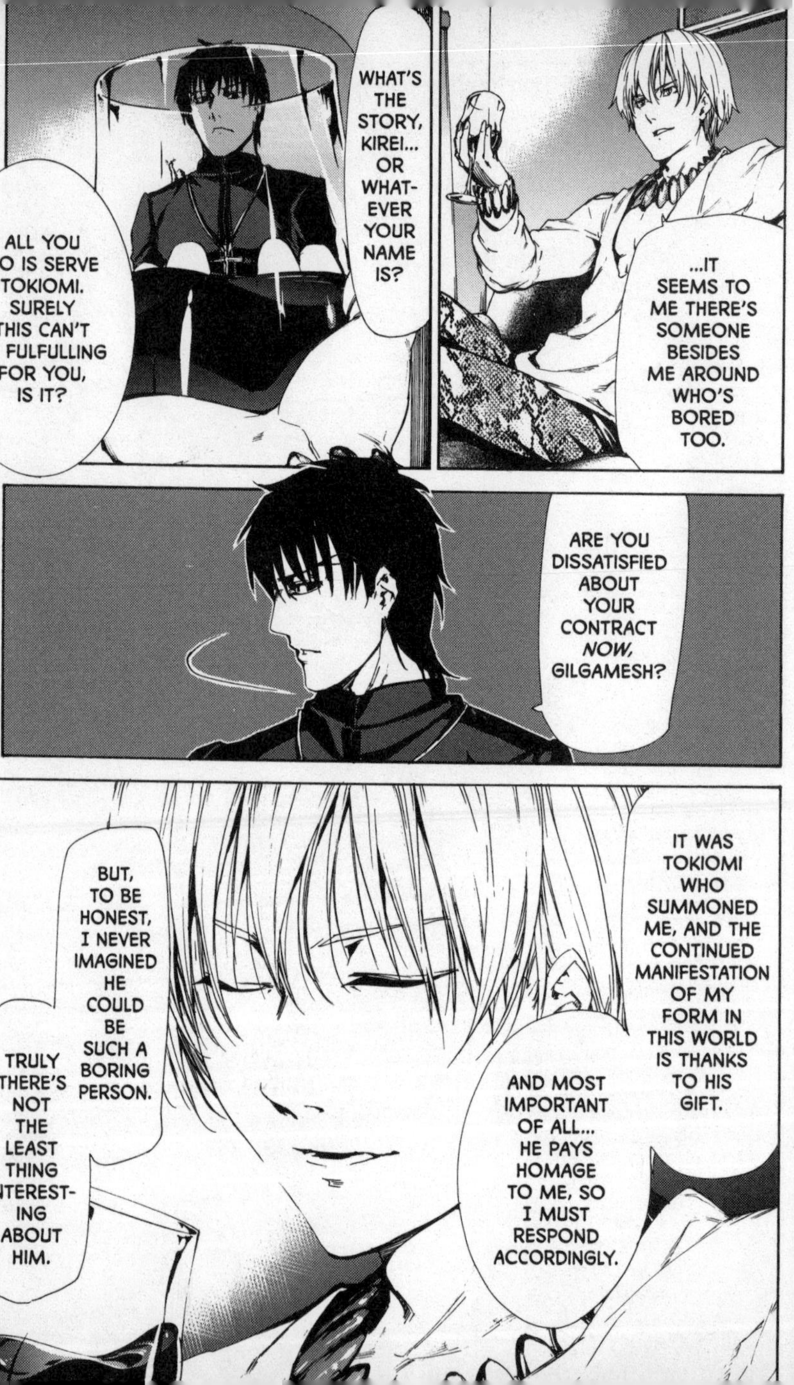
...IT SEEMS TO ME THERE'S SOMEONE BESIDES ME AROUND WHO'S BORED TOO.
WHAT'S THE STORY, KIREI... OR WHAT-EVER YOUR NAME IS?
ALL YOU DO IS SERVE TOKIOMI. SURELY THIS CAN'T BE FULFULLING FOR YOU, IS IT?
ARE YOU DISSATISFIED ABOUT YOUR CONTRACT *NOW,* GILGAMESH?
IT WAS TOKIOMI WHO SUMMONED ME, AND THE CONTINUED MANIFESTATION OF MY FORM IN THIS WORLD IS THANKS TO HIS GIFT.
AND MOST IMPORTANT OF ALL... HE PAYS HOMAGE TO ME, SO I MUST RESPOND ACCORDINGLY.
BUT, TO BE HONEST, I NEVER IMAGINED HE COULD BE SUCH A BORING PERSON.
TRULY THERE'S NOT THE LEAST THING INTEREST-ING ABOUT HIM.

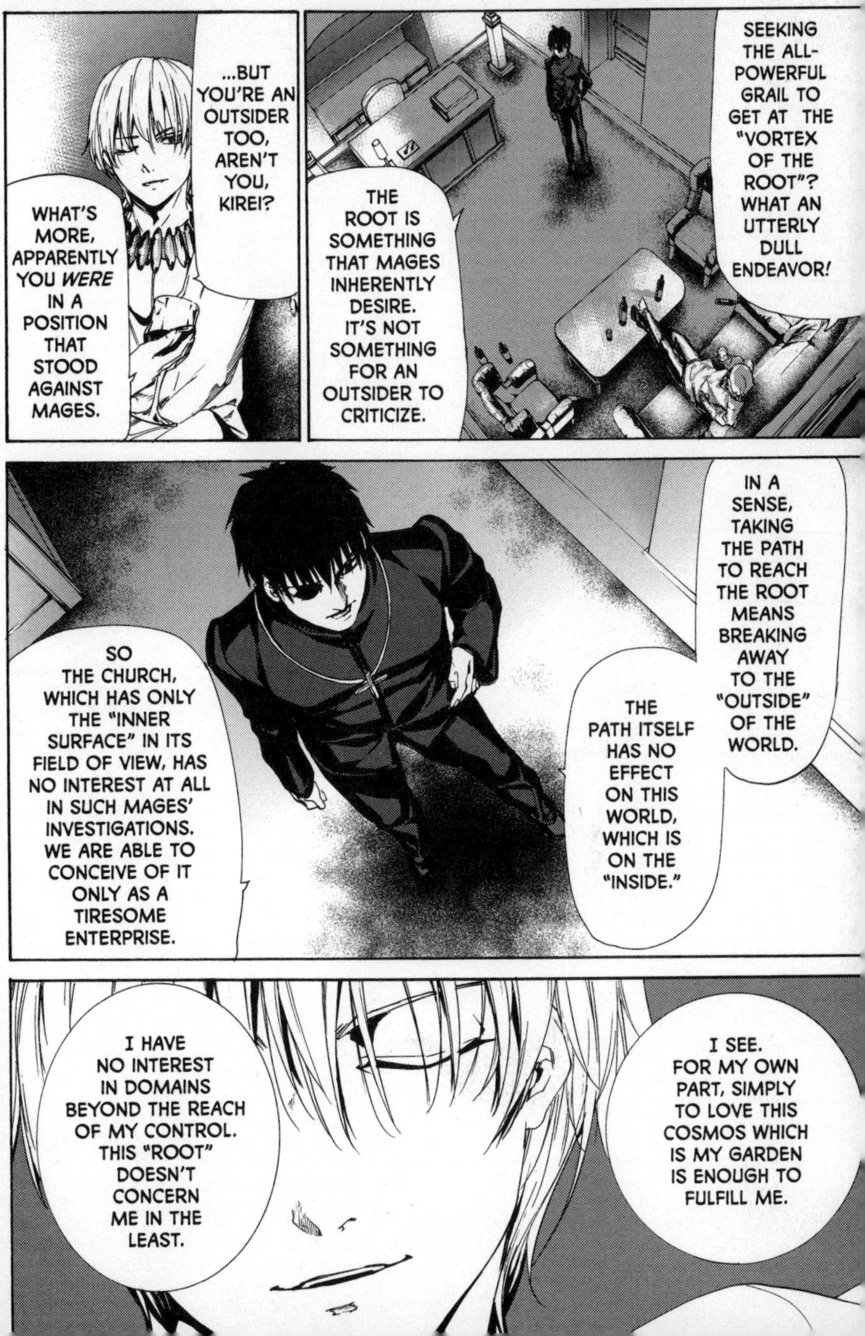
SEEKING THE ALL-POWERFUL GRAIL TO GET AT THE "VORTEX OF THE ROOT"? WHAT AN UTTERLY DULL ENDEAVOR!
THE ROOT IS SOMETHING THAT MAGES INHERENTLY DESIRE. IT'S NOT SOMETHING FOR AN OUTSIDER TO CRITICIZE.
...BUT YOU'RE AN OUTSIDER TOO, AREN'T YOU, KIREI?
WHAT'S MORE, APPARENTLY YOU *WERE* IN A POSITION THAT STOOD AGAINST MAGES.
IN A SENSE, TAKING THE PATH TO REACH THE ROOT MEANS BREAKING AWAY TO THE "OUTSIDE" OF THE WORLD.
THE PATH ITSELF HAS NO EFFECT ON THIS WORLD, WHICH IS ON THE "INSIDE."
SO THE CHURCH, WHICH HAS ONLY THE "INNER SURFACE" IN ITS FIELD OF VIEW, HAS NO INTEREST AT ALL IN SUCH MAGES' INVESTIGATIONS. WE ARE ABLE TO CONCEIVE OF IT ONLY AS A TIRESOME ENTERPRISE.
I SEE. FOR MY OWN PART, SIMPLY TO LOVE THIS COSMOS WHICH IS MY GARDEN IS ENOUGH TO FULFILL ME.
I HAVE NO INTEREST IN DOMAINS BEYOND THE REACH OF MY CONTROL. THIS "ROOT" DOESN'T CONCERN ME IN THE LEAST.

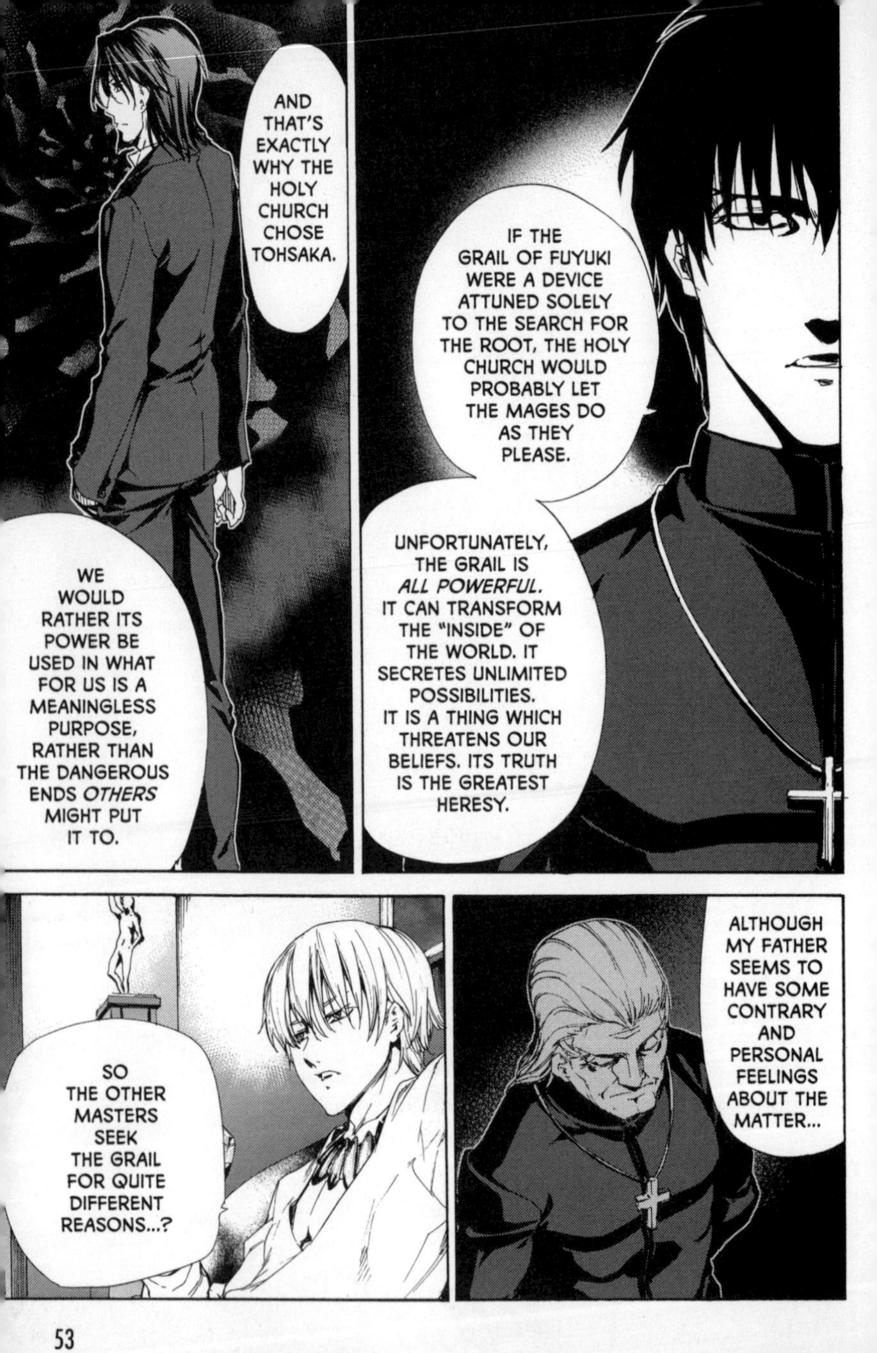
IF THE GRAIL OF FUYUKI WERE A DEVICE ATTUNED SOLELY TO THE SEARCH FOR THE ROOT, THE HOLY CHURCH WOULD PROBABLY LET THE MAGES DO AS THEY PLEASE.
UNFORTUNATELY, THE GRAIL IS *ALL POWERFUL.* IT CAN TRANSFORM THE "INSIDE" OF THE WORLD. IT SECRETES UNLIMITED POSSIBILITIES. IT IS A THING WHICH THREATENS OUR BELIEFS. ITS TRUTH IS THE GREATEST HERESY.
AND THAT'S EXACTLY WHY THE HOLY CHURCH CHOSE TOHSAKA.
WE WOULD RATHER ITS POWER BE USED IN WHAT FOR US IS A MEANINGLESS PURPOSE, RATHER THAN THE DANGEROUS ENDS *OTHERS* MIGHT PUT IT TO.
ALTHOUGH MY FATHER SEEMS TO HAVE SOME CONTRARY AND PERSONAL FEELINGS ABOUT THE MATTER...
SO THE OTHER MASTERS SEEK THE GRAIL FOR QUITE DIFFERENT REASONS...?

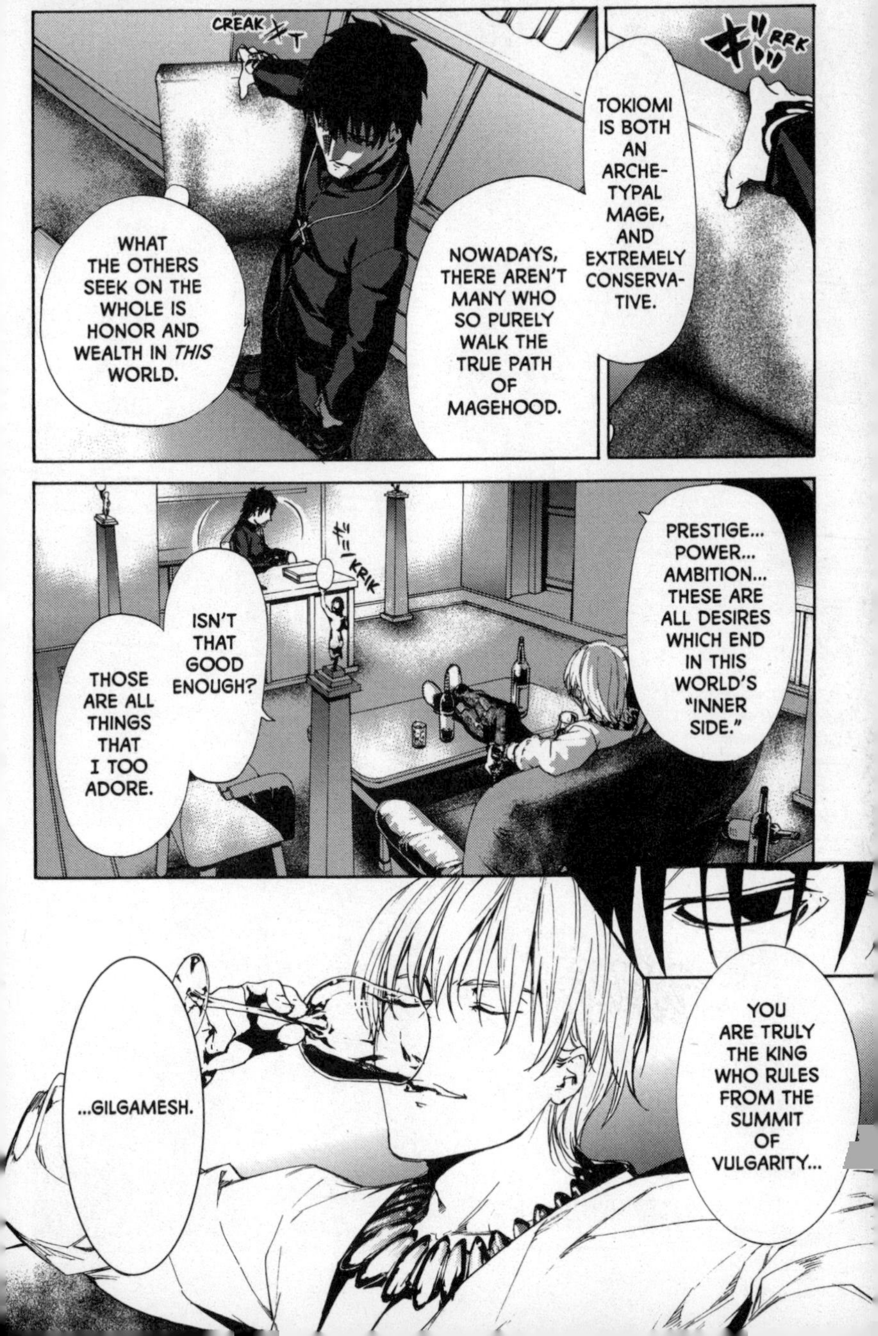
RRK
TOKIOMI IS BOTH AN ARCHE-TYPAL MAGE, AND EXTREMELY CONSERVA-TIVE.
CREAK
NOWADAYS, THERE AREN'T MANY WHO SO PURELY WALK THE TRUE PATH OF MAGEHOOD.
WHAT THE OTHERS SEEK ON THE WHOLE IS HONOR AND WEALTH IN *THIS* WORLD.
PRESTIGE... POWER... AMBITION... THESE ARE ALL DESIRES WHICH END IN THIS WORLD'S "INNER SIDE."
KRIK
ISN'T THAT GOOD ENOUGH?
THOSE ARE ALL THINGS THAT I TOO ADORE.
YOU ARE TRULY THE KING WHO RULES FROM THE SUMMIT OF VULGARITY...
...GILGAMESH.

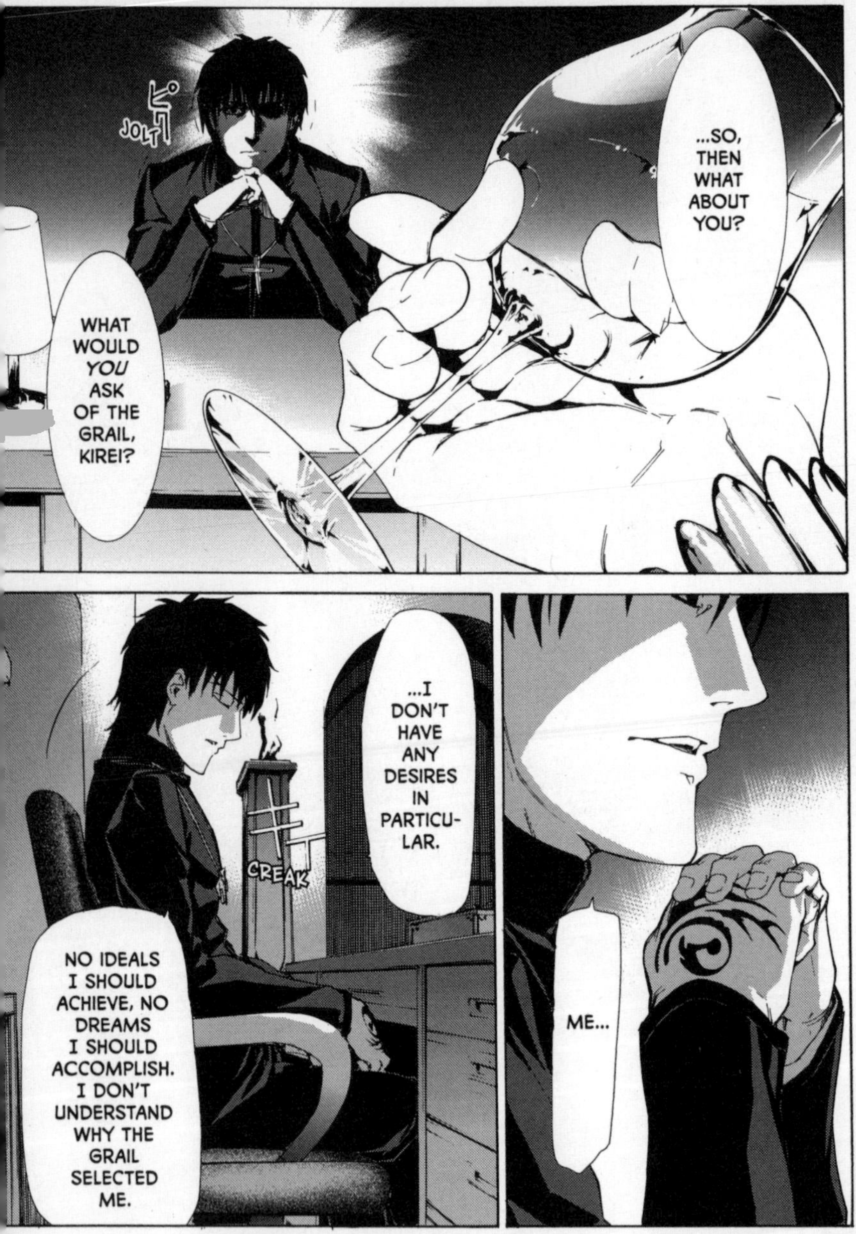
...SO, THEN WHAT ABOUT YOU?
JOLT
WHAT WOULD *YOU* ASK OF THE GRAIL, KIREI?
ME...
...I DON'T HAVE ANY DESIRES IN PARTICU-LAR.
CREAK
NO IDEALS I SHOULD ACHIEVE, NO DREAMS I SHOULD ACCOMPLISH. I DON'T UNDERSTAND WHY THE GRAIL SELECTED ME.

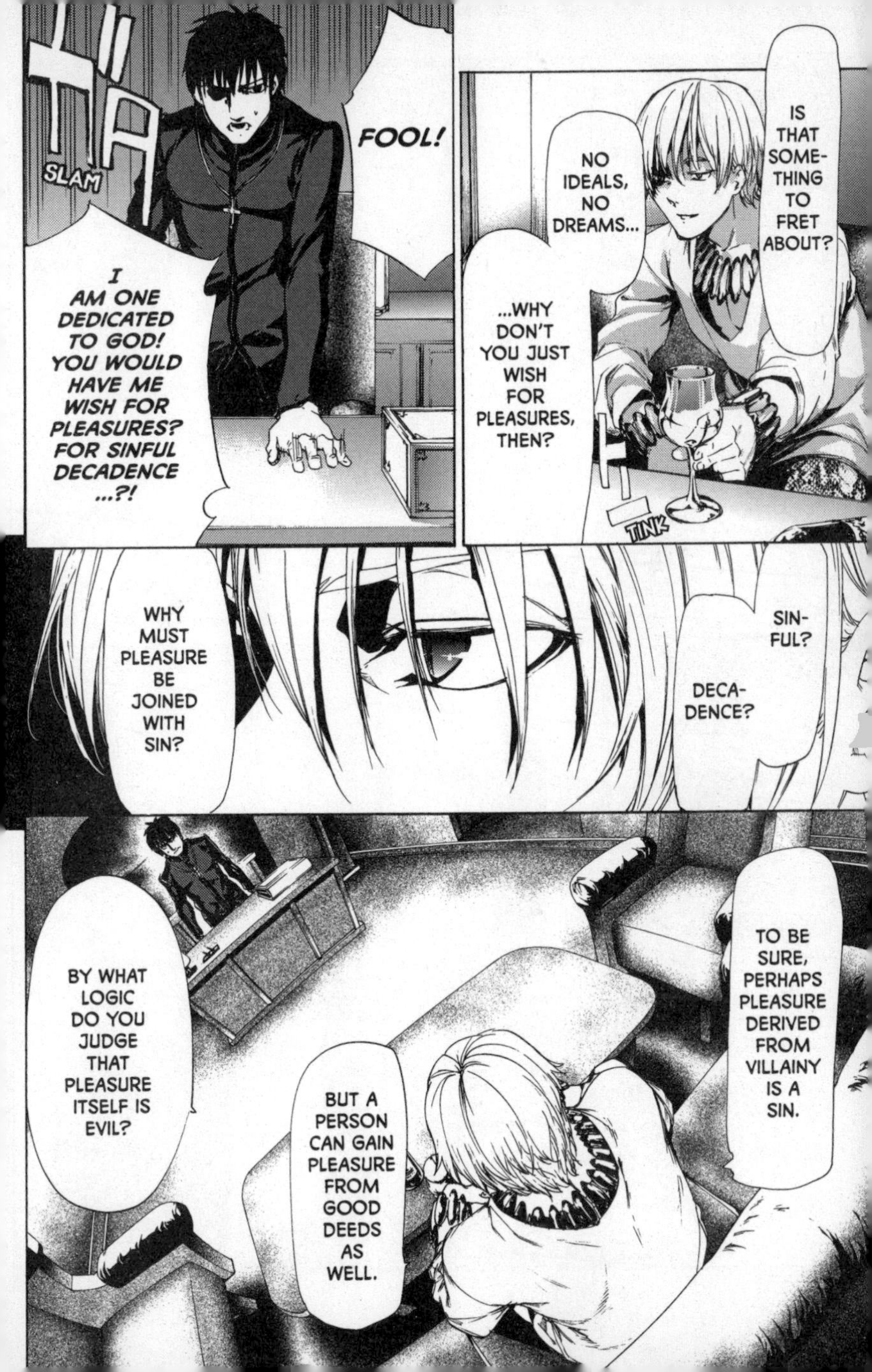
IS THAT SOMETHING TO FRET ABOUT?
NO IDEALS, NO DREAMS...
...WHY DON'T YOU JUST WISH FOR PLEASURES, THEN?
TINK
SLAM
FOOL!
I AM ONE DEDICATED TO GOD! YOU WOULD HAVE ME WISH FOR PLEASURES? FOR SINFUL DECADENCE ...?!
SINFUL?
DECADENCE?
WHY MUST PLEASURE BE JOINED WITH SIN?
TO BE SURE, PERHAPS PLEASURE DERIVED FROM VILLAINY IS A SIN.
BUT A PERSON CAN GAIN PLEASURE FROM GOOD DEEDS AS WELL.
BY WHAT LOGIC DO YOU JUDGE THAT PLEASURE ITSELF IS EVIL?

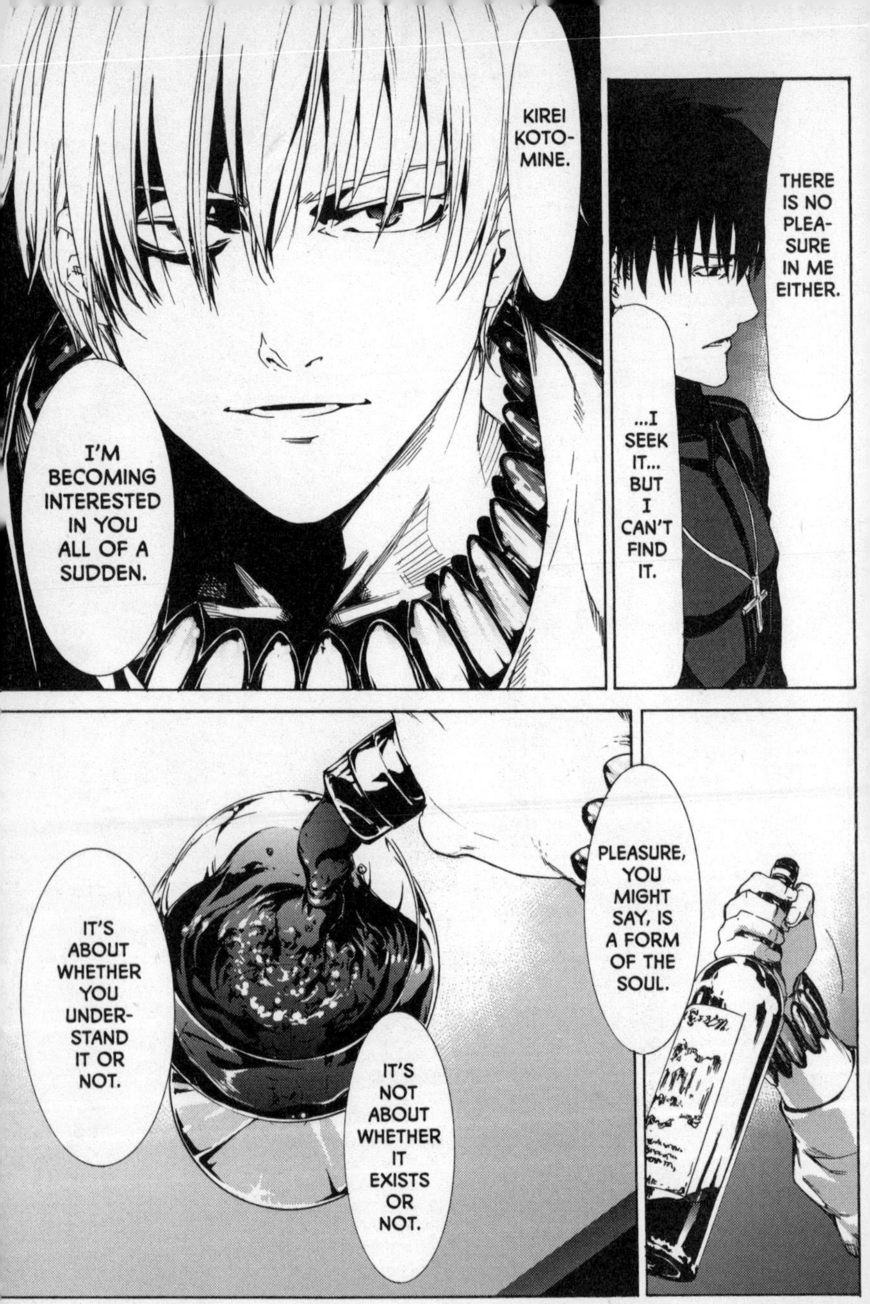
THERE IS NO PLEA-SURE IN ME EITHER.
...I SEEK IT... BUT I CAN'T FIND IT.
KIREI KOTO-MINE.
I'M BECOMING INTERESTED IN YOU ALL OF A SUDDEN.
PLEASURE, YOU MIGHT SAY, IS A FORM OF THE SOUL.
IT'S NOT ABOUT WHETHER IT EXISTS OR NOT.
IT'S ABOUT WHETHER YOU UNDER-STAND IT OR NOT.

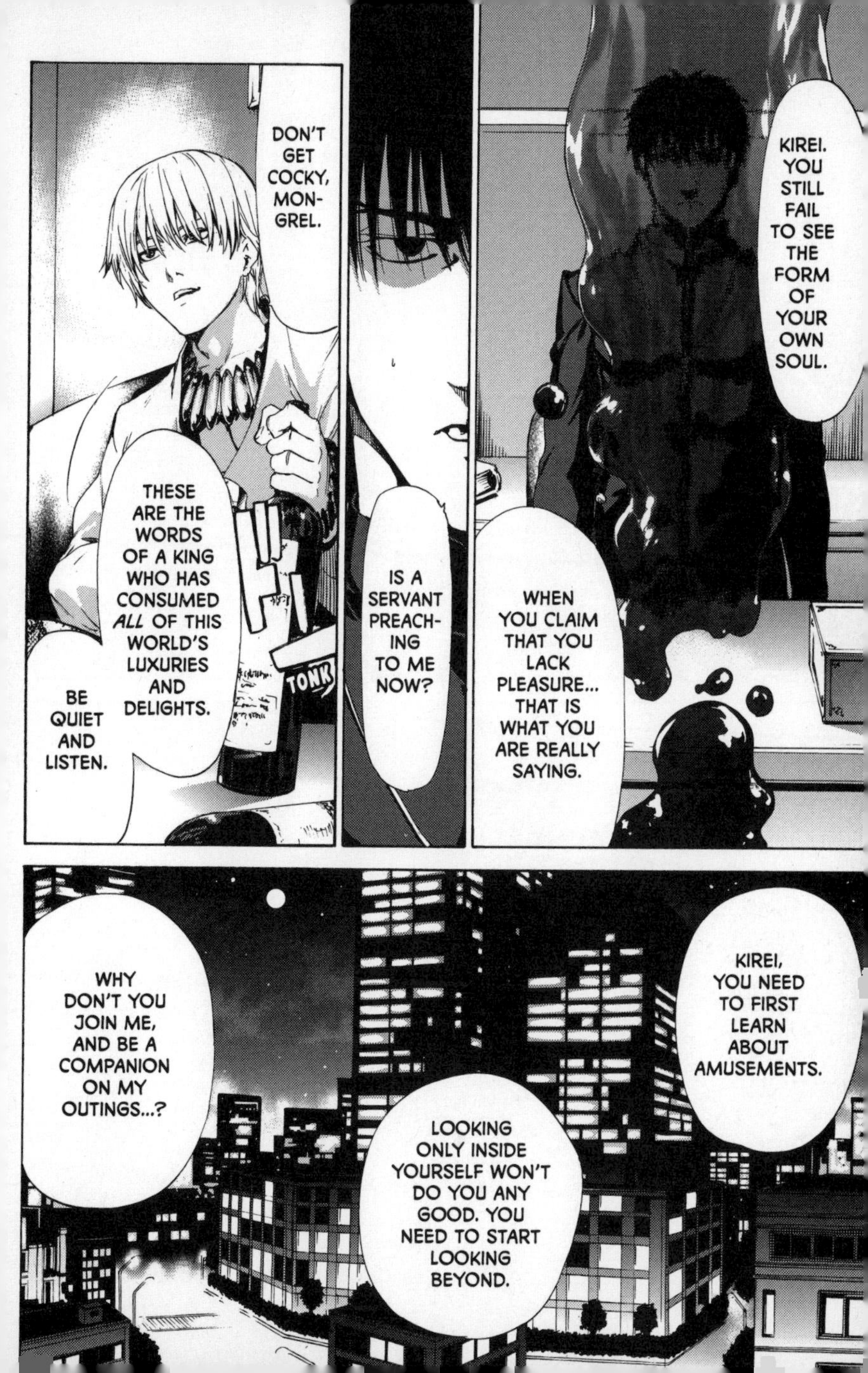
KIREI. YOU STILL FAIL TO SEE THE FORM OF YOUR OWN SOUL.
WHEN YOU CLAIM THAT YOU LACK PLEASURE... THAT IS WHAT YOU ARE REALLY SAYING.
IS A SERVANT PREACHING TO ME NOW?
DON'T GET COCKY, MONGREL.
TONK
THESE ARE THE WORDS OF A KING WHO HAS CONSUMED *ALL* OF THIS WORLD'S LUXURIES AND DELIGHTS.
BE QUIET AND LISTEN.
KIREI, YOU NEED TO FIRST LEARN ABOUT AMUSEMENTS.
LOOKING ONLY INSIDE YOURSELF WON'T DO YOU ANY GOOD. YOU NEED TO START LOOKING BEYOND.
WHY DON'T YOU JOIN ME, AND BE A COMPANION ON MY OUTINGS...?

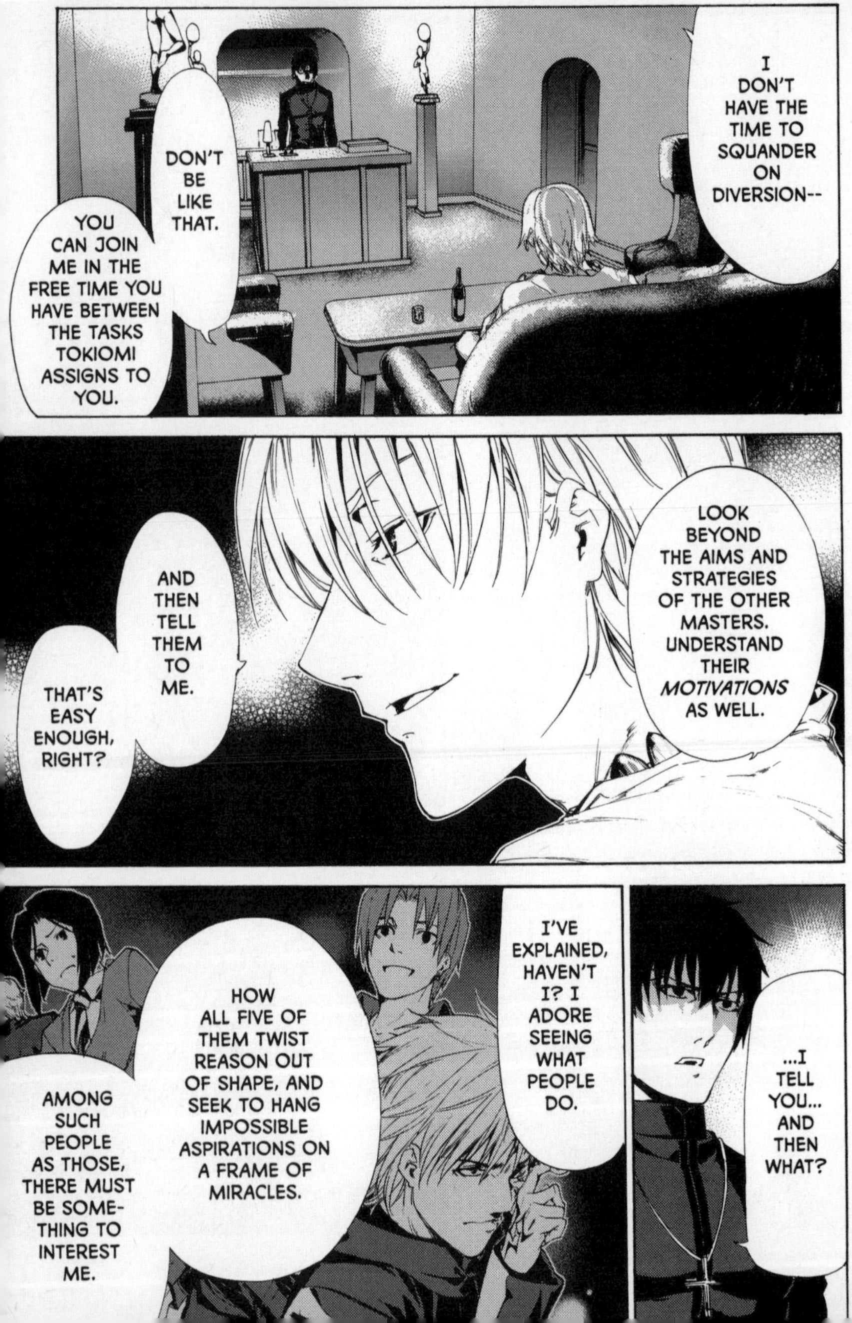
I DON'T HAVE THE TIME TO SQUANDER ON DIVERSION--
DON'T BE LIKE THAT.
YOU CAN JOIN ME IN THE FREE TIME YOU HAVE BETWEEN THE TASKS TOKIOMI ASSIGNS TO YOU.
LOOK BEYOND THE AIMS AND STRATEGIES OF THE OTHER MASTERS. UNDERSTAND THEIR *MOTIVATIONS* AS WELL.
AND THEN TELL THEM TO ME.
THAT'S EASY ENOUGH, RIGHT?
...I TELL YOU... AND THEN WHAT?
I'VE EXPLAINED, HAVEN'T I? I ADORE SEEING WHAT PEOPLE DO.
HOW ALL FIVE OF THEM TWIST REASON OUT OF SHAPE, AND SEEK TO HANG IMPOSSIBLE ASPIRATIONS ON A FRAME OF MIRACLES.
AMONG SUCH PEOPLE AS THOSE, THERE MUST BE SOME-THING TO INTEREST ME.

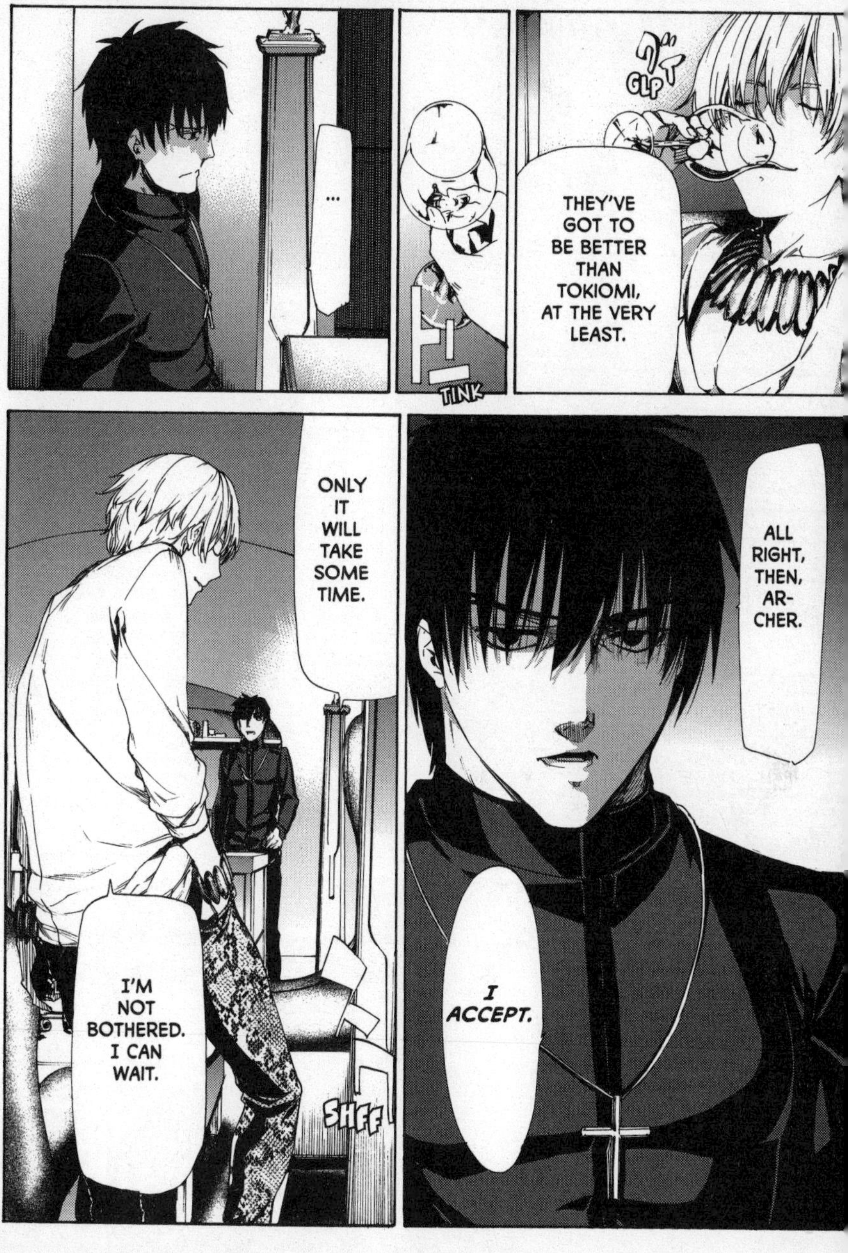
グイ
GLP
THEY'VE GOT TO BE BETTER THAN TOKIOMI, AT THE VERY LEAST.
TINK
...
ALL RIGHT, THEN, ARCHER.
I ACCEPT.
ONLY IT WILL TAKE SOME TIME.
I'M NOT BOTHERED. I CAN WAIT.
SHFF

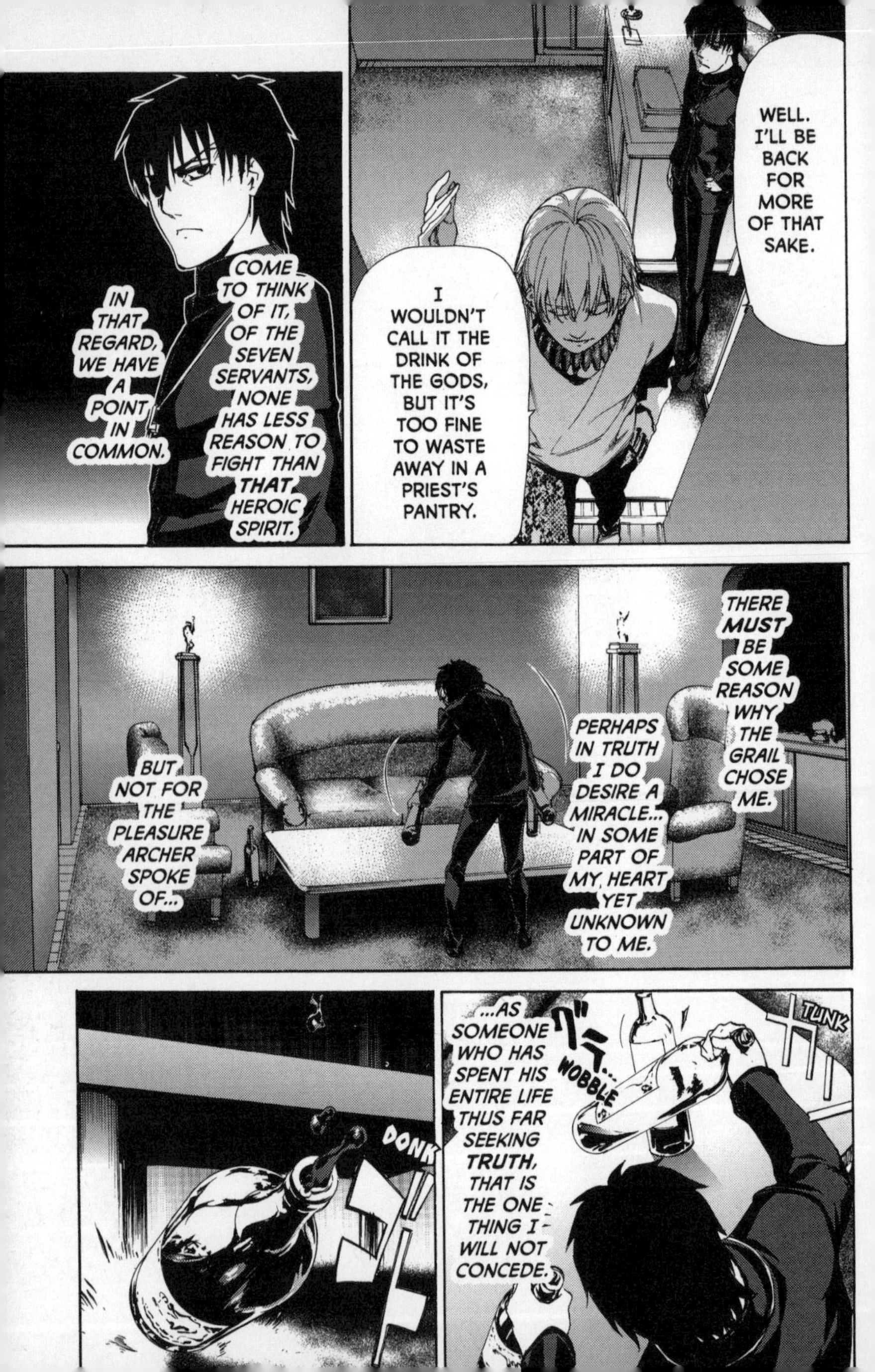
WELL. I'LL BE BACK FOR MORE OF THAT SAKE.
I WOULDN'T CALL IT THE DRINK OF THE GODS, BUT IT'S TOO FINE TO WASTE AWAY IN A PRIEST'S PANTRY.
COME TO THINK OF IT, OF THE SEVEN SERVANTS, NONE HAS LESS REASON TO FIGHT THAN THAT HEROIC SPIRIT.
IN THAT REGARD, WE HAVE A POINT IN COMMON.
THERE MUST BE SOME REASON WHY THE GRAIL CHOSE ME.
PERHAPS IN TRUTH I DO DESIRE A MIRACLE... IN SOME PART OF MY HEART YET UNKNOWN TO ME.
BUT NOT FOR THE PLEASURE ARCHER SPOKE OF...
TUNK
WOBBLE...
...AS SOMEONE WHO HAS SPENT HIS ENTIRE LIFE THUS FAR SEEKING TRUTH, THAT IS THE ONE THING I WILL NOT CONCEDE.
DONK

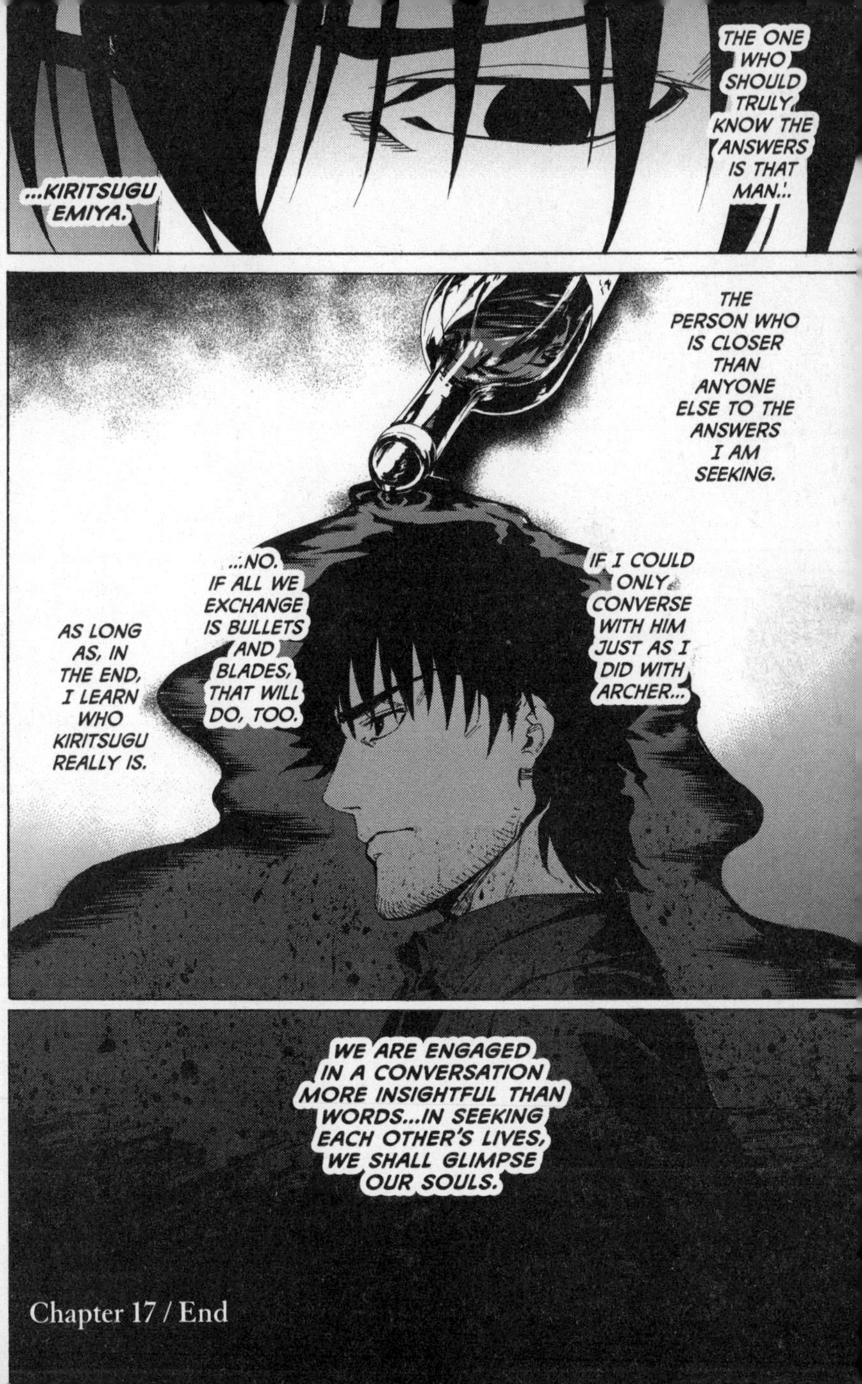
THE ONE WHO SHOULD TRULY KNOW THE ANSWERS IS THAT MAN...
...KIRITSUGU EMIYA.
THE PERSON WHO IS CLOSER THAN ANYONE ELSE TO THE ANSWERS I AM SEEKING.
IF I COULD ONLY CONVERSE WITH HIM JUST AS I DID WITH ARCHER...
...NO. IF ALL WE EXCHANGE IS BULLETS AND BLADES, THAT WILL DO, TOO.
AS LONG AS, IN THE END, I LEARN WHO KIRITSUGU REALLY IS.
WE ARE ENGAGED IN A CONVERSATION MORE INSIGHTFUL THAN WORDS...IN SEEKING EACH OTHER'S LIVES, WE SHALL GLIMPSE OUR SOULS.
Chapter 17 / End

Fate/Zero
フェイト／ゼロ

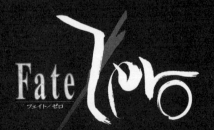

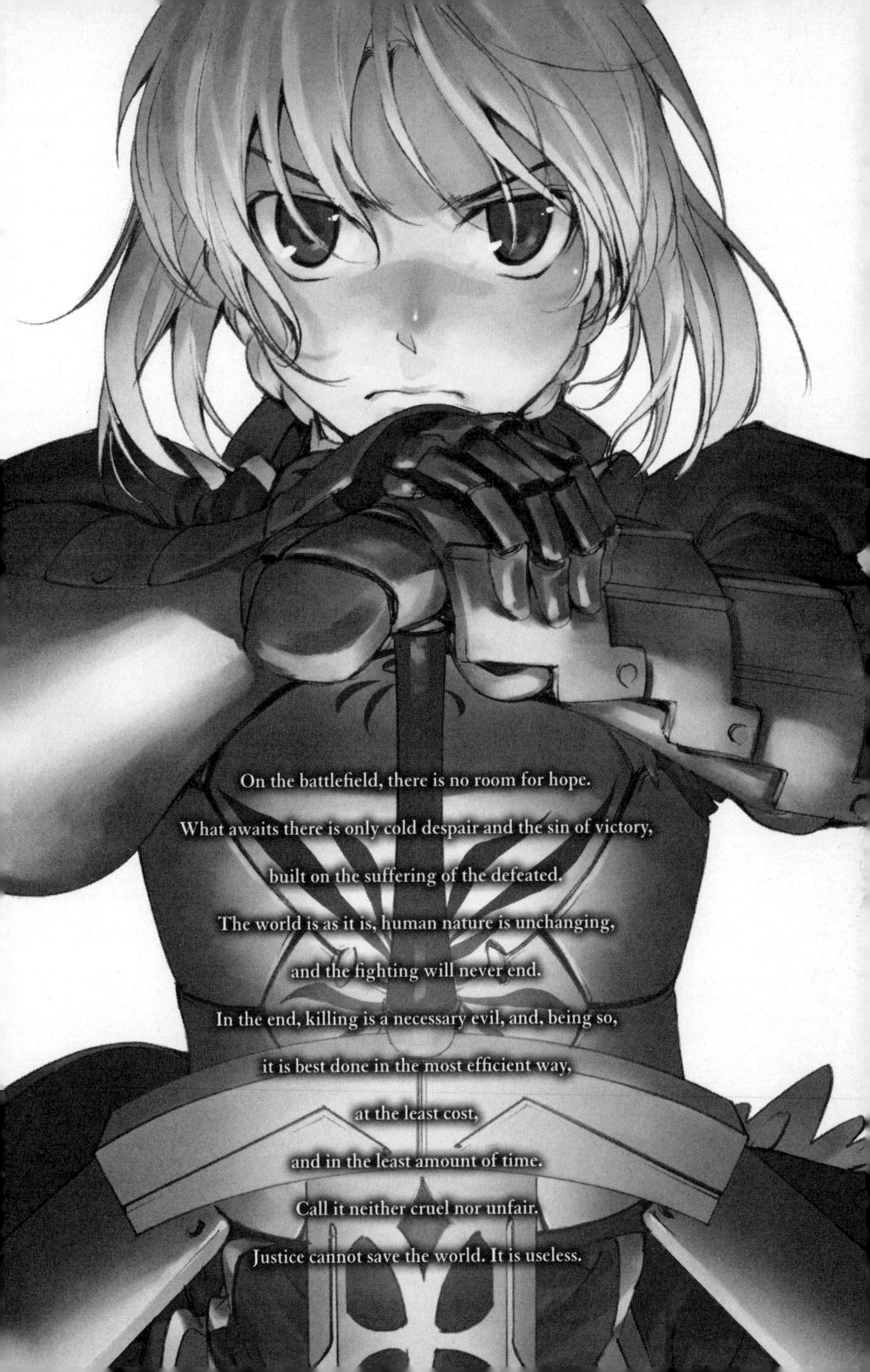
On the battlefield, there is no room for hope.
What awaits there is only cold despair and the sin of victory,
built on the suffering of the defeated.
The world is as it is, human nature is unchanging,
and the fighting will never end.
In the end, killing is a necessary evil, and, being so,
it is best done in the most efficient way,
at the least cost,
and in the least amount of time.
Call it neither cruel nor unfair.
Justice cannot save the world. It is useless.

CHAPTER 18

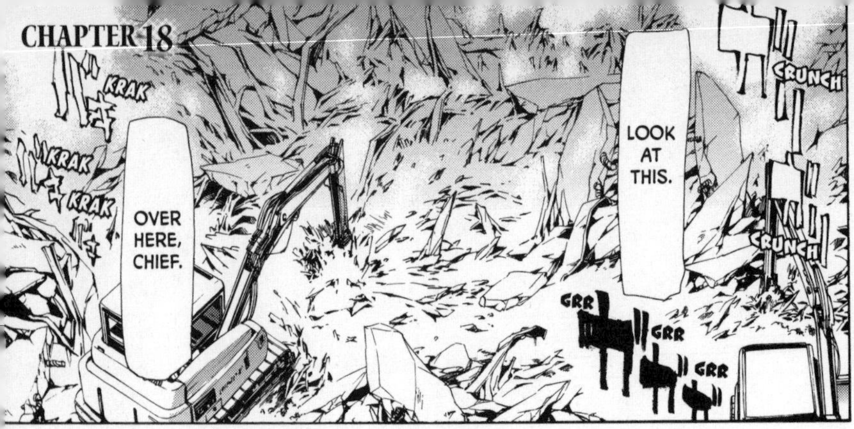
CRUNCH
CRUNCH
LOOK AT THIS.
GRR GRR GRR
KRAK KRAK KRAK
OVER HERE, CHIEF.

–140:41:54

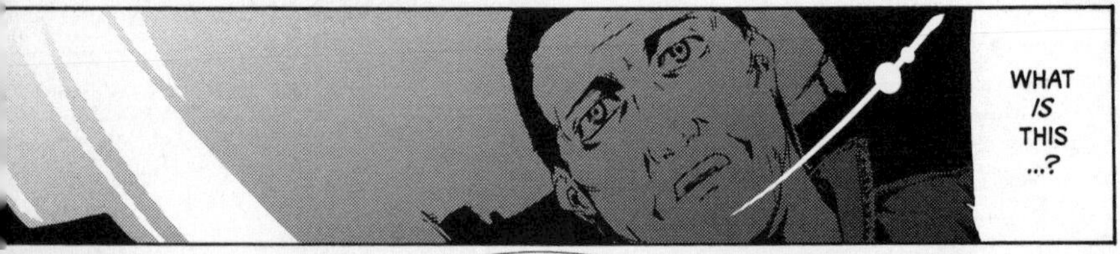
WHAT *IS* THIS ...?

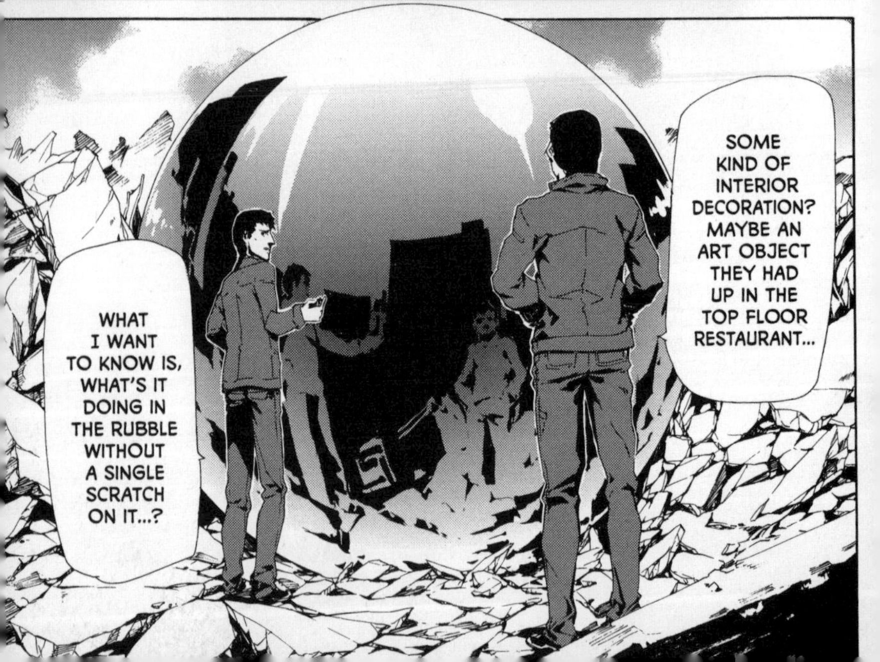
SOME KIND OF INTERIOR DECORATION? MAYBE AN ART OBJECT THEY HAD UP IN THE TOP FLOOR RESTAURANT...
WHAT I WANT TO KNOW IS, WHAT'S IT DOING IN THE RUBBLE WITHOUT A SINGLE SCRATCH ON IT...?

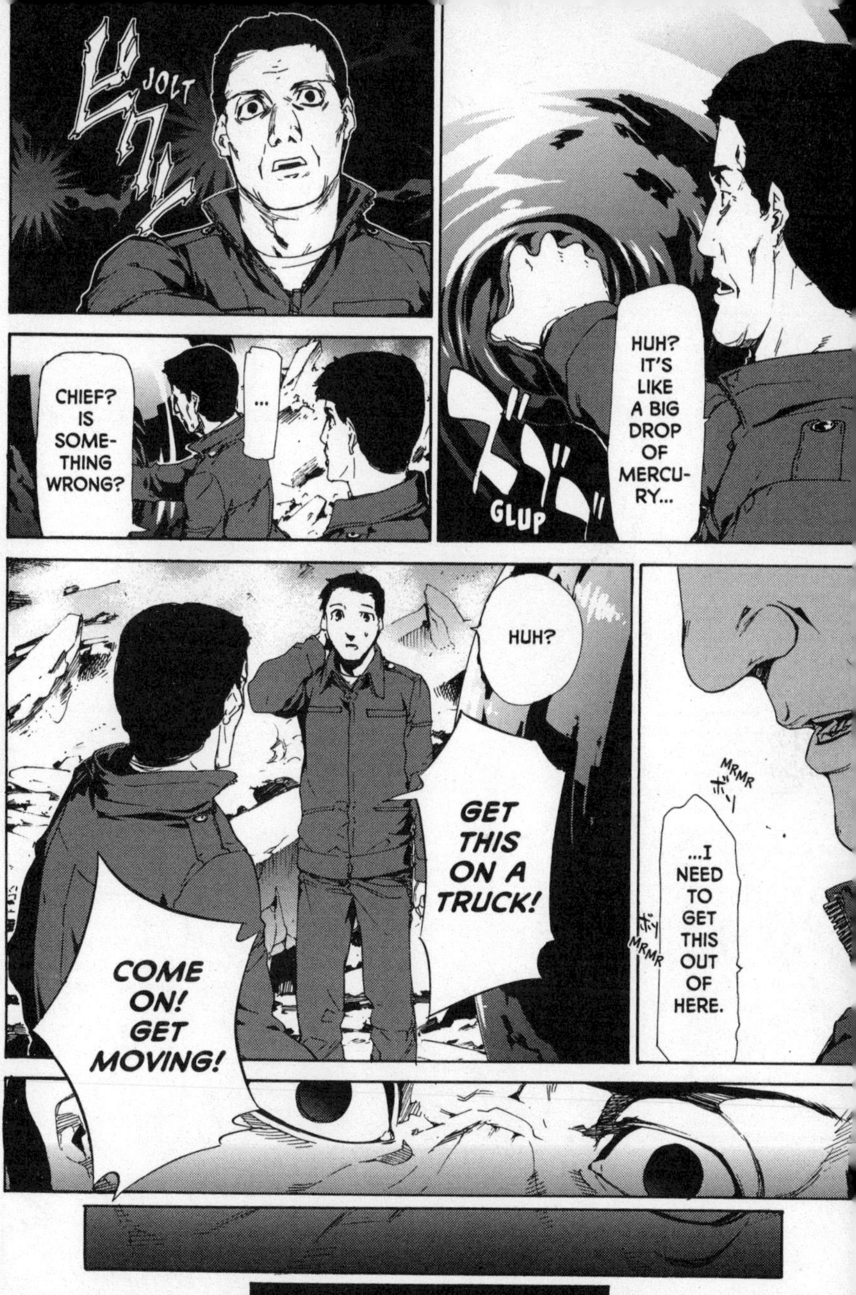
HUH? IT'S LIKE A BIG DROP OF MERCURY...
GLUP
JOLT
CHIEF? IS SOMETHING WRONG?
...
MRMR
...I NEED TO GET THIS OUT OF HERE.
MRMR
HUH?
GET THIS ON A TRUCK!
COME ON! GET MOVING!

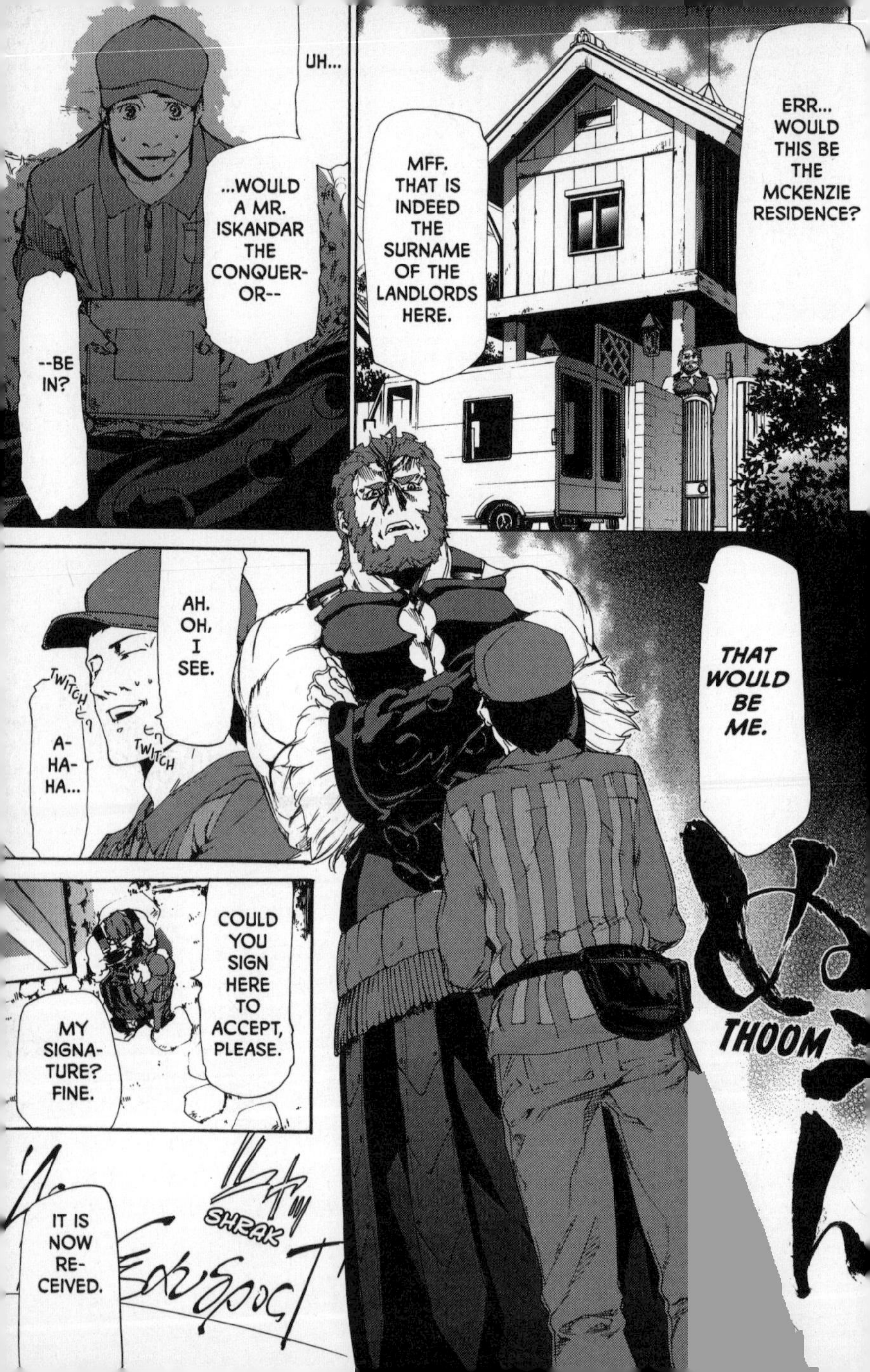
ERR... WOULD THIS BE THE MCKENZIE RESIDENCE?
MFF. THAT IS INDEED THE SURNAME OF THE LANDLORDS HERE.
UH...
...WOULD A MR. ISKANDAR THE CONQUER-OR--
--BE IN?
THAT WOULD BE ME.
THOOM
AH. OH, I SEE.
TWITCH
TWITCH
A-HA-HA...
COULD YOU SIGN HERE TO ACCEPT, PLEASE.
MY SIGNA-TURE? FINE.
SHRAK
IT IS NOW RE-CEIVED.

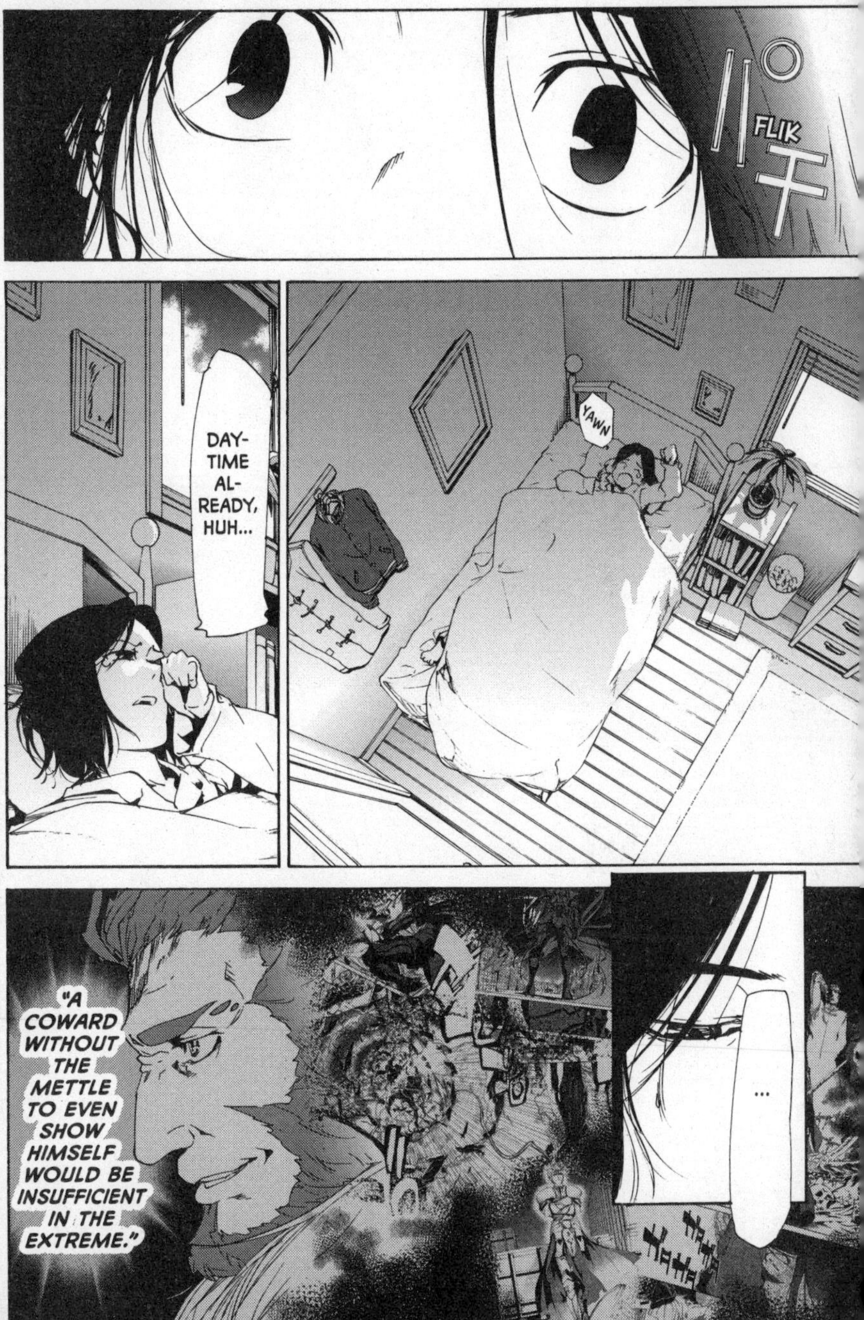
パチ
FLIK
YAWN
DAY-TIME AL-READY, HUH...
...
"A COWARD WITHOUT THE METTLE TO EVEN SHOW HIMSELF WOULD BE INSUFFICIENT IN THE EXTREME."

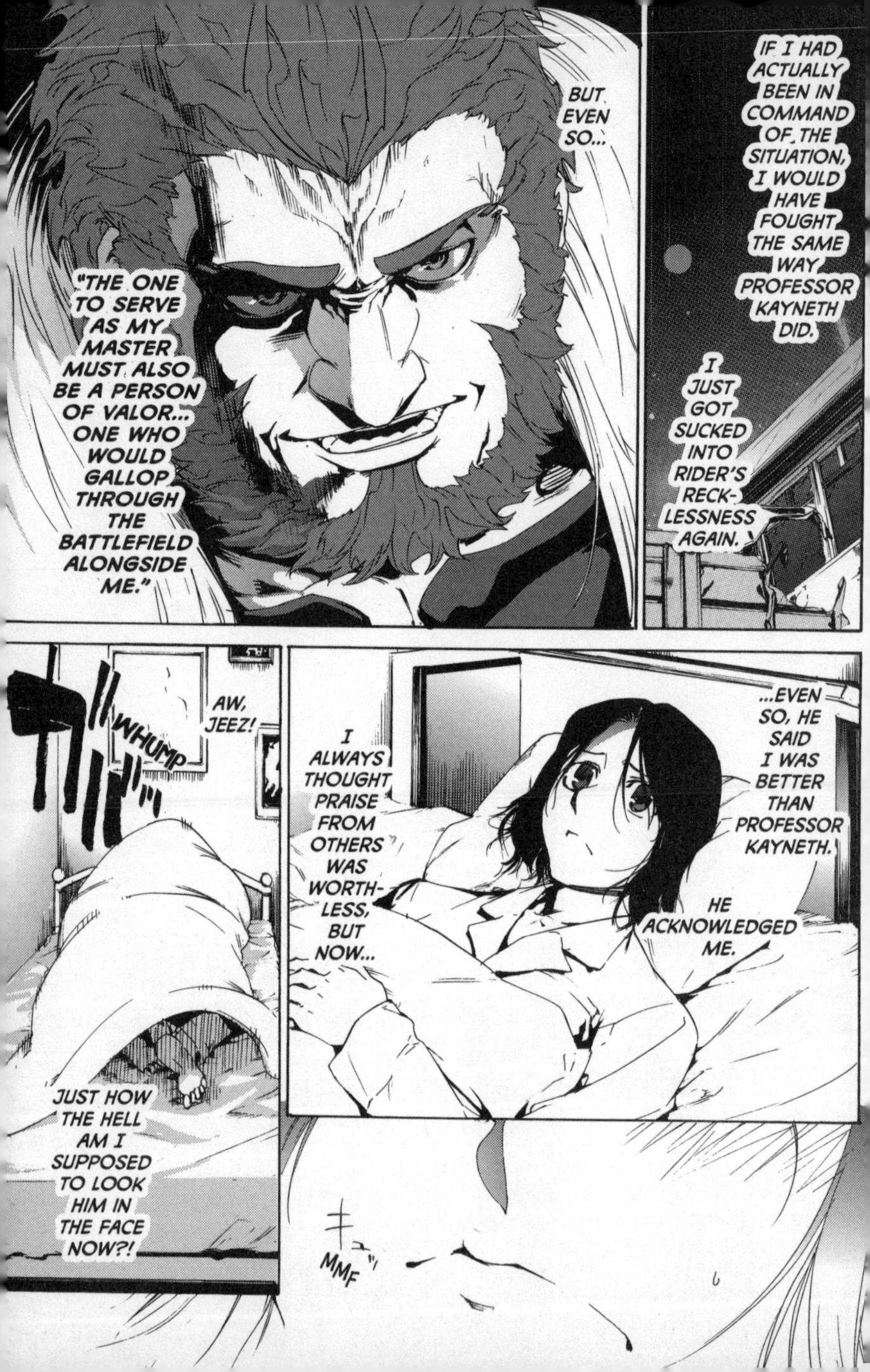
IF I HAD ACTUALLY BEEN IN COMMAND OF THE SITUATION, I WOULD HAVE FOUGHT THE SAME WAY PROFESSOR KAYNETH DID.
I JUST GOT SUCKED INTO RIDER'S RECK-LESSNESS AGAIN.
BUT EVEN SO...
"THE ONE TO SERVE AS MY MASTER MUST ALSO BE A PERSON OF VALOR... ONE WHO WOULD GALLOP THROUGH THE BATTLEFIELD ALONGSIDE ME."
...EVEN SO, HE SAID I WAS BETTER THAN PROFESSOR KAYNETH.
HE ACKNOWLEDGED ME.
I ALWAYS THOUGHT PRAISE FROM OTHERS WAS WORTH-LESS, BUT NOW...
MMF
WHUMP
AW, JEEZ!
JUST HOW THE HELL AM I SUPPOSED TO LOOK HIM IN THE FACE NOW?!

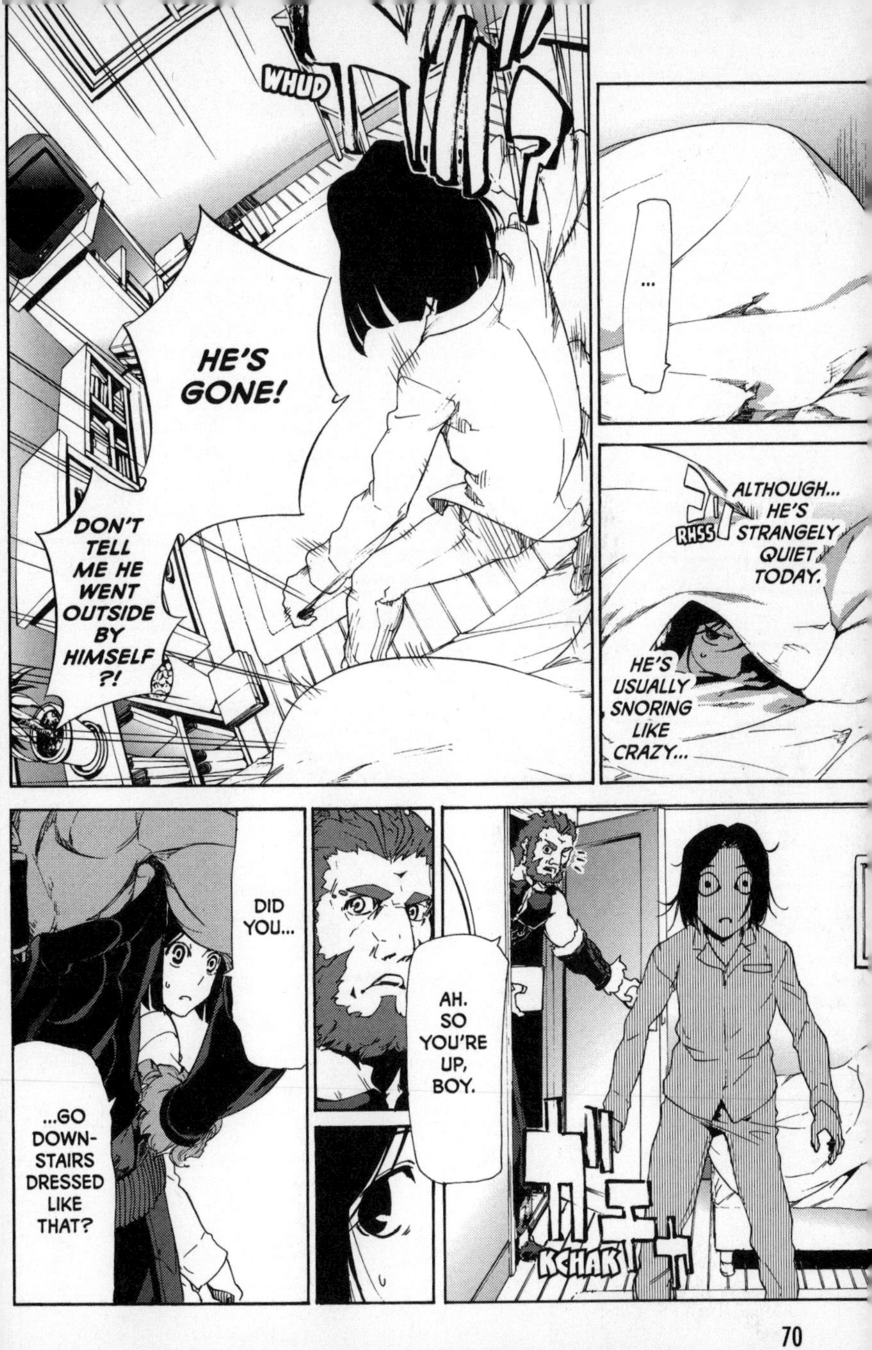
...
RHSS
ALTHOUGH... HE'S STRANGELY QUIET TODAY.
HE'S USUALLY SNORING LIKE CRAZY...
WHUD
HE'S GONE!
DON'T TELL ME HE WENT OUTSIDE BY HIMSELF?!
KCHAK
AH. SO YOU'RE UP, BOY.
DID YOU...
...GO DOWN-STAIRS DRESSED LIKE THAT?

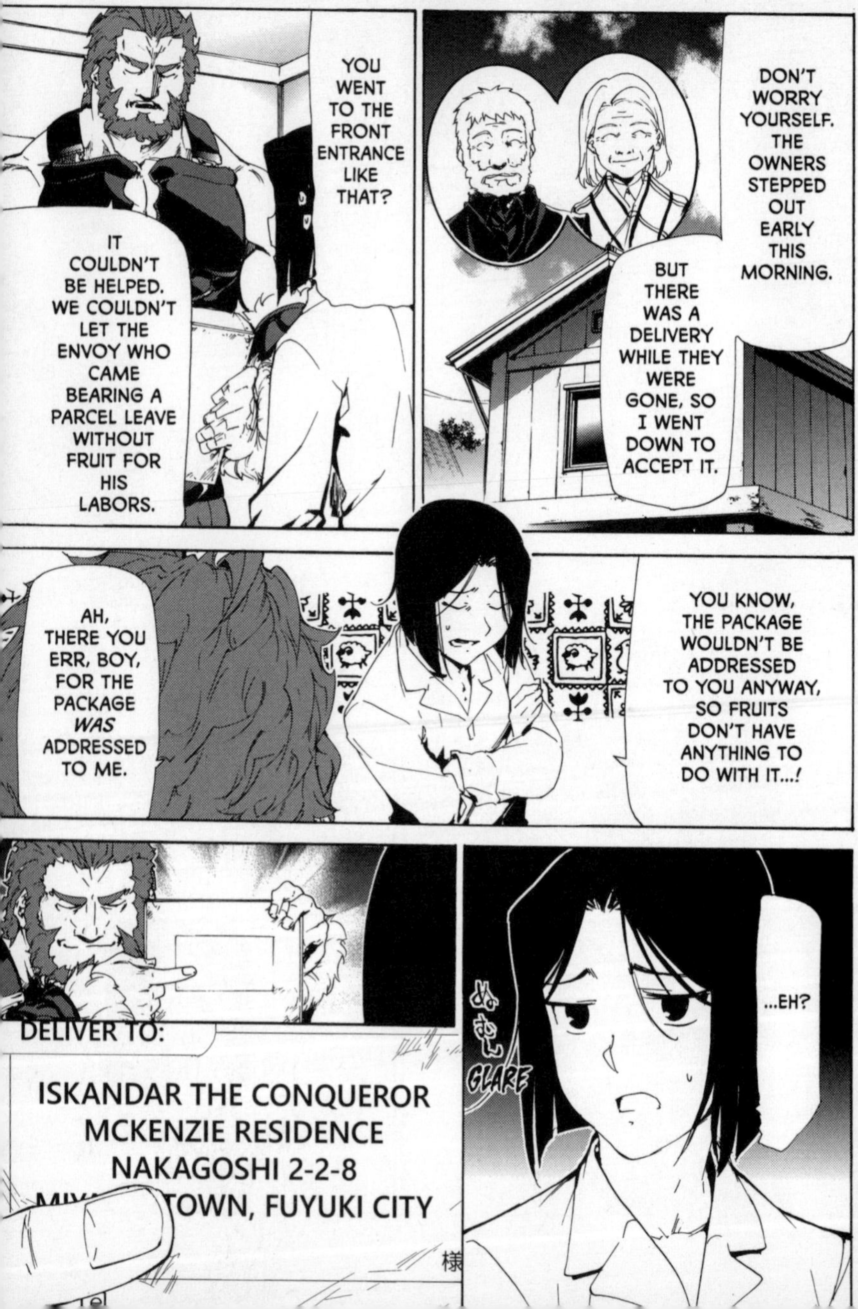
DON'T WORRY YOURSELF. THE OWNERS STEPPED OUT EARLY THIS MORNING.
BUT THERE WAS A DELIVERY WHILE THEY WERE GONE, SO I WENT DOWN TO ACCEPT IT.
YOU WENT TO THE FRONT ENTRANCE LIKE THAT?
IT COULDN'T BE HELPED. WE COULDN'T LET THE ENVOY WHO CAME BEARING A PARCEL LEAVE WITHOUT FRUIT FOR HIS LABORS.
YOU KNOW, THE PACKAGE WOULDN'T BE ADDRESSED TO YOU ANYWAY, SO FRUITS DON'T HAVE ANYTHING TO DO WITH IT...!
AH, THERE YOU ERR, BOY, FOR THE PACKAGE *WAS* ADDRESSED TO ME.
...EH?
GLARE
DELIVER TO:
ISKANDAR THE CONQUEROR
MCKENZIE RESIDENCE
NAKAGOSHI 2-2-8
TOWN, FUYUKI CITY
様

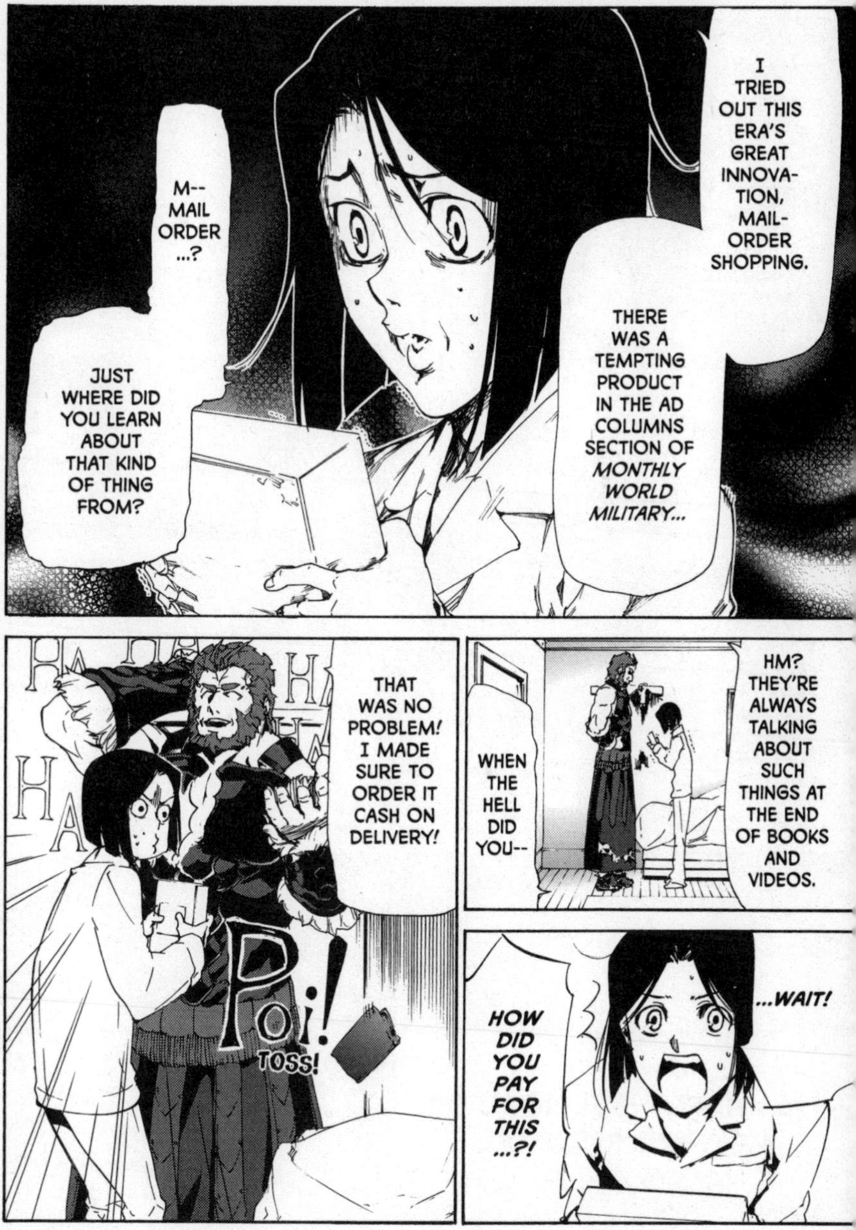
I TRIED OUT THIS ERA'S GREAT INNOVATION, MAIL-ORDER SHOPPING.
THERE WAS A TEMPTING PRODUCT IN THE AD COLUMNS SECTION OF *MONTHLY WORLD MILITARY*...
M-- MAIL ORDER ...?
JUST WHERE DID YOU LEARN ABOUT THAT KIND OF THING FROM?
WHEN THE HELL DID YOU--
HM? THEY'RE ALWAYS TALKING ABOUT SUCH THINGS AT THE END OF BOOKS AND VIDEOS.
...WAIT!
HOW DID YOU PAY FOR THIS ...?!
THAT WAS NO PROBLEM! I MADE SURE TO ORDER IT CASH ON DELIVERY!
HA HA HA HA HA HA
POI!
TOSS!

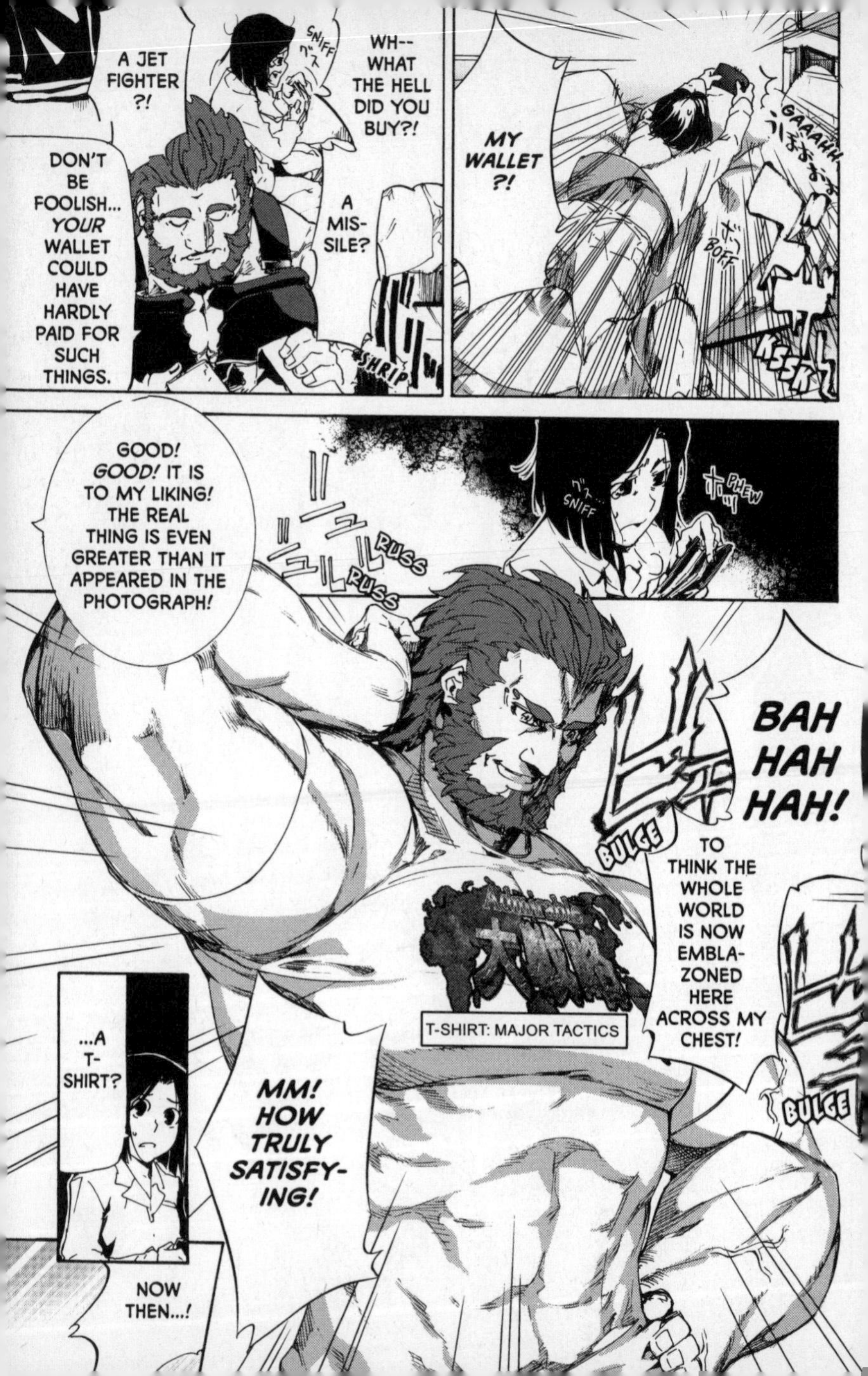
MY WALLET ?!
GAAAHH
BOFF
KSSK
SNIFF
WH-- WHAT THE HELL DID YOU BUY?!
A JET FIGHTER ?!
A MIS-SILE?
DON'T BE FOOLISH... *YOUR* WALLET COULD HAVE HARDLY PAID FOR SUCH THINGS.
SHRIP
SNIFF
PHEW
GOOD! *GOOD!* IT IS TO MY LIKING! THE REAL THING IS EVEN GREATER THAN IT APPEARED IN THE PHOTOGRAPH!
RUSS
RUSS
BAH HAH HAH!
BULGE
TO THINK THE WHOLE WORLD IS NOW EMBLA-ZONED HERE ACROSS MY CHEST!
BULGE
T-SHIRT: MAJOR TACTICS
MM! HOW TRULY SATISFY-ING!
...A T-SHIRT?
NOW THEN...!

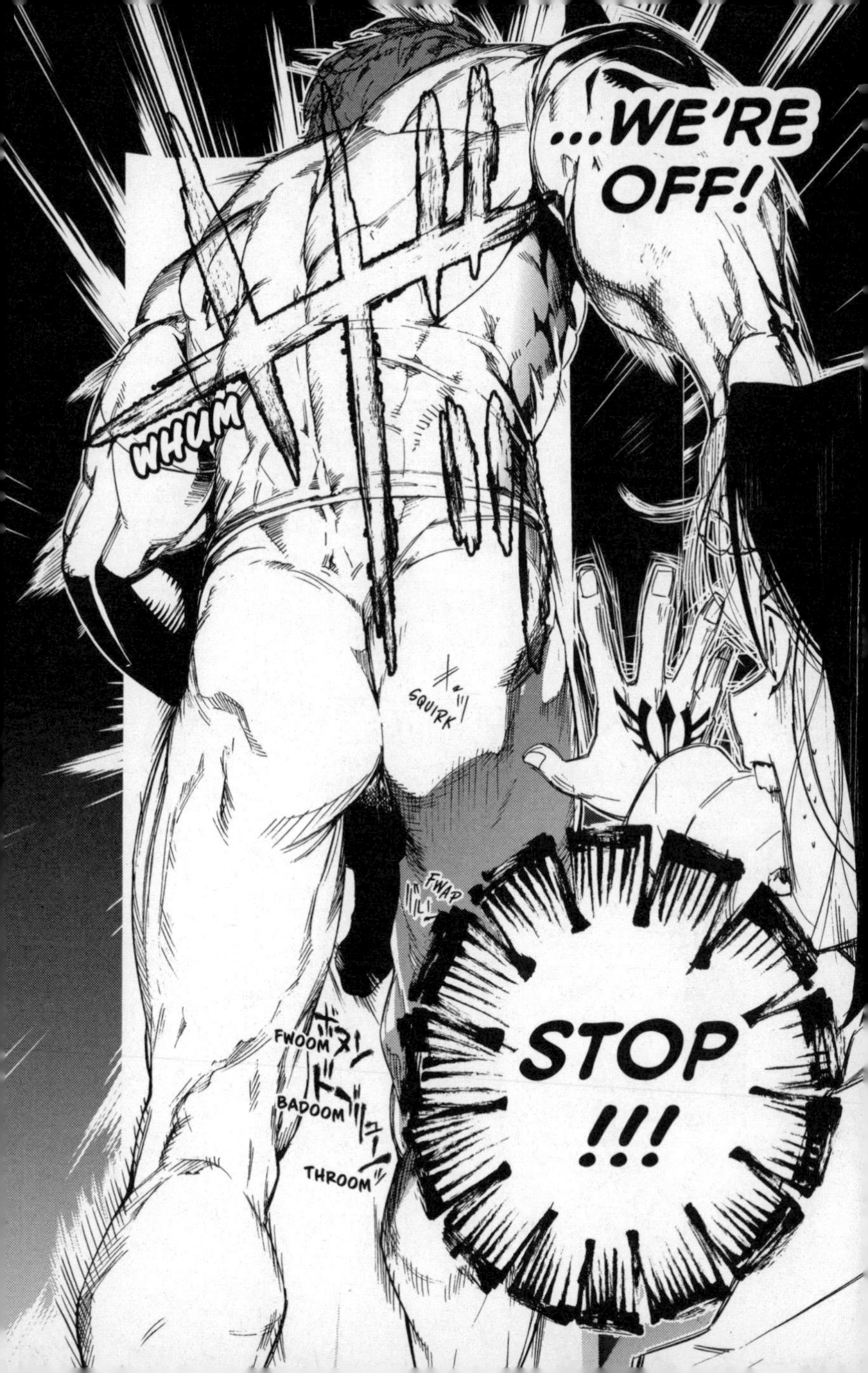
...WE'RE OFF!
WHUM
SQUIRK
FWAP
FWOOM
BADOOM
THROOM
STOP !!!

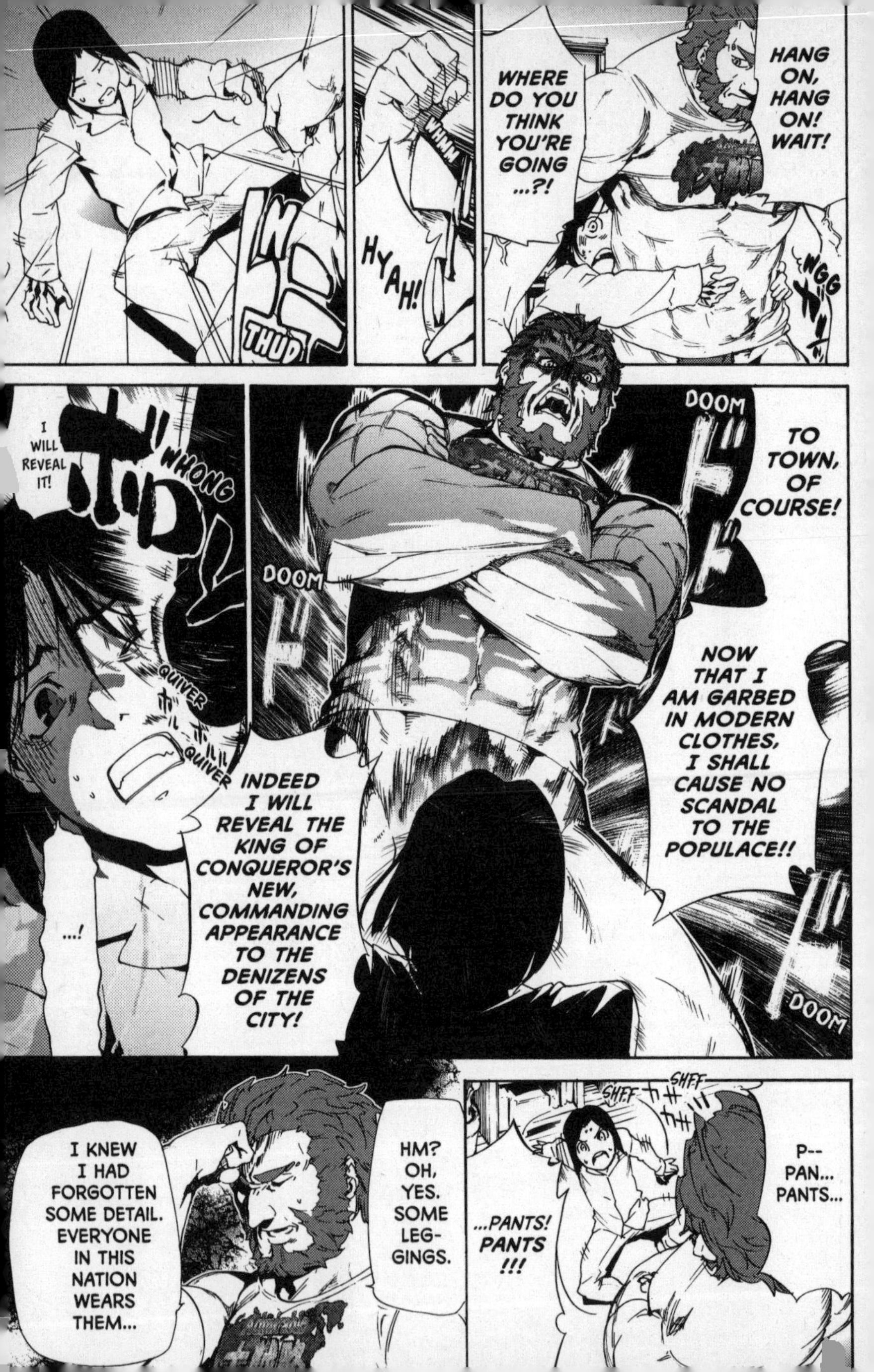
HANG ON, HANG ON! WAIT!
WHERE DO YOU THINK YOU'RE GOING ...?!
WGG
WHMM
HYAH!
THUD
TO TOWN, OF COURSE!
DOOM
NOW THAT I AM GARBED IN MODERN CLOTHES, I SHALL CAUSE NO SCANDAL TO THE POPULACE!!
DOOM
INDEED I WILL REVEAL THE KING OF CONQUEROR'S NEW, COMMANDING APPEARANCE TO THE DENIZENS OF THE CITY!
DOOM
I WILL REVEAL IT!
WHONG
QUIVER
QUIVER
...!
P-- PAN... PANTS...
SHFF
SHFF
...PANTS! PANTS !!!
HM? OH, YES. SOME LEG-GINGS.
I KNEW I HAD FORGOTTEN SOME DETAIL. EVERYONE IN THIS NATION WEARS THEM...

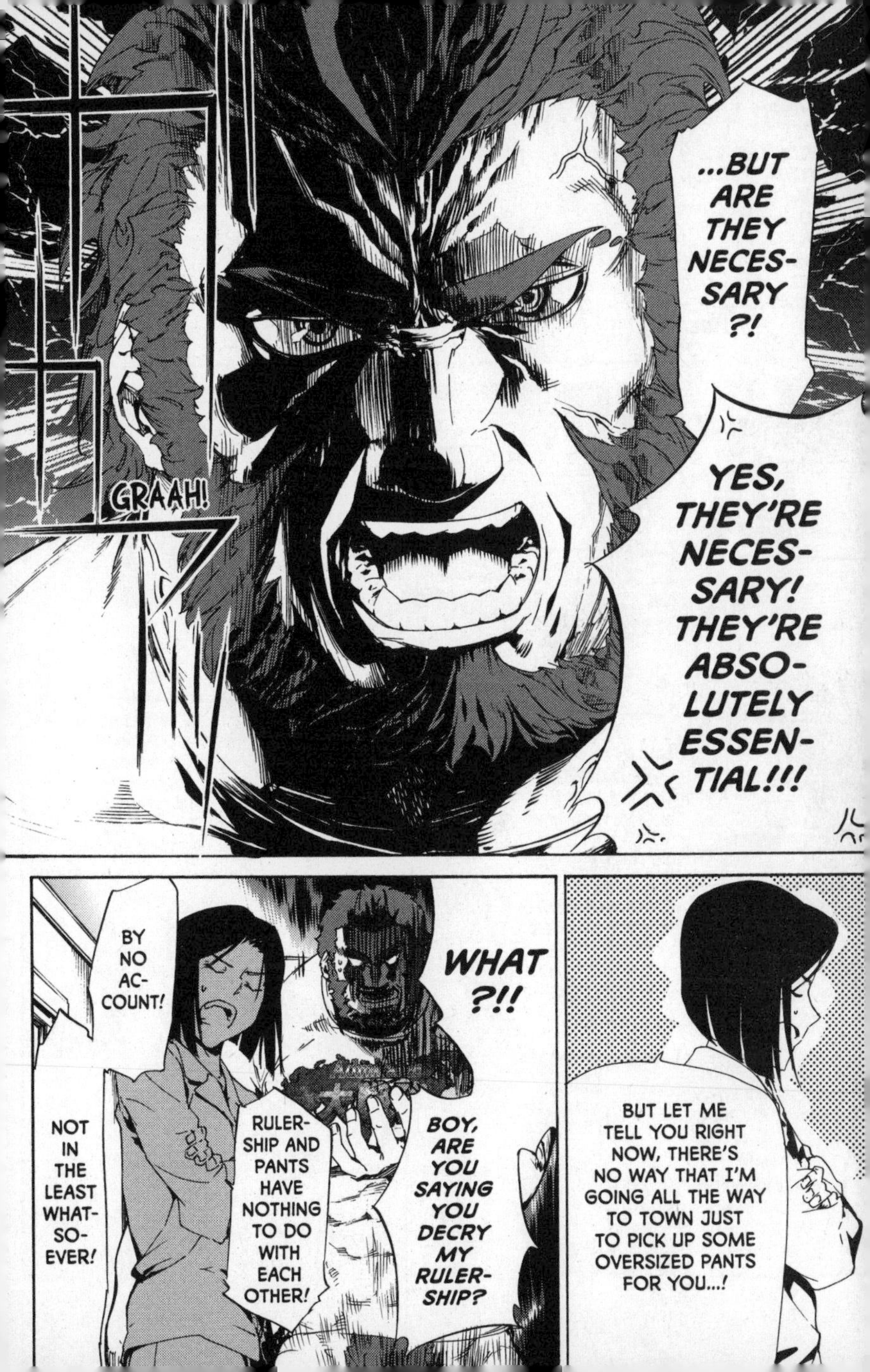
...BUT ARE THEY NECESSARY?!
YES, THEY'RE NECESSARY! THEY'RE ABSOLUTELY ESSENTIAL!!!
GRAAH!
BUT LET ME TELL YOU RIGHT NOW, THERE'S NO WAY THAT I'M GOING ALL THE WAY TO TOWN JUST TO PICK UP SOME OVERSIZED PANTS FOR YOU...!
WHAT?!!
BOY, ARE YOU SAYING YOU DECRY MY RULERSHIP?
BY NO ACCOUNT!
RULERSHIP AND PANTS HAVE NOTHING TO DO WITH EACH OTHER!
NOT IN THE LEAST WHATSOEVER!

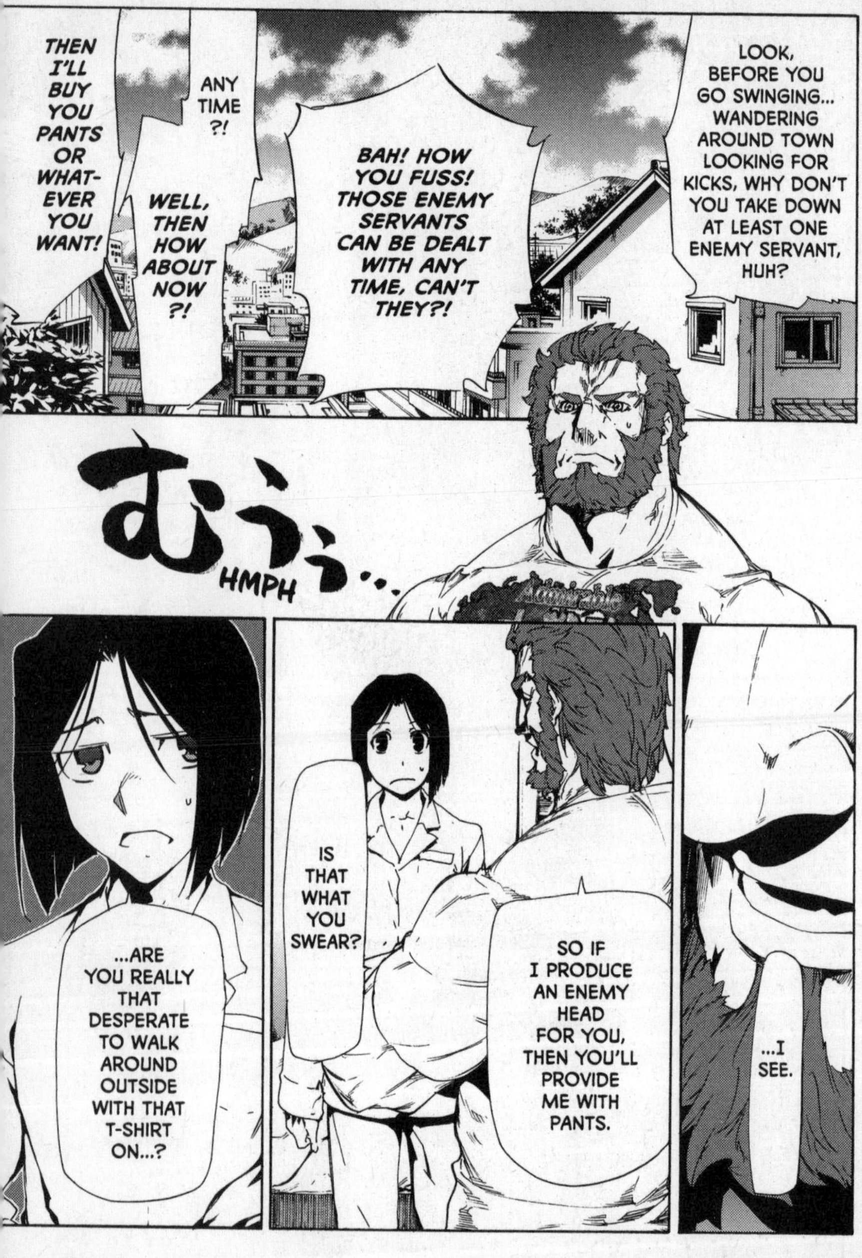
LOOK, BEFORE YOU GO SWINGING... WANDERING AROUND TOWN LOOKING FOR KICKS, WHY DON'T YOU TAKE DOWN AT LEAST ONE ENEMY SERVANT, HUH?
BAH! HOW YOU FUSS! THOSE ENEMY SERVANTS CAN BE DEALT WITH ANY TIME, CAN'T THEY?!
ANY TIME ?!
WELL, THEN HOW ABOUT NOW ?!
THEN I'LL BUY YOU PANTS OR WHAT-EVER YOU WANT!
むぅぅ...
HMPH
...I SEE.
SO IF I PRODUCE AN ENEMY HEAD FOR YOU, THEN YOU'LL PROVIDE ME WITH PANTS.
IS THAT WHAT YOU SWEAR?
...ARE YOU REALLY THAT DESPERATE TO WALK AROUND OUTSIDE WITH THAT T-SHIRT ON...?

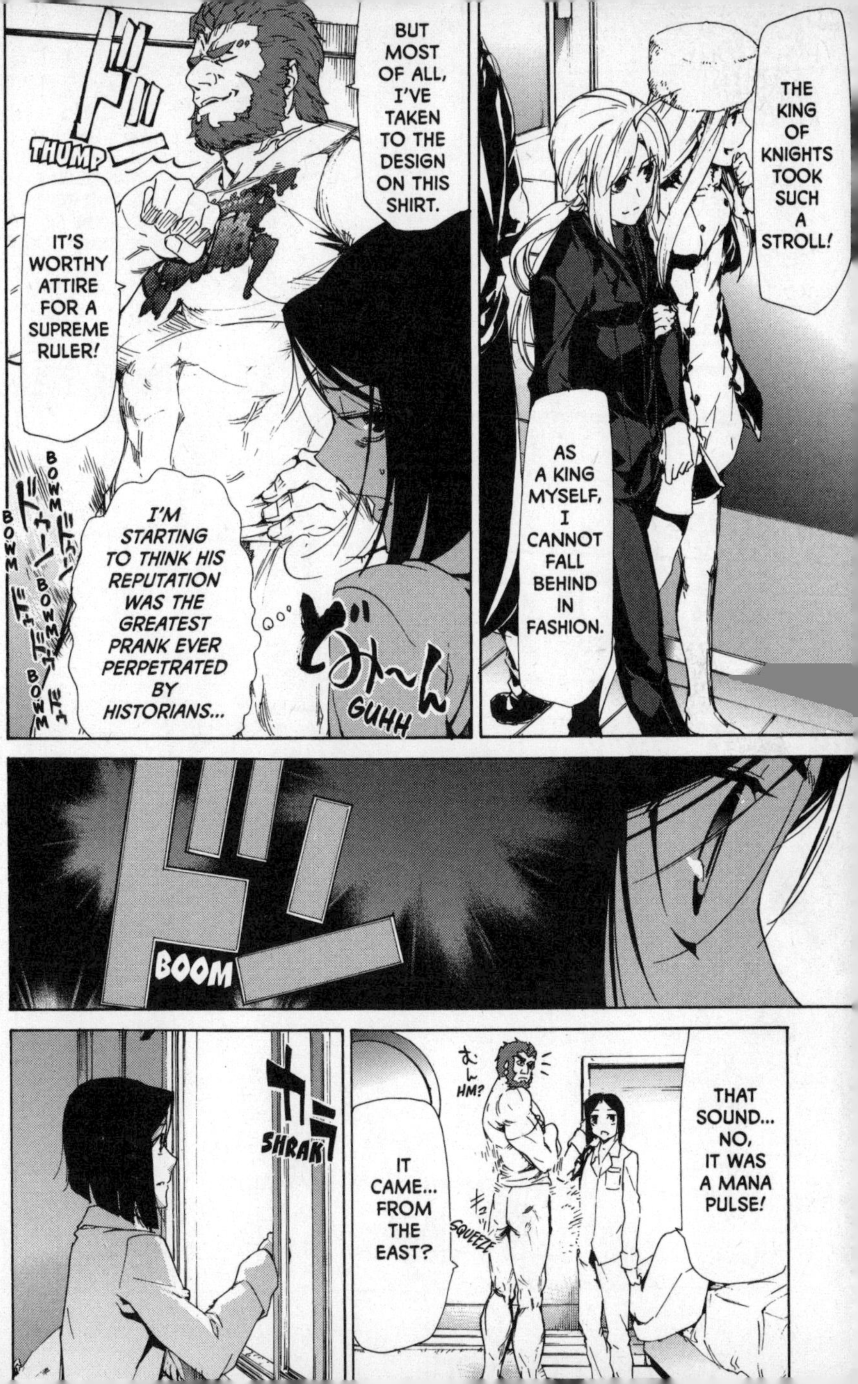

THE KING OF KNIGHTS TOOK SUCH A STROLL!
AS A KING MYSELF, I CANNOT FALL BEHIND IN FASHION.
BUT MOST OF ALL, I'VE TAKEN TO THE DESIGN ON THIS SHIRT.
THUMP
IT'S WORTHY ATTIRE FOR A SUPREME RULER!
I'M STARTING TO THINK HIS REPUTATION WAS THE GREATEST PRANK EVER PERPETRATED BY HISTORIANS...
GUHH
BOWM BOWM BOWM BOWM
BOOM
THAT SOUND... NO, IT WAS A MANA PULSE!
HM?
IT CAME... FROM THE EAST?
SQUEEZE
SHRAK

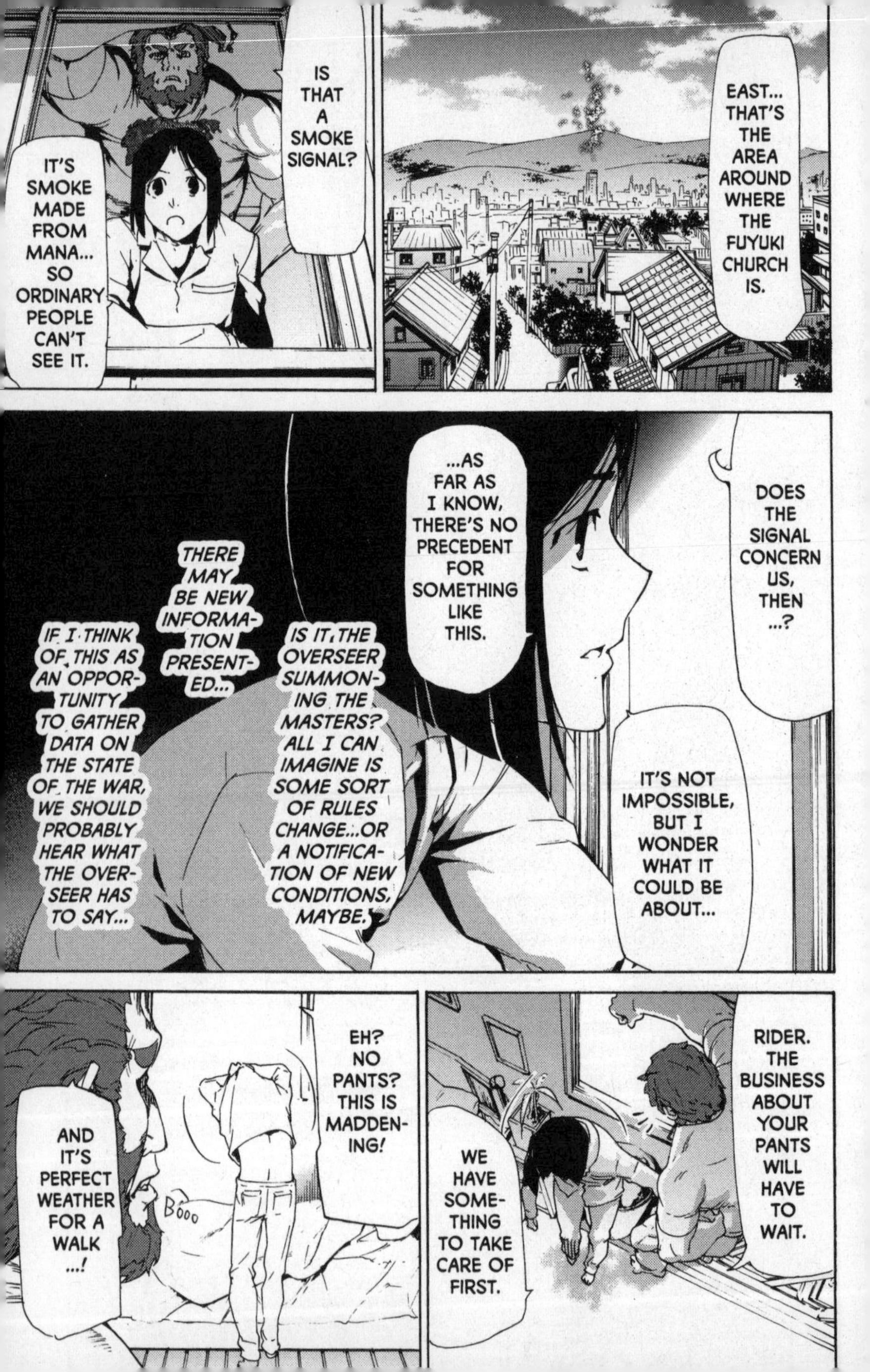
EAST... THAT'S THE AREA AROUND WHERE THE FUYUKI CHURCH IS.
IS THAT A SMOKE SIGNAL?
IT'S SMOKE MADE FROM MANA... SO ORDINARY PEOPLE CAN'T SEE IT.
DOES THE SIGNAL CONCERN US, THEN ...?
IT'S NOT IMPOSSIBLE, BUT I WONDER WHAT IT COULD BE ABOUT...
...AS FAR AS I KNOW, THERE'S NO PRECEDENT FOR SOMETHING LIKE THIS.
IS IT THE OVERSEER SUMMONING THE MASTERS? ALL I CAN IMAGINE IS SOME SORT OF RULES CHANGE...OR A NOTIFICATION OF NEW CONDITIONS, MAYBE.
THERE MAY BE NEW INFORMATION PRESENTED...
IF I THINK OF THIS AS AN OPPORTUNITY TO GATHER DATA ON THE STATE OF THE WAR, WE SHOULD PROBABLY HEAR WHAT THE OVERSEER HAS TO SAY...
RIDER. THE BUSINESS ABOUT YOUR PANTS WILL HAVE TO WAIT.
WE HAVE SOMETHING TO TAKE CARE OF FIRST.
EH? NO PANTS? THIS IS MADDENING!
AND IT'S PERFECT WEATHER FOR A WALK ...!
Booo

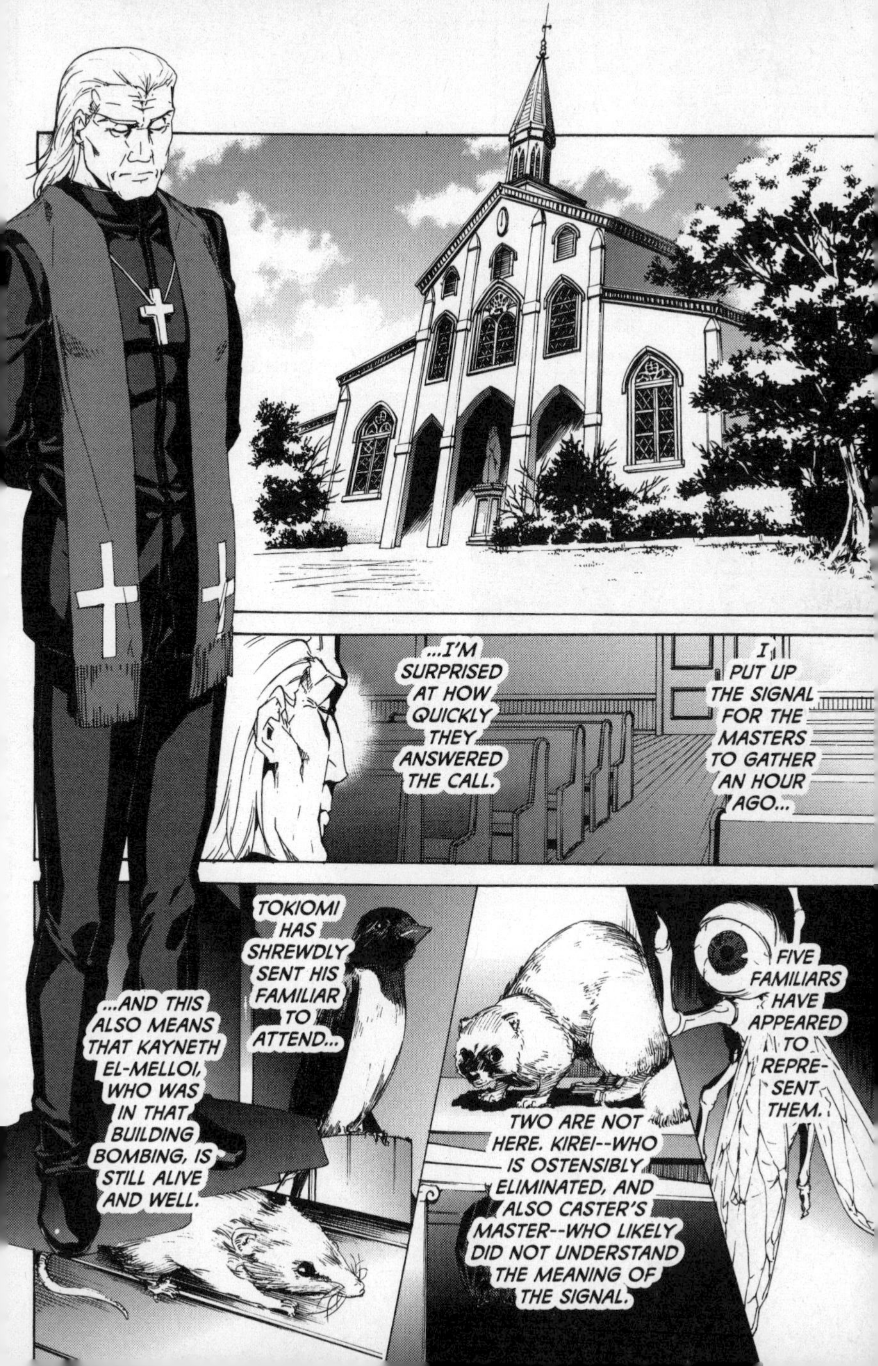
I PUT UP THE SIGNAL FOR THE MASTERS TO GATHER AN HOUR AGO...
...I'M SURPRISED AT HOW QUICKLY THEY ANSWERED THE CALL.
FIVE FAMILIARS HAVE APPEARED TO REPRESENT THEM.
TWO ARE NOT HERE. KIREI--WHO IS OSTENSIBLY ELIMINATED, AND ALSO CASTER'S MASTER--WHO LIKELY DID NOT UNDERSTAND THE MEANING OF THE SIGNAL.
TOKIOMI HAS SHREWDLY SENT HIS FAMILIAR TO ATTEND...
...AND THIS ALSO MEANS THAT KAYNETH EL-MELLOI, WHO WAS IN THAT BUILDING BOMBING, IS STILL ALIVE AND WELL.

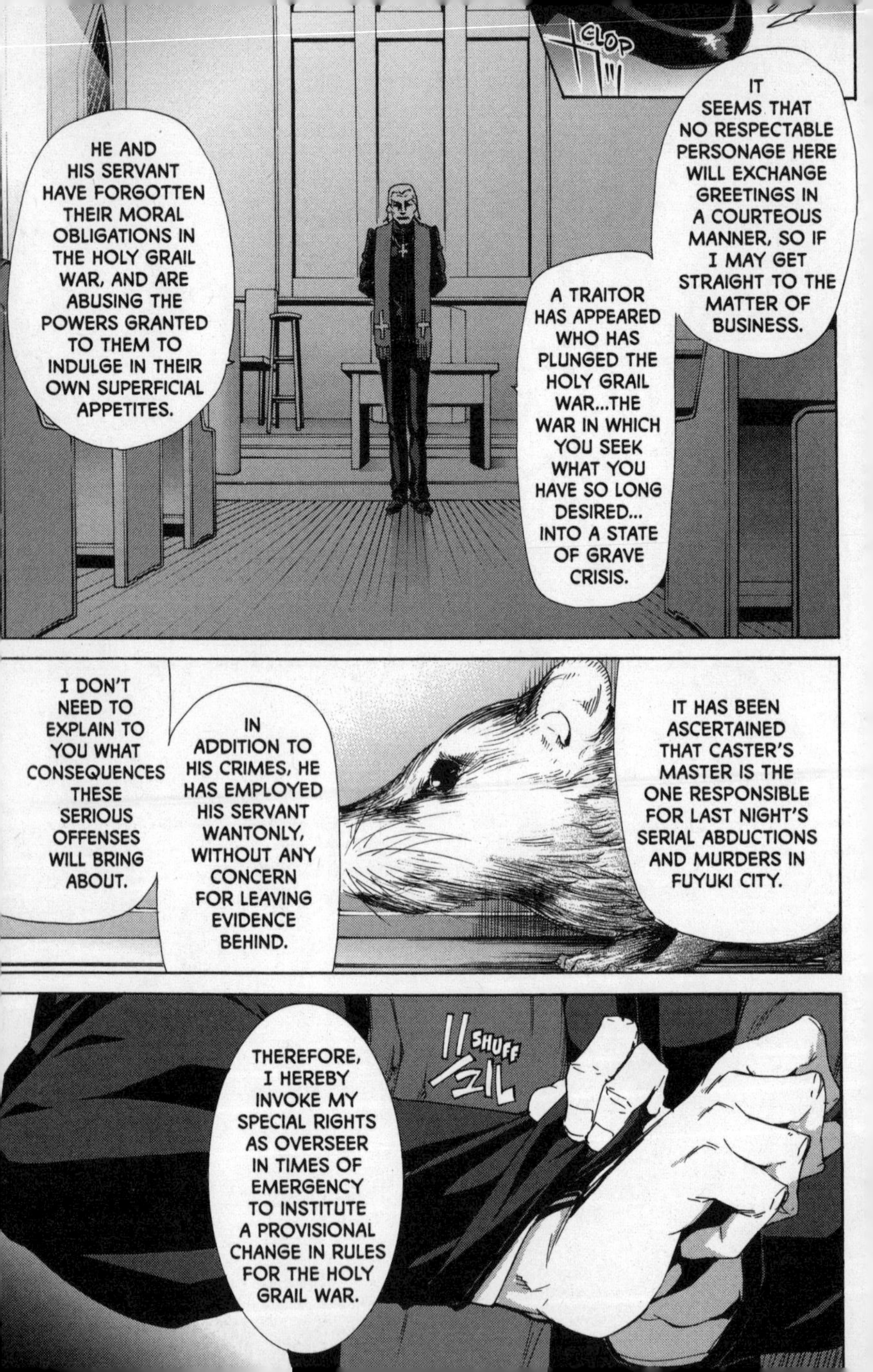
CLOP
IT SEEMS THAT NO RESPECTABLE PERSONAGE HERE WILL EXCHANGE GREETINGS IN A COURTEOUS MANNER, SO IF I MAY GET STRAIGHT TO THE MATTER OF BUSINESS.
A TRAITOR HAS APPEARED WHO HAS PLUNGED THE HOLY GRAIL WAR...THE WAR IN WHICH YOU SEEK WHAT YOU HAVE SO LONG DESIRED... INTO A STATE OF GRAVE CRISIS.
HE AND HIS SERVANT HAVE FORGOTTEN THEIR MORAL OBLIGATIONS IN THE HOLY GRAIL WAR, AND ARE ABUSING THE POWERS GRANTED TO THEM TO INDULGE IN THEIR OWN SUPERFICIAL APPETITES.
IT HAS BEEN ASCERTAINED THAT CASTER'S MASTER IS THE ONE RESPONSIBLE FOR LAST NIGHT'S SERIAL ABDUCTIONS AND MURDERS IN FUYUKI CITY.
IN ADDITION TO HIS CRIMES, HE HAS EMPLOYED HIS SERVANT WANTONLY, WITHOUT ANY CONCERN FOR LEAVING EVIDENCE BEHIND.
I DON'T NEED TO EXPLAIN TO YOU WHAT CONSEQUENCES THESE SERIOUS OFFENSES WILL BRING ABOUT.
SHUFF
THEREFORE, I HEREBY INVOKE MY SPECIAL RIGHTS AS OVERSEER IN TIMES OF EMERGENCY TO INSTITUTE A PROVISIONAL CHANGE IN RULES FOR THE HOLY GRAIL WAR.

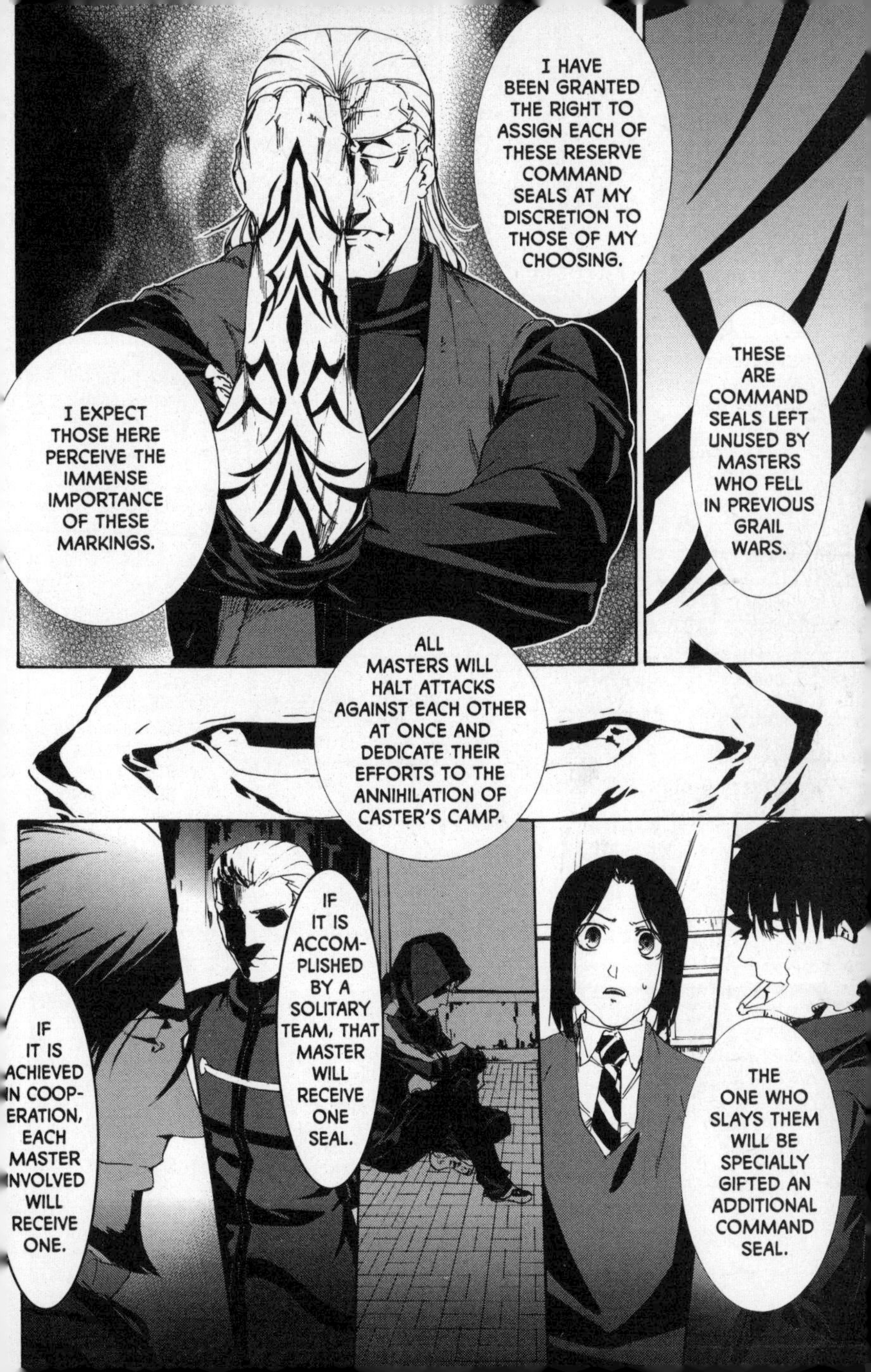
THESE ARE COMMAND SEALS LEFT UNUSED BY MASTERS WHO FELL IN PREVIOUS GRAIL WARS.
I HAVE BEEN GRANTED THE RIGHT TO ASSIGN EACH OF THESE RESERVE COMMAND SEALS AT MY DISCRETION TO THOSE OF MY CHOOSING.
I EXPECT THOSE HERE PERCEIVE THE IMMENSE IMPORTANCE OF THESE MARKINGS.
ALL MASTERS WILL HALT ATTACKS AGAINST EACH OTHER AT ONCE AND DEDICATE THEIR EFFORTS TO THE ANNIHILATION OF CASTER'S CAMP.
THE ONE WHO SLAYS THEM WILL BE SPECIALLY GIFTED AN ADDITIONAL COMMAND SEAL.
IF IT IS ACCOMPLISHED BY A SOLITARY TEAM, THAT MASTER WILL RECEIVE ONE SEAL.
IF IT IS ACHIEVED IN COOPERATION, EACH MASTER INVOLVED WILL RECEIVE ONE.

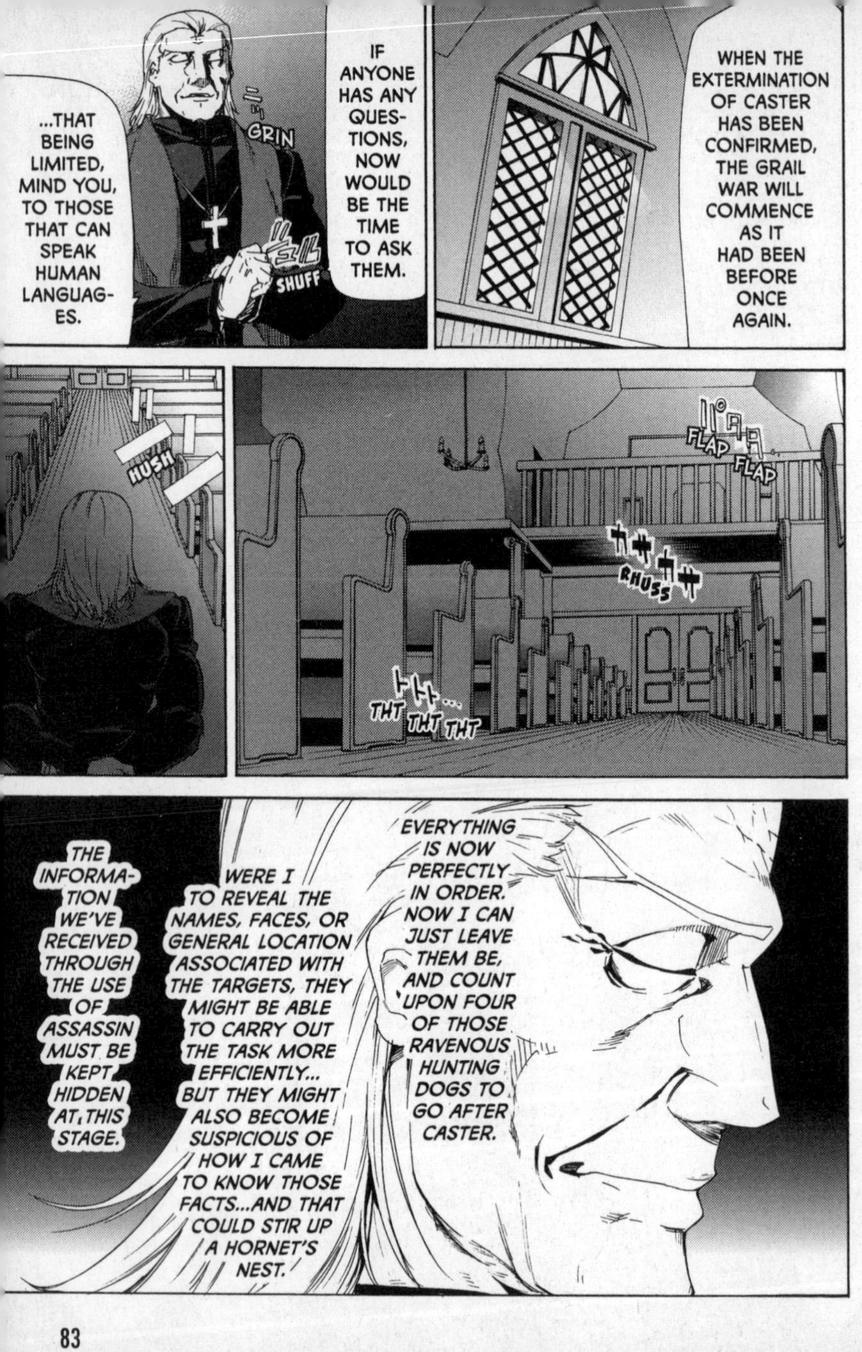
WHEN THE EXTERMINATION OF CASTER HAS BEEN CONFIRMED, THE GRAIL WAR WILL COMMENCE AS IT HAD BEEN BEFORE ONCE AGAIN.
IF ANYONE HAS ANY QUES-TIONS, NOW WOULD BE THE TIME TO ASK THEM.
GRIN
...THAT BEING LIMITED, MIND YOU, TO THOSE THAT CAN SPEAK HUMAN LANGUAG-ES.
SHUFF
FLAP FLAP
RHUSS
THT THT THT
HUSH
EVERYTHING IS NOW PERFECTLY IN ORDER. NOW I CAN JUST LEAVE THEM BE, AND COUNT UPON FOUR OF THOSE RAVENOUS HUNTING DOGS TO GO AFTER CASTER.
WERE I TO REVEAL THE NAMES, FACES, OR GENERAL LOCATION ASSOCIATED WITH THE TARGETS, THEY MIGHT BE ABLE TO CARRY OUT THE TASK MORE EFFICIENTLY... BUT THEY MIGHT ALSO BECOME SUSPICIOUS OF HOW I CAME TO KNOW THOSE FACTS...AND THAT COULD STIR UP A HORNET'S NEST.
THE INFORMA-TION WE'VE RECEIVED THROUGH THE USE OF ASSASSIN MUST BE KEPT HIDDEN AT THIS STAGE.

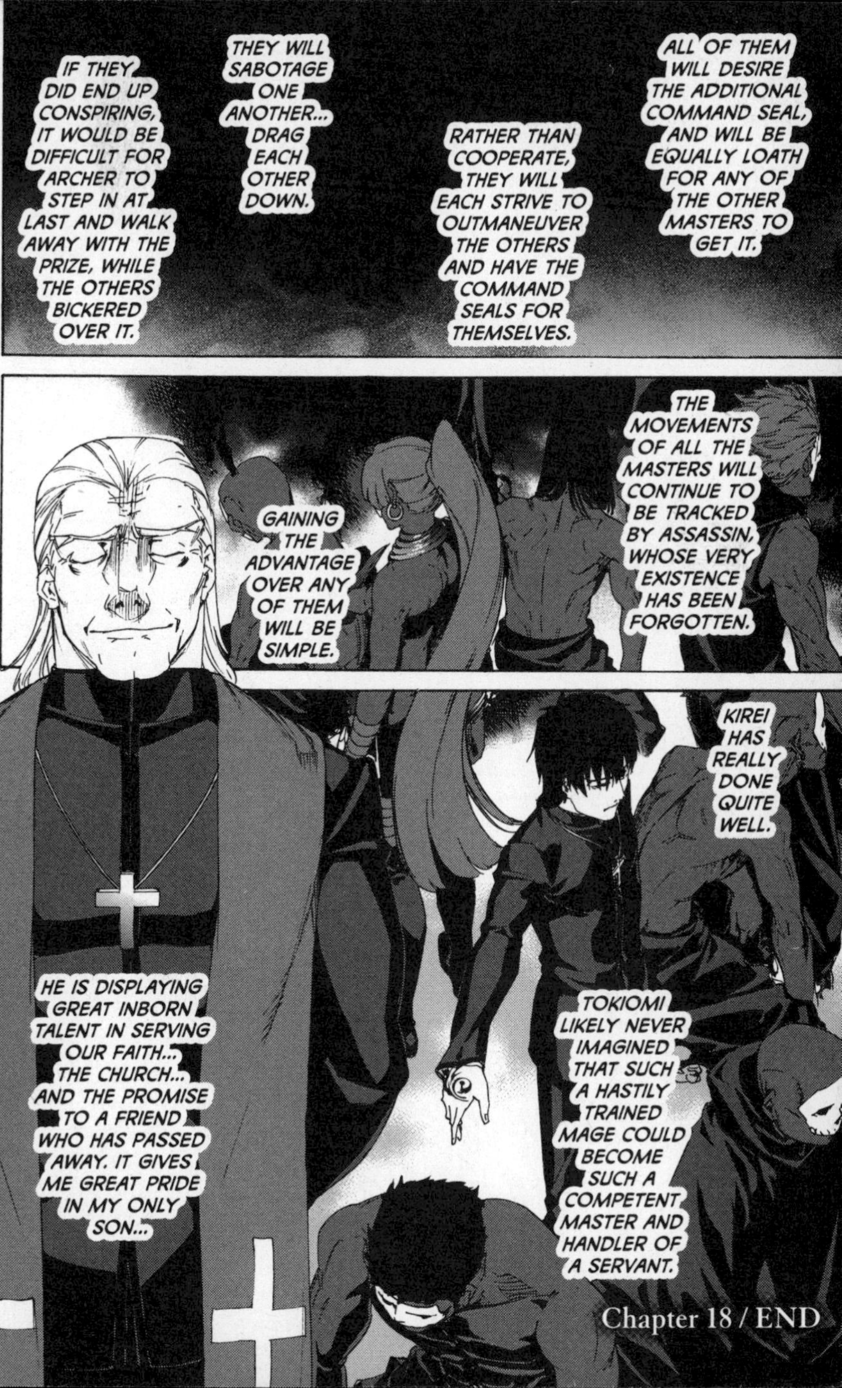
ALL OF THEM WILL DESIRE THE ADDITIONAL COMMAND SEAL, AND WILL BE EQUALLY LOATH FOR ANY OF THE OTHER MASTERS TO GET IT.
RATHER THAN COOPERATE, THEY WILL EACH STRIVE TO OUTMANEUVER THE OTHERS AND HAVE THE COMMAND SEALS FOR THEMSELVES.
THEY WILL SABOTAGE ONE ANOTHER... DRAG EACH OTHER DOWN.
IF THEY DID END UP CONSPIRING, IT WOULD BE DIFFICULT FOR ARCHER TO STEP IN AT LAST AND WALK AWAY WITH THE PRIZE, WHILE THE OTHERS BICKERED OVER IT.
THE MOVEMENTS OF ALL THE MASTERS WILL CONTINUE TO BE TRACKED BY ASSASSIN, WHOSE VERY EXISTENCE HAS BEEN FORGOTTEN.
GAINING THE ADVANTAGE OVER ANY OF THEM WILL BE SIMPLE.
KIREI HAS REALLY DONE QUITE WELL.
TOKIOMI LIKELY NEVER IMAGINED THAT SUCH A HASTILY TRAINED MAGE COULD BECOME SUCH A COMPETENT MASTER AND HANDLER OF A SERVANT.
HE IS DISPLAYING GREAT INBORN TALENT IN SERVING OUR FAITH... THE CHURCH... AND THE PROMISE TO A FRIEND WHO HAS PASSED AWAY. IT GIVES ME GREAT PRIDE IN MY ONLY SON...
Chapter 18 / END

Fate/Zero
フェイト／ゼロ

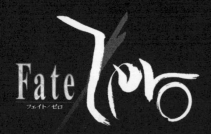

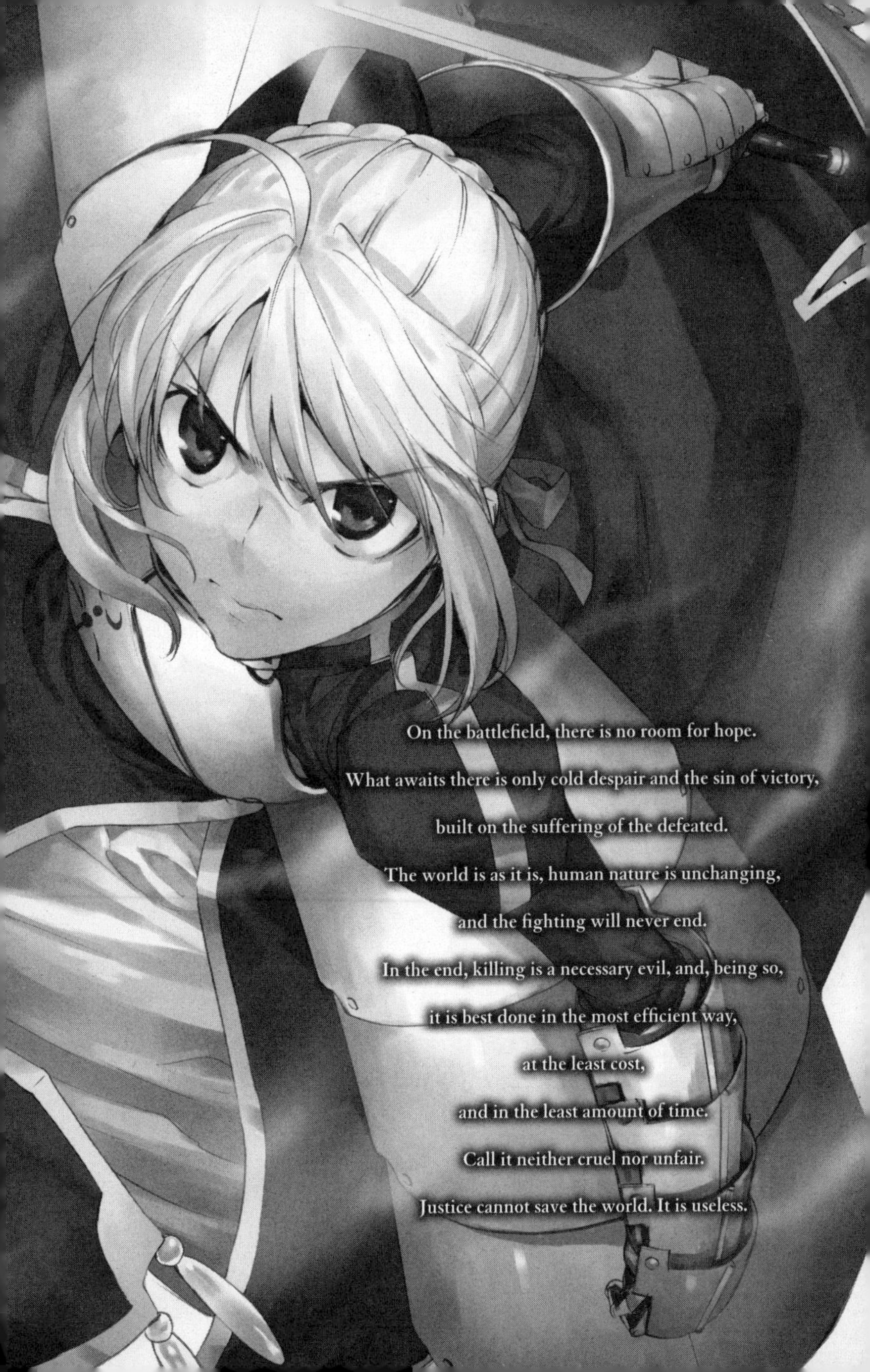
On the battlefield, there is no room for hope.
What awaits there is only cold despair and the sin of victory,
built on the suffering of the defeated.
The world is as it is, human nature is unchanging,
and the fighting will never end.
In the end, killing is a necessary evil, and, being so,
it is best done in the most efficient way,
at the least cost,
and in the least amount of time.
Call it neither cruel nor unfair.
Justice cannot save the world. It is useless.

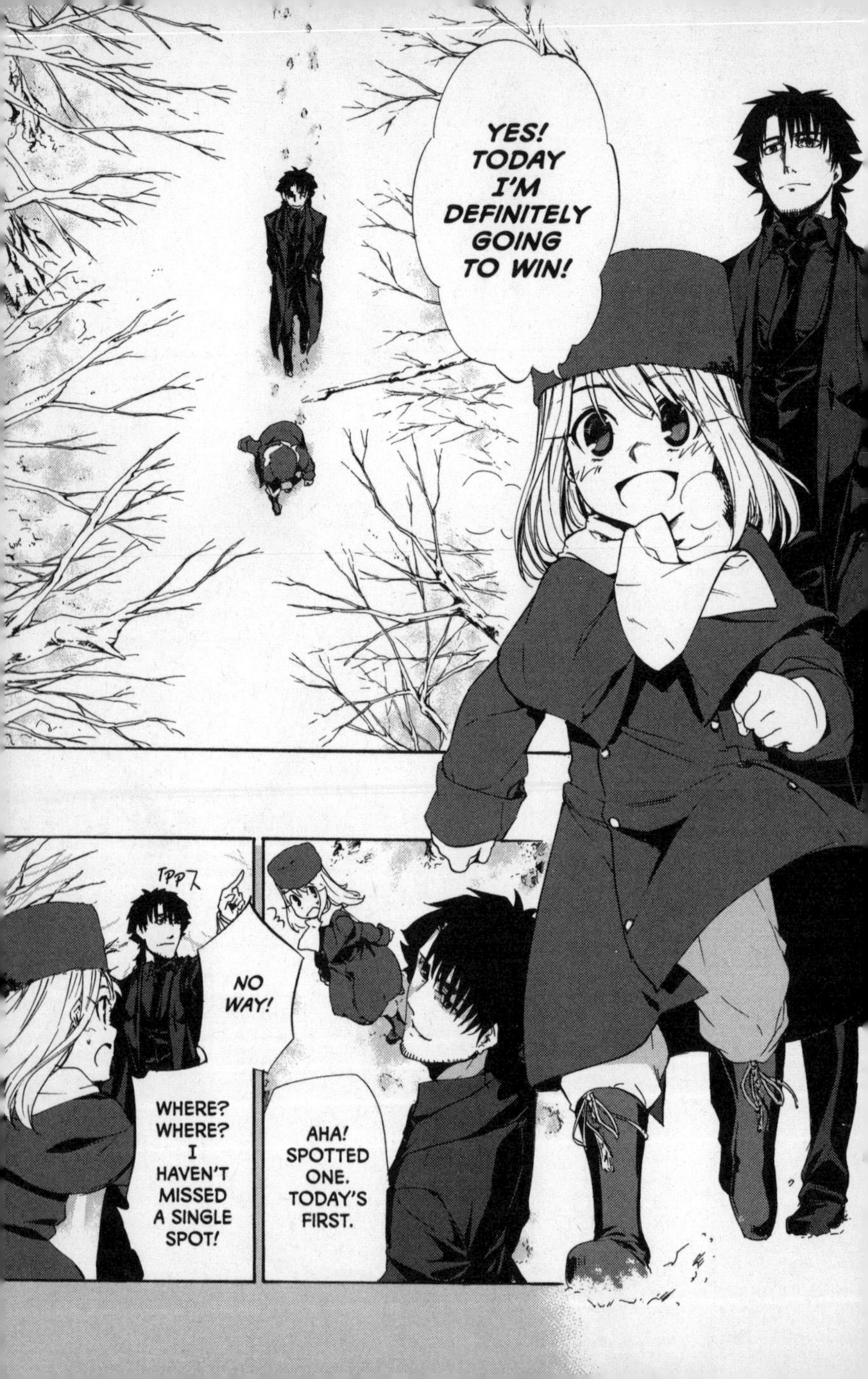
YES! TODAY I'M DEFINITELY GOING TO WIN!
AHA! SPOTTED ONE. TODAY'S FIRST.
NO WAY!
WHERE? WHERE? I HAVEN'T MISSED A SINGLE SPOT!

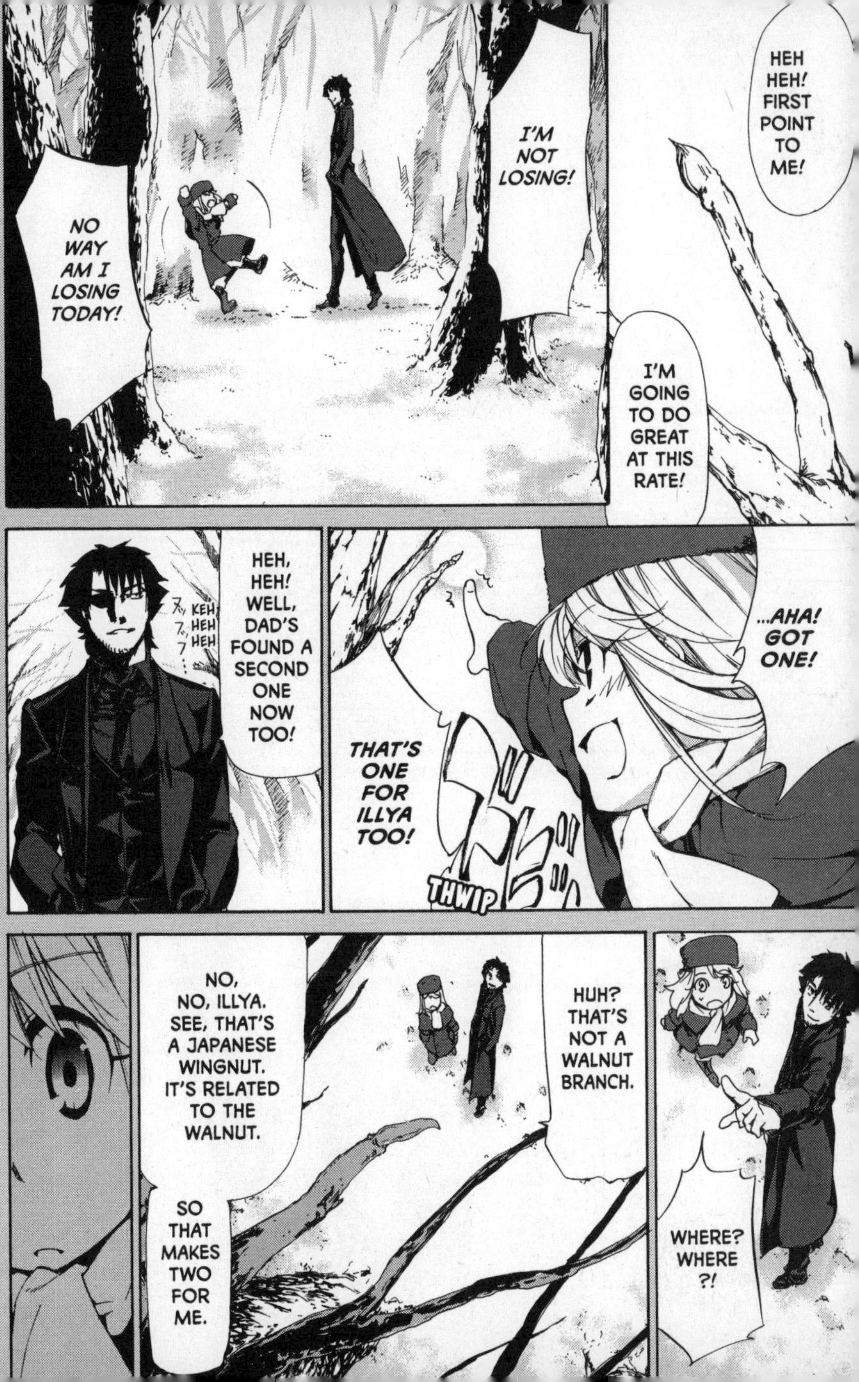
HEH HEH! FIRST POINT TO ME!
I'M GOING TO DO GREAT AT THIS RATE!
I'M NOT LOSING!
NO WAY AM I LOSING TODAY!
...AHA! GOT ONE!
THAT'S ONE FOR ILLYA TOO!
THWIP
HEH, HEH! WELL, DAD'S FOUND A SECOND ONE NOW TOO!
KEH HEH HEH
WHERE? WHERE ?!
HUH? THAT'S NOT A WALNUT BRANCH.
NO, NO, ILLYA. SEE, THAT'S A JAPANESE WINGNUT. IT'S RELATED TO THE WALNUT.
SO THAT MAKES TWO FOR ME.

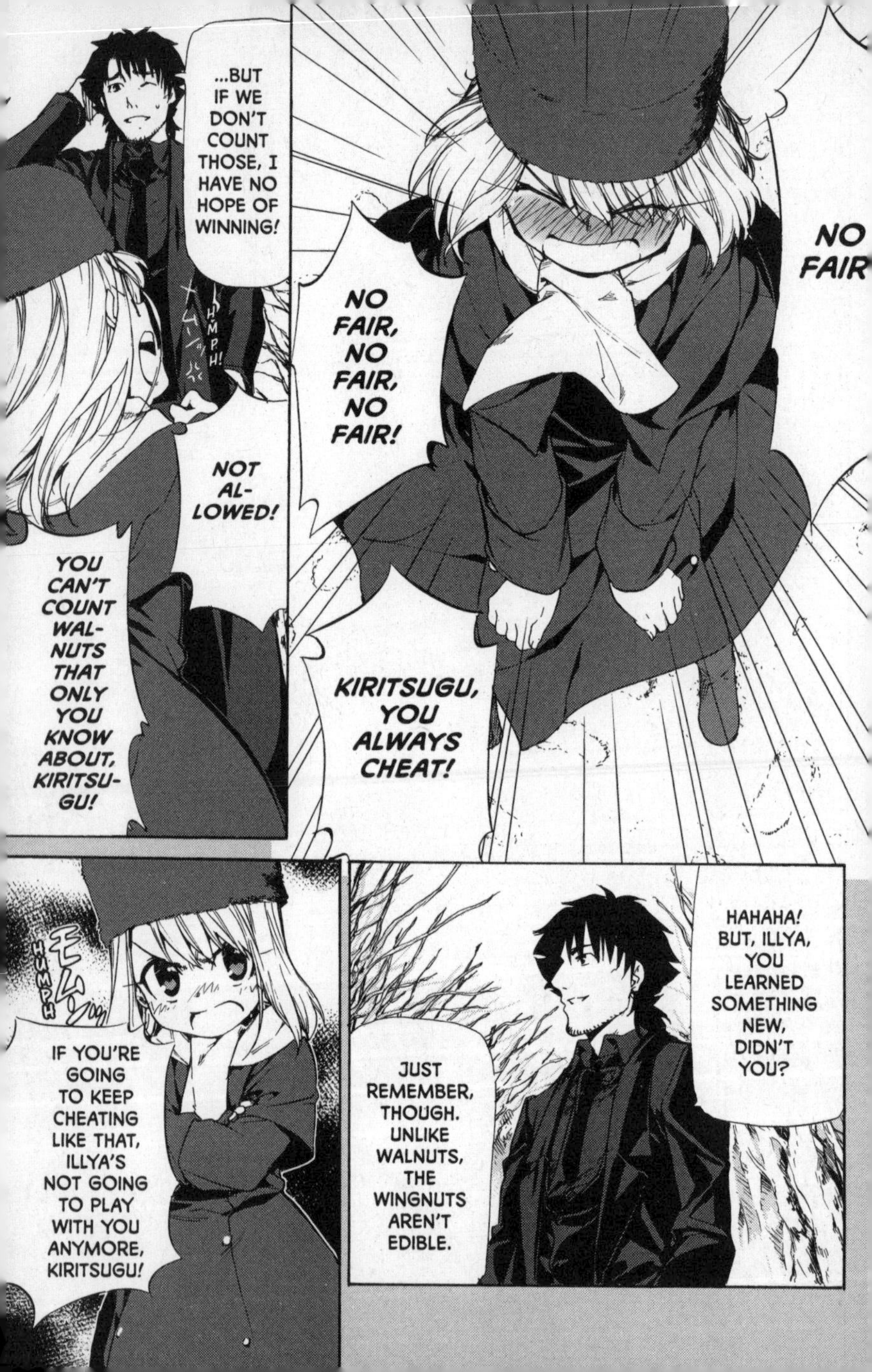
NO FAIR
NO FAIR, NO FAIR, NO FAIR!
KIRITSUGU, YOU ALWAYS CHEAT!
...BUT IF WE DON'T COUNT THOSE, I HAVE NO HOPE OF WINNING!
HMPH!
NOT AL-LOWED!
YOU CAN'T COUNT WAL-NUTS THAT ONLY YOU KNOW ABOUT, KIRITSU-GU!
HAHAHA! BUT, ILLYA, YOU LEARNED SOMETHING NEW, DIDN'T YOU?
JUST REMEMBER, THOUGH. UNLIKE WALNUTS, THE WINGNUTS AREN'T EDIBLE.
HUMPH
IF YOU'RE GOING TO KEEP CHEATING LIKE THAT, ILLYA'S NOT GOING TO PLAY WITH YOU ANYMORE, KIRITSUGU!

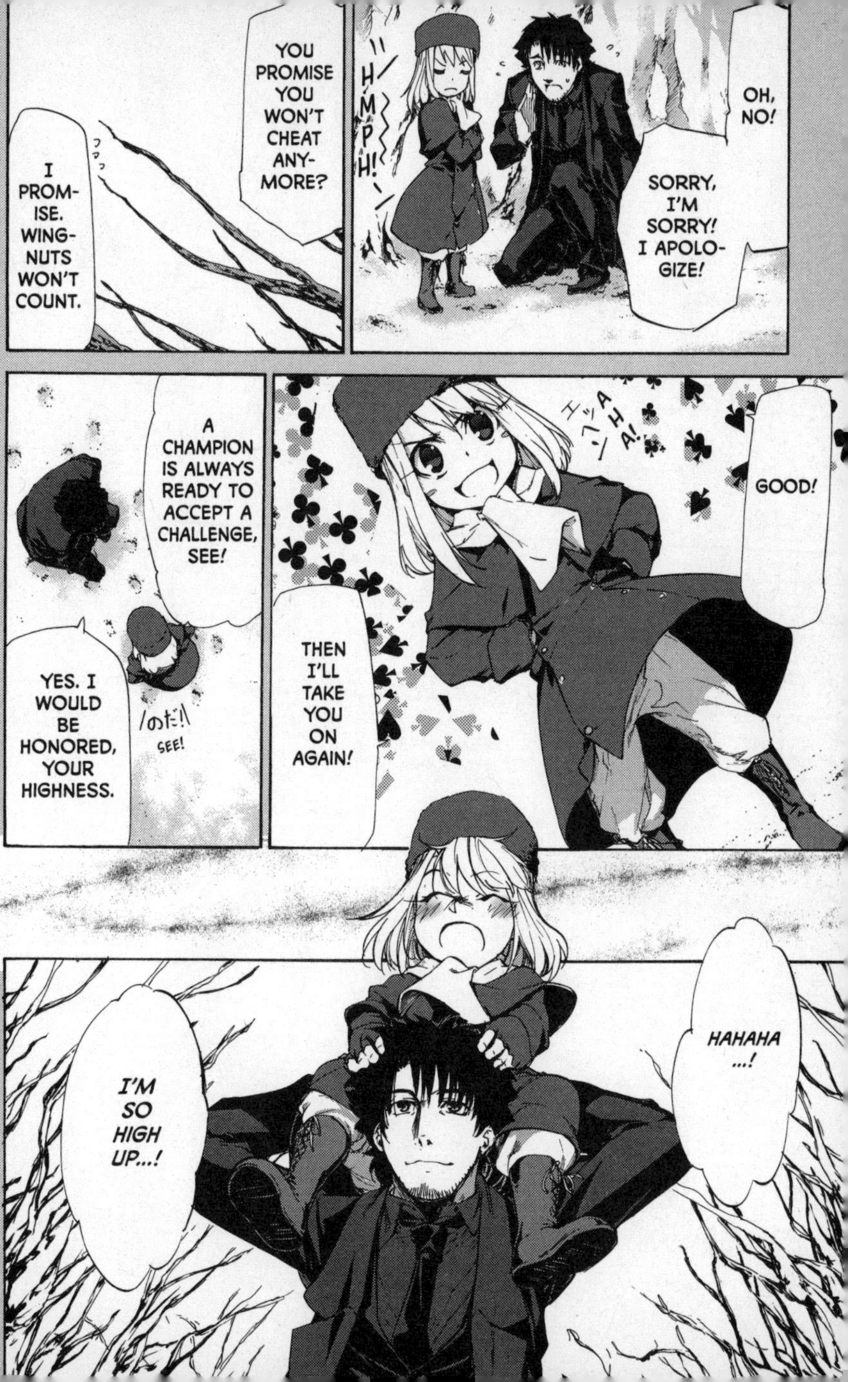
OH, NO!
SORRY, I'M SORRY! I APOLOGIZE!
HMPH!
YOU PROMISE YOU WON'T CHEAT ANYMORE?
I PROMISE. WING-NUTS WON'T COUNT.
GOOD!
AHA!
THEN I'LL TAKE YOU ON AGAIN!
A CHAMPION IS ALWAYS READY TO ACCEPT A CHALLENGE, SEE!
のだ!
SEE!
YES. I WOULD BE HONORED, YOUR HIGHNESS.
HAHAHA...!
I'M SO HIGH UP...!

CHAPTER 19

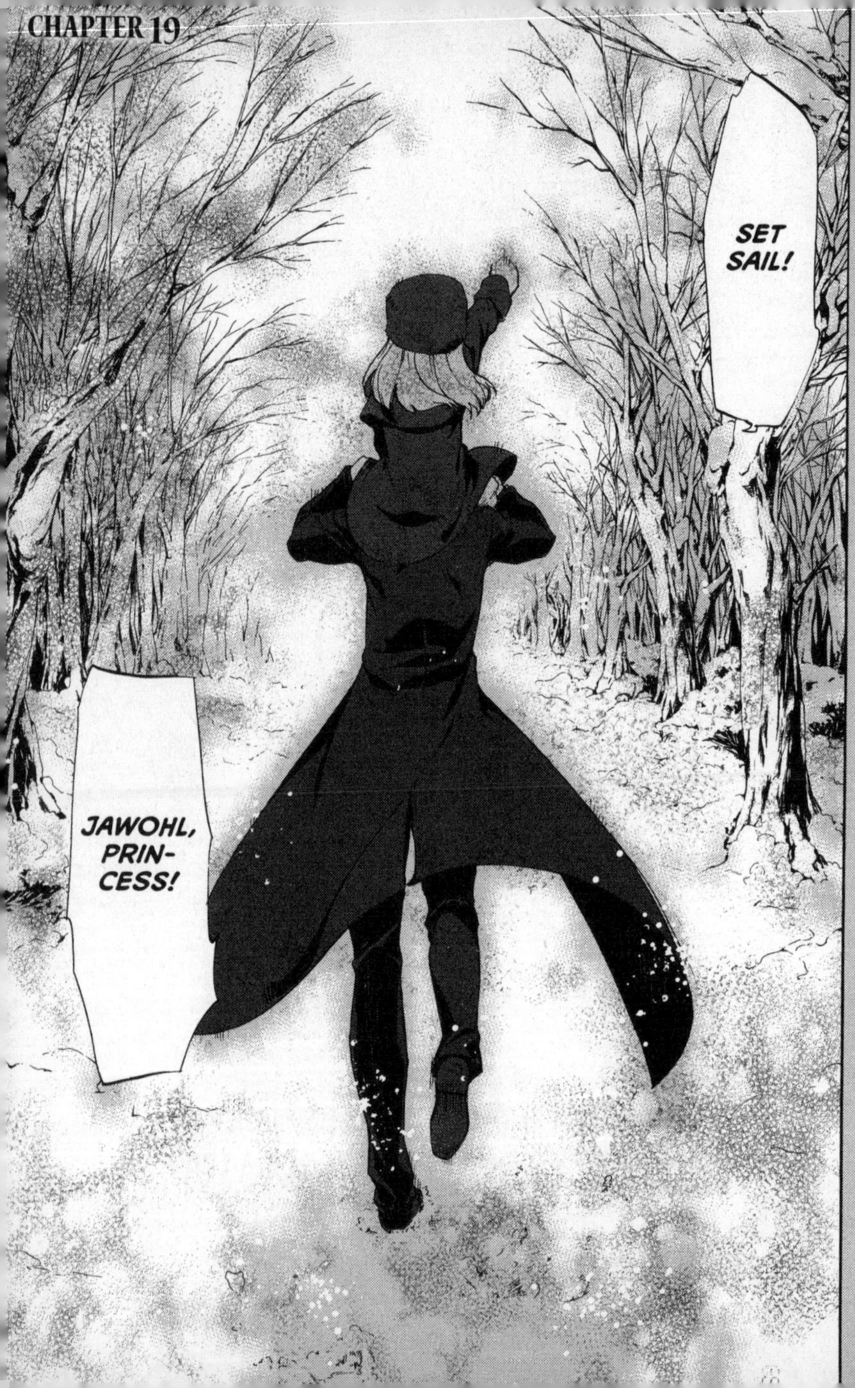
SET SAIL!
JAWOHL, PRIN-CESS!

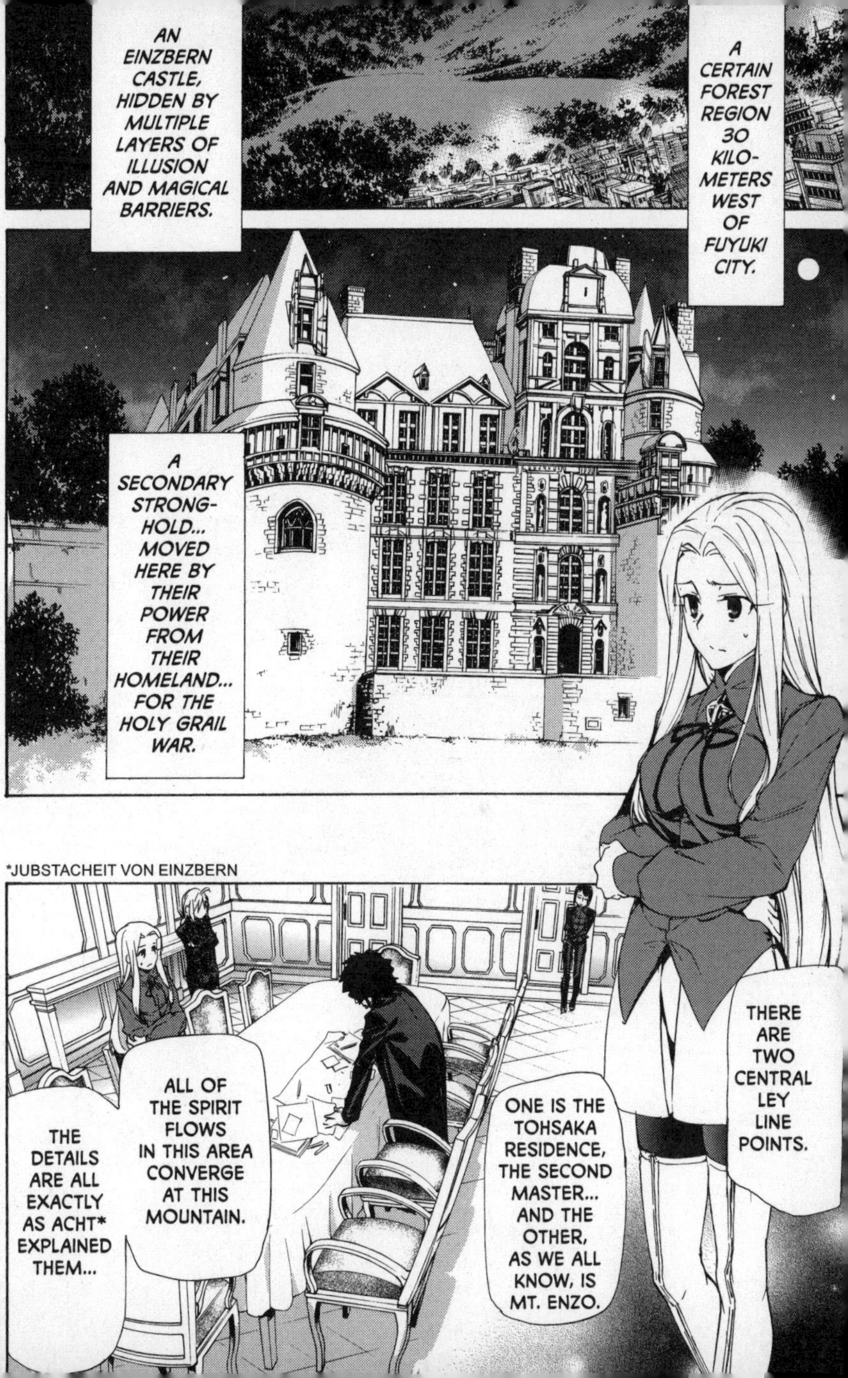
A CERTAIN FOREST REGION 30 KILO-METERS WEST OF FUYUKI CITY.
AN EINZBERN CASTLE, HIDDEN BY MULTIPLE LAYERS OF ILLUSION AND MAGICAL BARRIERS.
A SECONDARY STRONG-HOLD... MOVED HERE BY THEIR POWER FROM THEIR HOMELAND... FOR THE HOLY GRAIL WAR.
THERE ARE TWO CENTRAL LEY LINE POINTS.
ONE IS THE TOHSAKA RESIDENCE, THE SECOND MASTER... AND THE OTHER, AS WE ALL KNOW, IS MT. ENZO.
ALL OF THE SPIRIT FLOWS IN THIS AREA CONVERGE AT THIS MOUNTAIN.
THE DETAILS ARE ALL EXACTLY AS ACHT* EXPLAINED THEM...

*JUBSTACHEIT VON EINZBERN

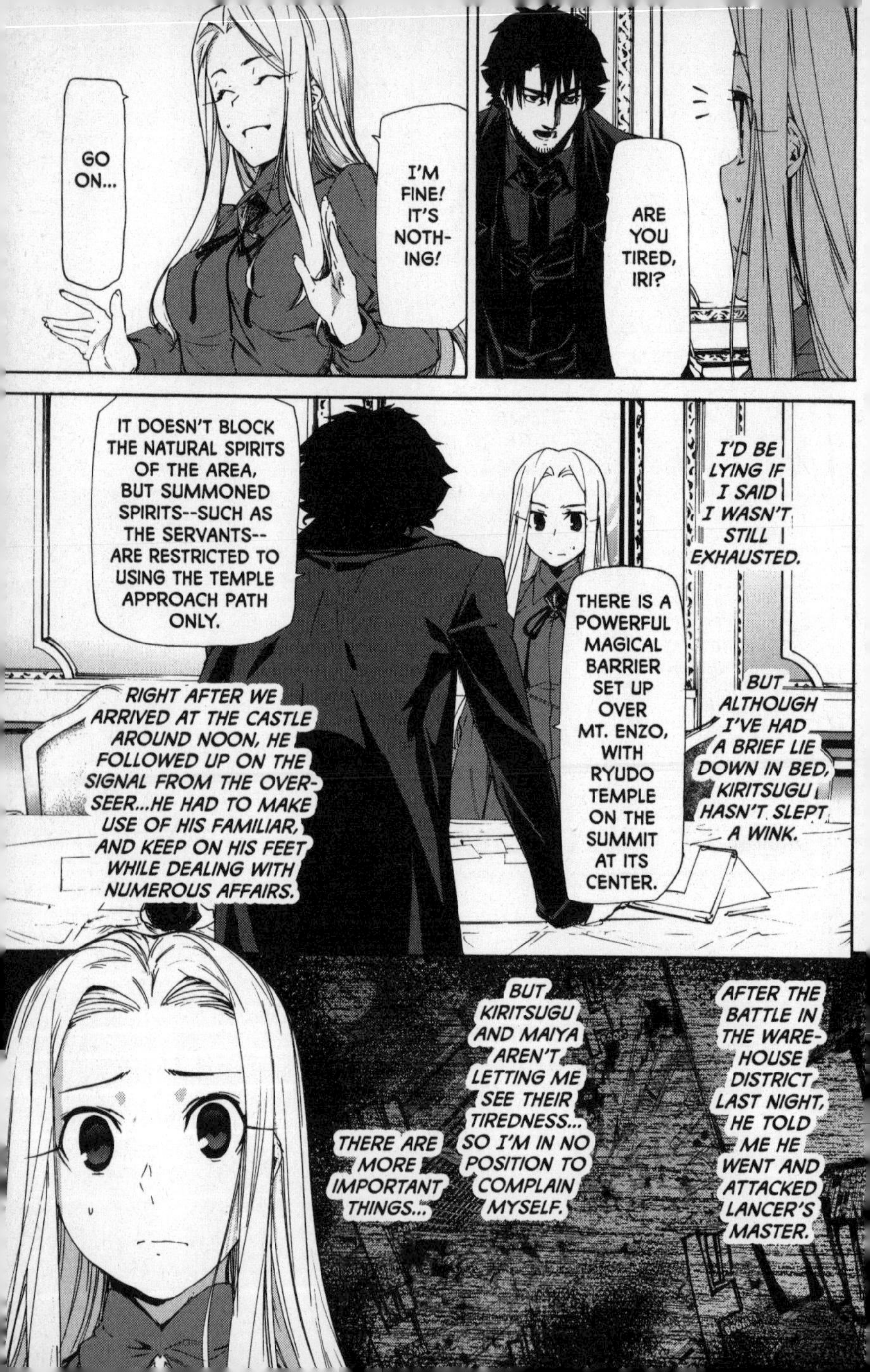

ARE YOU TIRED, IRI?
I'M FINE! IT'S NOTHING!
GO ON...
I'D BE LYING IF I SAID I WASN'T STILL EXHAUSTED.
THERE IS A POWERFUL MAGICAL BARRIER SET UP OVER MT. ENZO, WITH RYUDO TEMPLE ON THE SUMMIT AT ITS CENTER.
IT DOESN'T BLOCK THE NATURAL SPIRITS OF THE AREA, BUT SUMMONED SPIRITS--SUCH AS THE SERVANTS--ARE RESTRICTED TO USING THE TEMPLE APPROACH PATH ONLY.
BUT ALTHOUGH I'VE HAD A BRIEF LIE DOWN IN BED, KIRITSUGU HASN'T SLEPT A WINK.
RIGHT AFTER WE ARRIVED AT THE CASTLE AROUND NOON, HE FOLLOWED UP ON THE SIGNAL FROM THE OVERSEER...HE HAD TO MAKE USE OF HIS FAMILIAR, AND KEEP ON HIS FEET WHILE DEALING WITH NUMEROUS AFFAIRS.
AFTER THE BATTLE IN THE WAREHOUSE DISTRICT LAST NIGHT, HE TOLD ME HE WENT AND ATTACKED LANCER'S MASTER.
BUT KIRITSUGU AND MAIYA AREN'T LETTING ME SEE THEIR TIREDNESS... SO I'M IN NO POSITION TO COMPLAIN MYSELF.
THERE ARE MORE IMPORTANT THINGS...

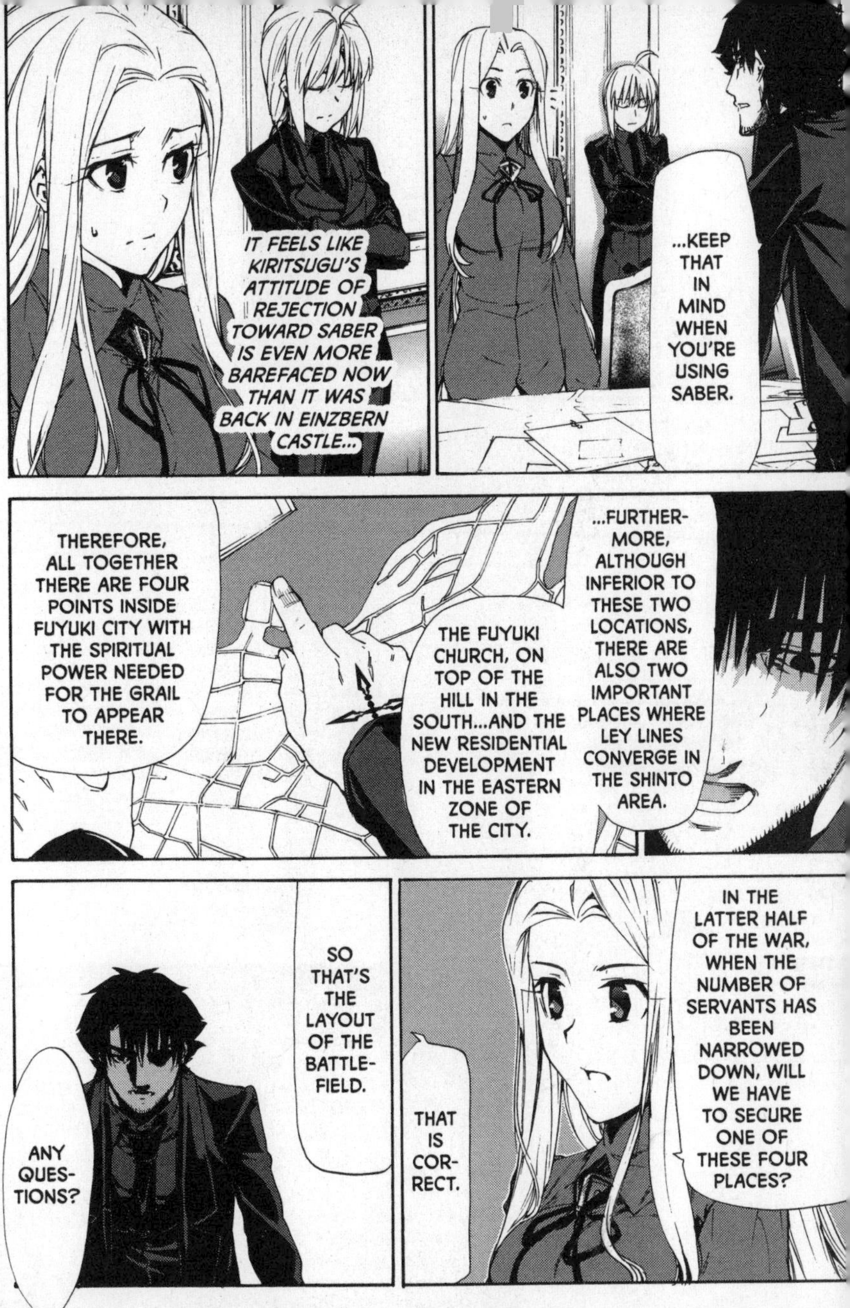
IT FEELS LIKE KIRITSUGU'S ATTITUDE OF REJECTION TOWARD SABER IS EVEN MORE BAREFACED NOW THAN IT WAS BACK IN EINZBERN CASTLE...
...KEEP THAT IN MIND WHEN YOU'RE USING SABER.
THEREFORE, ALL TOGETHER THERE ARE FOUR POINTS INSIDE FUYUKI CITY WITH THE SPIRITUAL POWER NEEDED FOR THE GRAIL TO APPEAR THERE.
THE FUYUKI CHURCH, ON TOP OF THE HILL IN THE SOUTH...AND THE NEW RESIDENTIAL DEVELOPMENT IN THE EASTERN ZONE OF THE CITY.
...FURTHER-MORE, ALTHOUGH INFERIOR TO THESE TWO LOCATIONS, THERE ARE ALSO TWO IMPORTANT PLACES WHERE LEY LINES CONVERGE IN THE SHINTO AREA.
SO THAT'S THE LAYOUT OF THE BATTLE-FIELD.
ANY QUES-TIONS?
IN THE LATTER HALF OF THE WAR, WHEN THE NUMBER OF SERVANTS HAS BEEN NARROWED DOWN, WILL WE HAVE TO SECURE ONE OF THESE FOUR PLACES?
THAT IS COR-RECT.

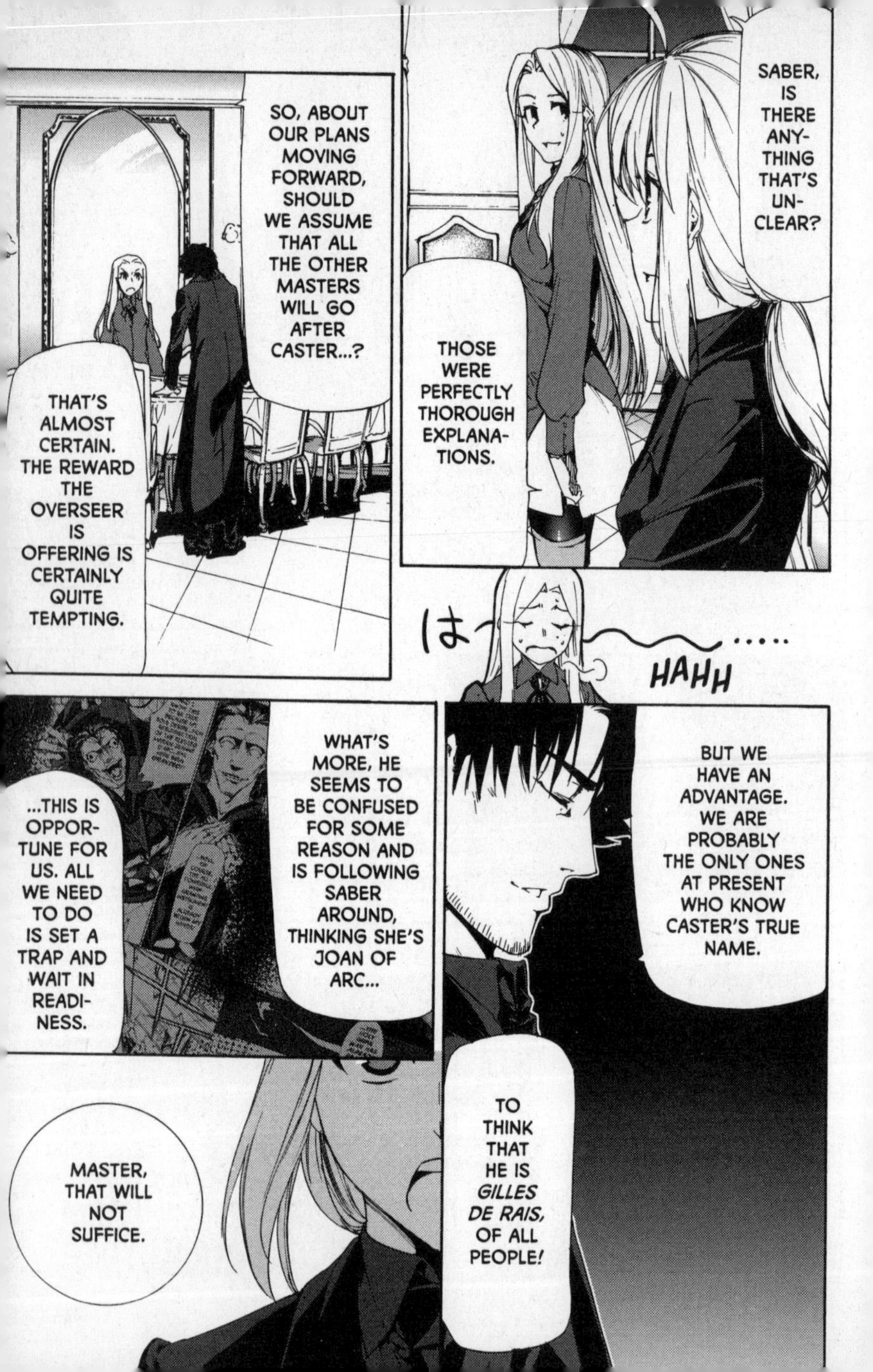
SABER, IS THERE ANYTHING THAT'S UNCLEAR?
THOSE WERE PERFECTLY THOROUGH EXPLANATIONS.
SO, ABOUT OUR PLANS MOVING FORWARD, SHOULD WE ASSUME THAT ALL THE OTHER MASTERS WILL GO AFTER CASTER...?
THAT'S ALMOST CERTAIN. THE REWARD THE OVERSEER IS OFFERING IS CERTAINLY QUITE TEMPTING.
は〜〜〜……
HAHH
BUT WE HAVE AN ADVANTAGE. WE ARE PROBABLY THE ONLY ONES AT PRESENT WHO KNOW CASTER'S TRUE NAME.
WHAT'S MORE, HE SEEMS TO BE CONFUSED FOR SOME REASON AND IS FOLLOWING SABER AROUND, THINKING SHE'S JOAN OF ARC...
...THIS IS OPPORTUNE FOR US. ALL WE NEED TO DO IS SET A TRAP AND WAIT IN READINESS.
TO THINK THAT HE IS *GILLES DE RAIS*, OF ALL PEOPLE!
MASTER, THAT WILL NOT SUFFICE.

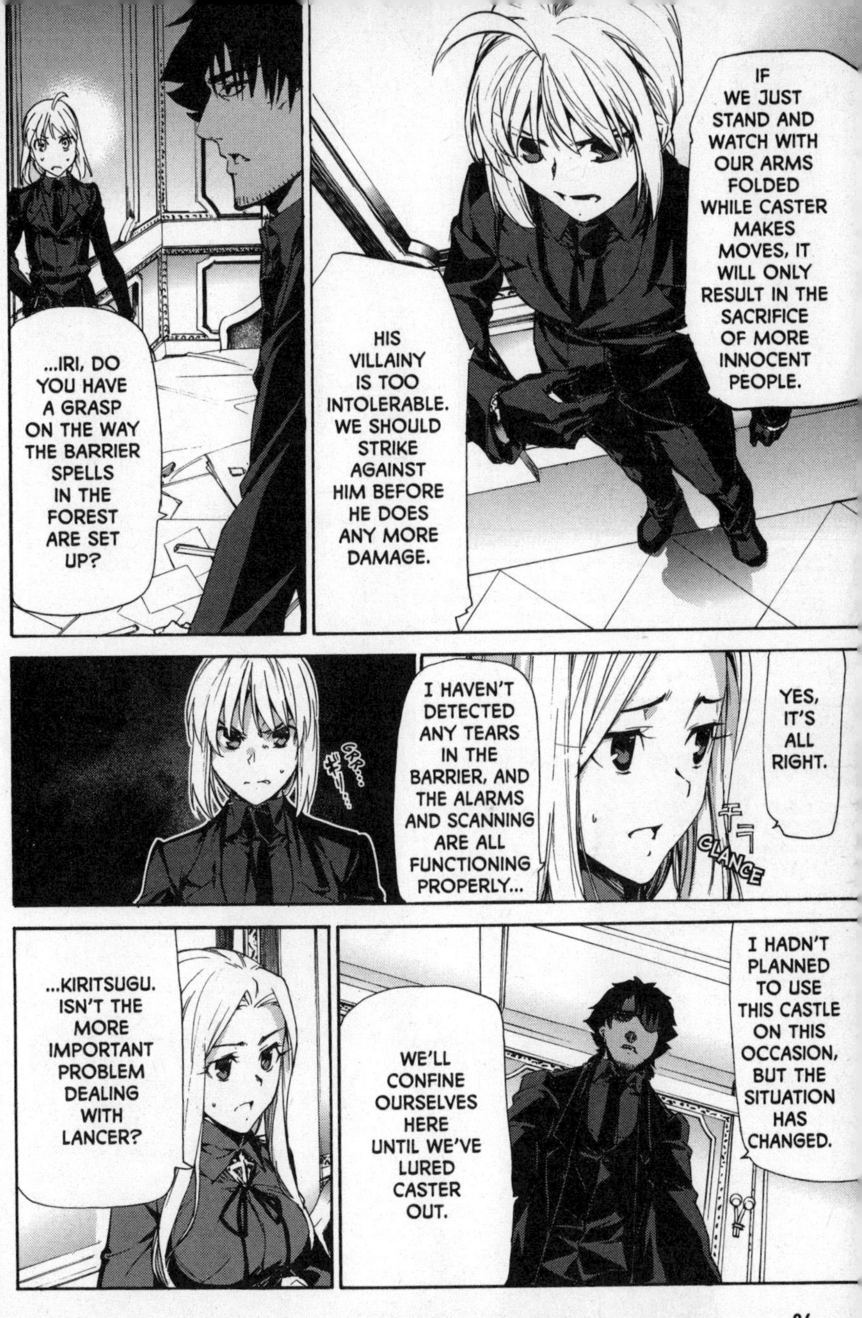
IF WE JUST STAND AND WATCH WITH OUR ARMS FOLDED WHILE CASTER MAKES MOVES, IT WILL ONLY RESULT IN THE SACRIFICE OF MORE INNOCENT PEOPLE.
HIS VILLAINY IS TOO INTOLERABLE. WE SHOULD STRIKE AGAINST HIM BEFORE HE DOES ANY MORE DAMAGE.
...IRI, DO YOU HAVE A GRASP ON THE WAY THE BARRIER SPELLS IN THE FOREST ARE SET UP?
YES, IT'S ALL RIGHT.
I HAVEN'T DETECTED ANY TEARS IN THE BARRIER, AND THE ALARMS AND SCANNING ARE ALL FUNCTIONING PROPERLY...
GLANCE
GRR...
I HADN'T PLANNED TO USE THIS CASTLE ON THIS OCCASION, BUT THE SITUATION HAS CHANGED.
WE'LL CONFINE OURSELVES HERE UNTIL WE'VE LURED CASTER OUT.
...KIRITSUGU. ISN'T THE MORE IMPORTANT PROBLEM DEALING WITH LANCER?

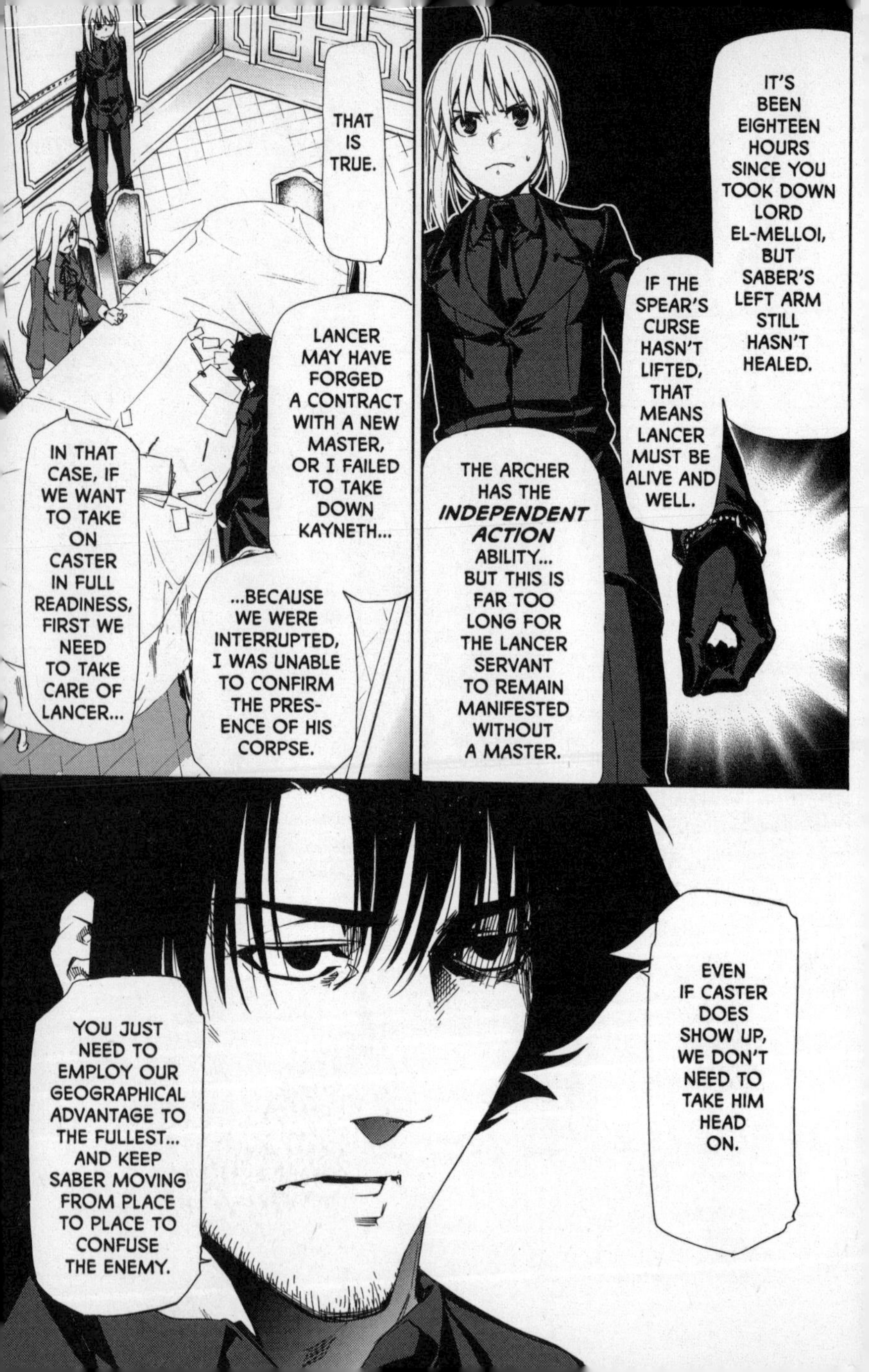
IT'S BEEN EIGHTEEN HOURS SINCE YOU TOOK DOWN LORD EL-MELLOI, BUT SABER'S LEFT ARM STILL HASN'T HEALED.
IF THE SPEAR'S CURSE HASN'T LIFTED, THAT MEANS LANCER MUST BE ALIVE AND WELL.
THE ARCHER HAS THE *INDEPENDENT ACTION* ABILITY... BUT THIS IS FAR TOO LONG FOR THE LANCER SERVANT TO REMAIN MANIFESTED WITHOUT A MASTER.
THAT IS TRUE.
LANCER MAY HAVE FORGED A CONTRACT WITH A NEW MASTER, OR I FAILED TO TAKE DOWN KAYNETH...
...BECAUSE WE WERE INTERRUPTED, I WAS UNABLE TO CONFIRM THE PRESENCE OF HIS CORPSE.
IN THAT CASE, IF WE WANT TO TAKE ON CASTER IN FULL READINESS, FIRST WE NEED TO TAKE CARE OF LANCER...
EVEN IF CASTER DOES SHOW UP, WE DON'T NEED TO TAKE HIM HEAD ON.
YOU JUST NEED TO EMPLOY OUR GEOGRAPHICAL ADVANTAGE TO THE FULLEST... AND KEEP SABER MOVING FROM PLACE TO PLACE TO CONFUSE THE ENEMY.

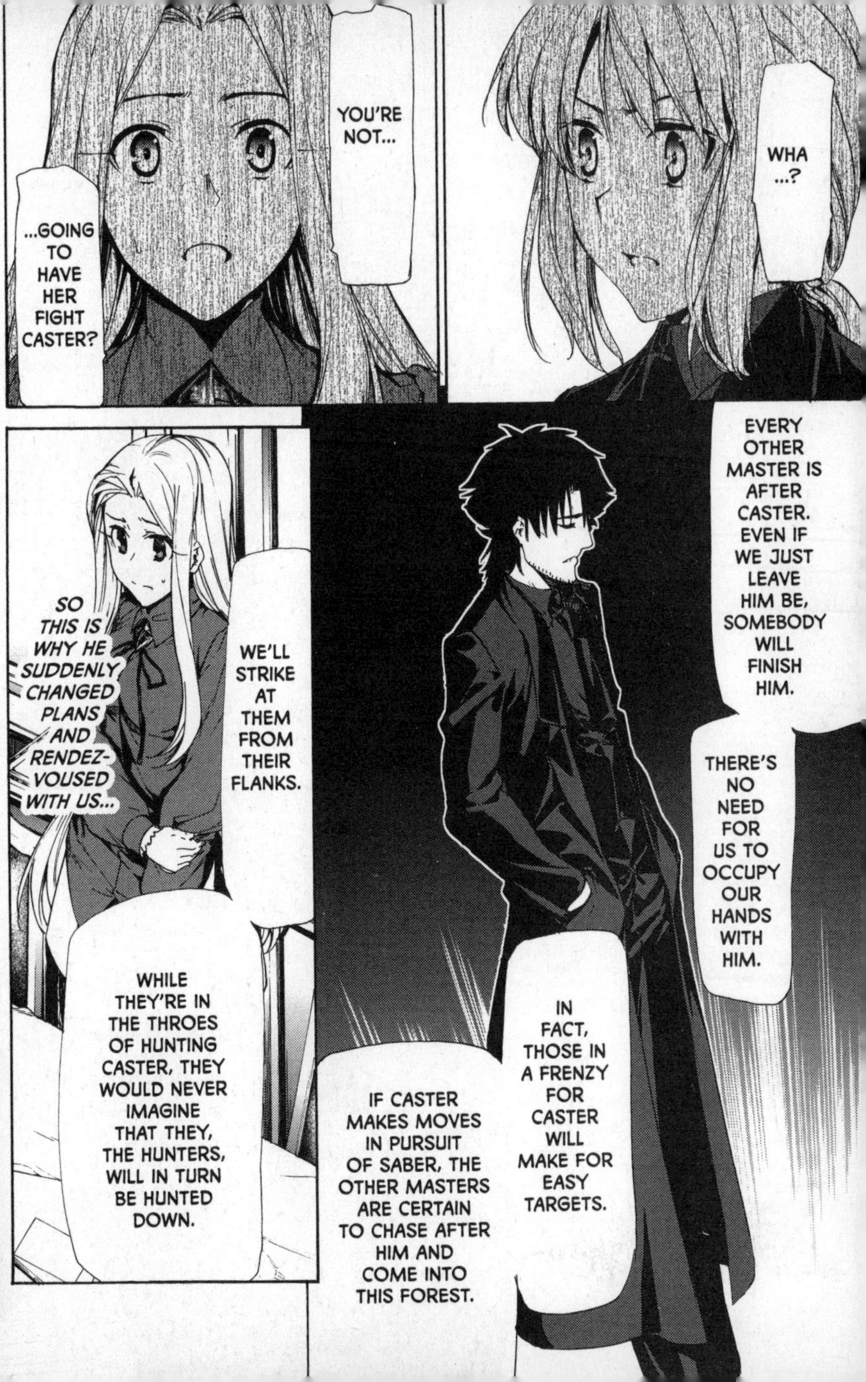
WHA ...?
YOU'RE NOT...
...GOING TO HAVE HER FIGHT CASTER?
EVERY OTHER MASTER IS AFTER CASTER. EVEN IF WE JUST LEAVE HIM BE, SOMEBODY WILL FINISH HIM.
THERE'S NO NEED FOR US TO OCCUPY OUR HANDS WITH HIM.
IN FACT, THOSE IN A FRENZY FOR CASTER WILL MAKE FOR EASY TARGETS.
IF CASTER MAKES MOVES IN PURSUIT OF SABER, THE OTHER MASTERS ARE CERTAIN TO CHASE AFTER HIM AND COME INTO THIS FOREST.
WE'LL STRIKE AT THEM FROM THEIR FLANKS.
WHILE THEY'RE IN THE THROES OF HUNTING CASTER, THEY WOULD NEVER IMAGINE THAT THEY, THE HUNTERS, WILL IN TURN BE HUNTED DOWN.
SO THIS IS WHY HE SUDDENLY CHANGED PLANS AND RENDEZ-VOUSED WITH US...

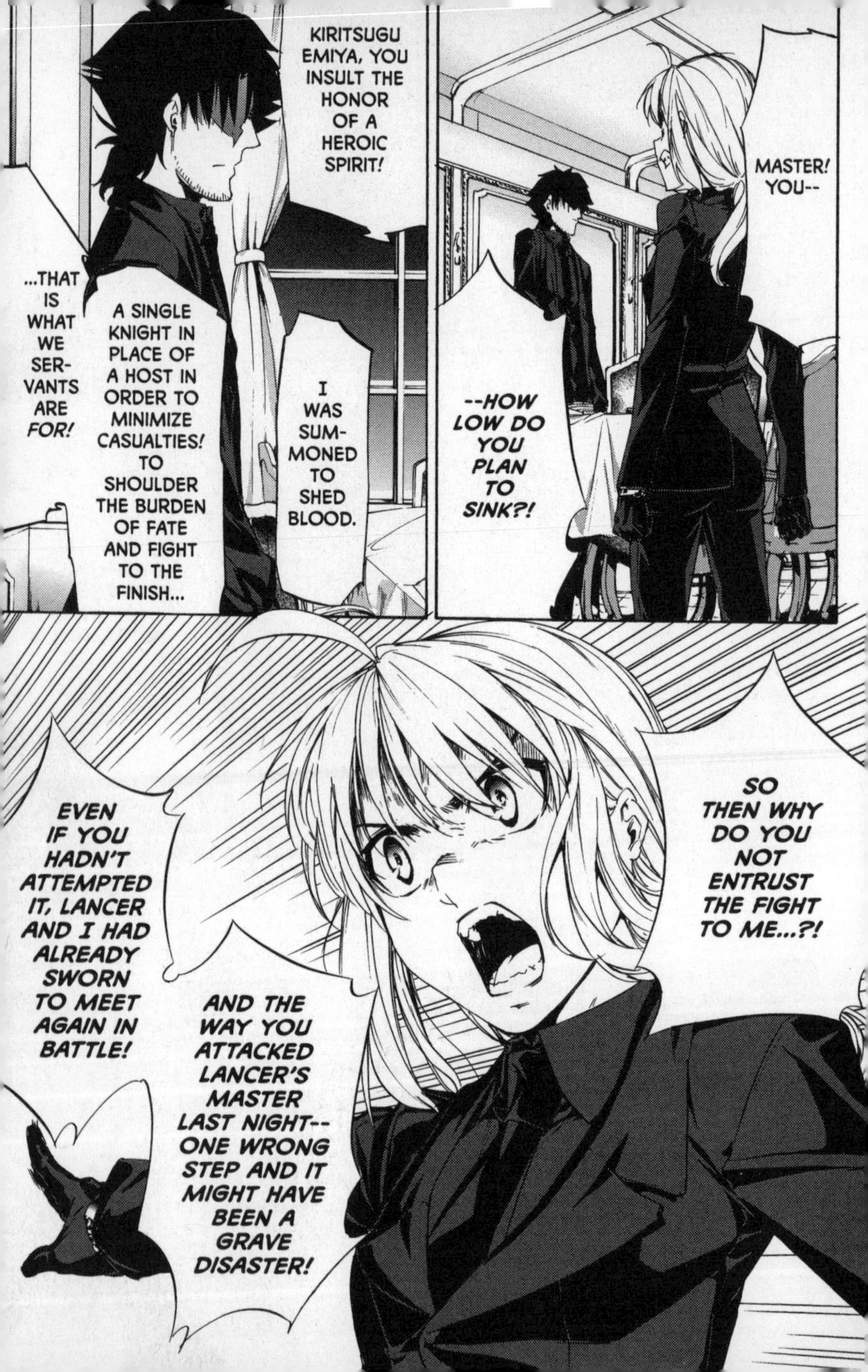
MASTER! YOU--
--HOW LOW DO YOU PLAN TO SINK?!
KIRITSUGU EMIYA, YOU INSULT THE HONOR OF A HEROIC SPIRIT!
I WAS SUMMONED TO SHED BLOOD.
A SINGLE KNIGHT IN PLACE OF A HOST IN ORDER TO MINIMIZE CASUALTIES! TO SHOULDER THE BURDEN OF FATE AND FIGHT TO THE FINISH...
...THAT IS WHAT WE SERVANTS ARE FOR!
SO THEN WHY DO YOU NOT ENTRUST THE FIGHT TO ME...?!
EVEN IF YOU HADN'T ATTEMPTED IT, LANCER AND I HAD ALREADY SWORN TO MEET AGAIN IN BATTLE!
AND THE WAY YOU ATTACKED LANCER'S MASTER LAST NIGHT-- ONE WRONG STEP AND IT MIGHT HAVE BEEN A GRAVE DISASTER!

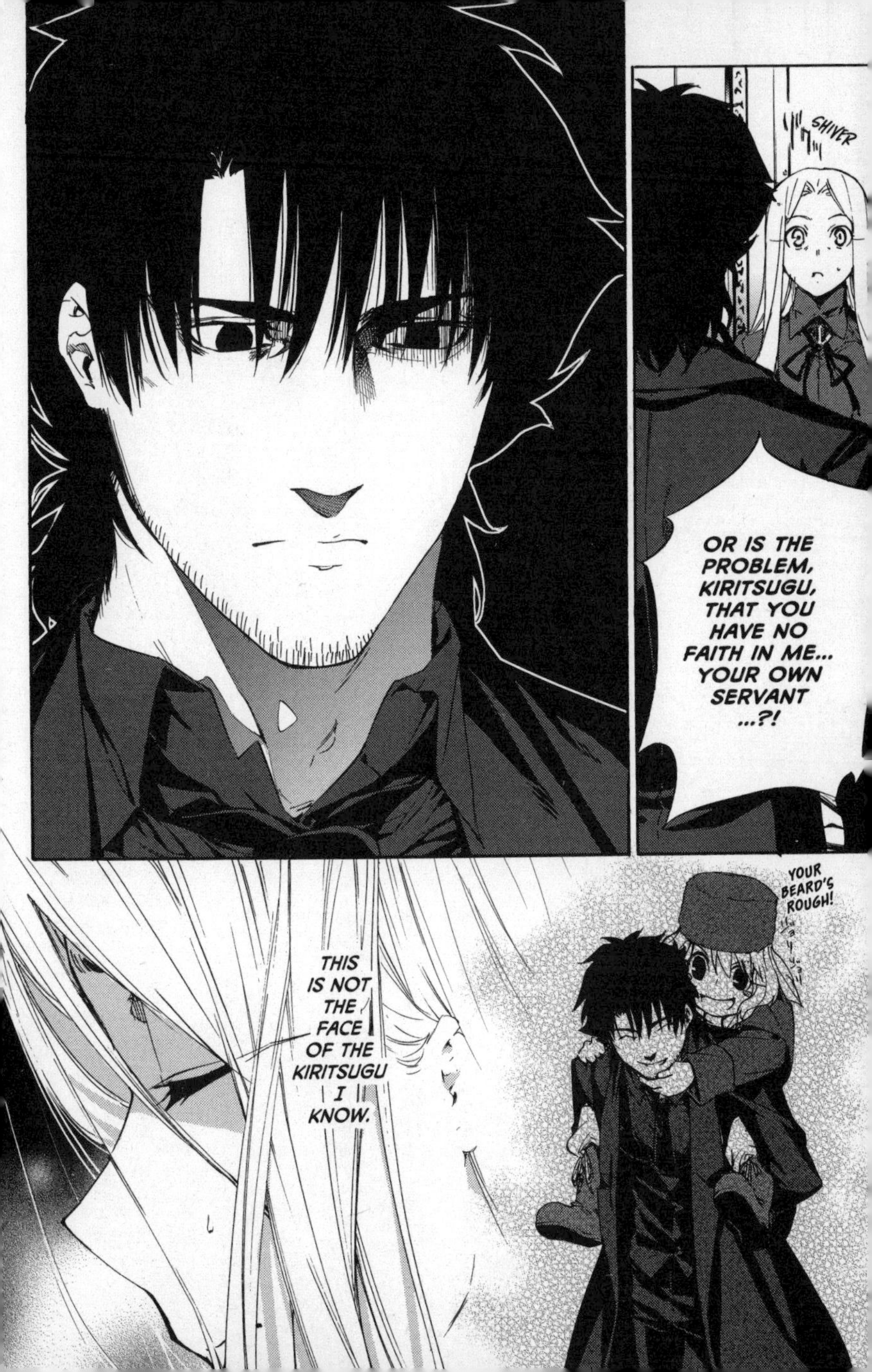
SHIVER
OR IS THE PROBLEM, KIRITSUGU, THAT YOU HAVE NO FAITH IN ME... YOUR OWN SERVANT ...?!
YOUR BEARD'S ROUGH!
THIS IS NOT THE FACE OF THE KIRITSUGU I KNOW.

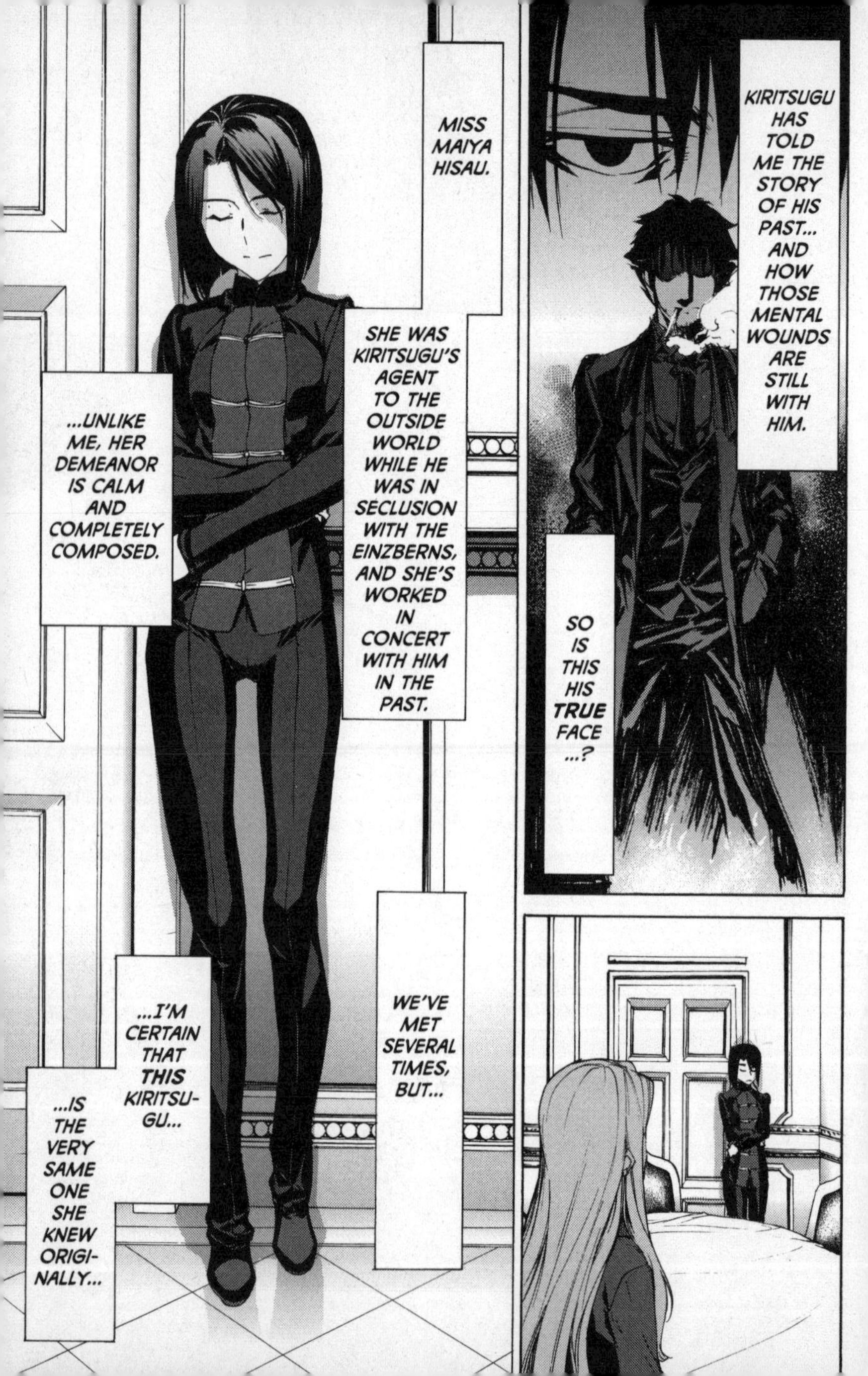
KIRITSUGU HAS TOLD ME THE STORY OF HIS PAST... AND HOW THOSE MENTAL WOUNDS ARE STILL WITH HIM.
SO IS THIS HIS TRUE FACE ...?
MISS MAIYA HISAU.
SHE WAS KIRITSUGU'S AGENT TO THE OUTSIDE WORLD WHILE HE WAS IN SECLUSION WITH THE EINZBERNS, AND SHE'S WORKED IN CONCERT WITH HIM IN THE PAST.
...UNLIKE ME, HER DEMEANOR IS CALM AND COMPLETELY COMPOSED.
WE'VE MET SEVERAL TIMES, BUT...
...I'M CERTAIN THAT THIS KIRITSU-GU...
...IS THE VERY SAME ONE SHE KNEW ORIGI-NALLY...

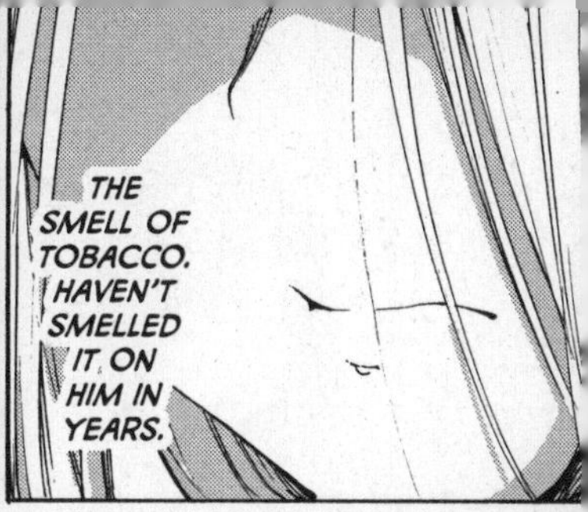
THE SMELL OF TOBACCO. HAVEN'T SMELLED IT ON HIM IN YEARS.
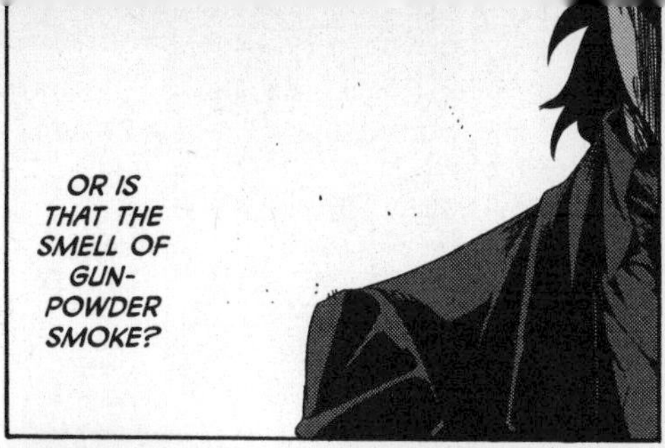
OR IS THAT THE SMELL OF GUN-POWDER SMOKE?
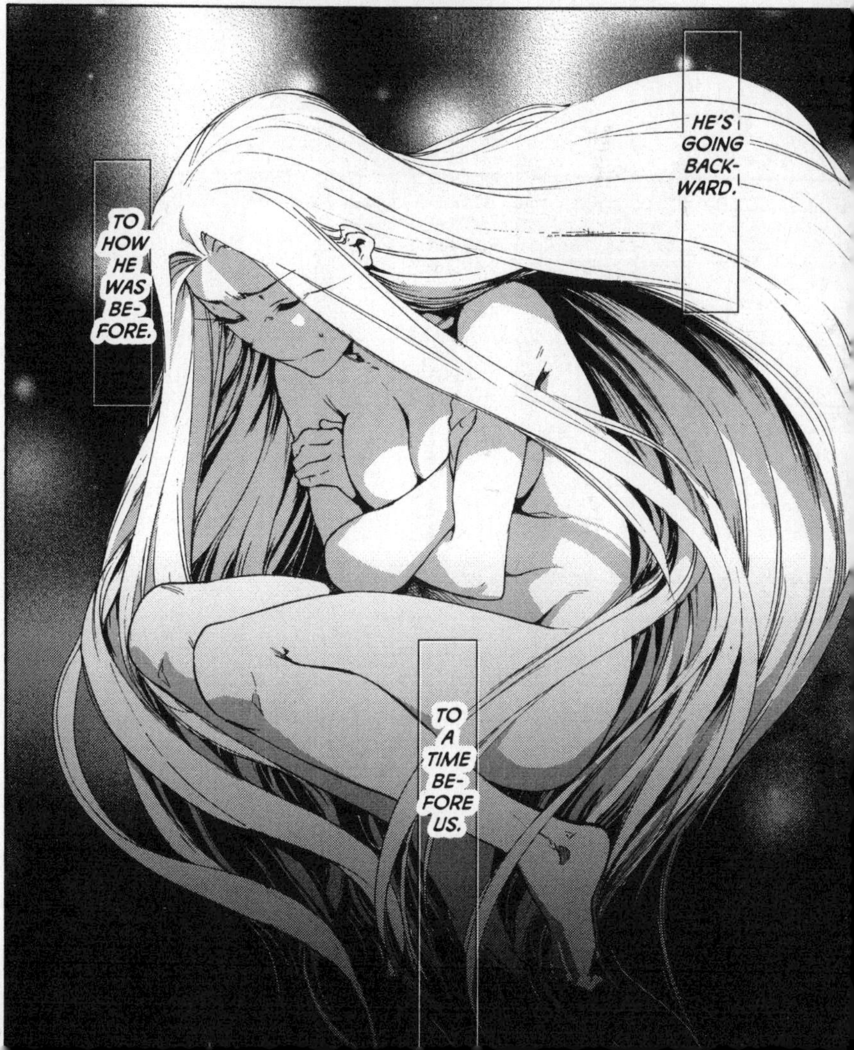
HE'S GOING BACK-WARD.
TO HOW HE WAS BE-FORE.
TO A TIME BE-FORE US.

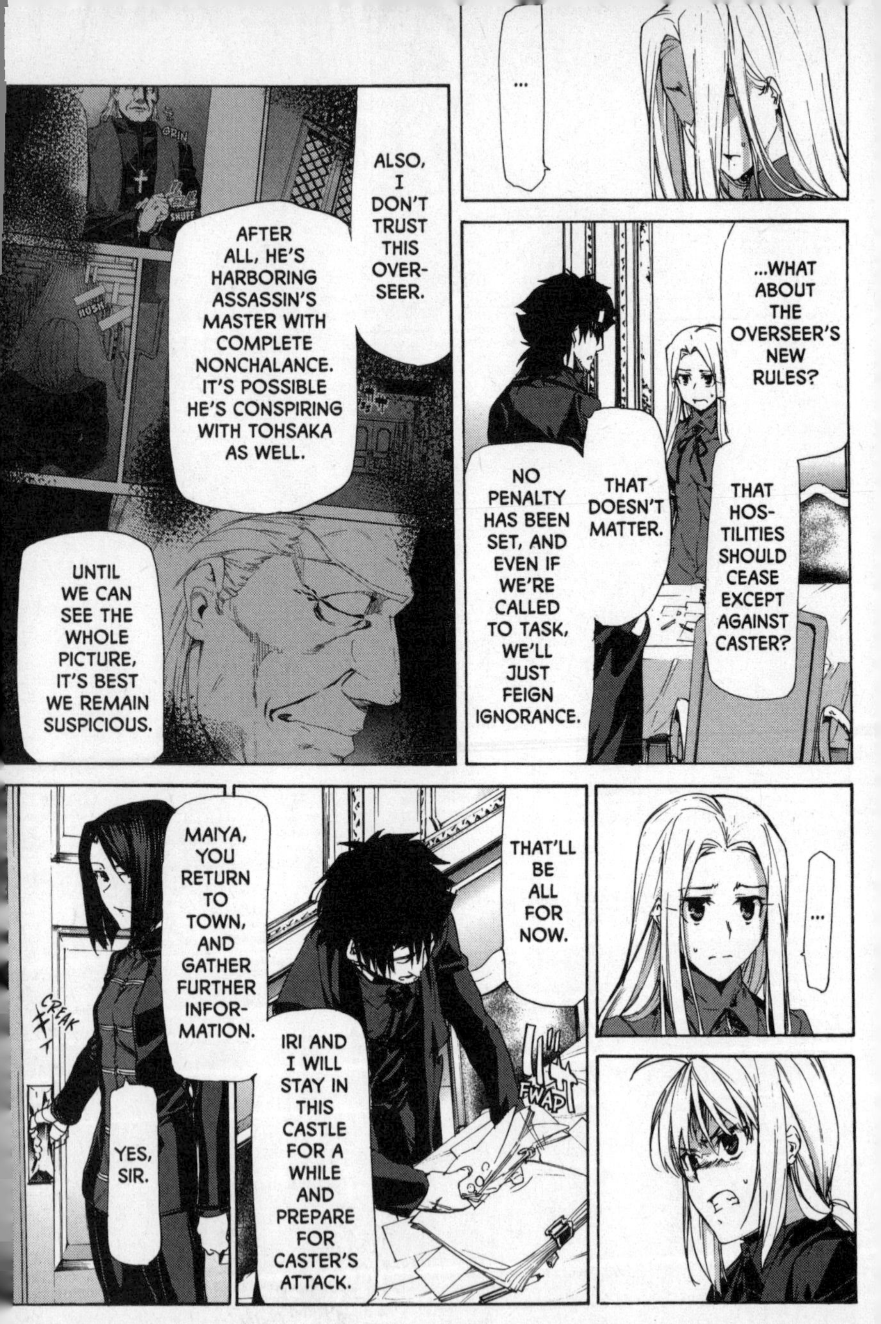
...
...WHAT ABOUT THE OVERSEER'S NEW RULES?
THAT HOSTILITIES SHOULD CEASE EXCEPT AGAINST CASTER?
THAT DOESN'T MATTER.
NO PENALTY HAS BEEN SET, AND EVEN IF WE'RE CALLED TO TASK, WE'LL JUST FEIGN IGNORANCE.
GRIN
SNUFF
ALSO, I DON'T TRUST THIS OVER-SEER.
AFTER ALL, HE'S HARBORING ASSASSIN'S MASTER WITH COMPLETE NONCHALANCE. IT'S POSSIBLE HE'S CONSPIRING WITH TOHSAKA AS WELL.
UNTIL WE CAN SEE THE WHOLE PICTURE, IT'S BEST WE REMAIN SUSPICIOUS.
...
THAT'LL BE ALL FOR NOW.
MAIYA, YOU RETURN TO TOWN, AND GATHER FURTHER INFOR-MATION.
IRI AND I WILL STAY IN THIS CASTLE FOR A WHILE AND PREPARE FOR CASTER'S ATTACK.
FWAP
CREAK
YES, SIR.

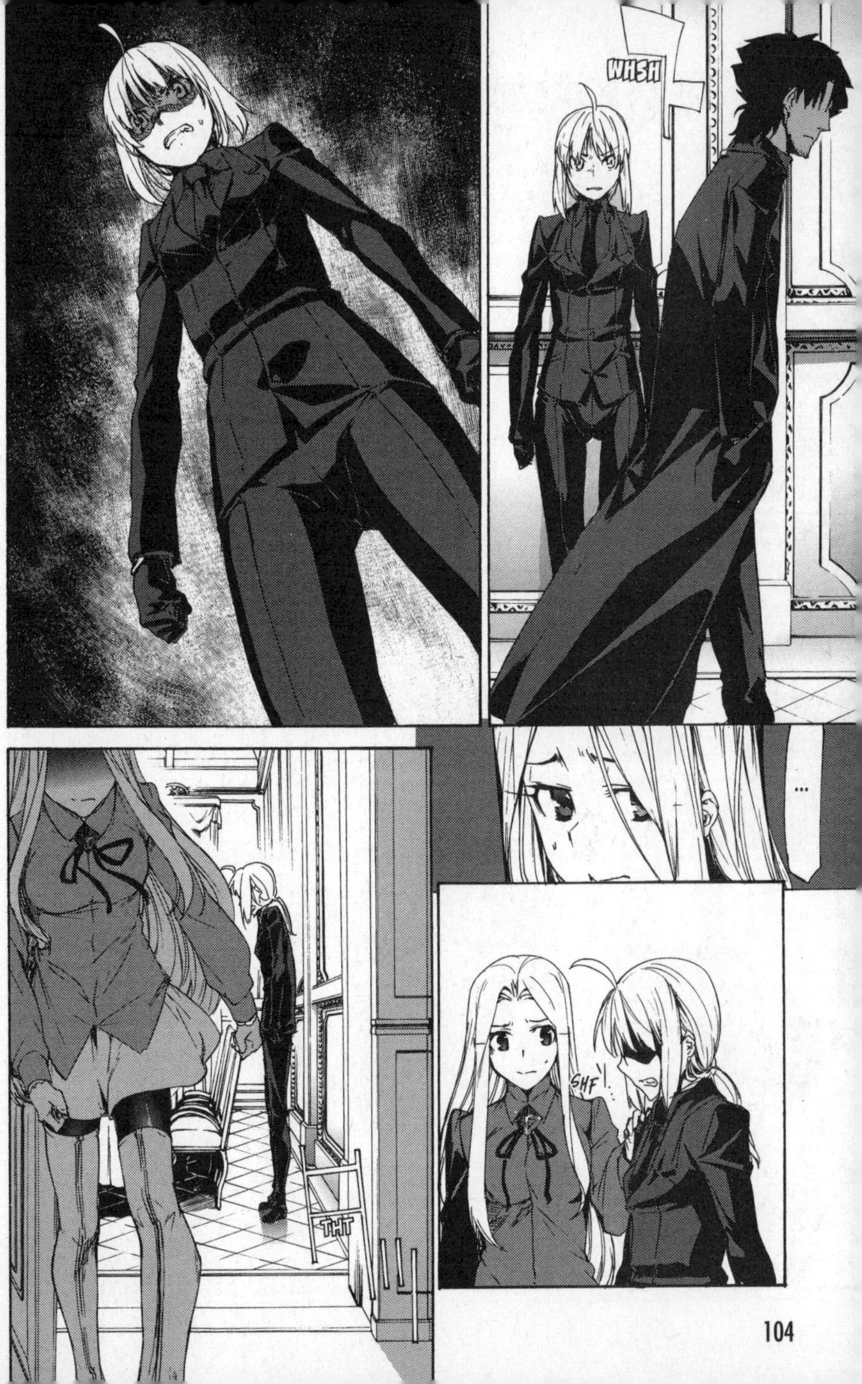
WHSH
...
SHF
!...
THT

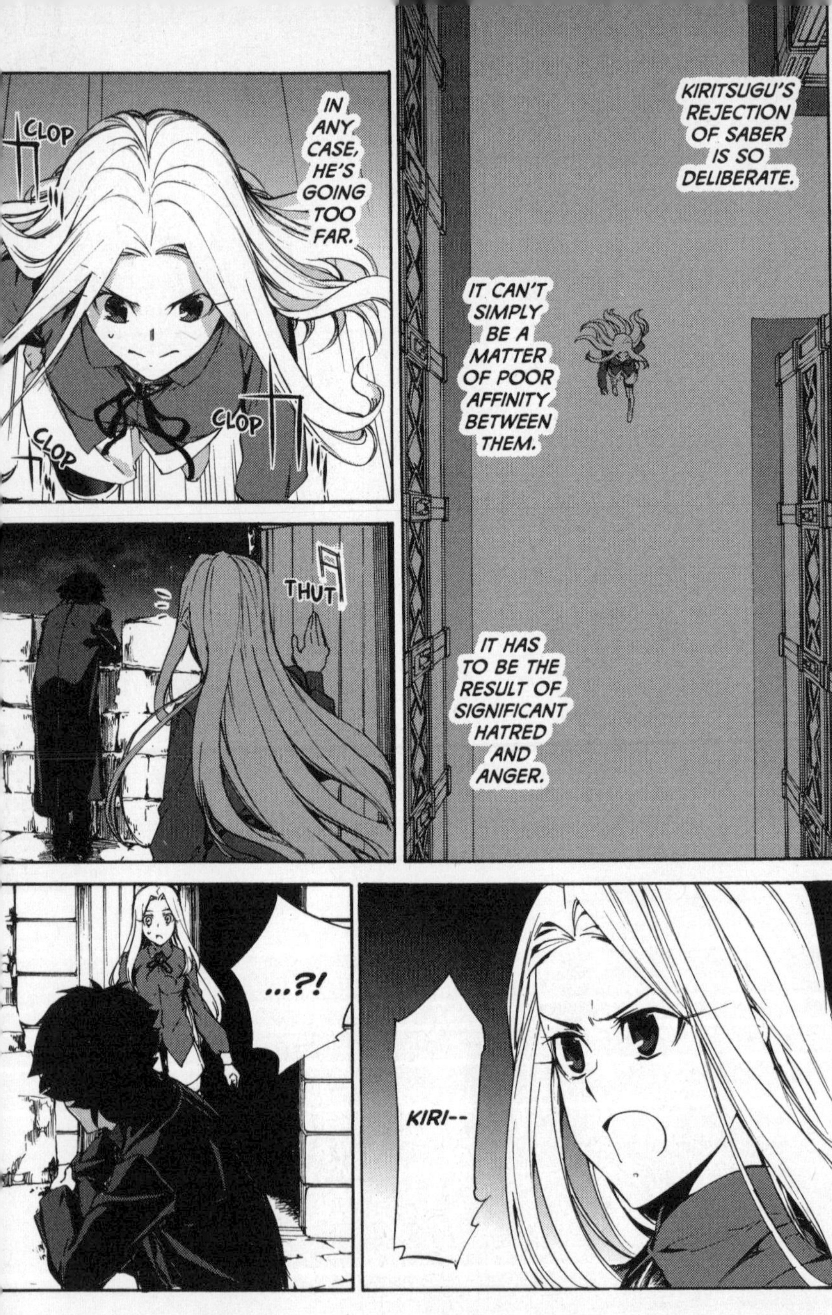
KIRITSUGU'S REJECTION OF SABER IS SO DELIBERATE.
IT CAN'T SIMPLY BE A MATTER OF POOR AFFINITY BETWEEN THEM.
IT HAS TO BE THE RESULT OF SIGNIFICANT HATRED AND ANGER.
IN ANY CASE, HE'S GOING TOO FAR.
CLOP
CLOP
CLOP
THUT
KIRI--
...?!

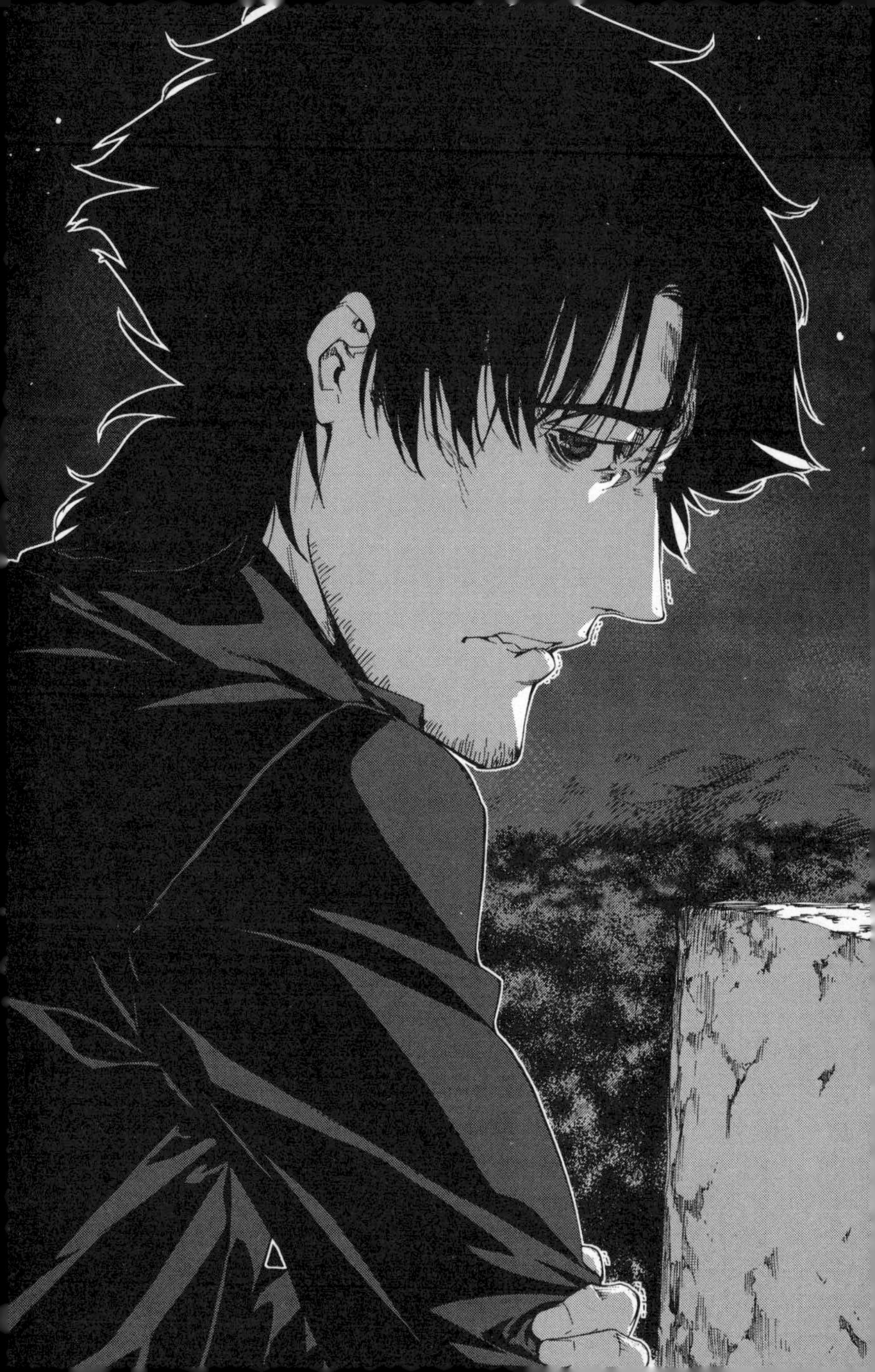

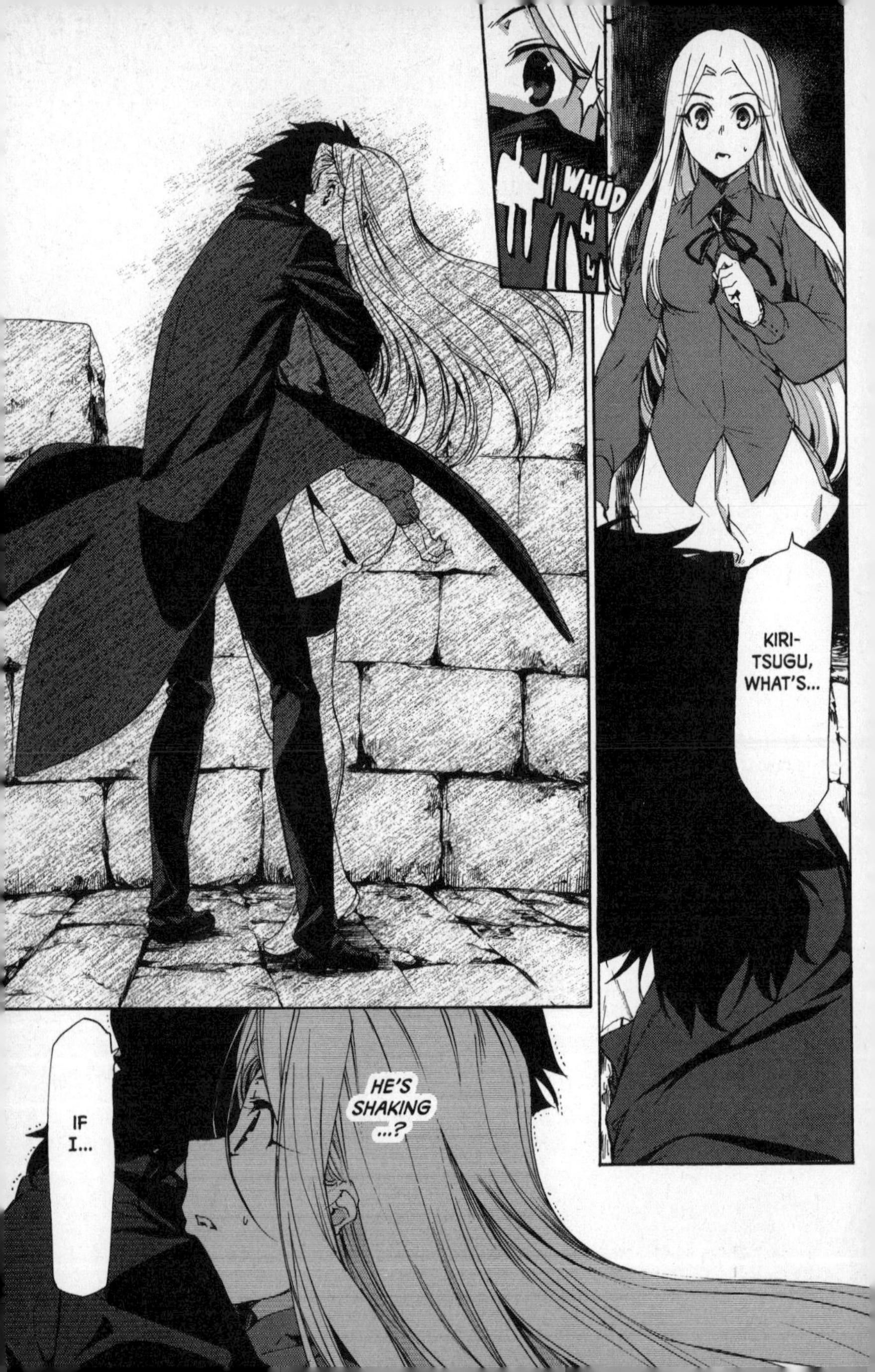
WHUD
KIRI-TSUGU, WHAT'S...
HE'S SHAKING ...?
IF I...

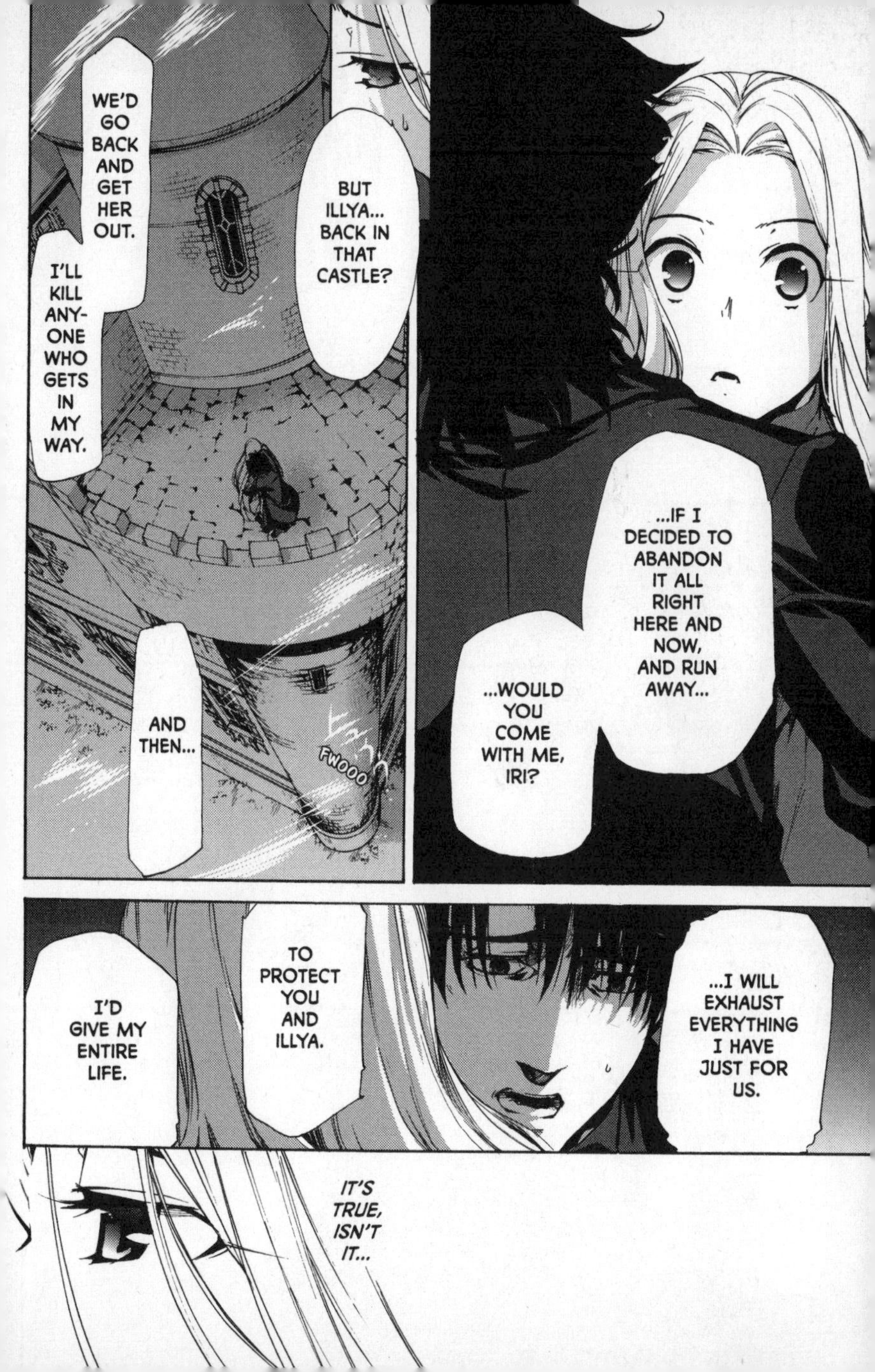
...IF I DECIDED TO ABANDON IT ALL RIGHT HERE AND NOW, AND RUN AWAY...
...WOULD YOU COME WITH ME, IRI?
BUT ILLYA... BACK IN THAT CASTLE?
WE'D GO BACK AND GET HER OUT.
I'LL KILL ANY-ONE WHO GETS IN MY WAY.
AND THEN...
FWOOO
...I WILL EXHAUST EVERYTHING I HAVE JUST FOR US.
TO PROTECT YOU AND ILLYA.
I'D GIVE MY ENTIRE LIFE.
IT'S TRUE, ISN'T IT...

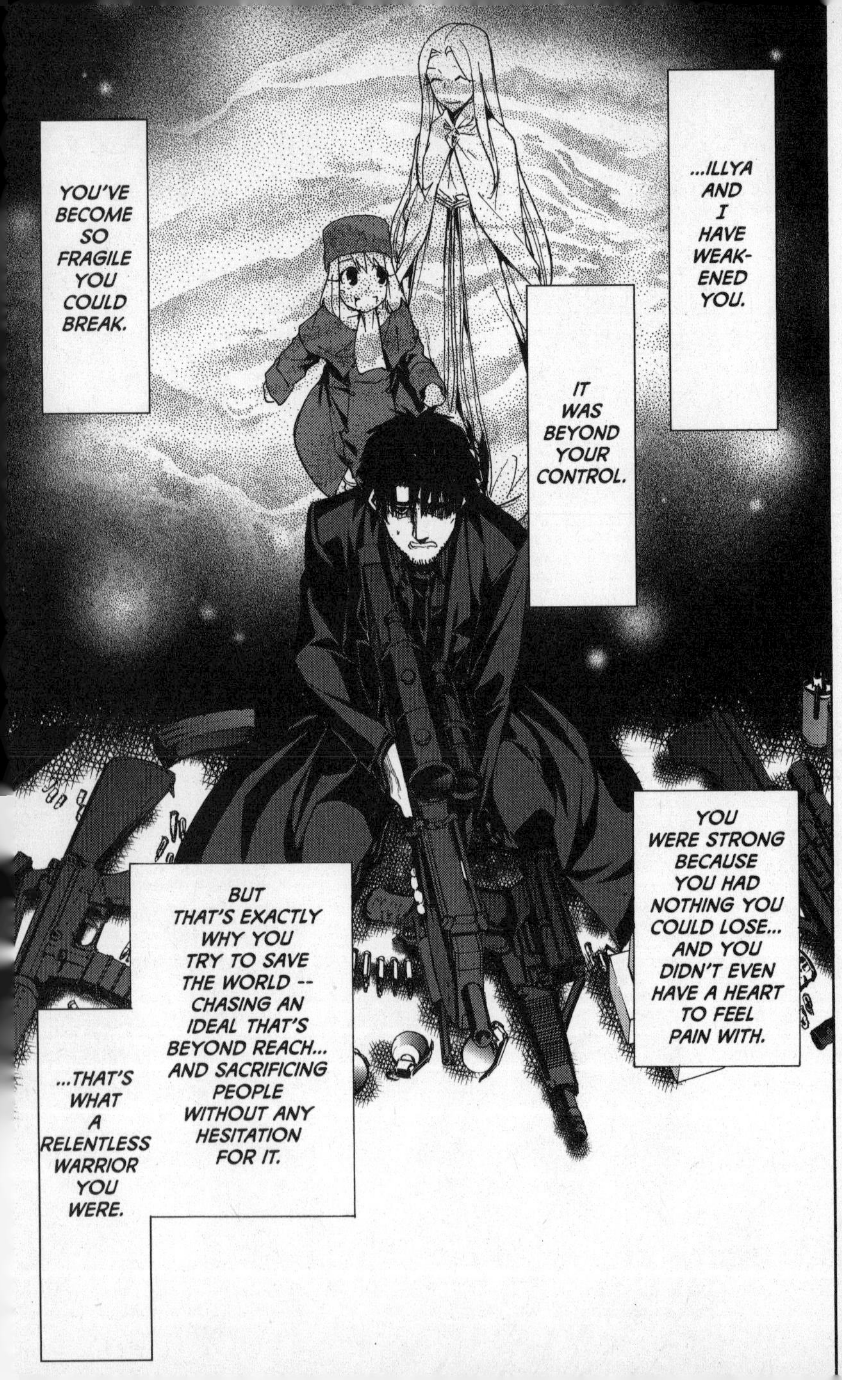
...ILLYA AND I HAVE WEAK-ENED YOU.
IT WAS BEYOND YOUR CONTROL.
YOU'VE BECOME SO FRAGILE YOU COULD BREAK.
YOU WERE STRONG BECAUSE YOU HAD NOTHING YOU COULD LOSE... AND YOU DIDN'T EVEN HAVE A HEART TO FEEL PAIN WITH.
BUT THAT'S EXACTLY WHY YOU TRY TO SAVE THE WORLD -- CHASING AN IDEAL THAT'S BEYOND REACH... AND SACRIFICING PEOPLE WITHOUT ANY HESITATION FOR IT.
...THAT'S WHAT A RELENTLESS WARRIOR YOU WERE.

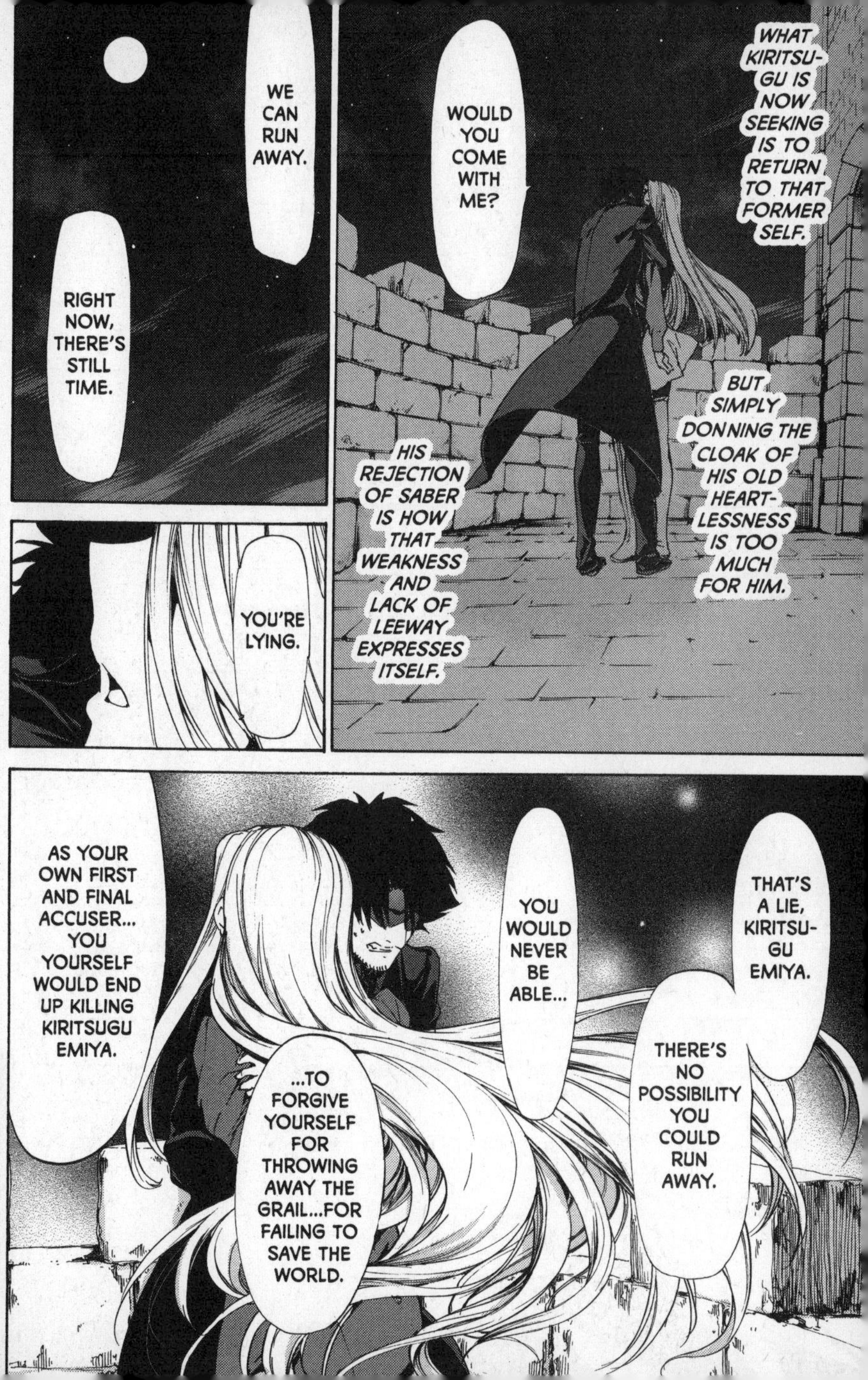

WHAT KIRITSU-GU IS NOW SEEKING IS TO RETURN TO THAT FORMER SELF.
WOULD YOU COME WITH ME?
BUT SIMPLY DONNING THE CLOAK OF HIS OLD HEART-LESSNESS IS TOO MUCH FOR HIM.
HIS REJECTION OF SABER IS HOW THAT WEAKNESS AND LACK OF LEEWAY EXPRESSES ITSELF.
WE CAN RUN AWAY.
RIGHT NOW, THERE'S STILL TIME.
YOU'RE LYING.
THAT'S A LIE, KIRITSU-GU EMIYA.
THERE'S NO POSSIBILITY YOU COULD RUN AWAY.
YOU WOULD NEVER BE ABLE...
...TO FORGIVE YOURSELF FOR THROWING AWAY THE GRAIL...FOR FAILING TO SAVE THE WORLD.
AS YOUR OWN FIRST AND FINAL ACCUSER... YOU YOURSELF WOULD END UP KILLING KIRITSUGU EMIYA.

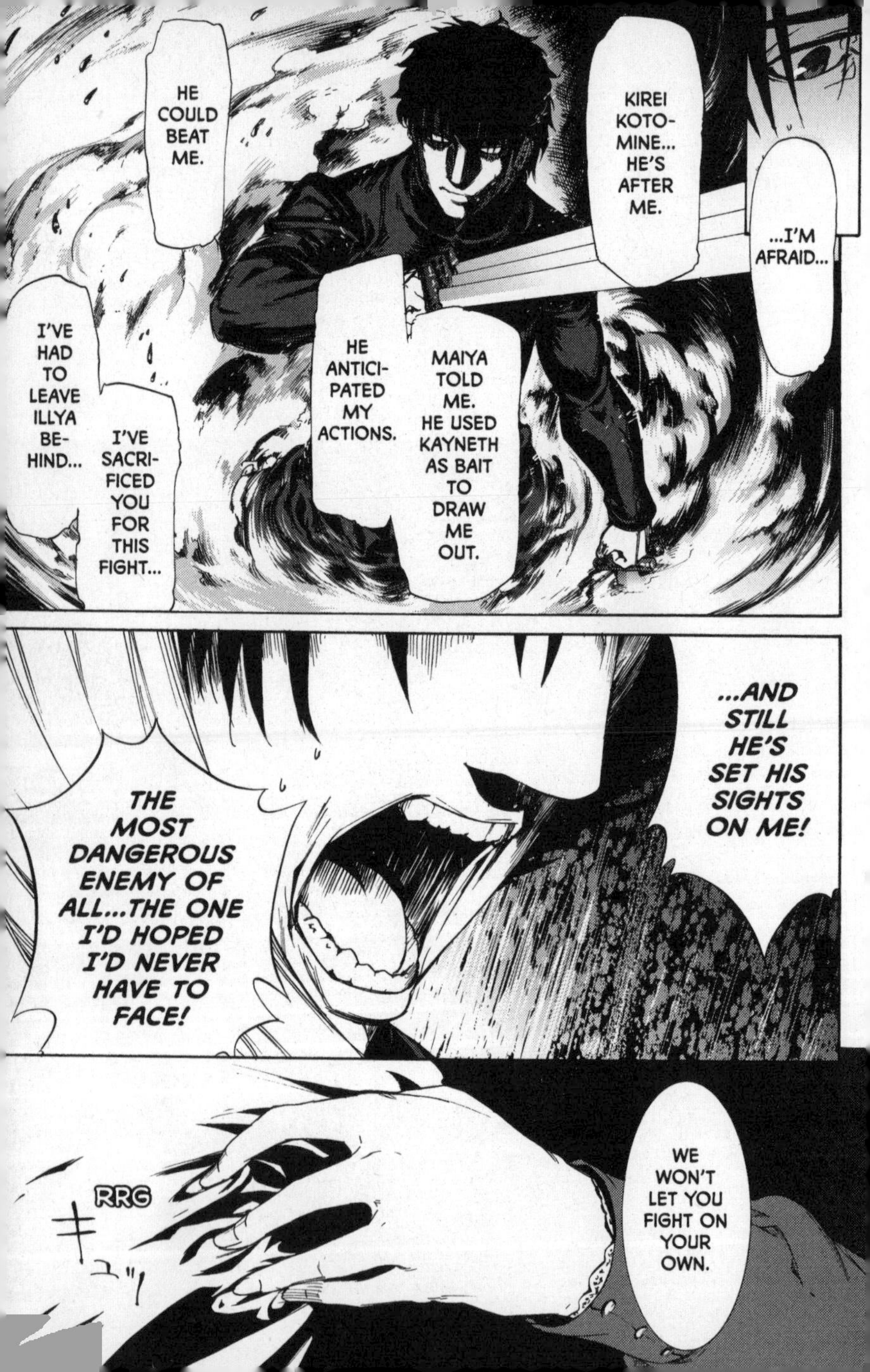
KIREI KOTO-MINE... HE'S AFTER ME.
...I'M AFRAID...
MAIYA TOLD ME. HE USED KAYNETH AS BAIT TO DRAW ME OUT.
HE ANTICI-PATED MY ACTIONS.
HE COULD BEAT ME.
I'VE SACRI-FICED YOU FOR THIS FIGHT...
I'VE HAD TO LEAVE ILLYA BE-HIND...
THE MOST DANGEROUS ENEMY OF ALL...THE ONE I'D HOPED I'D NEVER HAVE TO FACE!
...AND STILL HE'S SET HIS SIGHTS ON ME!
WE WON'T LET YOU FIGHT ON YOUR OWN.
RRG
キュッ

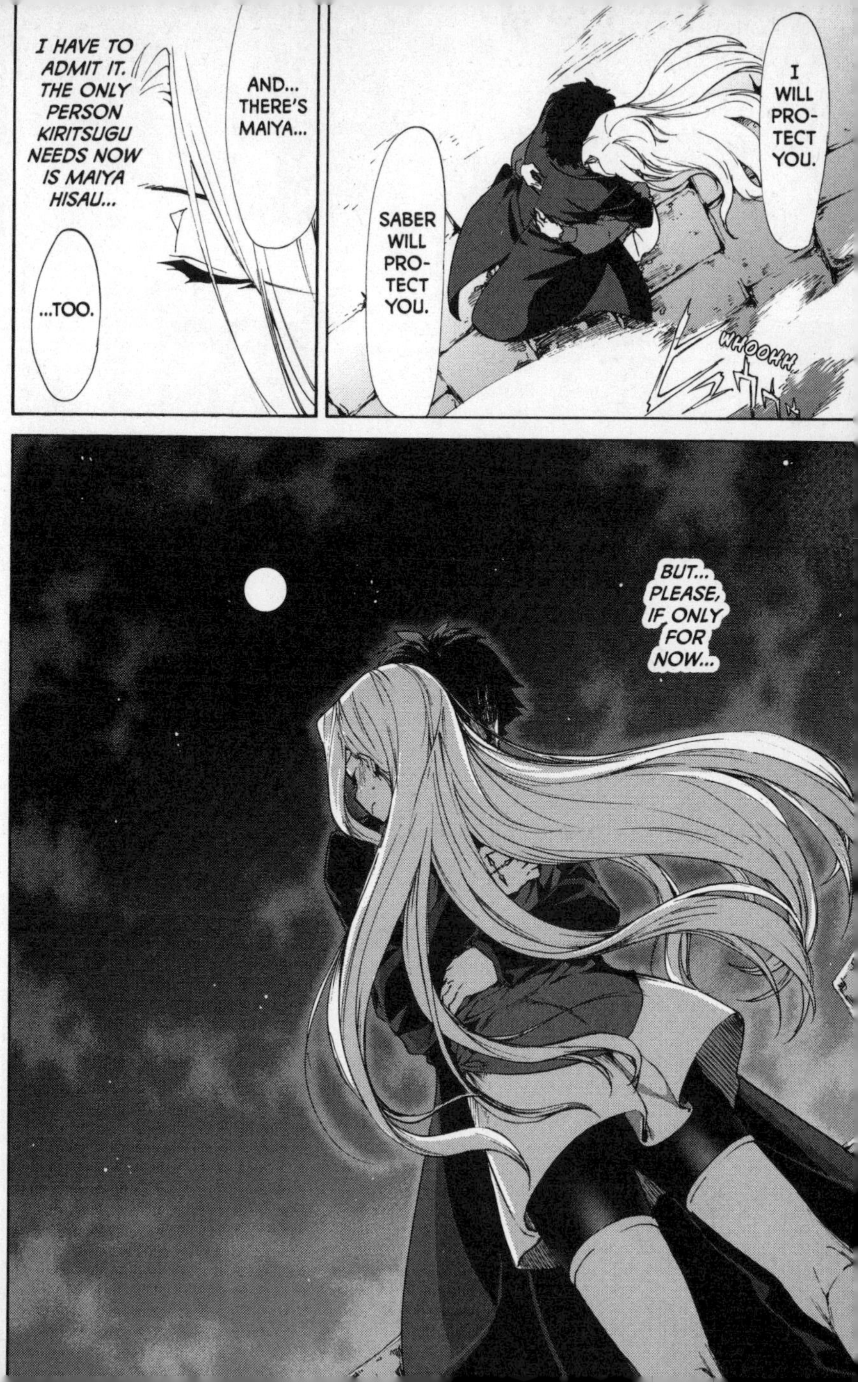
I WILL PROTECT YOU.
SABER WILL PROTECT YOU.
WHOOHH...
AND... THERE'S MAIYA...
I HAVE TO ADMIT IT. THE ONLY PERSON KIRITSUGU NEEDS NOW IS MAIYA HISAU...
...TOO.
BUT... PLEASE, IF ONLY FOR NOW...

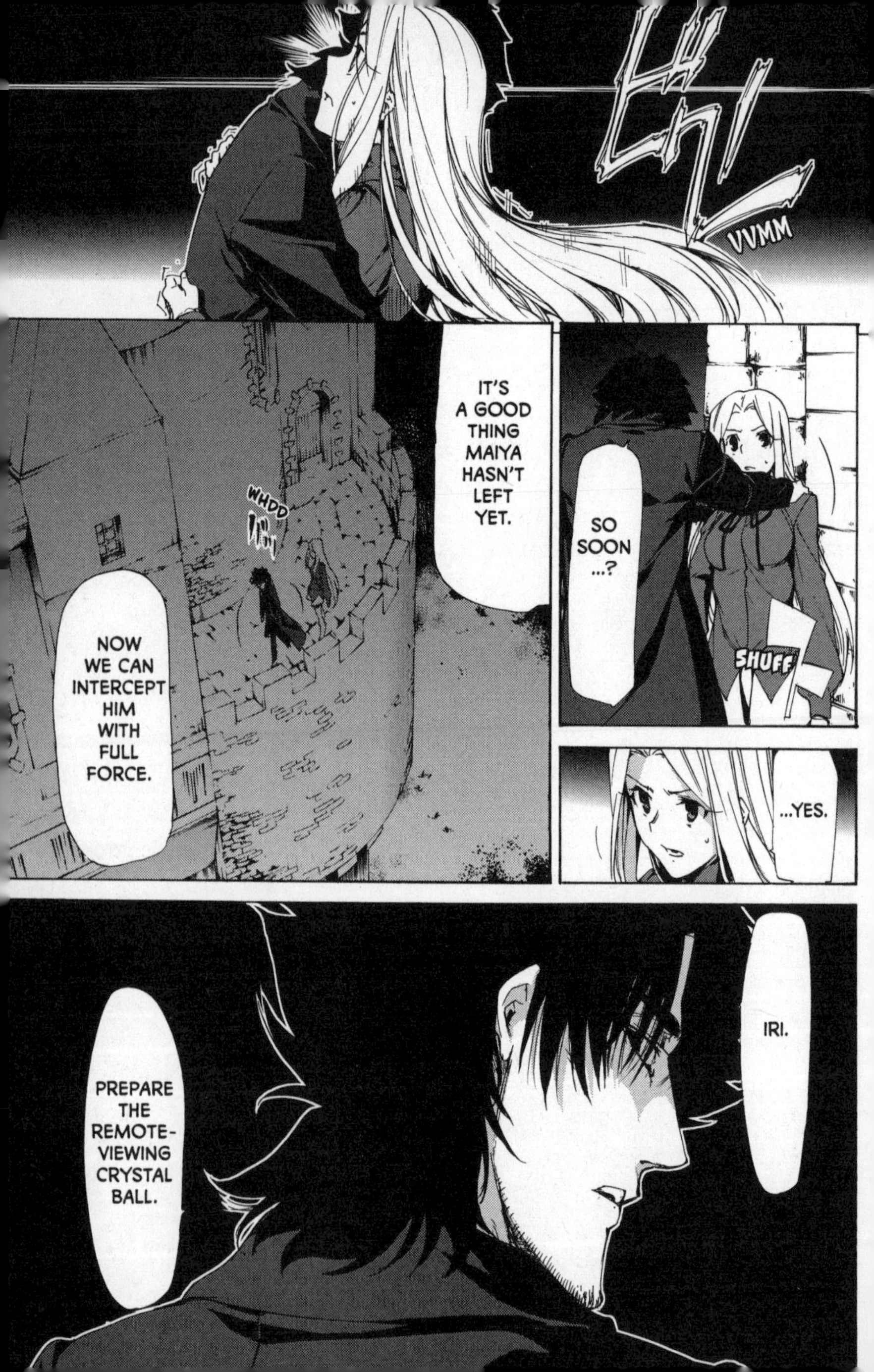
VVMM
SO SOON ...?
SHUFF
...YES.
IT'S A GOOD THING MAIYA HASN'T LEFT YET.
WHDD
NOW WE CAN INTERCEPT HIM WITH FULL FORCE.
IRI.
PREPARE THE REMOTE-VIEWING CRYSTAL BALL.

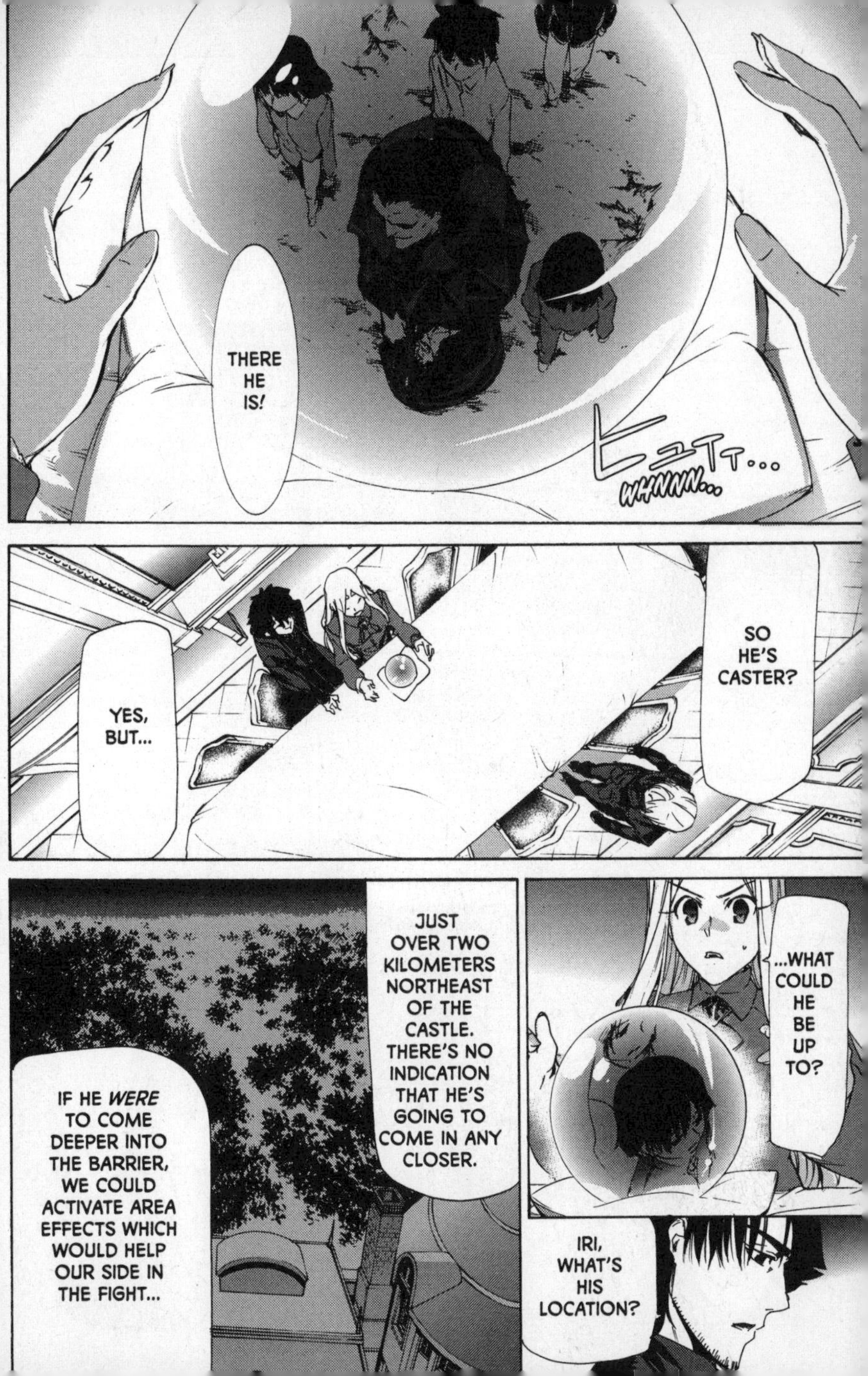
THERE HE IS!
WHNNN...
SO HE'S CASTER?
YES, BUT...
...WHAT COULD HE BE UP TO?
IRI, WHAT'S HIS LOCATION?
JUST OVER TWO KILOMETERS NORTHEAST OF THE CASTLE. THERE'S NO INDICATION THAT HE'S GOING TO COME IN ANY CLOSER.
IF HE *WERE* TO COME DEEPER INTO THE BARRIER, WE COULD ACTIVATE AREA EFFECTS WHICH WOULD HELP OUR SIDE IN THE FIGHT...

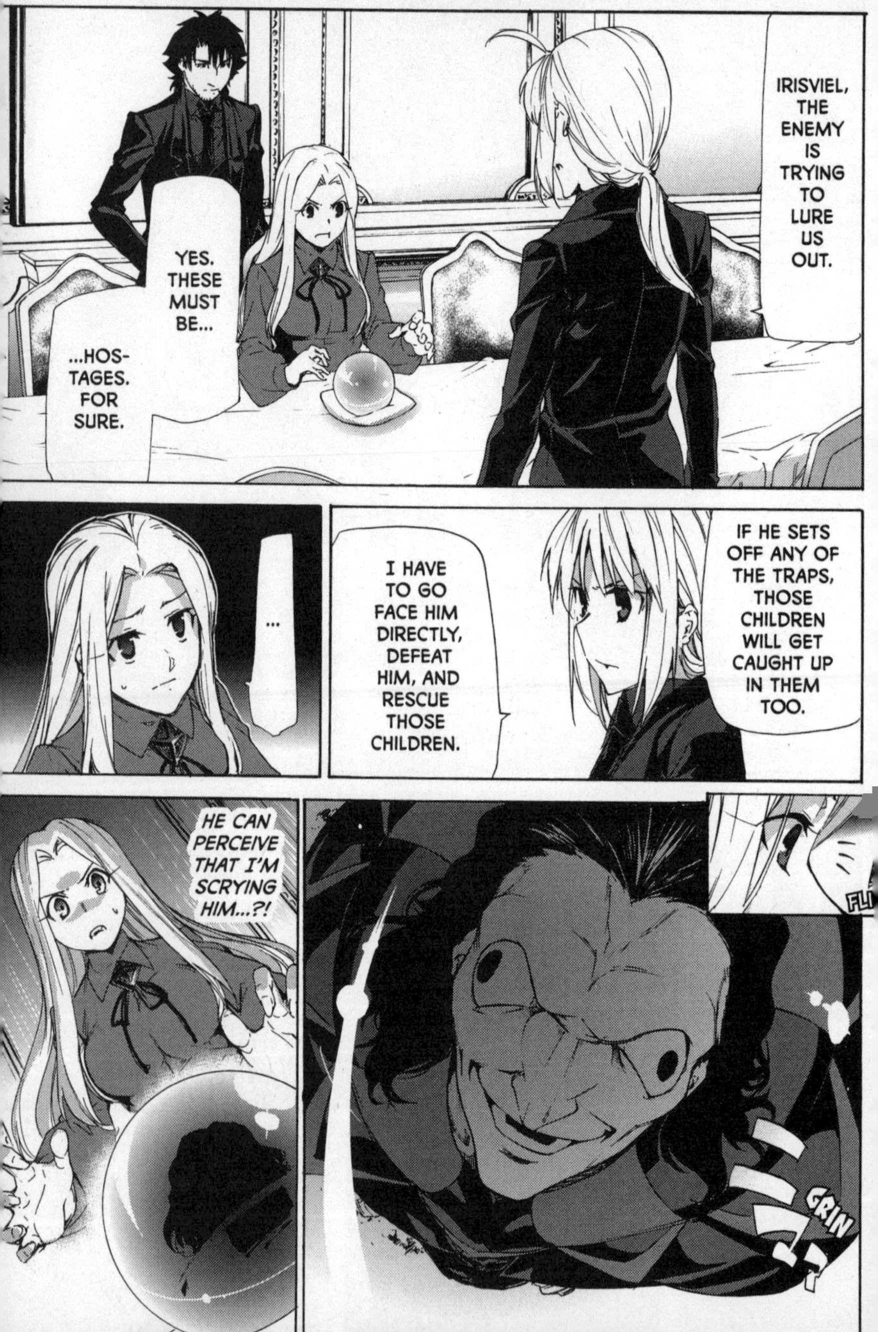
IRISVIEL, THE ENEMY IS TRYING TO LURE US OUT.
YES. THESE MUST BE...
...HOS-TAGES. FOR SURE.
IF HE SETS OFF ANY OF THE TRAPS, THOSE CHILDREN WILL GET CAUGHT UP IN THEM TOO.
I HAVE TO GO FACE HIM DIRECTLY, DEFEAT HIM, AND RESCUE THOSE CHILDREN.
...
FLI
GRIN
HE CAN PERCEIVE THAT I'M SCRYING HIM...?!

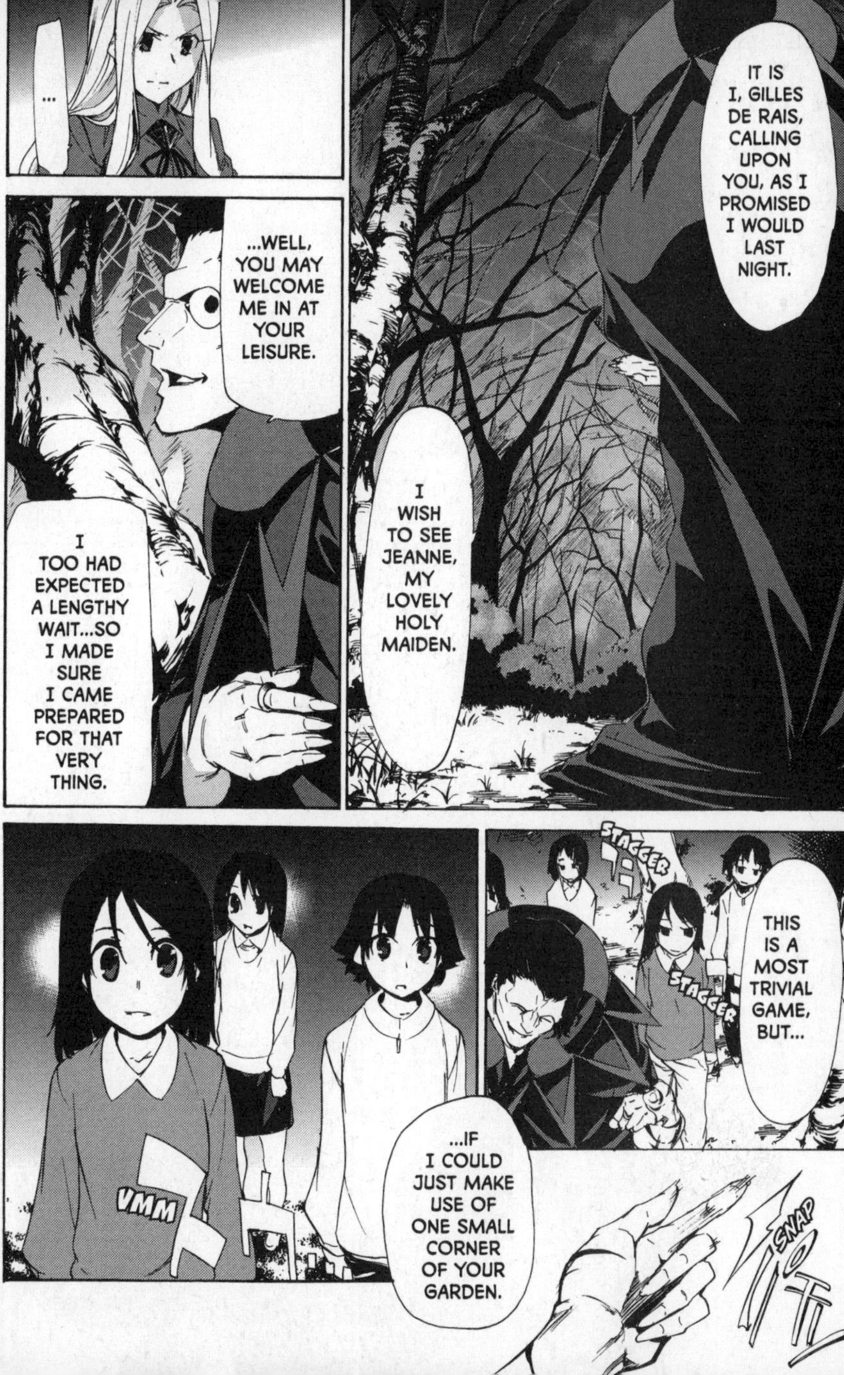
IT IS I, GILLES DE RAIS, CALLING UPON YOU, AS I PROMISED I WOULD LAST NIGHT.
I WISH TO SEE JEANNE, MY LOVELY HOLY MAIDEN.
...
...WELL, YOU MAY WELCOME ME IN AT YOUR LEISURE.
I TOO HAD EXPECTED A LENGTHY WAIT...SO I MADE SURE I CAME PREPARED FOR THAT VERY THING.
STAGGER
STAGGER
THIS IS A MOST TRIVIAL GAME, BUT...
...IF I COULD JUST MAKE USE OF ONE SMALL CORNER OF YOUR GARDEN.
SNAP
VMM

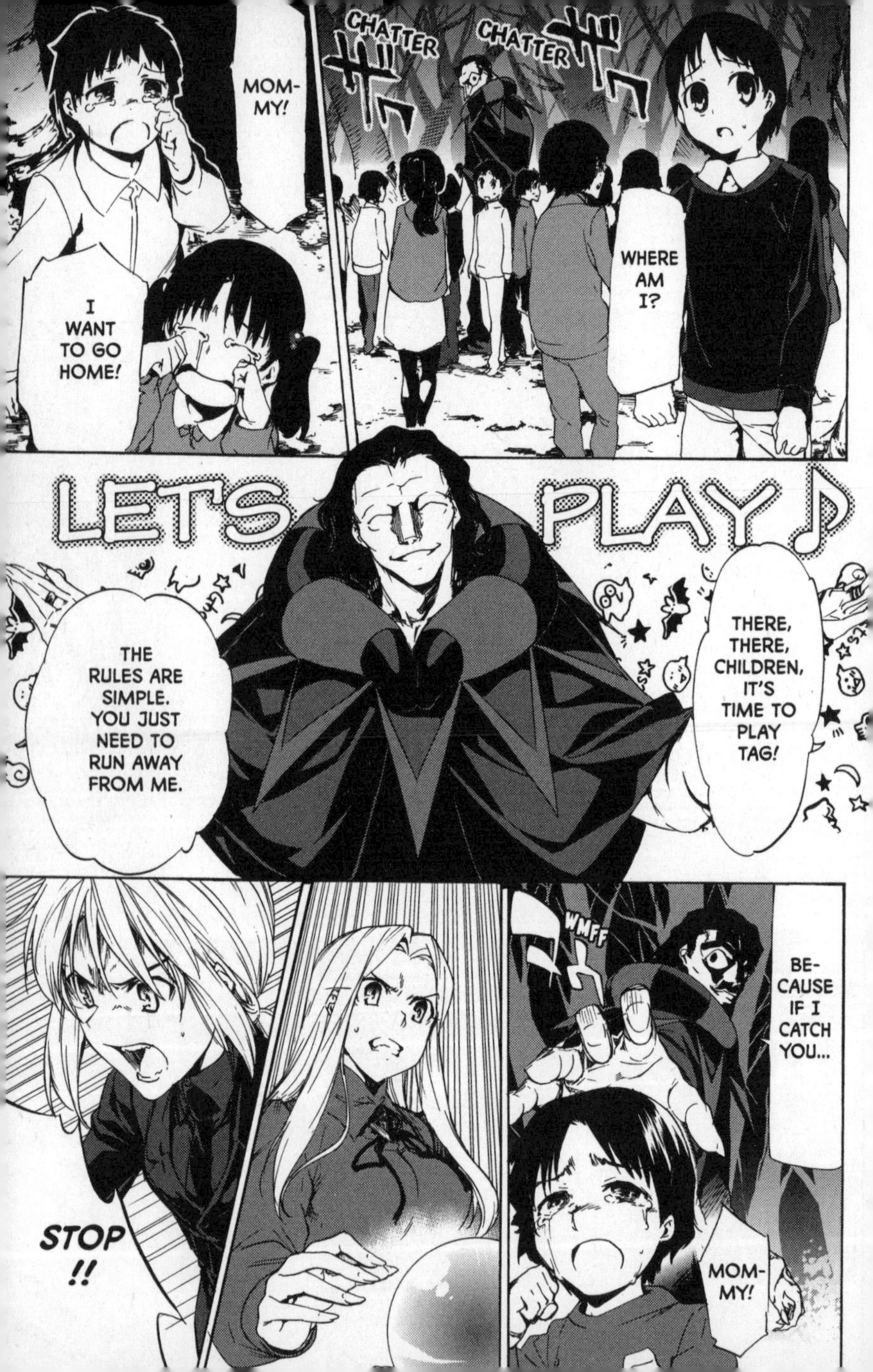
CHATTER
CHATTER
WHERE AM I?
MOM-MY!
I WANT TO GO HOME!
LET'S PLAY ♪
THERE, THERE, CHILDREN, IT'S TIME TO PLAY TAG!
THE RULES ARE SIMPLE. YOU JUST NEED TO RUN AWAY FROM ME.
BE-CAUSE IF I CATCH YOU...
WMFF
MOM-MY!
STOP!!

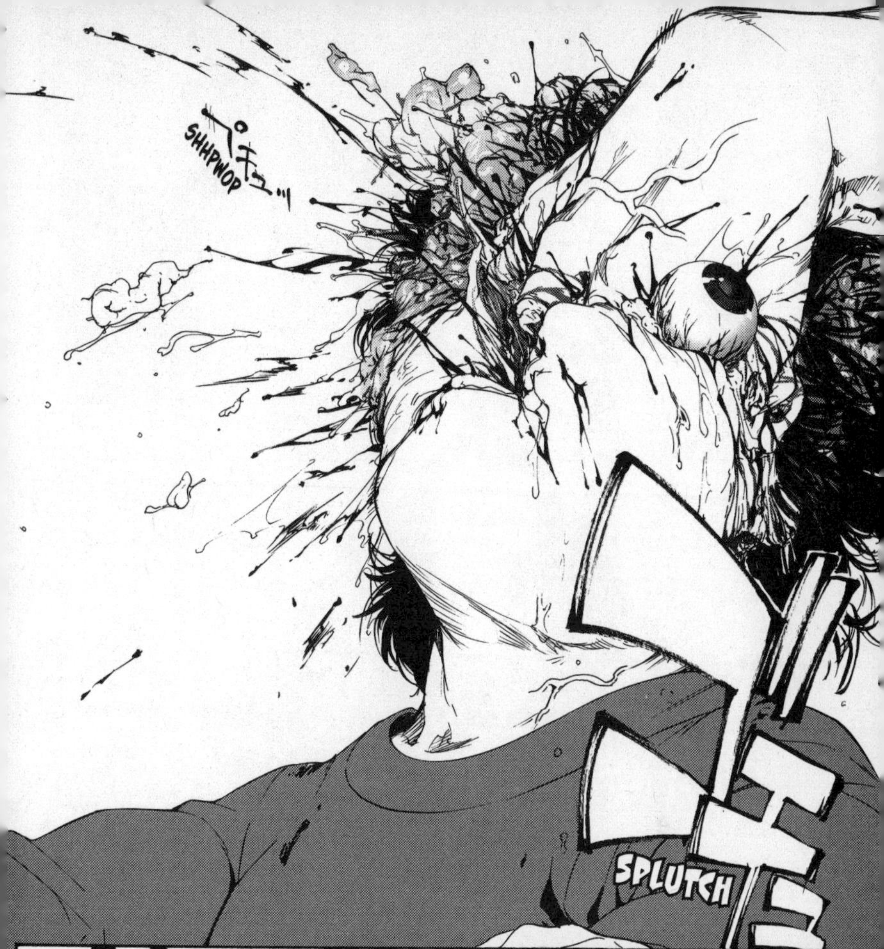
SHHPWOP
SPLUTCH

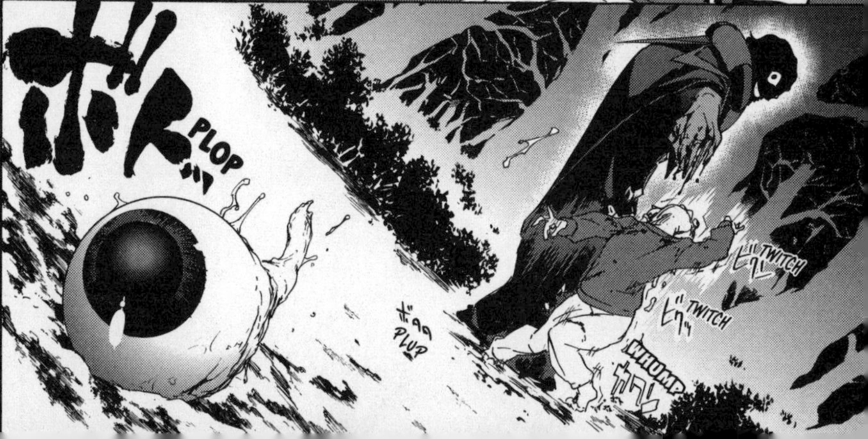
TWITCH
TWITCH
WHUMP
PLUP
PLOP

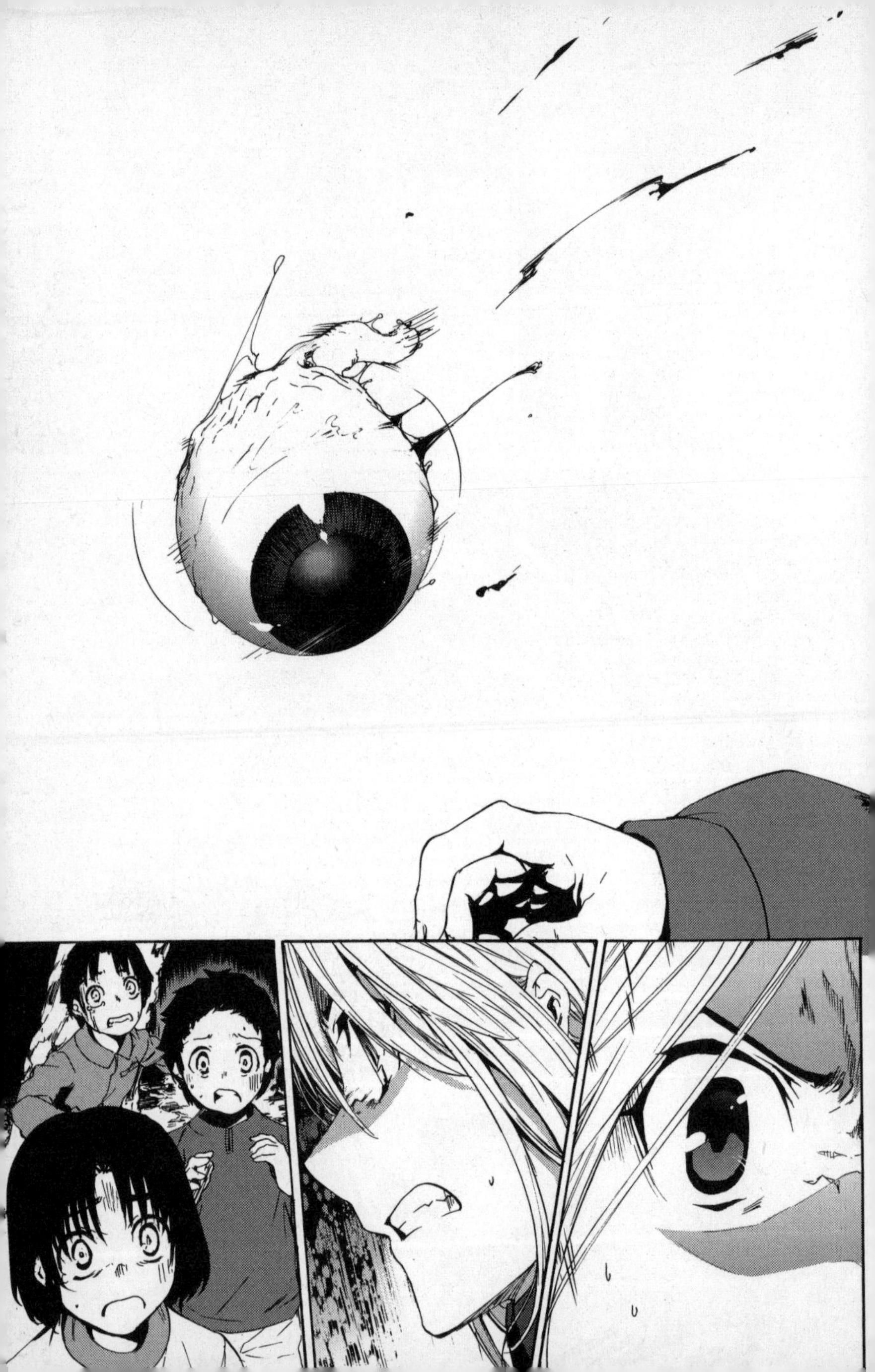

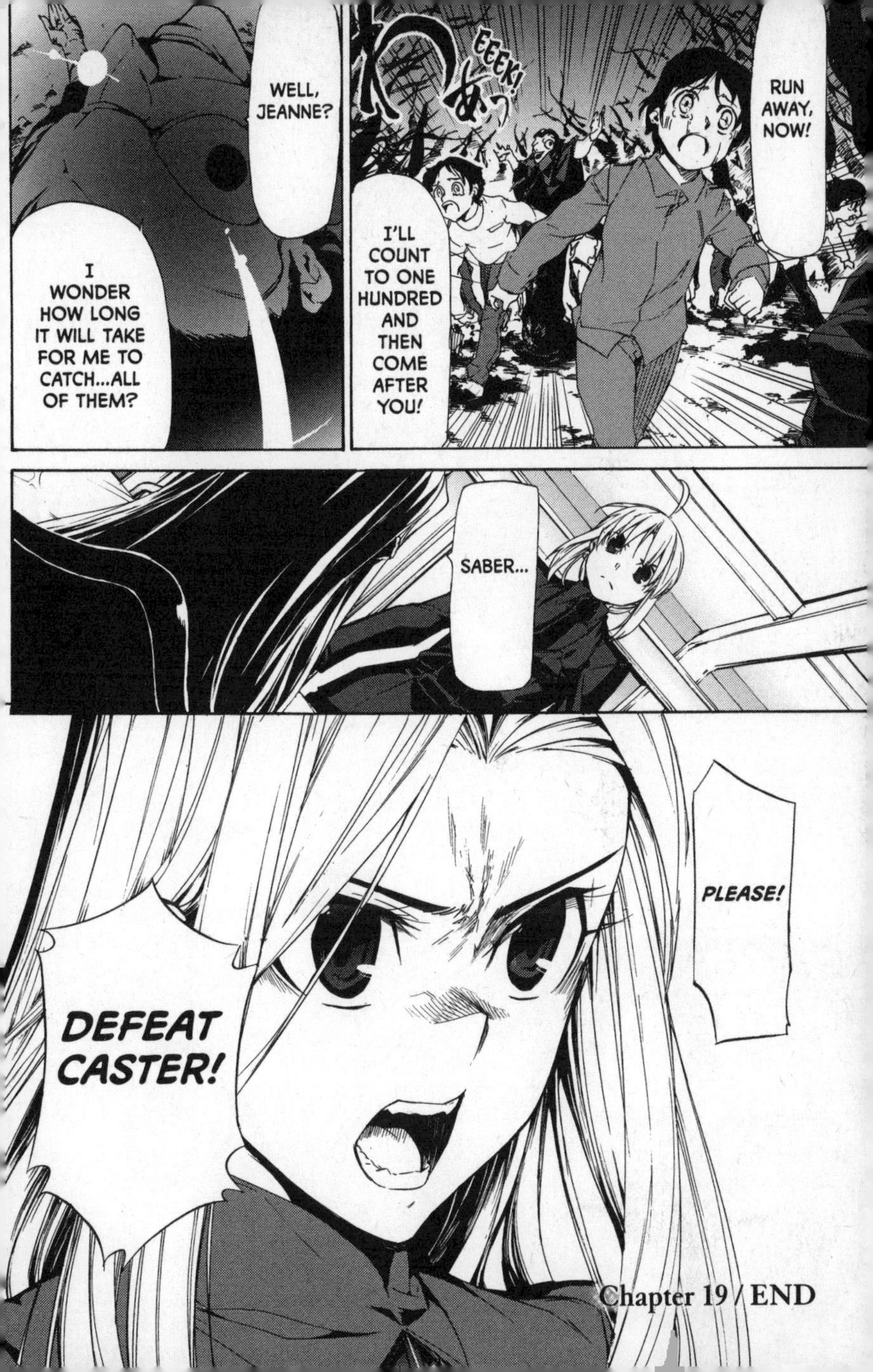
RUN AWAY, NOW!
EEEK!
あっ
I'LL COUNT TO ONE HUNDRED AND THEN COME AFTER YOU!
WELL, JEANNE?
I WONDER HOW LONG IT WILL TAKE FOR ME TO CATCH...ALL OF THEM?
SABER...
PLEASE!
DEFEAT CASTER!
Chapter 19 / END

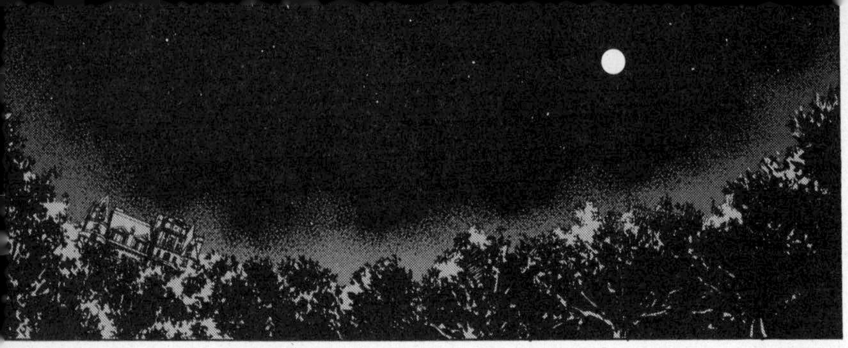

— 130 : 55 : 11

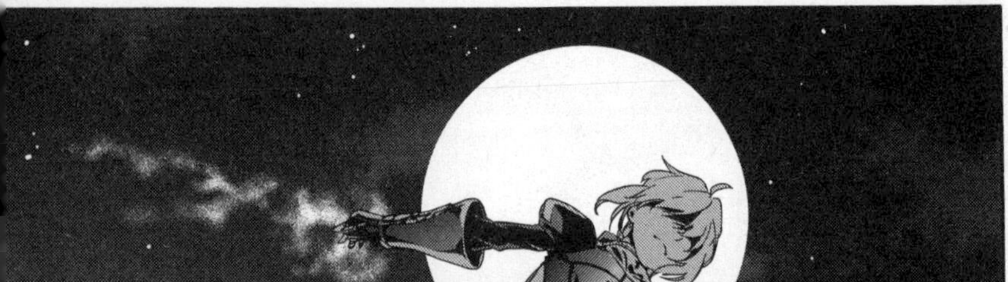

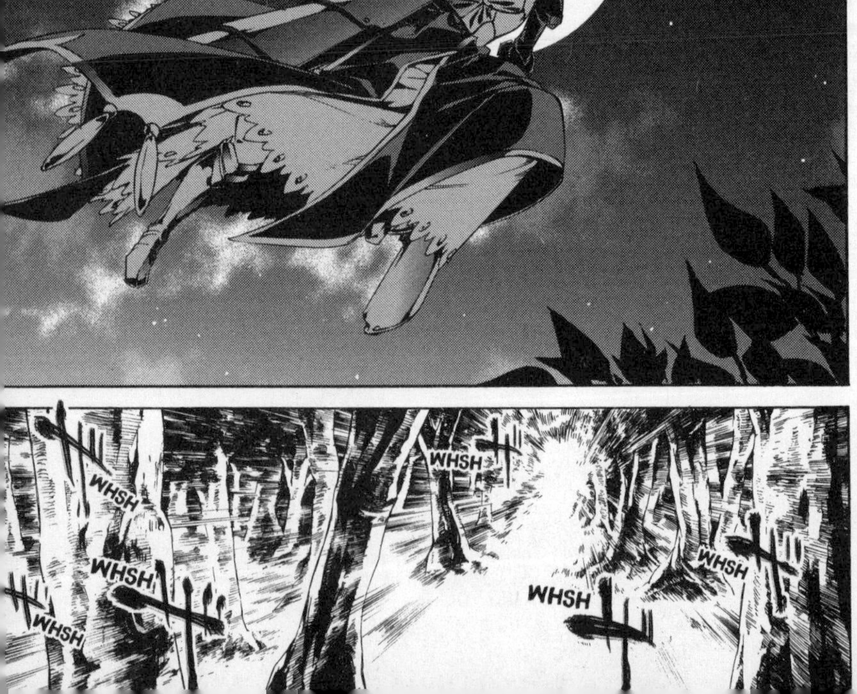
WHSH
WHSH
WHSH
WHSH
WHSH
WHSH

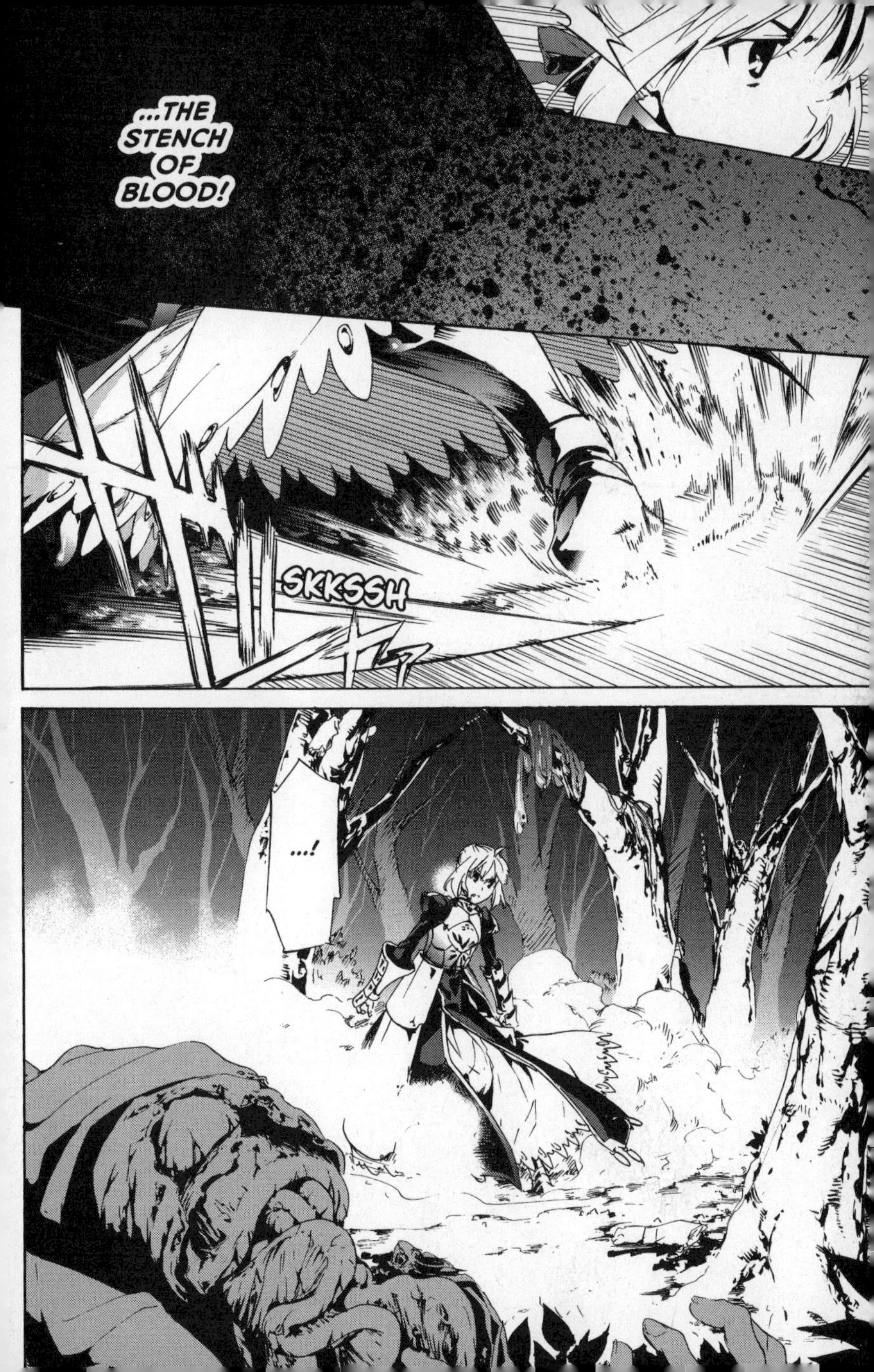
...THE STENCH OF BLOOD!
SKKSSH
...!

CHAPTER 20

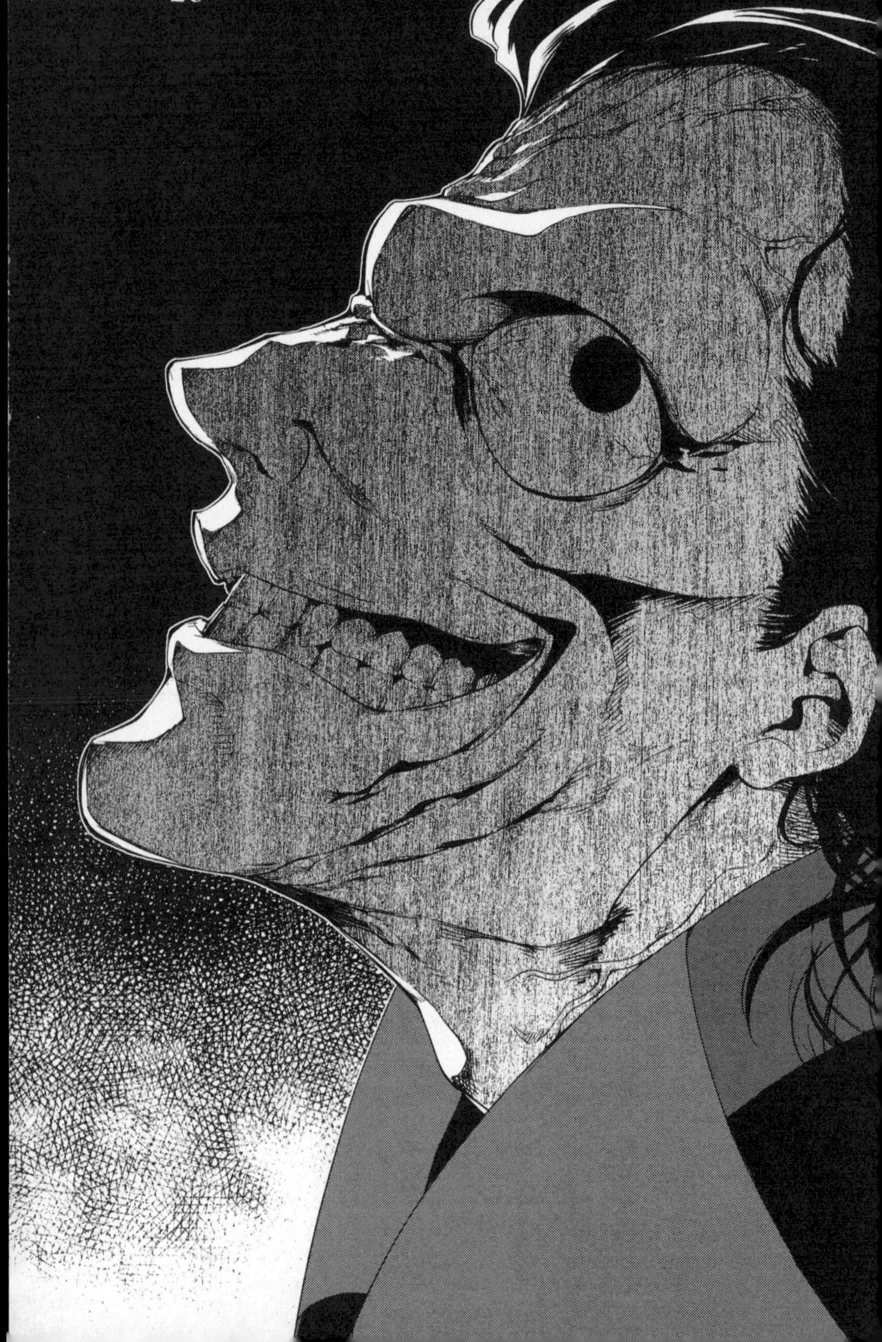

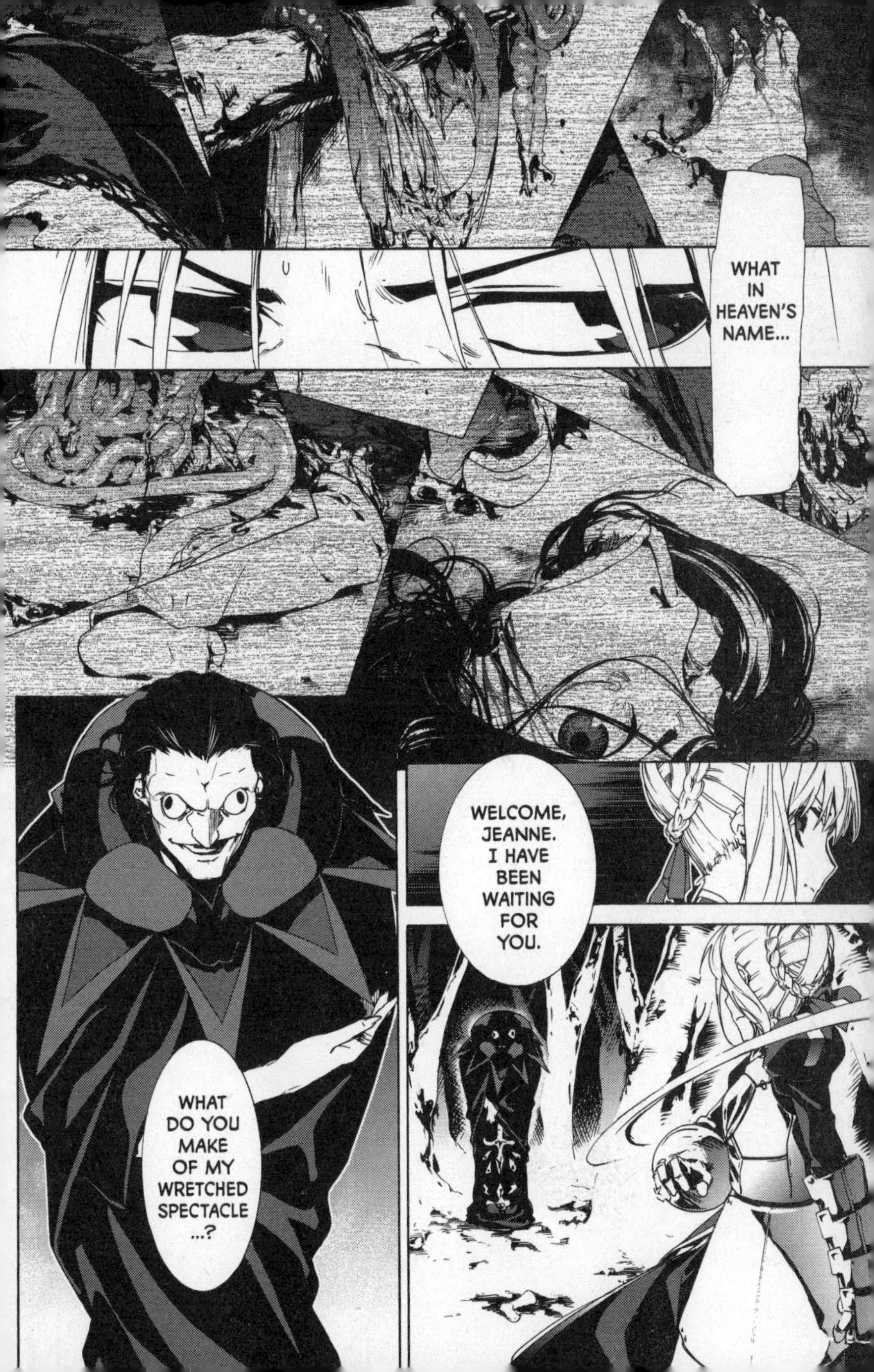
WHAT IN HEAVEN'S NAME...
WELCOME, JEANNE. I HAVE BEEN WAITING FOR YOU.
WHAT DO YOU MAKE OF MY WRETCHED SPECTACLE ...?

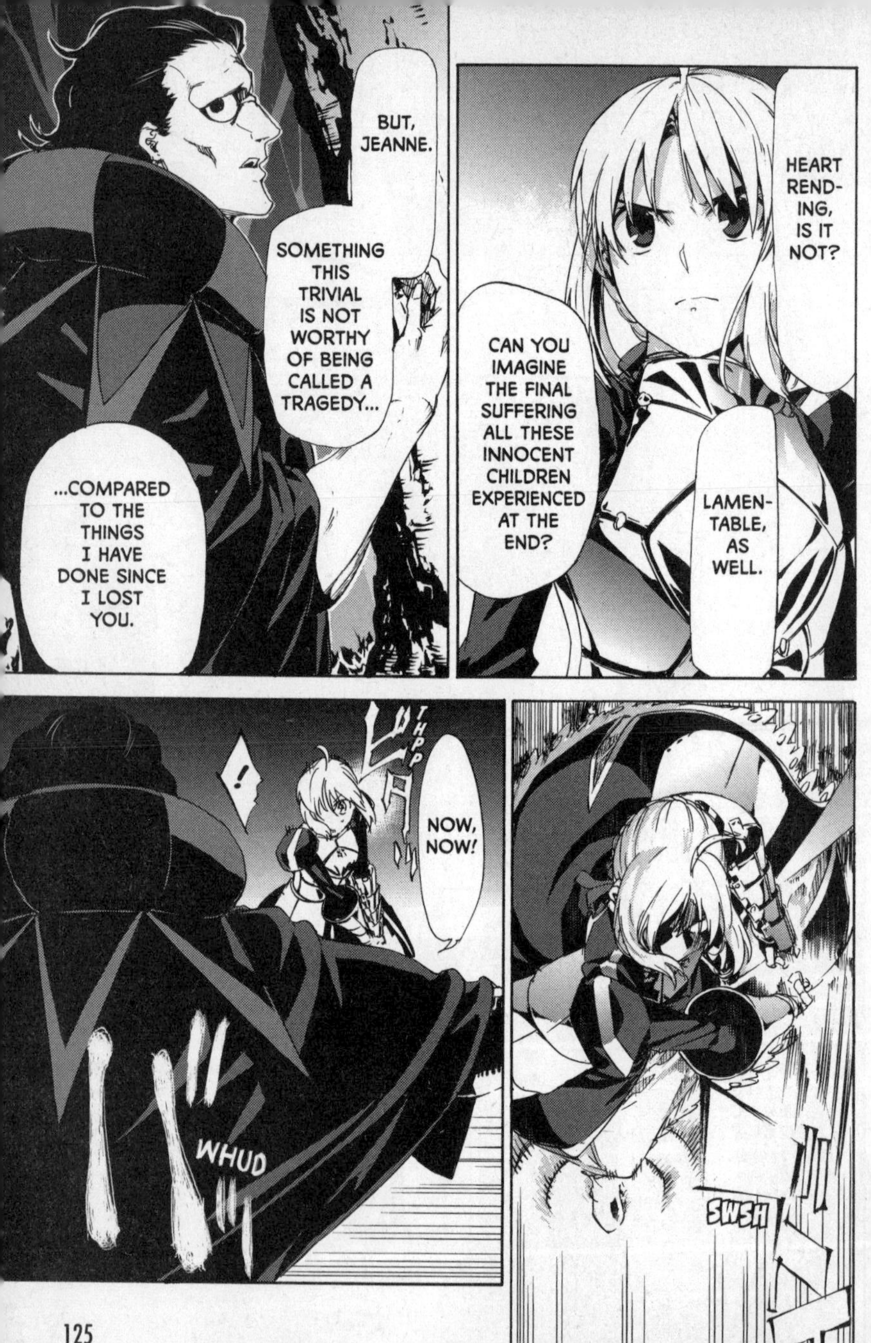
HEART RENDING, IS IT NOT?
LAMENTABLE, AS WELL.
CAN YOU IMAGINE THE FINAL SUFFERING ALL THESE INNOCENT CHILDREN EXPERIENCED AT THE END?
BUT, JEANNE.
SOMETHING THIS TRIVIAL IS NOT WORTHY OF BEING CALLED A TRAGEDY...
...COMPARED TO THE THINGS I HAVE DONE SINCE I LOST YOU.
SWSH
NOW, NOW!
THPP
!
WHUD

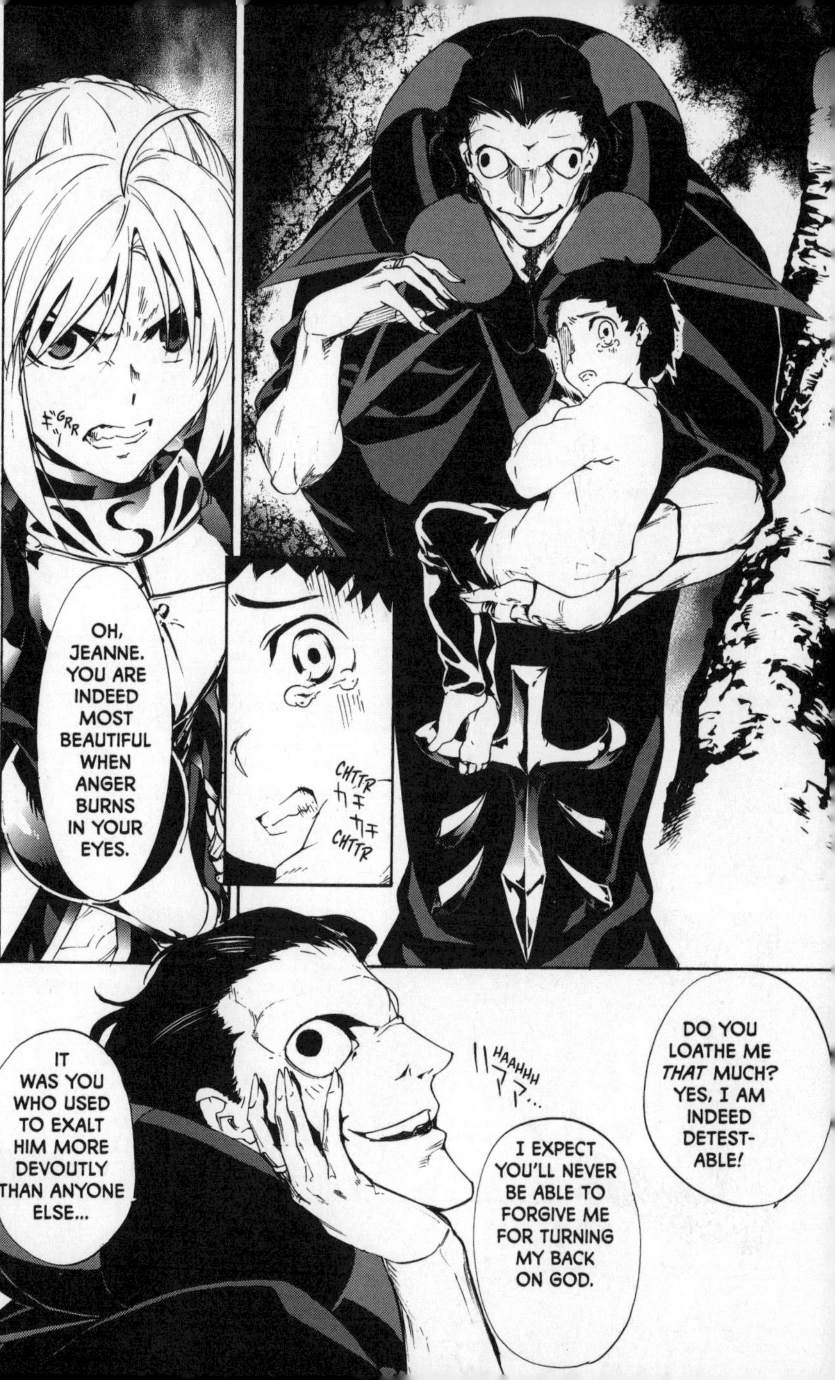
OH, JEANNE. YOU ARE INDEED MOST BEAUTIFUL WHEN ANGER BURNS IN YOUR EYES.
CHTTR
CHTTR
GRR
DO YOU LOATHE ME *THAT* MUCH? YES, I AM INDEED DETEST-ABLE!
HAAHHH
I EXPECT YOU'LL NEVER BE ABLE TO FORGIVE ME FOR TURNING MY BACK ON GOD.
IT WAS YOU WHO USED TO EXALT HIM MORE DEVOUTLY THAN ANYONE ELSE...

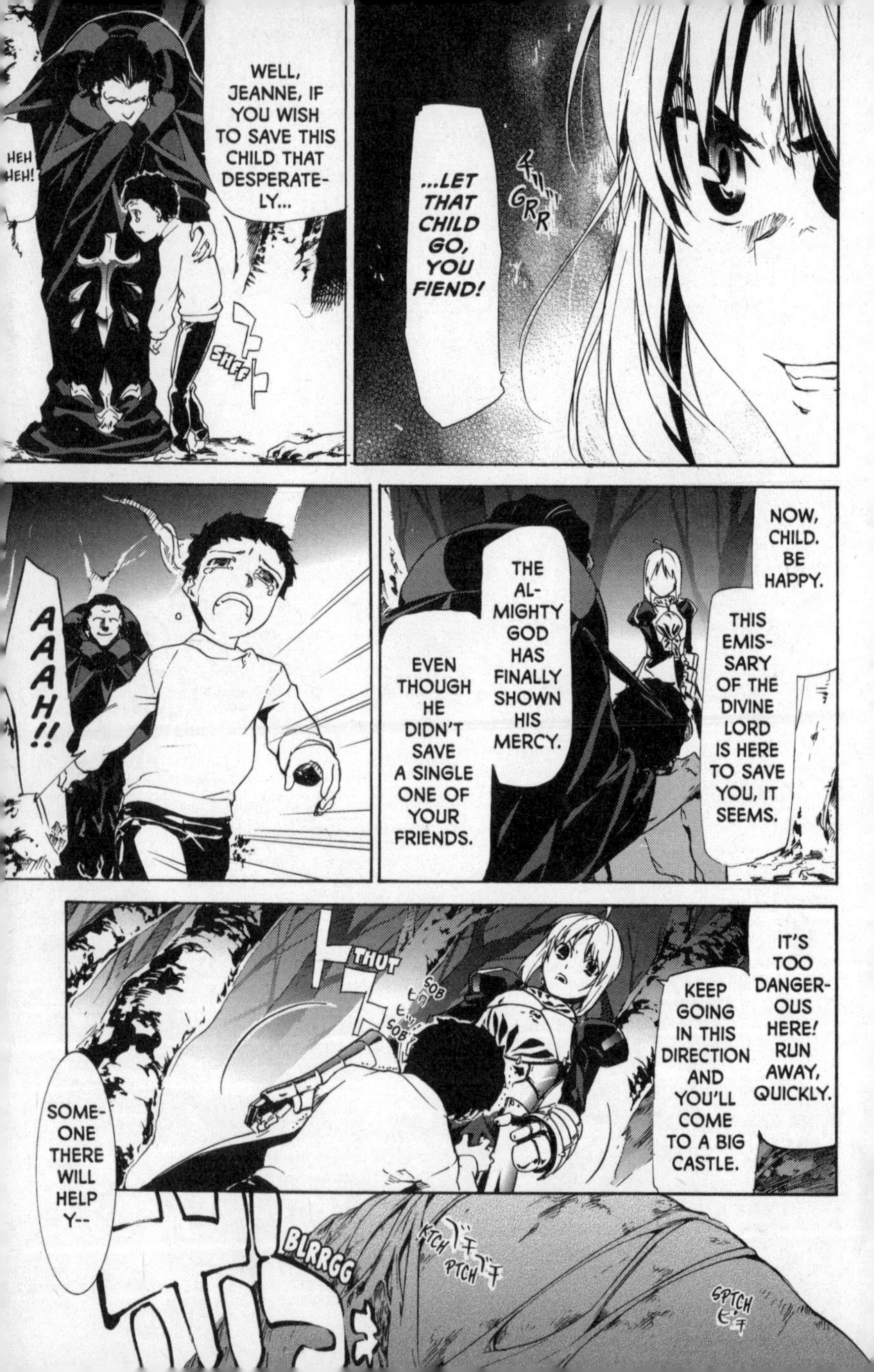
...LET THAT CHILD GO, YOU FIEND!
GRR
WELL, JEANNE, IF YOU WISH TO SAVE THIS CHILD THAT DESPERATE-LY...
HEH HEH!
SHFF
NOW, CHILD. BE HAPPY.
THIS EMIS-SARY OF THE DIVINE LORD IS HERE TO SAVE YOU, IT SEEMS.
THE AL-MIGHTY GOD HAS FINALLY SHOWN HIS MERCY.
EVEN THOUGH HE DIDN'T SAVE A SINGLE ONE OF YOUR FRIENDS.
AAAAH!!
IT'S TOO DANGER-OUS HERE! RUN AWAY, QUICKLY.
KEEP GOING IN THIS DIRECTION AND YOU'LL COME TO A BIG CASTLE.
THUT
SOB
SOB
SOME-ONE THERE WILL HELP Y--
KTCH
PTCH
BLRRGG
SPTCH

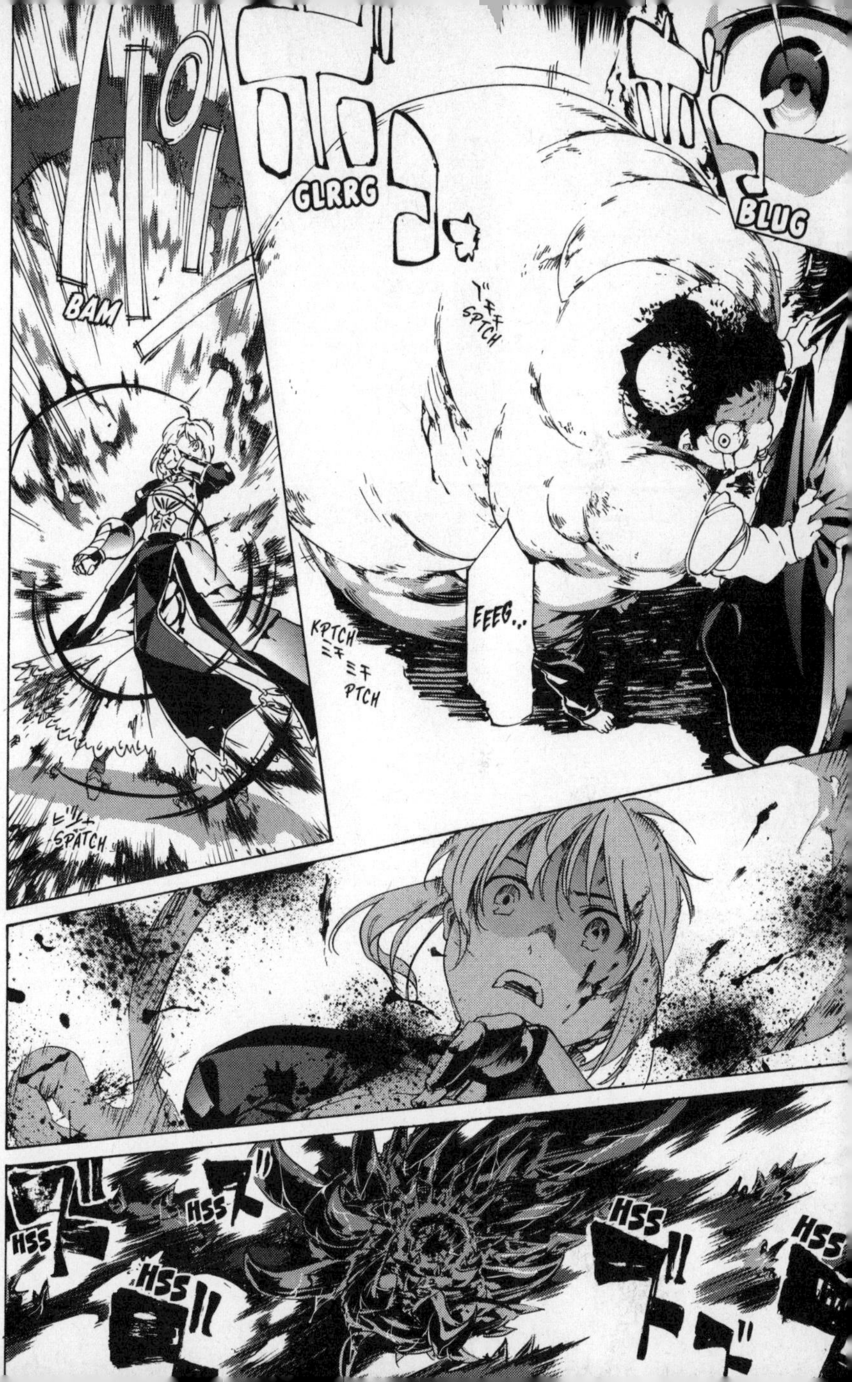
BLUG
GLRRG
SPTCH
EEEG...
KPTCH
PTCH
BAM
SPATCH
HSS
HSS
HSS
HSS
HSS

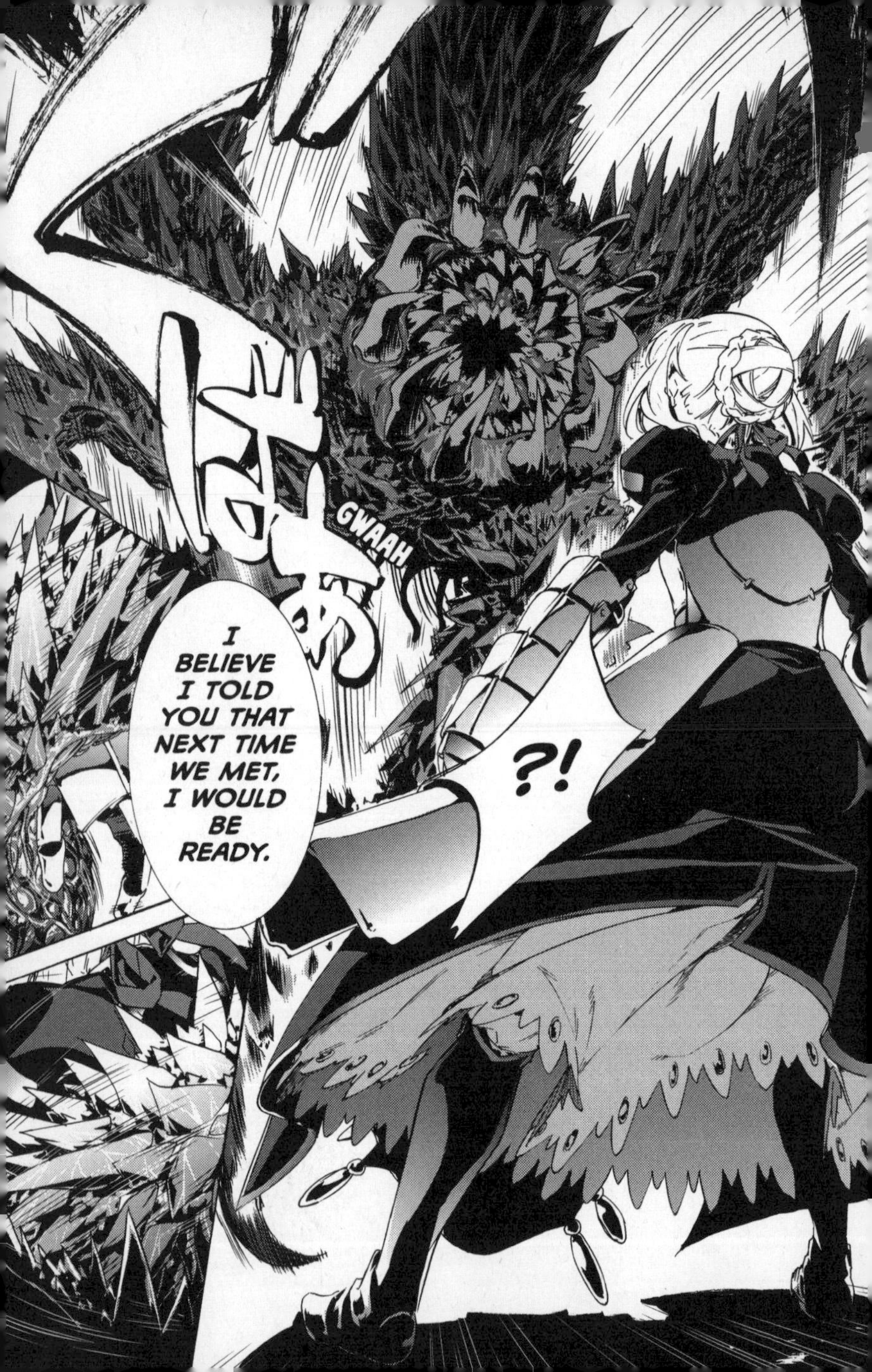
GWAAH
I BELIEVE I TOLD YOU THAT NEXT TIME WE MET, I WOULD BE READY.
?!

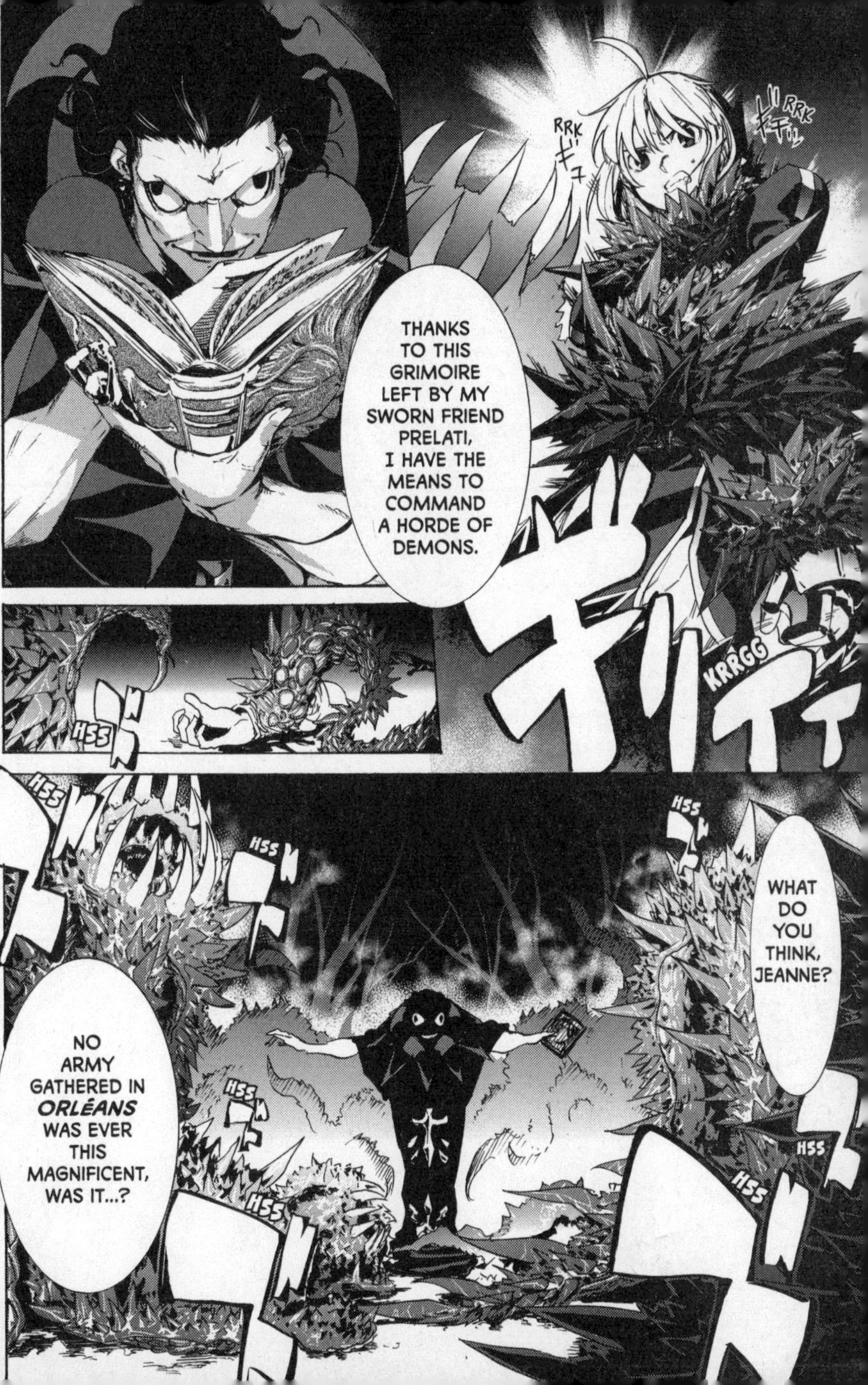
RRK
RRK
THANKS TO THIS GRIMOIRE LEFT BY MY SWORN FRIEND PRELATI, I HAVE THE MEANS TO COMMAND A HORDE OF DEMONS.
KRRGG
HSS
HSS
HSS
HSS
WHAT DO YOU THINK, JEANNE?
NO ARMY GATHERED IN *ORLÉANS* WAS EVER THIS MAGNIFICENT, WAS IT...?
HSS
HSS
HSS

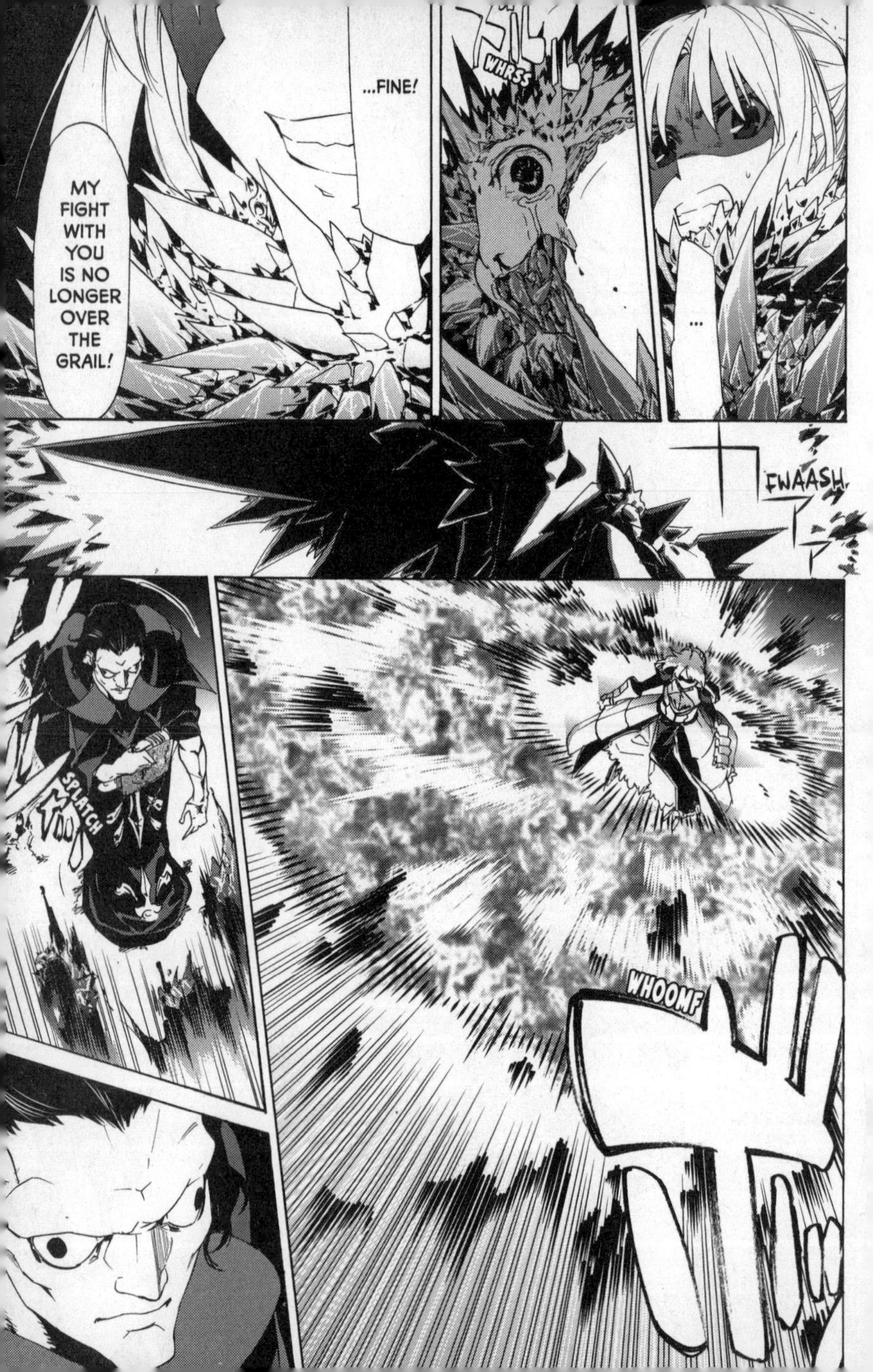
...
WHRSS
...FINE!
MY FIGHT WITH YOU IS NO LONGER OVER THE GRAIL!
FWAASH
WHOOMF
SPLATCH

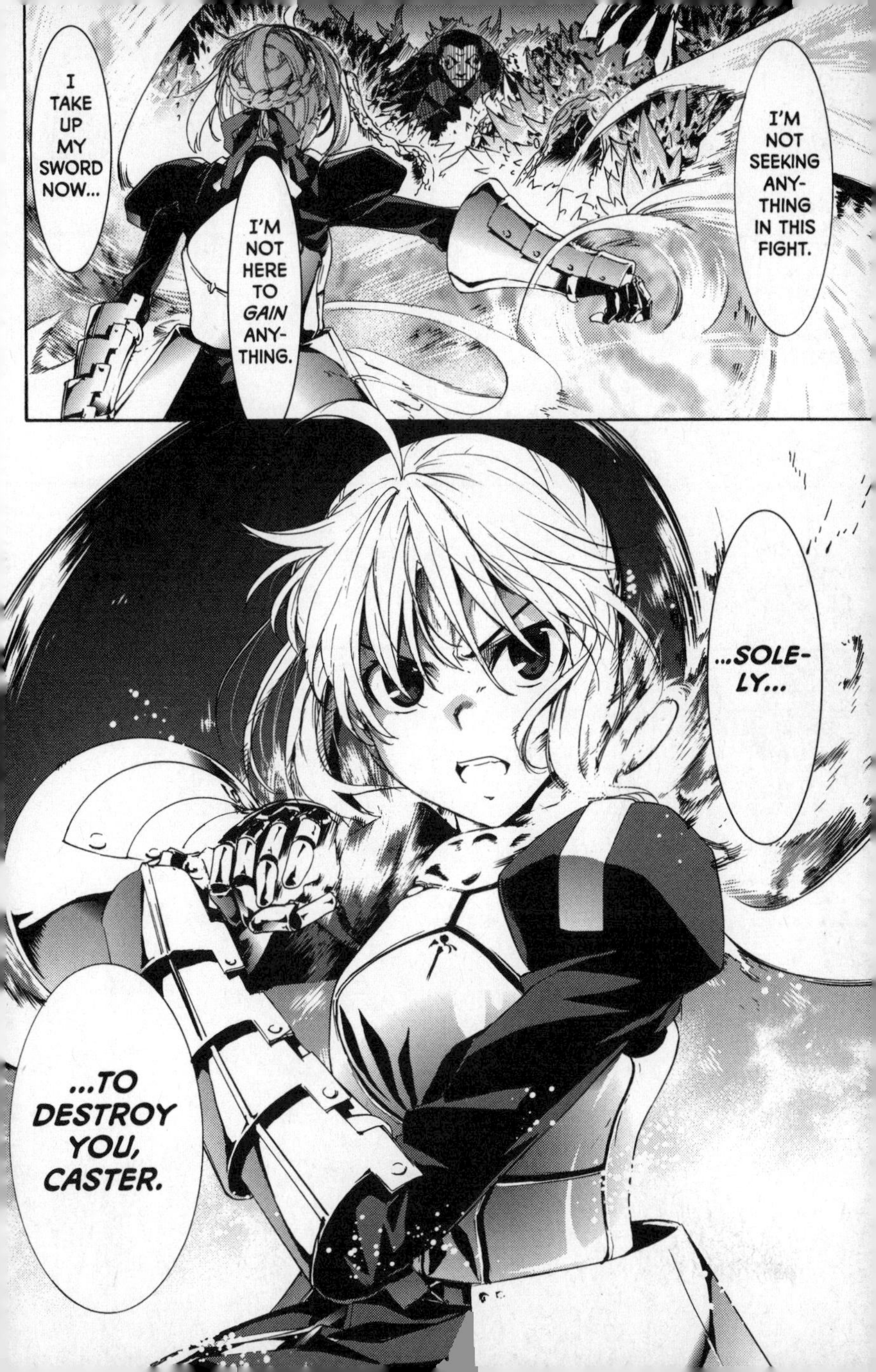
I'M NOT SEEKING ANYTHING IN THIS FIGHT.
I TAKE UP MY SWORD NOW...
I'M NOT HERE TO *GAIN* ANYTHING.
...SOLELY...
...TO DESTROY YOU, CASTER.

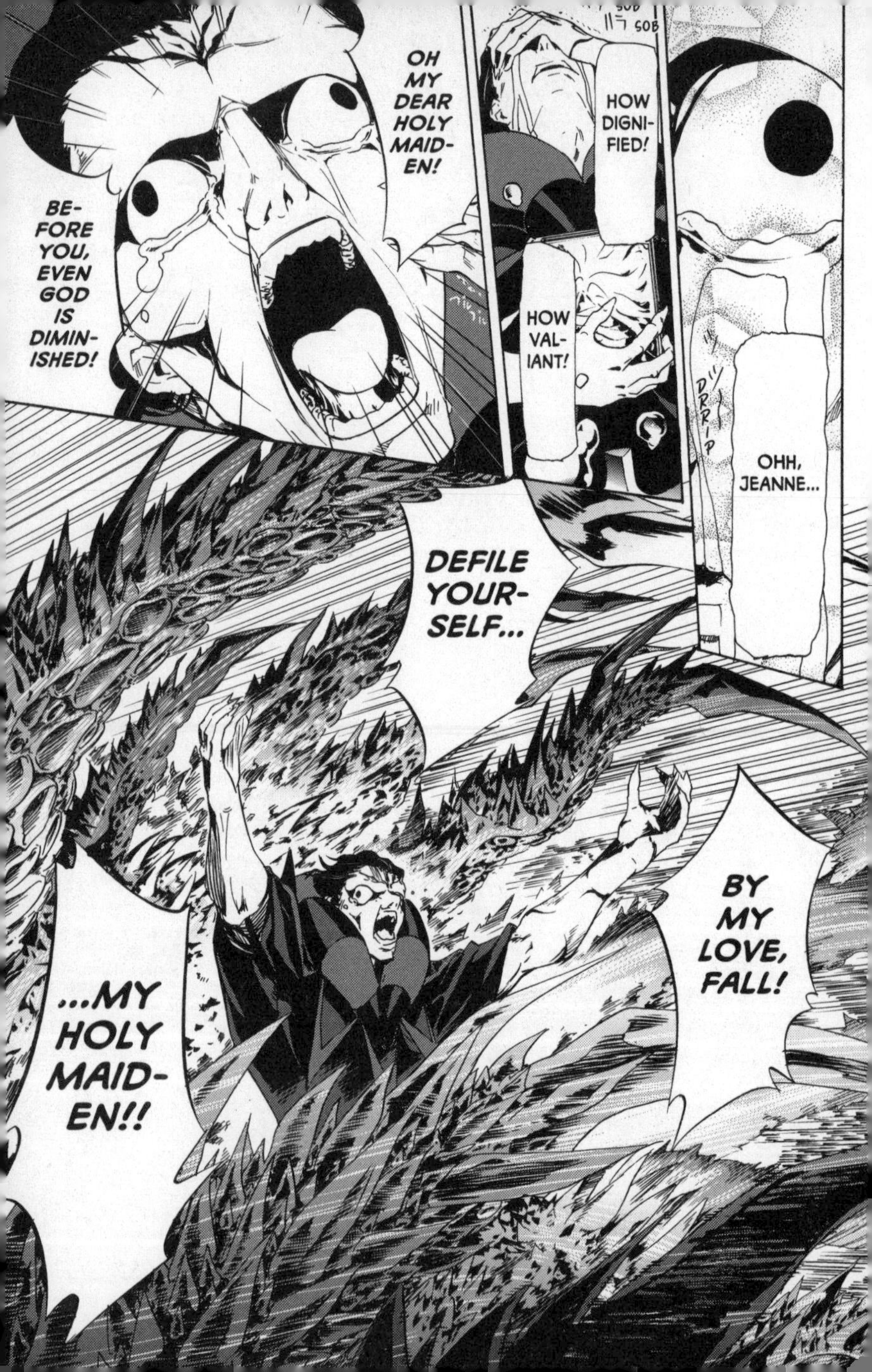
DRRRIP
OHH, JEANNE...
SOB SOB
HOW DIGNIFIED!
HOW VALIANT!
OH MY DEAR HOLY MAIDEN!
BEFORE YOU, EVEN GOD IS DIMINISHED!
DEFILE YOURSELF...
BY MY LOVE, FALL!
...MY HOLY MAIDEN!!

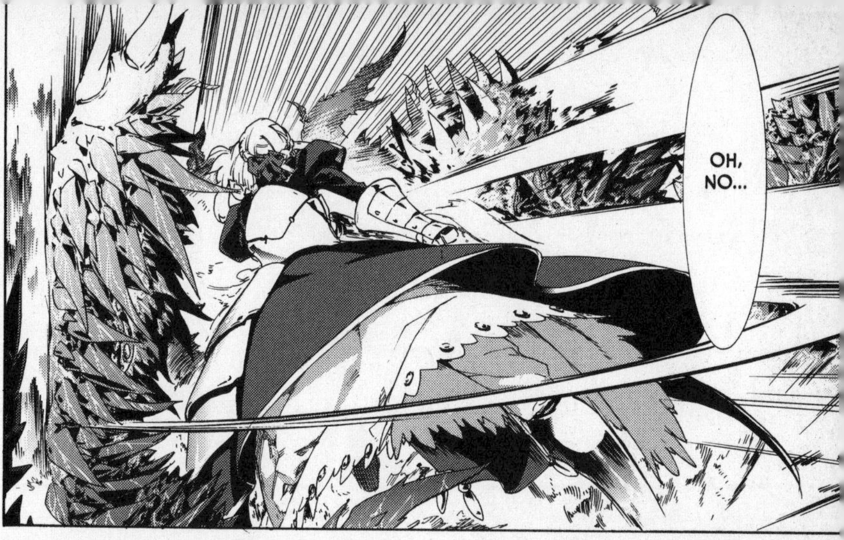
OH, NO...

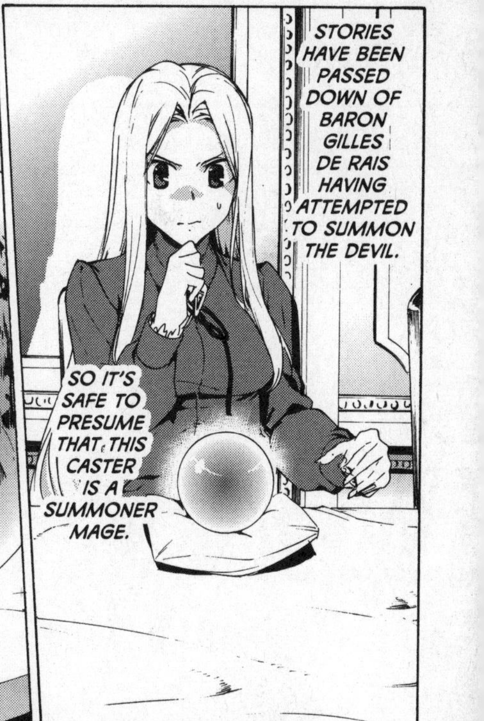
STORIES HAVE BEEN PASSED DOWN OF BARON GILLES DE RAIS HAVING ATTEMPTED TO SUMMON THE DEVIL.
SO IT'S SAFE TO PRESUME THAT THIS CASTER IS A SUMMONER MAGE.

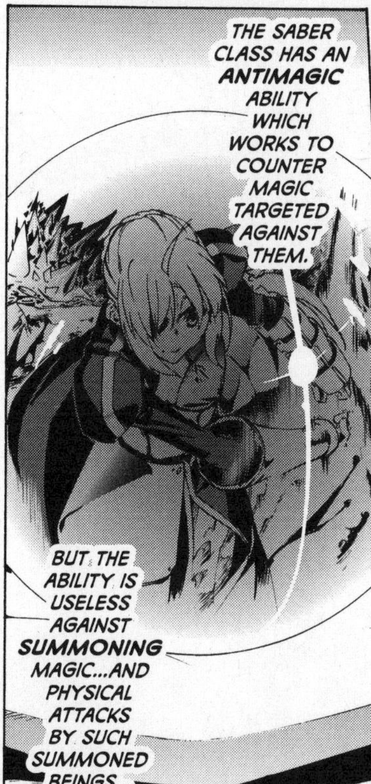
THE SABER CLASS HAS AN **ANTIMAGIC** ABILITY WHICH WORKS TO COUNTER MAGIC TARGETED AGAINST THEM.
BUT THE ABILITY IS USELESS AGAINST **SUMMONING** MAGIC...AND PHYSICAL ATTACKS BY SUCH SUMMONED BEINGS...

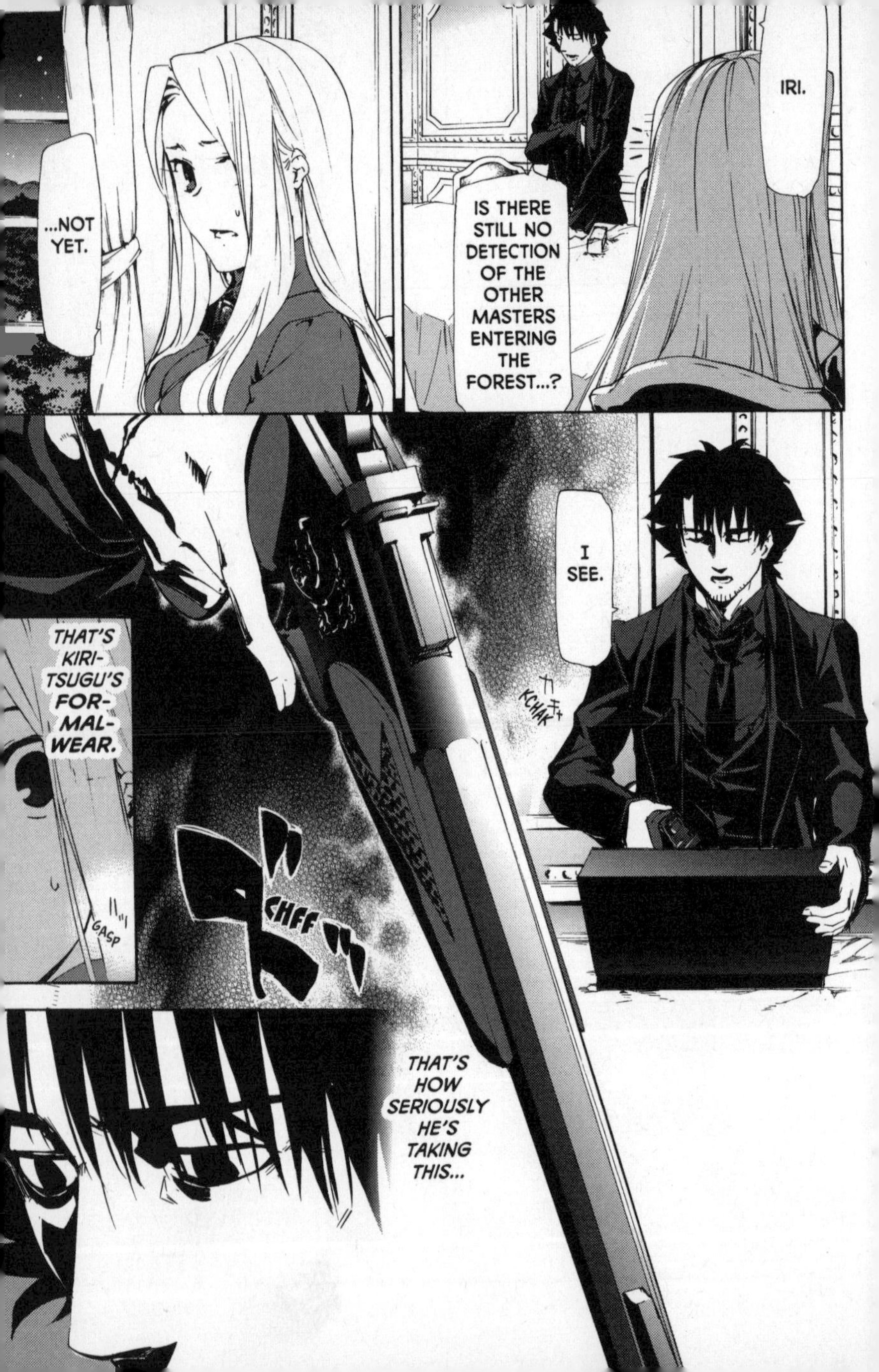
IRI.
IS THERE STILL NO DETECTION OF THE OTHER MASTERS ENTERING THE FOREST...?
...NOT YET.
I SEE.
KCHAK
CHFF
THAT'S KIRI-TSUGU'S FOR-MAL-WEAR.
GASP
THAT'S HOW SERIOUSLY HE'S TAKING THIS...

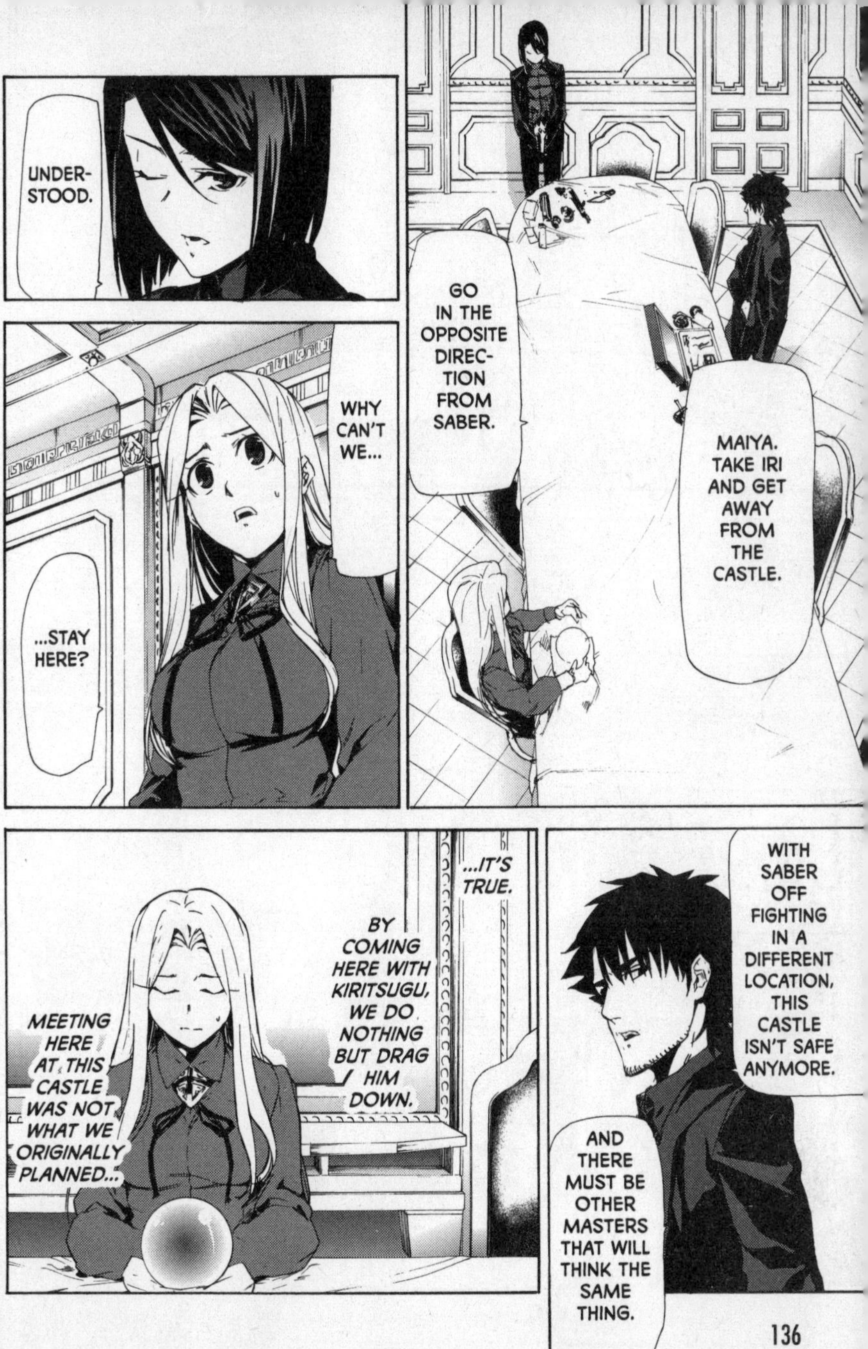
MAIYA. TAKE IRI AND GET AWAY FROM THE CASTLE.
GO IN THE OPPOSITE DIREC- TION FROM SABER.
UNDER- STOOD.
WHY CAN'T WE...
...STAY HERE?
WITH SABER OFF FIGHTING IN A DIFFERENT LOCATION, THIS CASTLE ISN'T SAFE ANYMORE.
AND THERE MUST BE OTHER MASTERS THAT WILL THINK THE SAME THING.
...IT'S TRUE.
BY COMING HERE WITH KIRITSUGU, WE DO NOTHING BUT DRAG HIM DOWN.
MEETING HERE AT THIS CASTLE WAS NOT WHAT WE ORIGINALLY PLANNED...

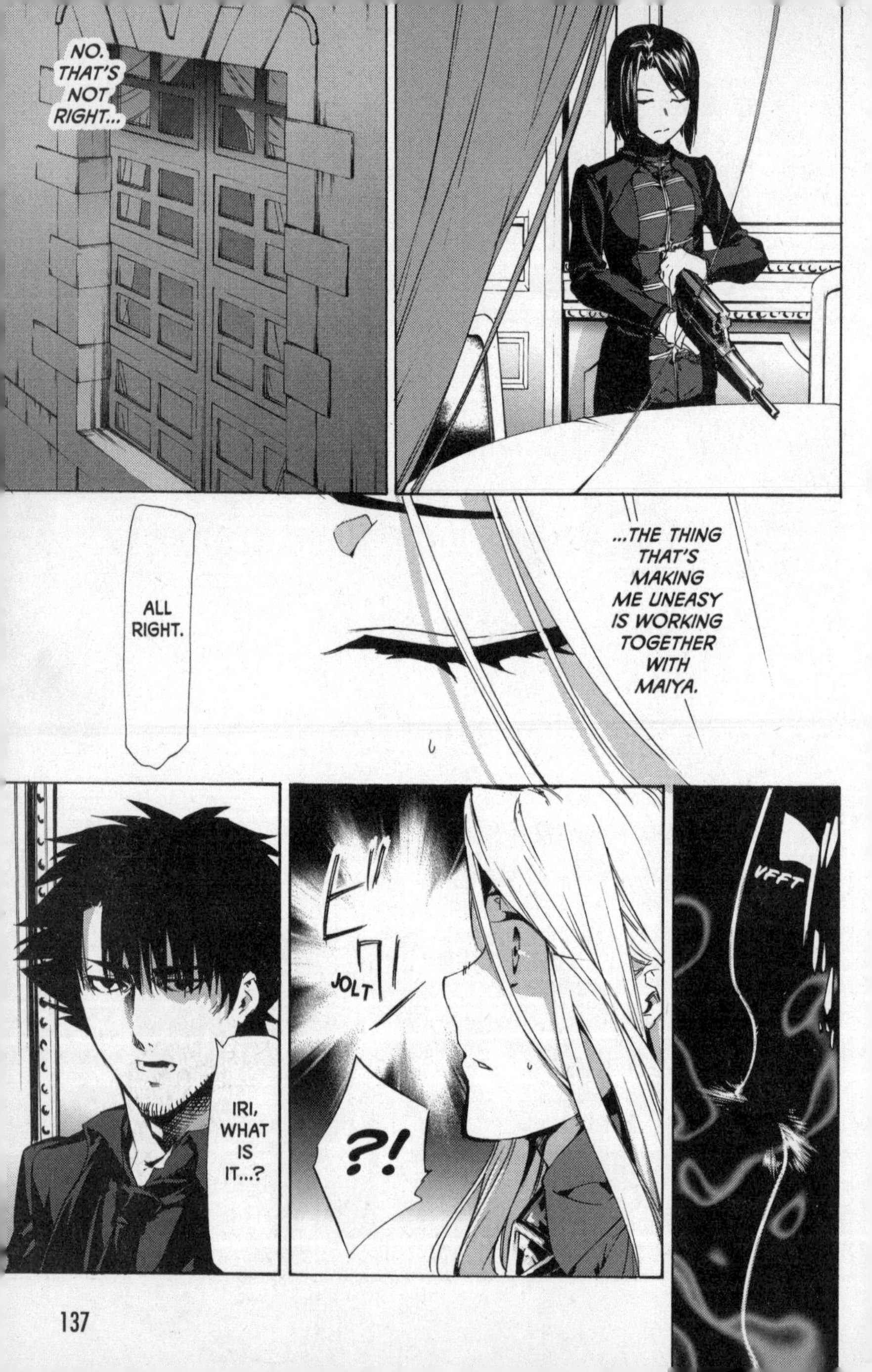
NO. THAT'S NOT RIGHT...
...THE THING THAT'S MAKING ME UNEASY IS WORKING TOGETHER WITH MAIYA.
ALL RIGHT.
VFFT
JOLT
?!
IRI, WHAT IS IT...?

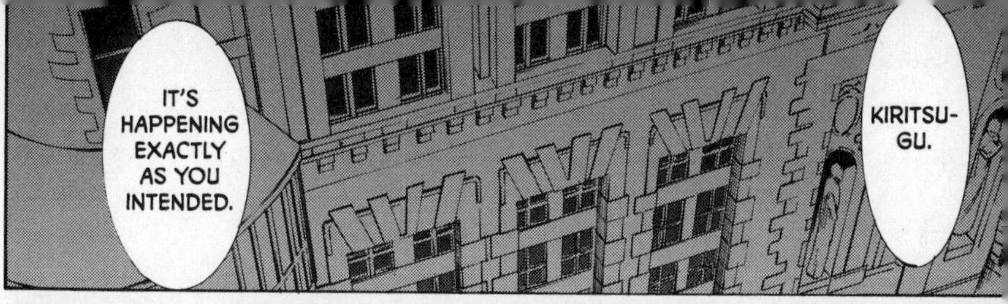
KIRITSU-GU.
IT'S HAPPENING EXACTLY AS YOU INTENDED.

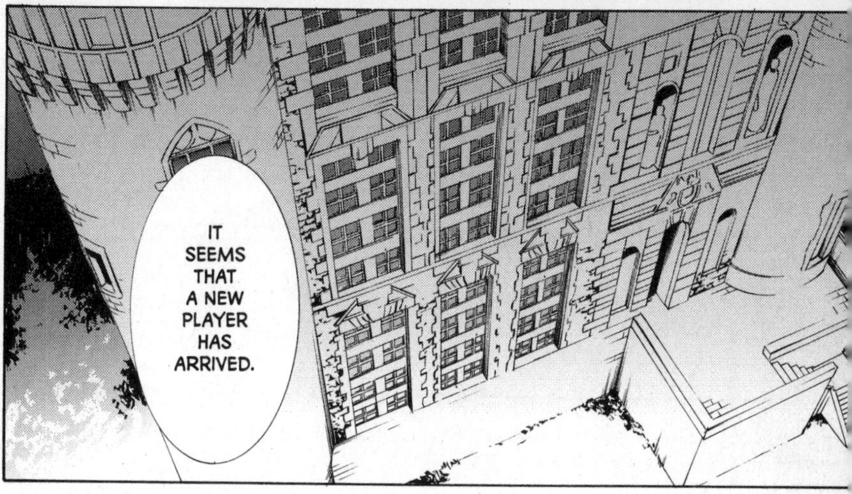
IT SEEMS THAT A NEW PLAYER HAS ARRIVED.

— 130:48:29

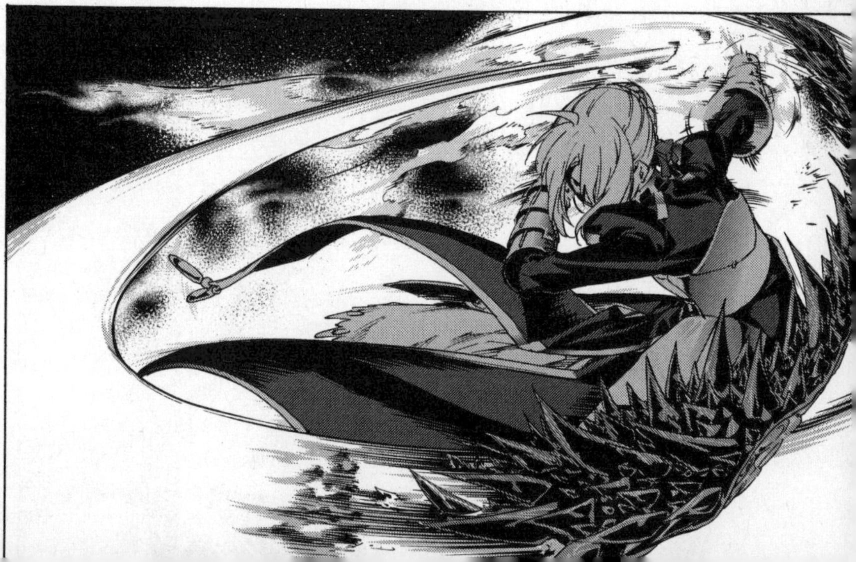

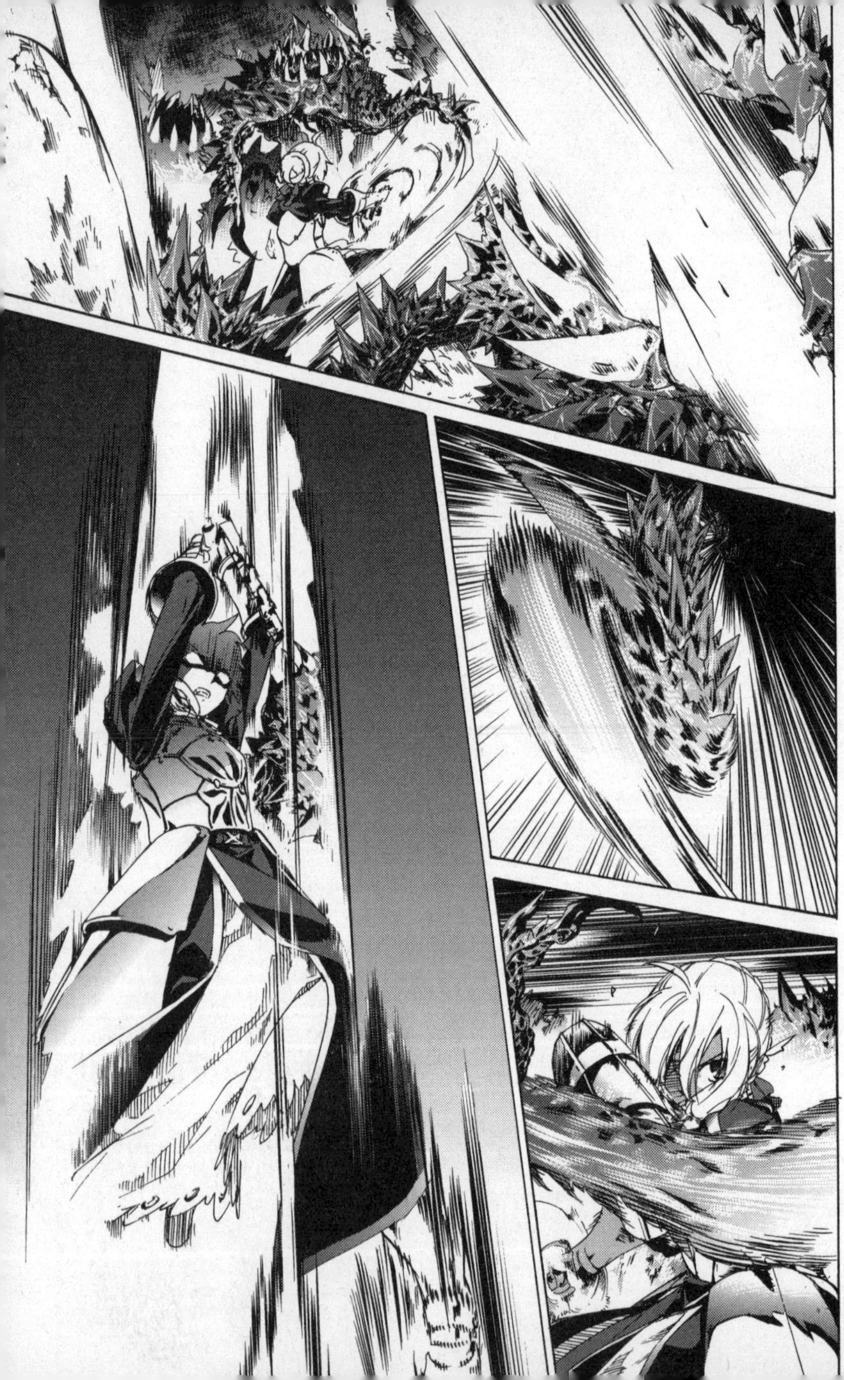

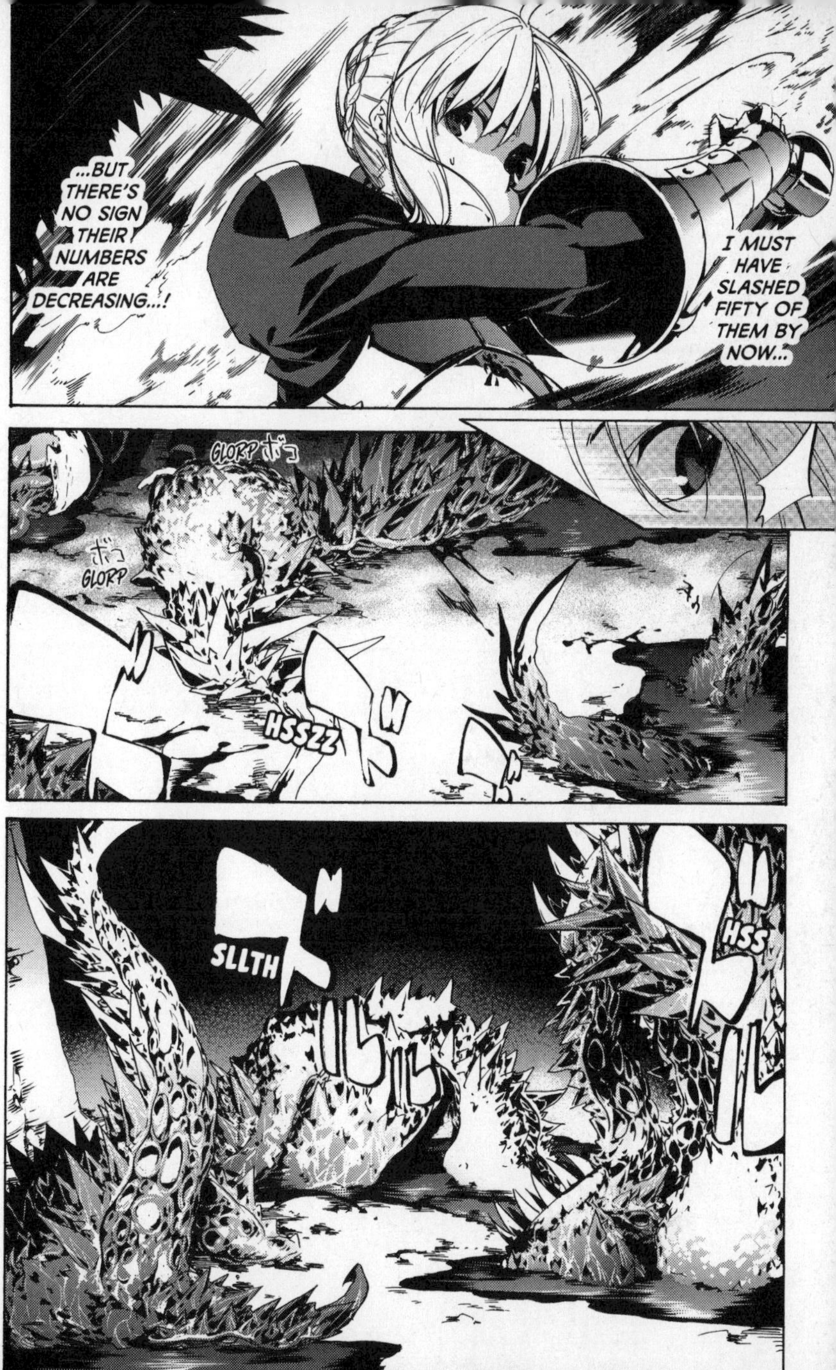
I MUST HAVE SLASHED FIFTY OF THEM BY NOW...
...BUT THERE'S NO SIGN THEIR NUMBERS ARE DECREASING...!
GLORP ボコ
ボコ GLORP
HSSZZ
HSS
SLLTH

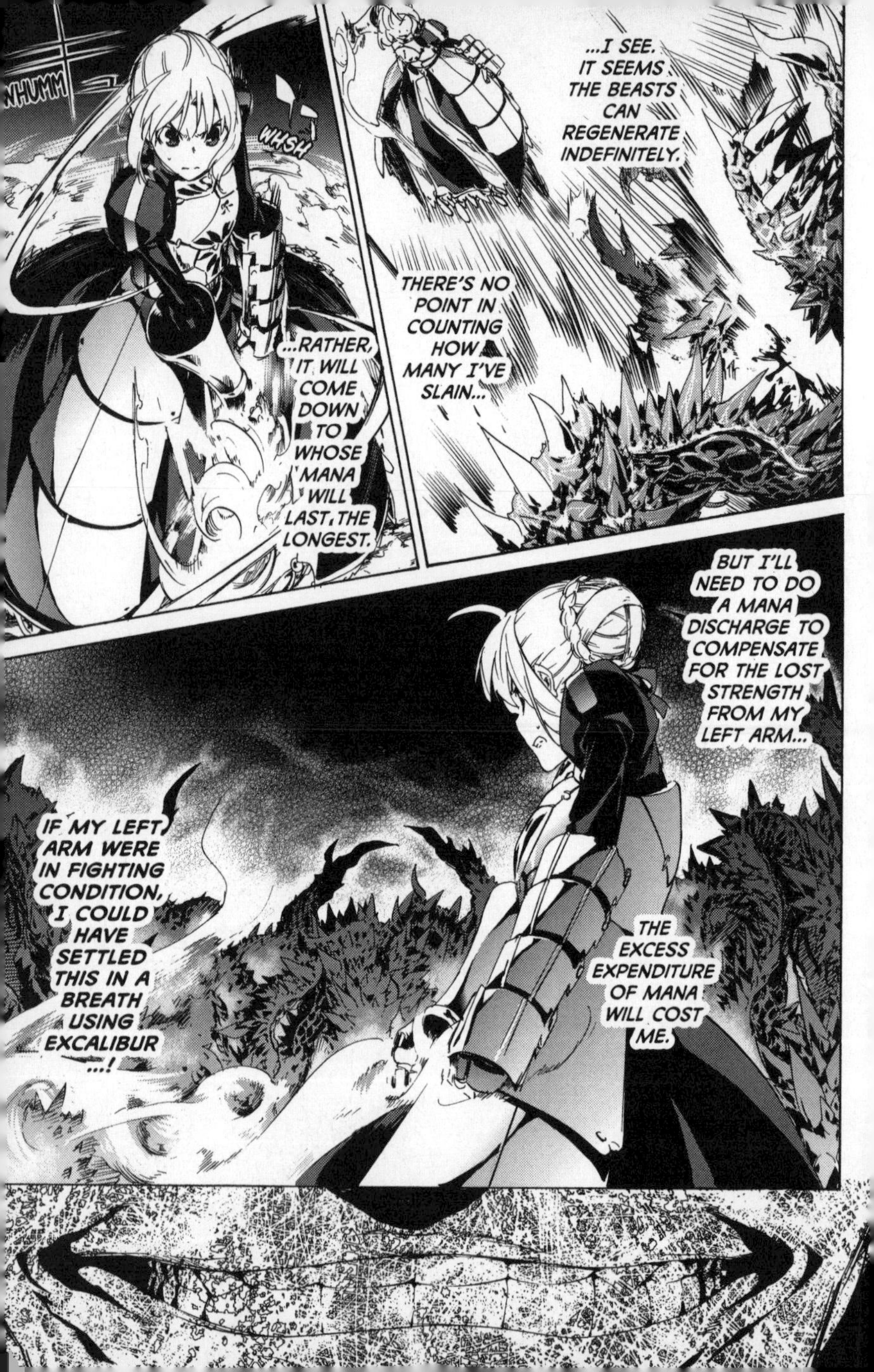

...I SEE. IT SEEMS THE BEASTS CAN REGENERATE INDEFINITELY.
THERE'S NO POINT IN COUNTING HOW MANY I'VE SLAIN...
WHSH
...RATHER, IT WILL COME DOWN TO WHOSE MANA WILL LAST THE LONGEST.
BUT I'LL NEED TO DO A MANA DISCHARGE TO COMPENSATE FOR THE LOST STRENGTH FROM MY LEFT ARM...
THE EXCESS EXPENDITURE OF MANA WILL COST ME.
IF MY LEFT ARM WERE IN FIGHTING CONDITION, I COULD HAVE SETTLED THIS IN A BREATH USING EXCALIBUR ...!

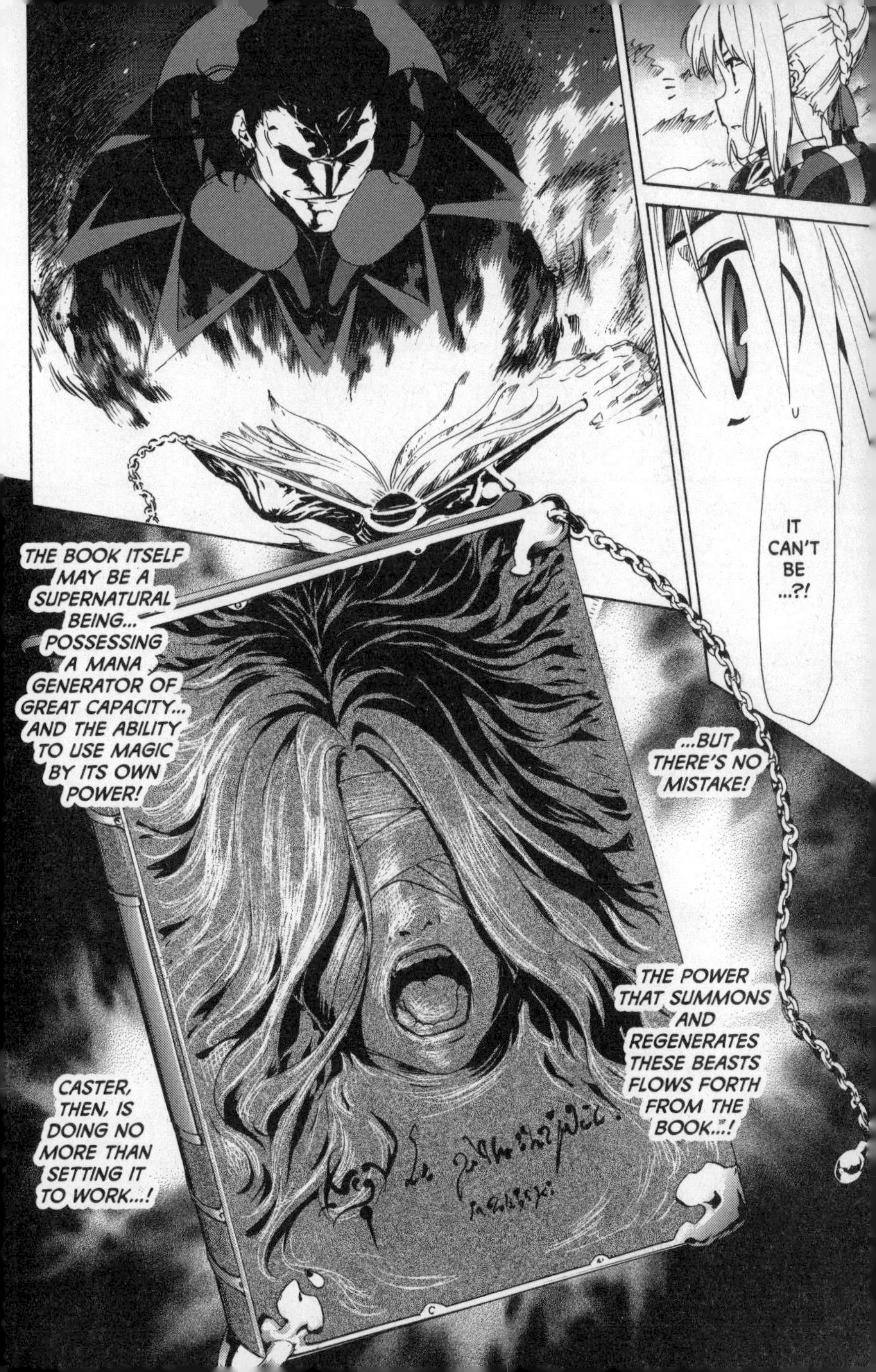
IT CAN'T BE ...?!
...BUT THERE'S NO MISTAKE!
THE BOOK ITSELF MAY BE A SUPERNATURAL BEING... POSSESSING A MANA GENERATOR OF GREAT CAPACITY... AND THE ABILITY TO USE MAGIC BY ITS OWN POWER!
THE POWER THAT SUMMONS AND REGENERATES THESE BEASTS FLOWS FORTH FROM THE BOOK...!
CASTER, THEN, IS DOING NO MORE THAN SETTING IT TO WORK...!

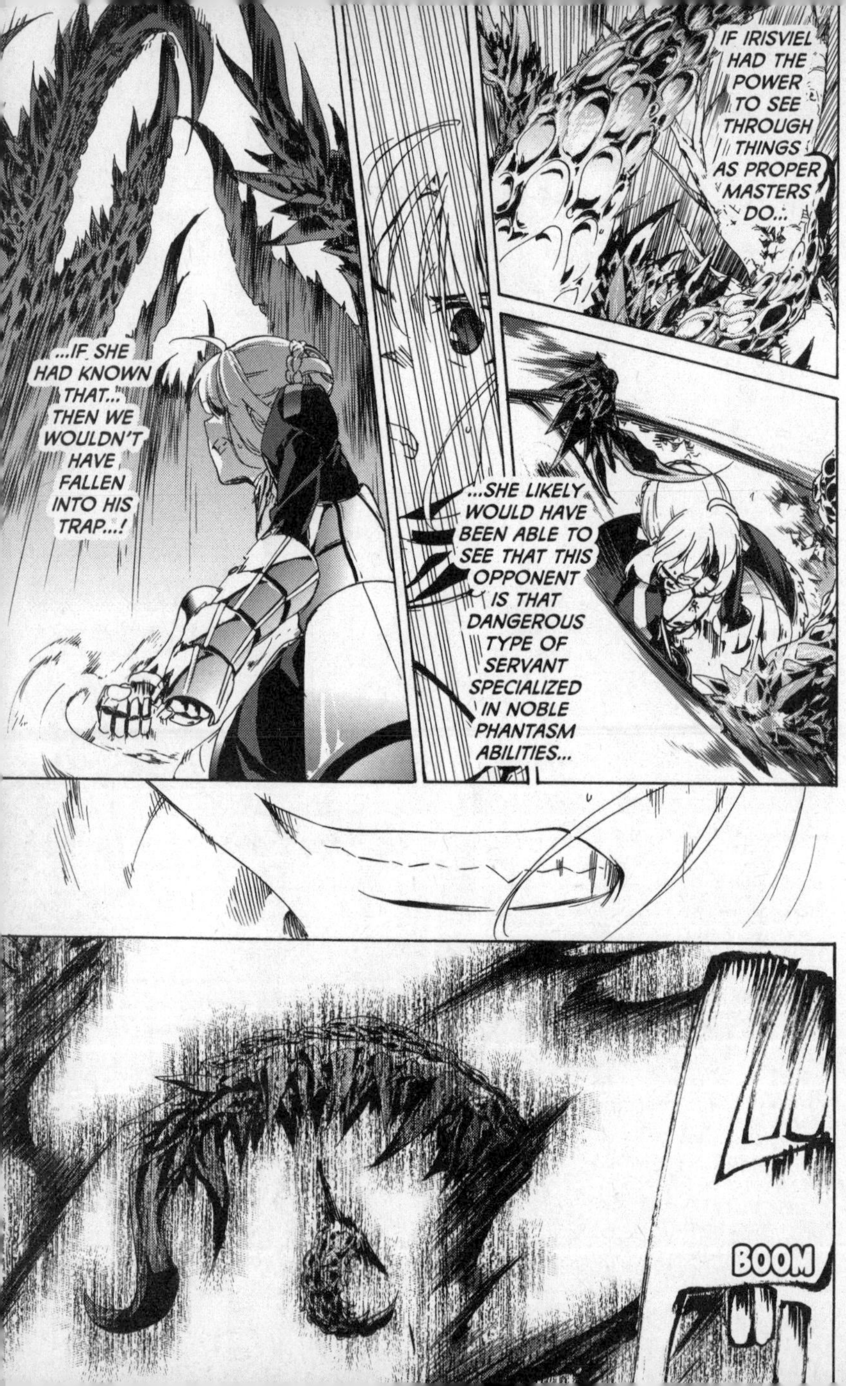
IF IRISVIEL HAD THE POWER TO SEE THROUGH THINGS AS PROPER MASTERS DO...
...SHE LIKELY WOULD HAVE BEEN ABLE TO SEE THAT THIS OPPONENT IS THAT DANGEROUS TYPE OF SERVANT SPECIALIZED IN NOBLE PHANTASM ABILITIES...
...IF SHE HAD KNOWN THAT... THEN WE WOULDN'T HAVE FALLEN INTO HIS TRAP...!
BOOM

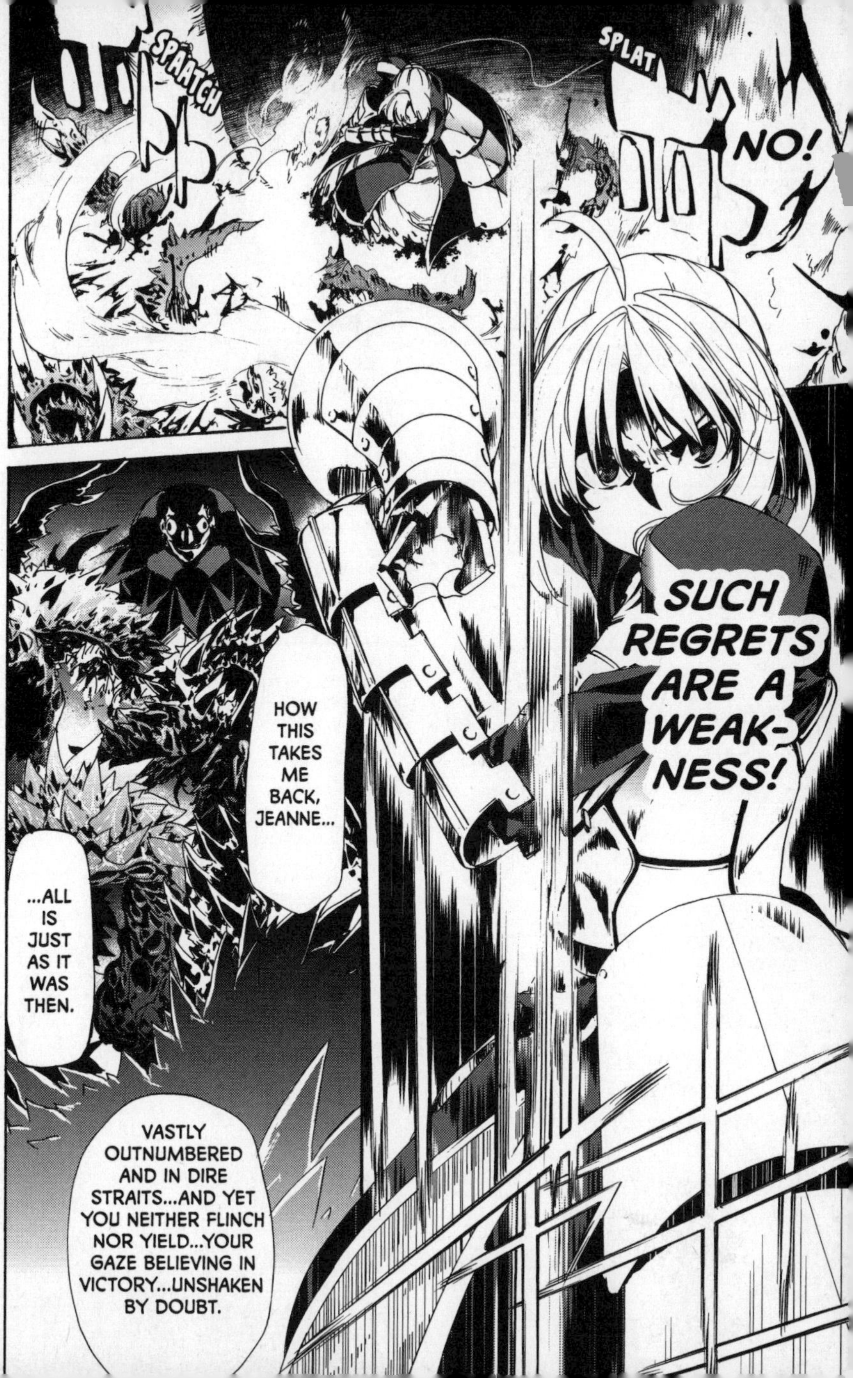
SPLAT
NO!
SPAATCH
SUCH REGRETS ARE A WEAK-NESS!
HOW THIS TAKES ME BACK, JEANNE...
...ALL IS JUST AS IT WAS THEN.
VASTLY OUTNUMBERED AND IN DIRE STRAITS...AND YET YOU NEITHER FLINCH NOR YIELD...YOUR GAZE BELIEVING IN VICTORY...UNSHAKEN BY DOUBT.

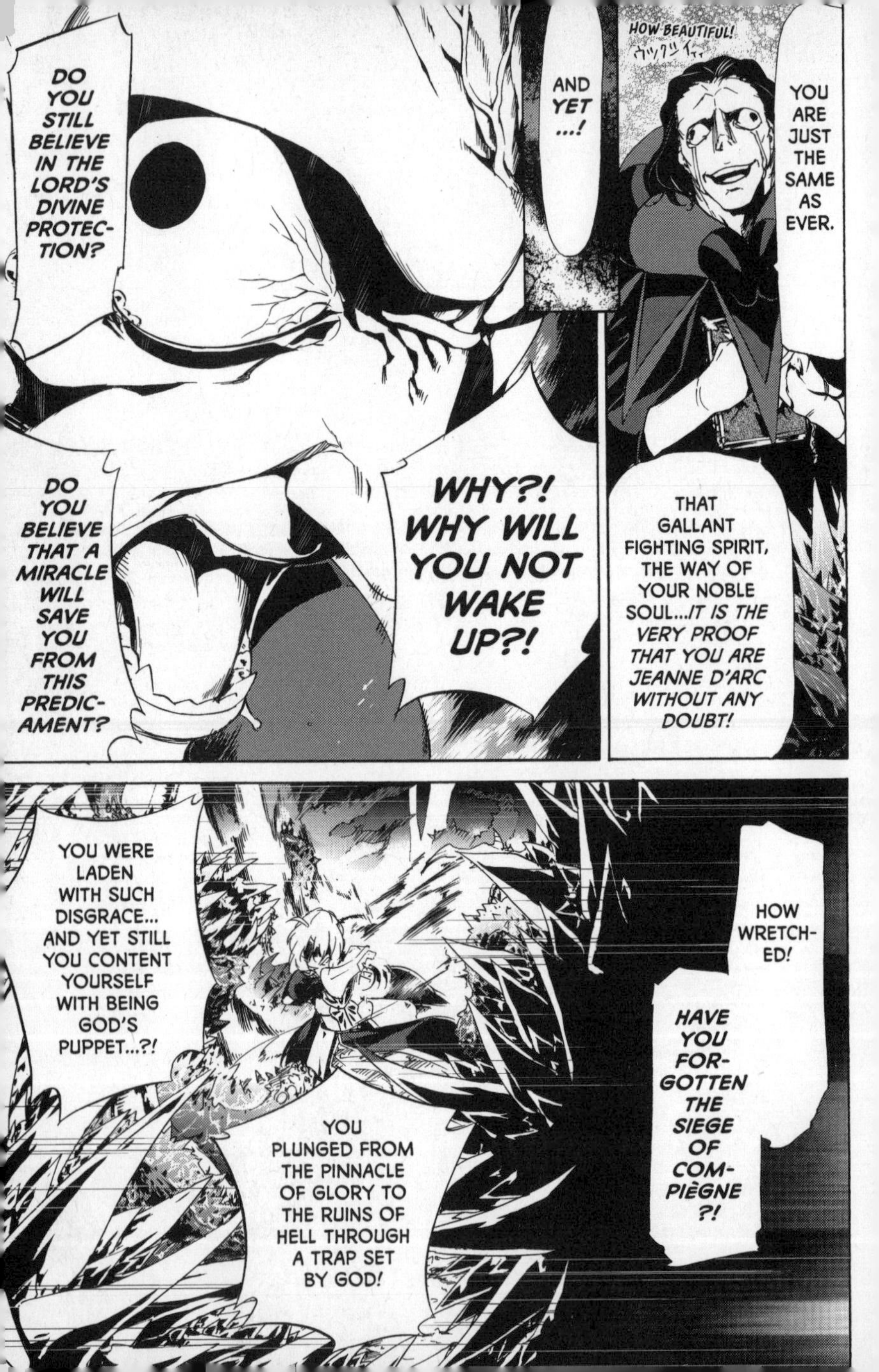
HOW BEAUTIFUL!
YOU ARE JUST THE SAME AS EVER.
THAT GALLANT FIGHTING SPIRIT, THE WAY OF YOUR NOBLE SOUL...*IT IS THE VERY PROOF THAT YOU ARE JEANNE D'ARC WITHOUT ANY DOUBT!*
AND *YET* ...!
WHY?! WHY WILL YOU NOT WAKE UP?!
DO YOU STILL BELIEVE IN THE LORD'S DIVINE PROTECTION?
DO YOU BELIEVE THAT A MIRACLE WILL SAVE YOU FROM THIS PREDICAMENT?
HOW WRETCHED!
HAVE YOU FORGOTTEN THE SIEGE OF COMPIÈGNE?!
YOU PLUNGED FROM THE PINNACLE OF GLORY TO THE RUINS OF HELL THROUGH A TRAP SET BY GOD!
YOU WERE LADEN WITH SUCH DISGRACE... AND YET STILL YOU CONTENT YOURSELF WITH BEING GOD'S PUPPET...?!

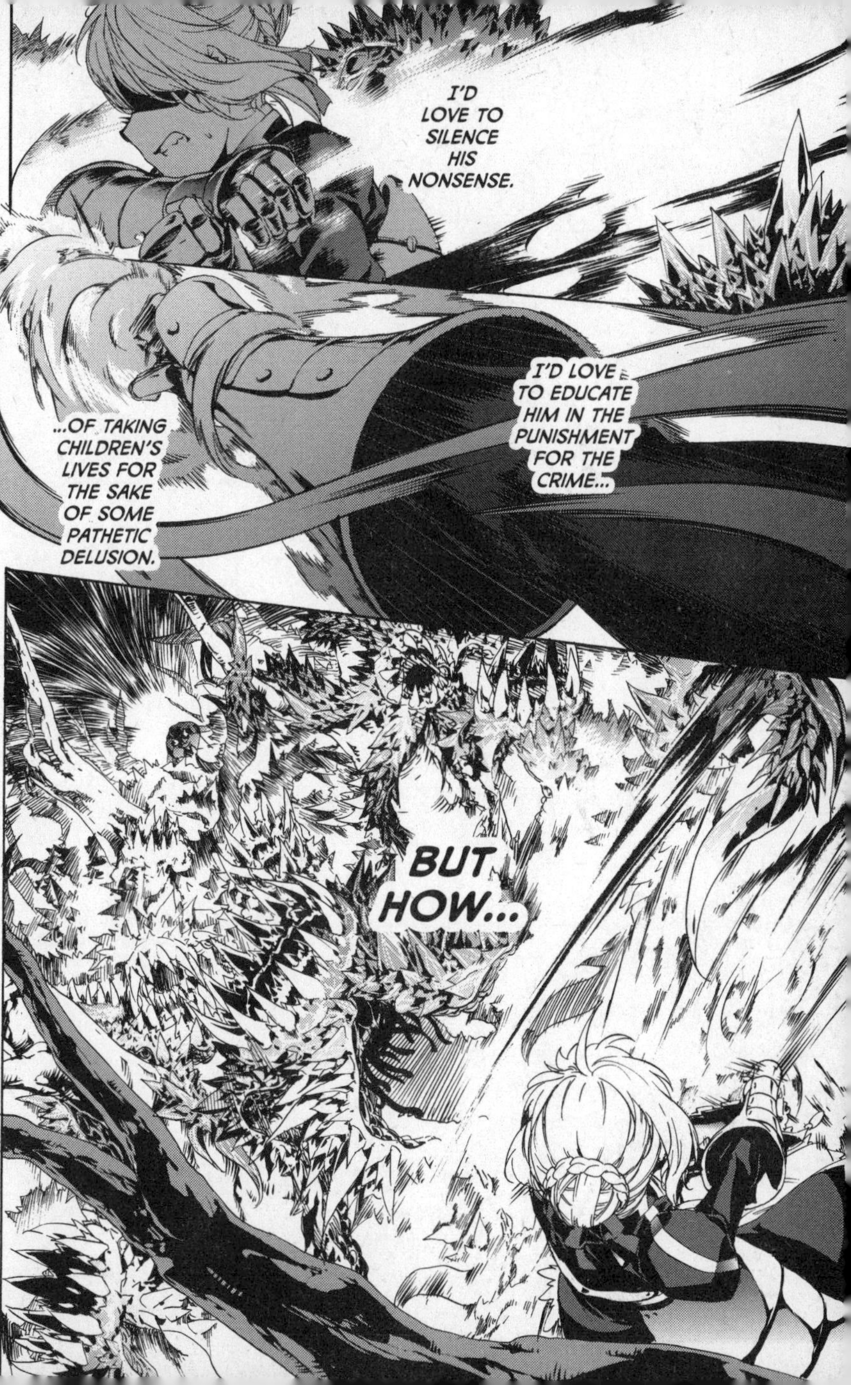
I'D LOVE TO SILENCE HIS NONSENSE.
I'D LOVE TO EDUCATE HIM IN THE PUNISHMENT FOR THE CRIME...
...OF TAKING CHILDREN'S LIVES FOR THE SAKE OF SOME PATHETIC DELUSION.
BUT HOW...

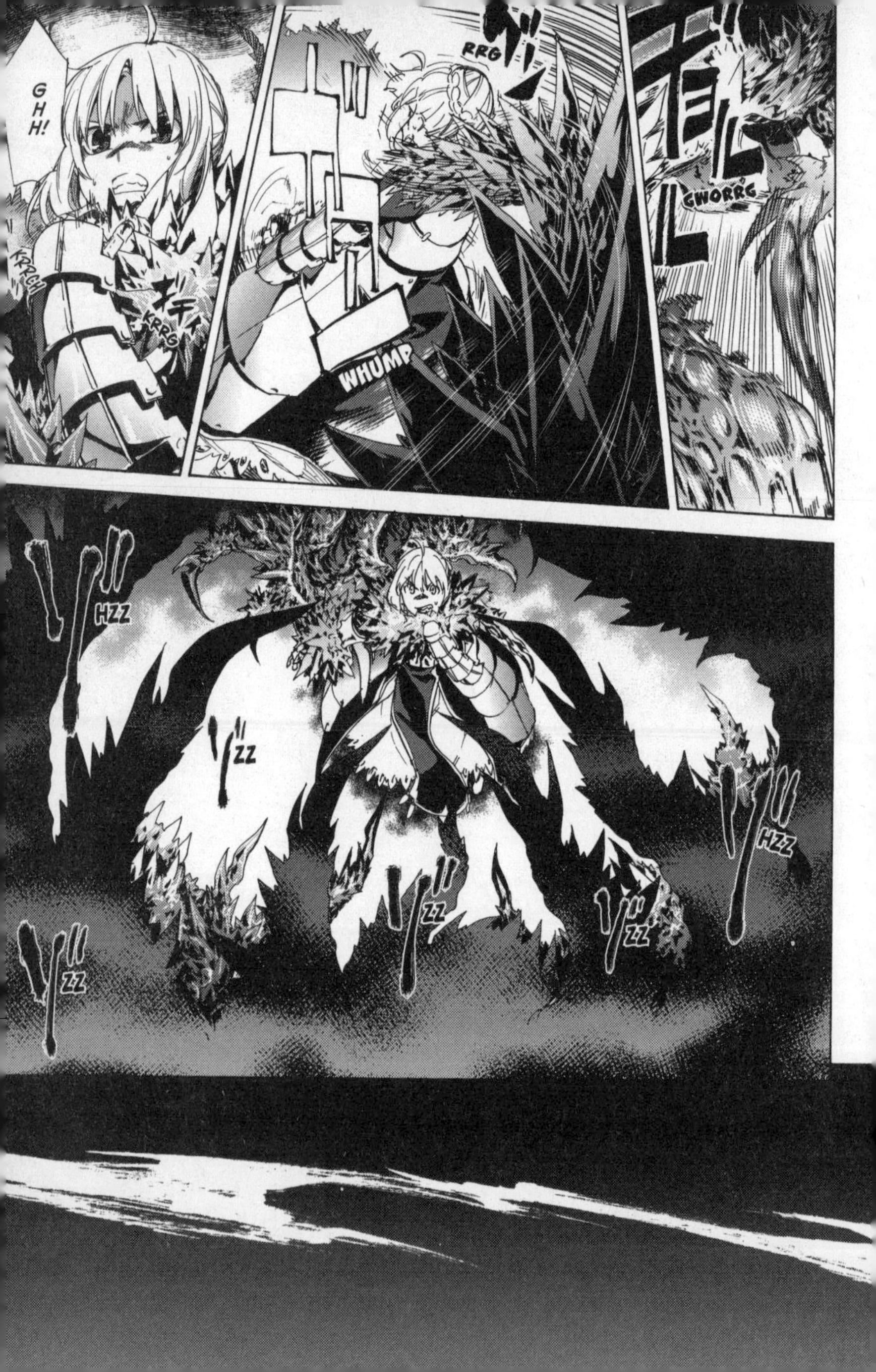
GWORRG
RRG
WHUMP
GHH!
KRRCH
KRRG
HZZ
ZZ
ZZ
HZZ
ZZ
ZZ

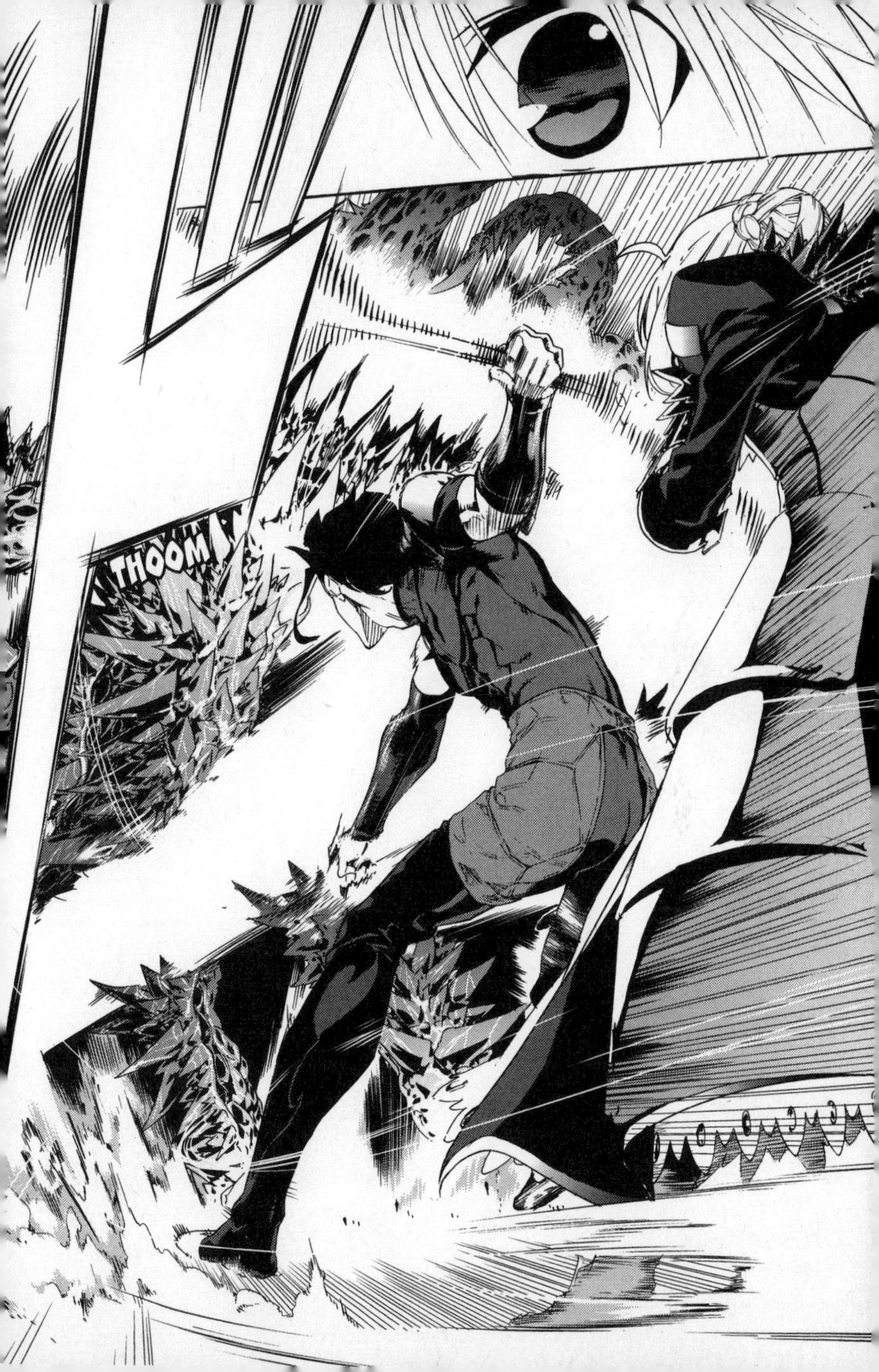
THOOM

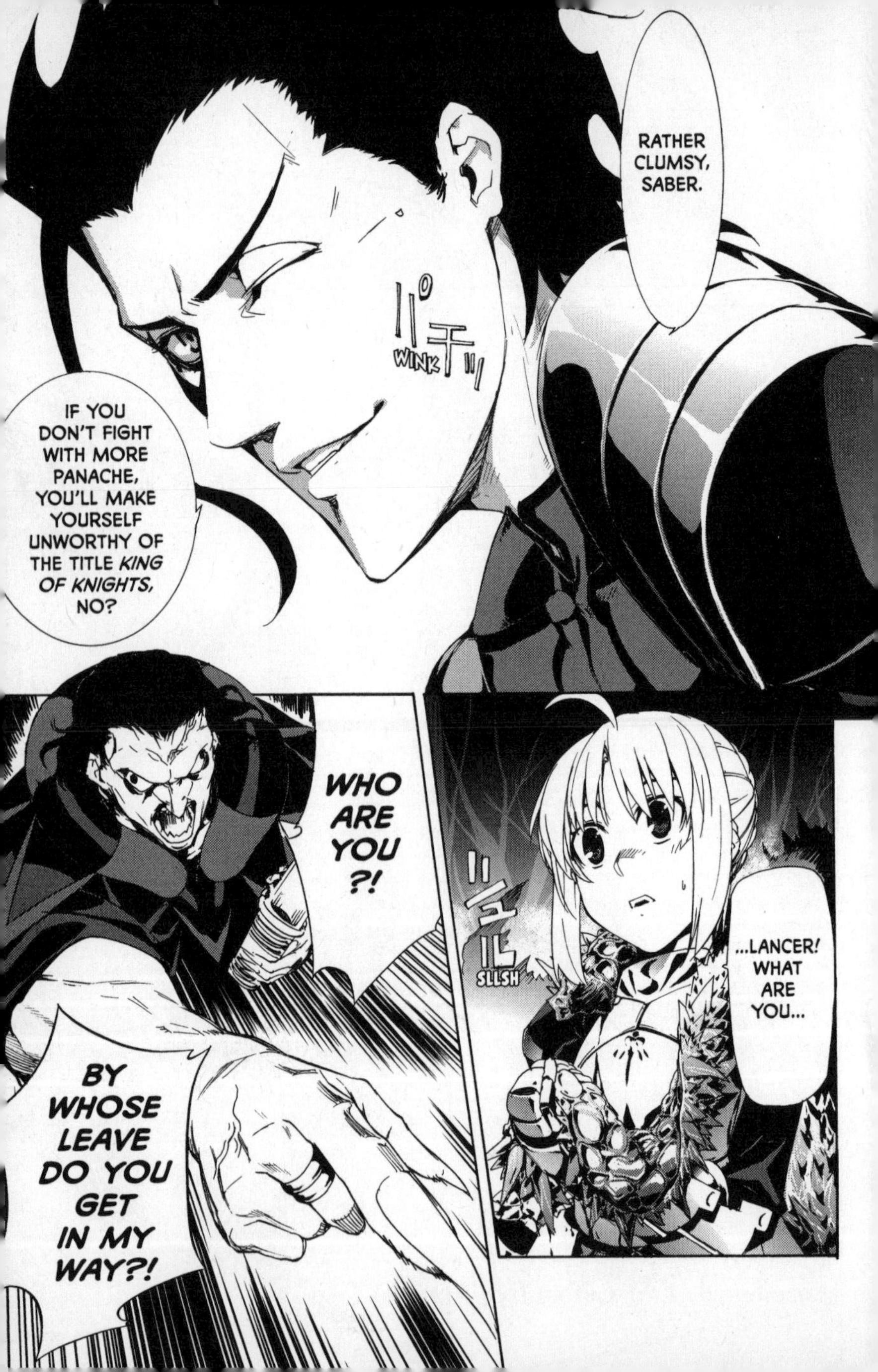
RATHER CLUMSY, SABER.
パチッ
WINK
IF YOU DON'T FIGHT WITH MORE PANACHE, YOU'LL MAKE YOURSELF UNWORTHY OF THE TITLE *KING OF KNIGHTS,* NO?
シュル
SLLSH
...LANCER! WHAT ARE YOU...
WHO ARE YOU?!
BY WHOSE LEAVE DO YOU GET IN MY WAY?!

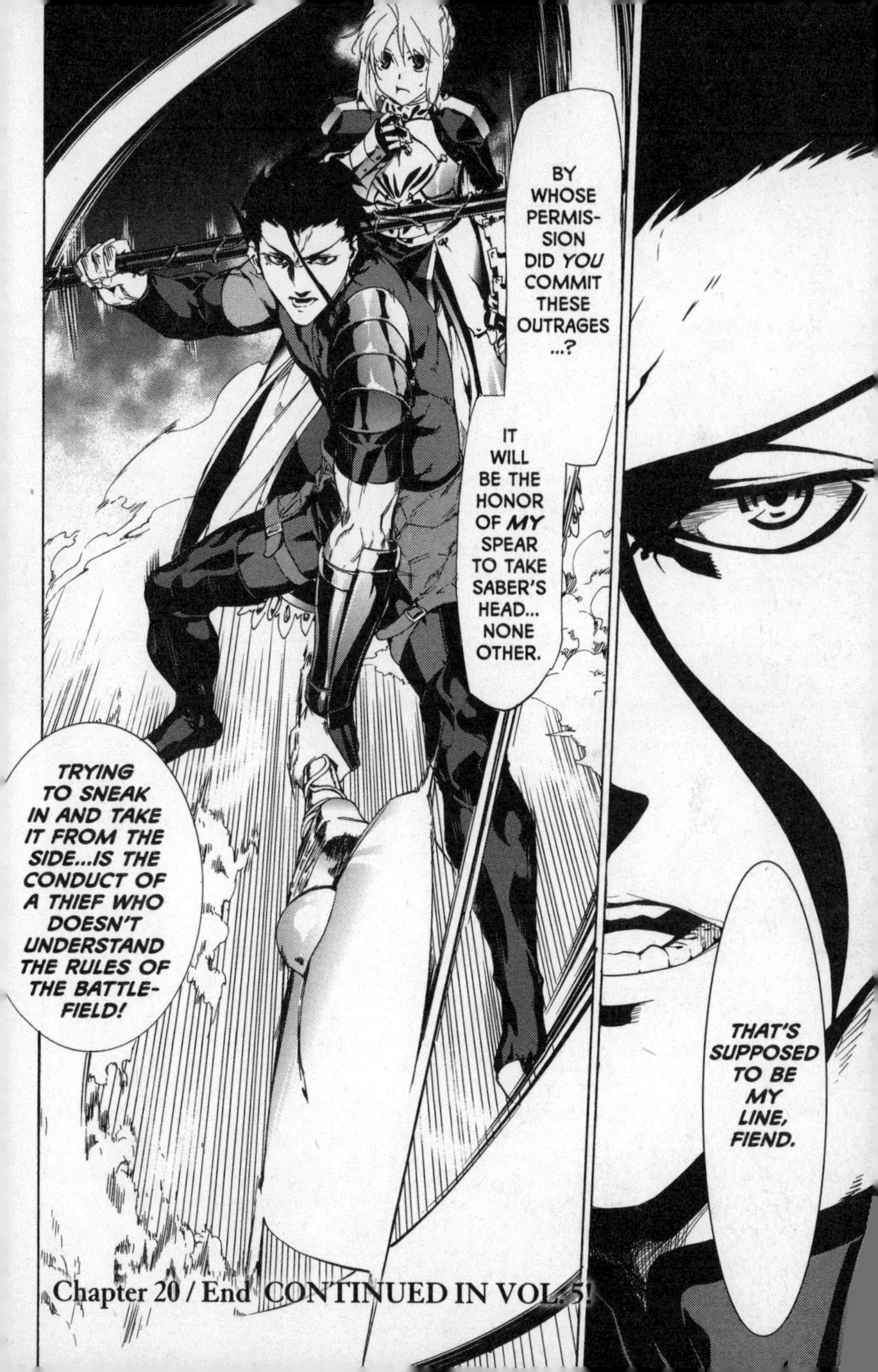
BY WHOSE PERMISSION DID YOU COMMIT THESE OUTRAGES ...?
IT WILL BE THE HONOR OF MY SPEAR TO TAKE SABER'S HEAD... NONE OTHER.
TRYING TO SNEAK IN AND TAKE IT FROM THE SIDE...IS THE CONDUCT OF A THIEF WHO DOESN'T UNDERSTAND THE RULES OF THE BATTLEFIELD!
THAT'S SUPPOSED TO BE MY LINE, FIEND.
Chapter 20 / End CONTINUED IN VOL. 5!

Fate/Zero
フェイト／ゼロ

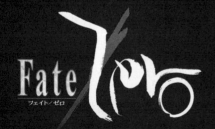

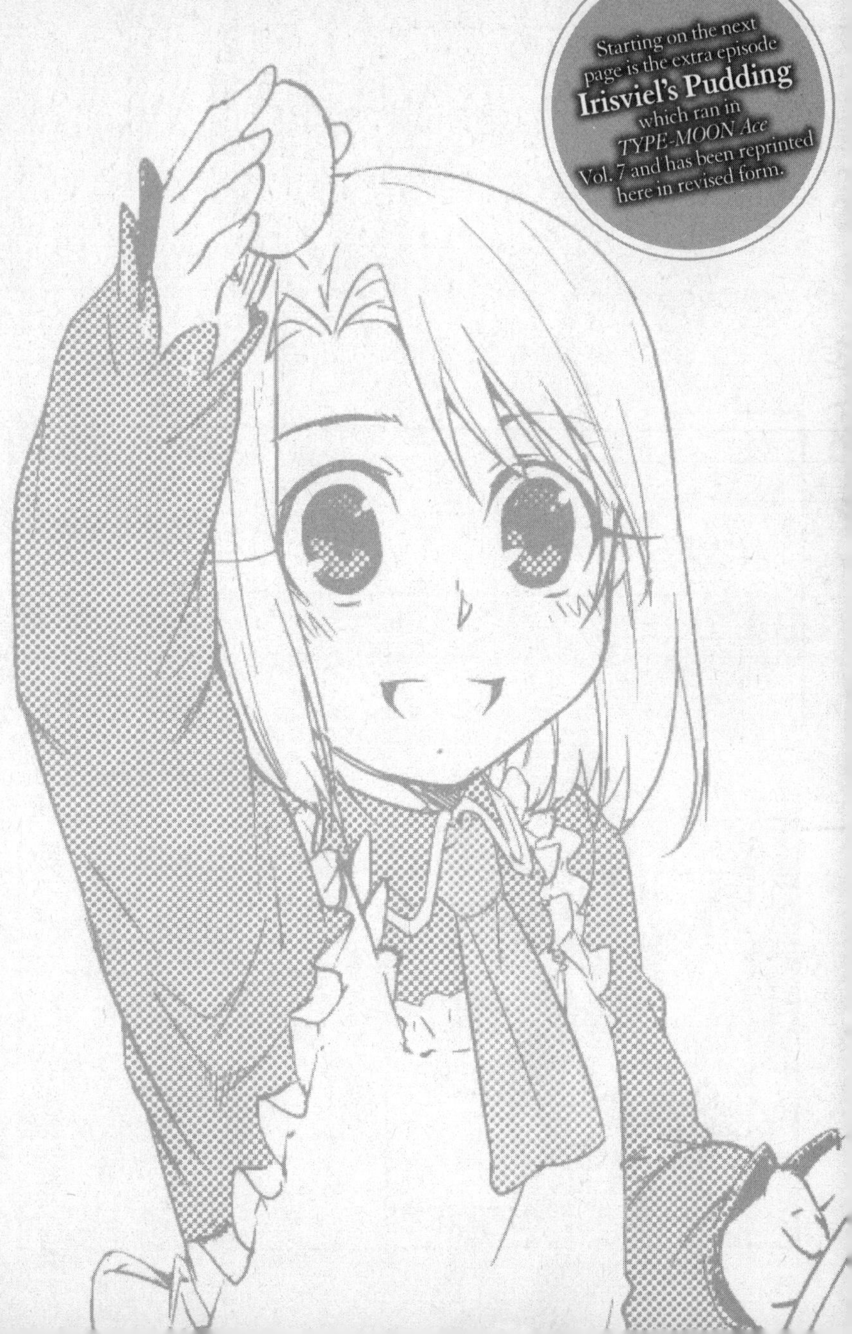
Starting on the next page is the extra episode
Irisviel's Pudding
which ran in *TYPE-MOON Ace* Vol. 7 and has been reprinted here in revised form.

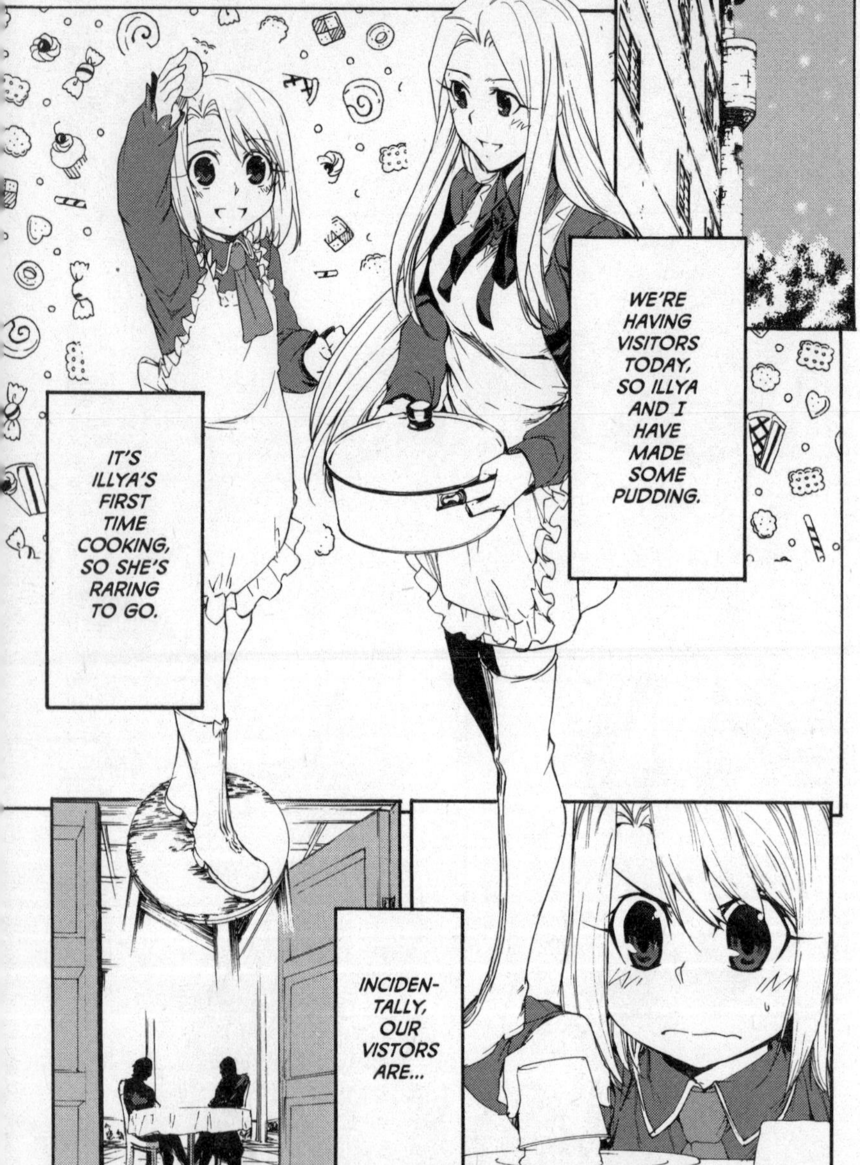
WE'RE HAVING VISITORS TODAY, SO ILLYA AND I HAVE MADE SOME PUDDING.
IT'S ILLYA'S FIRST TIME COOKING, SO SHE'S RARING TO GO.
INCIDEN-TALLY, OUR VISTORS ARE...

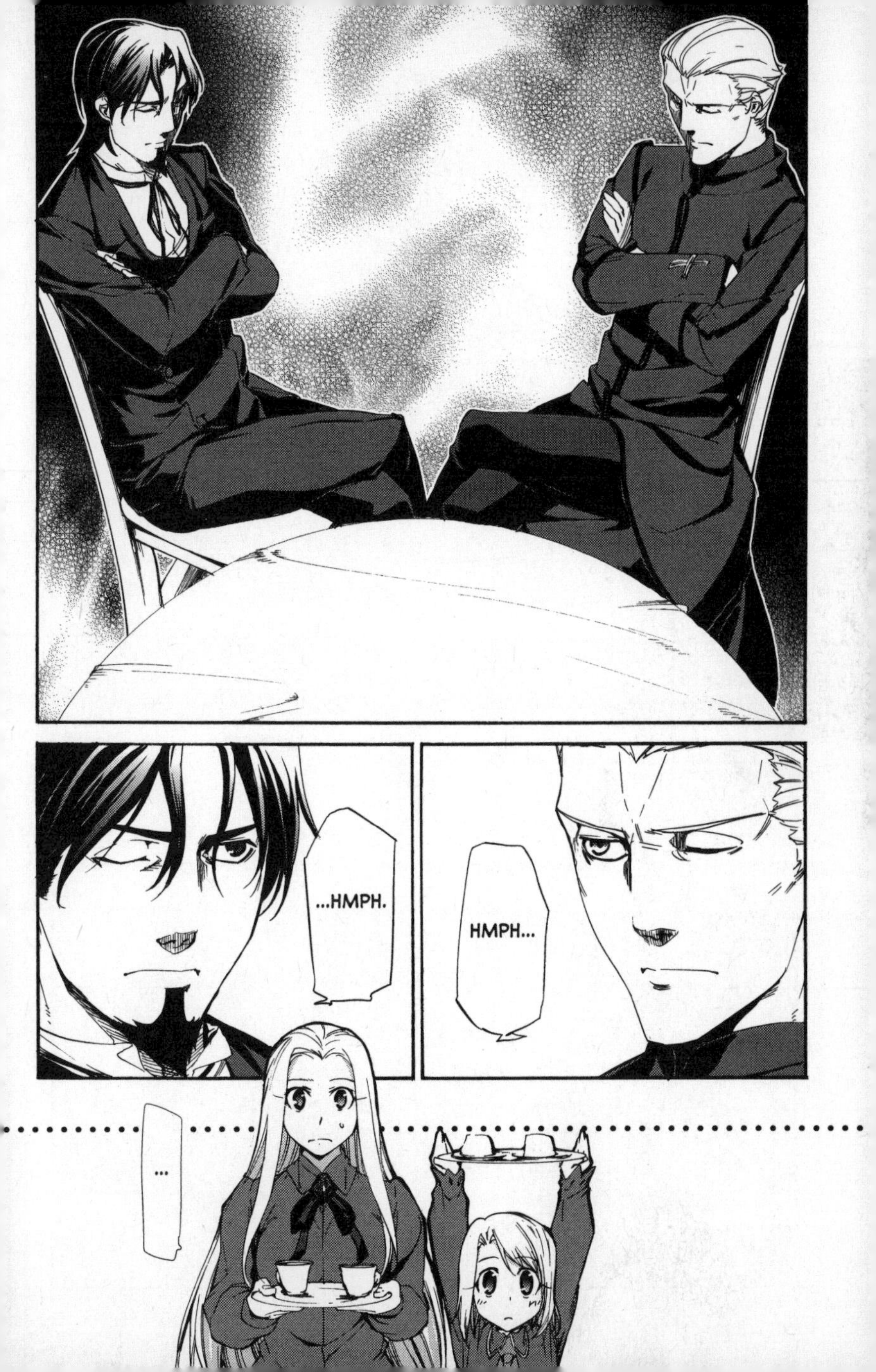
HMPH...
...HMPH.
...

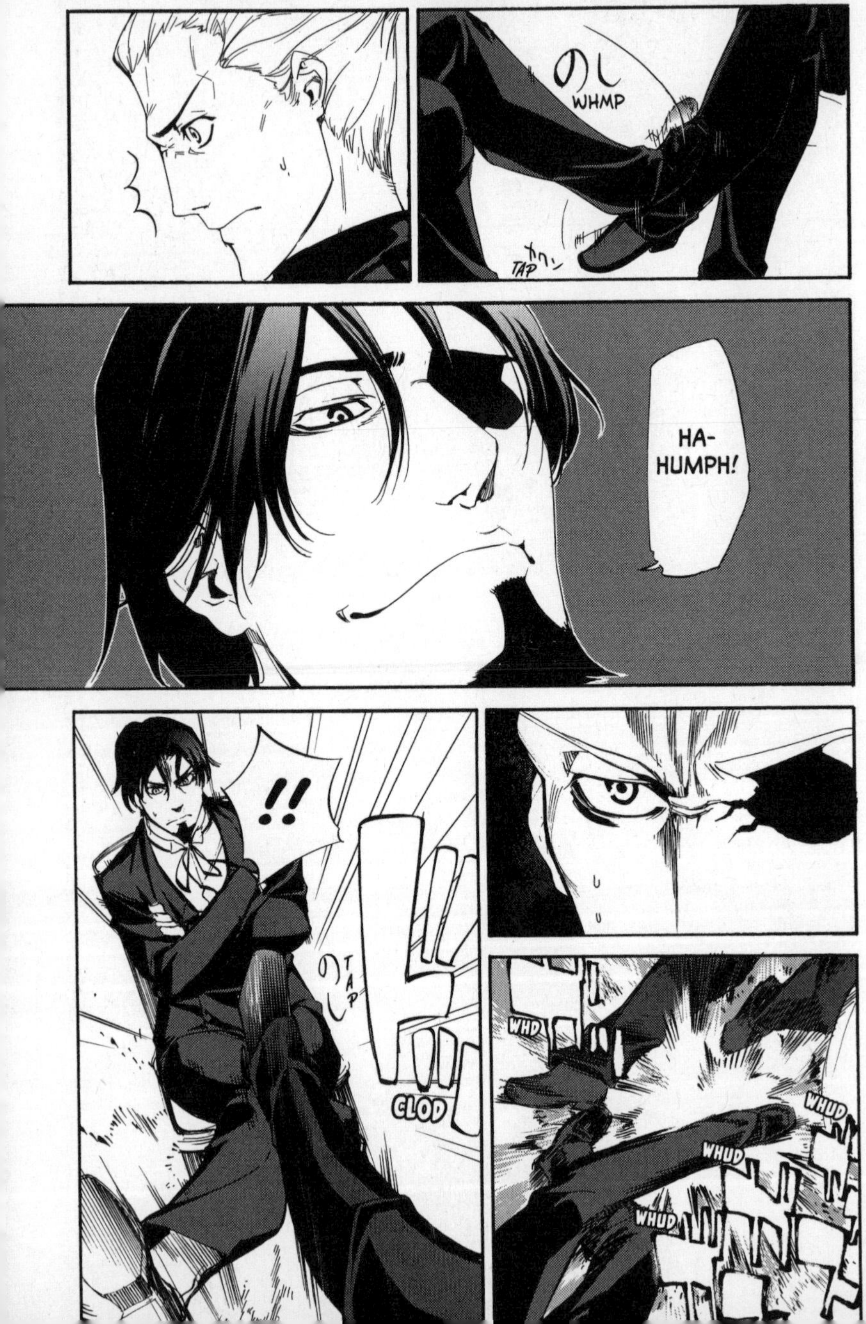
のし
WHMP
カツン
TAP
HA-HUMPH!
WHD
WHUD
WHUD
WHUD
!!
のし
TAP
CLOD

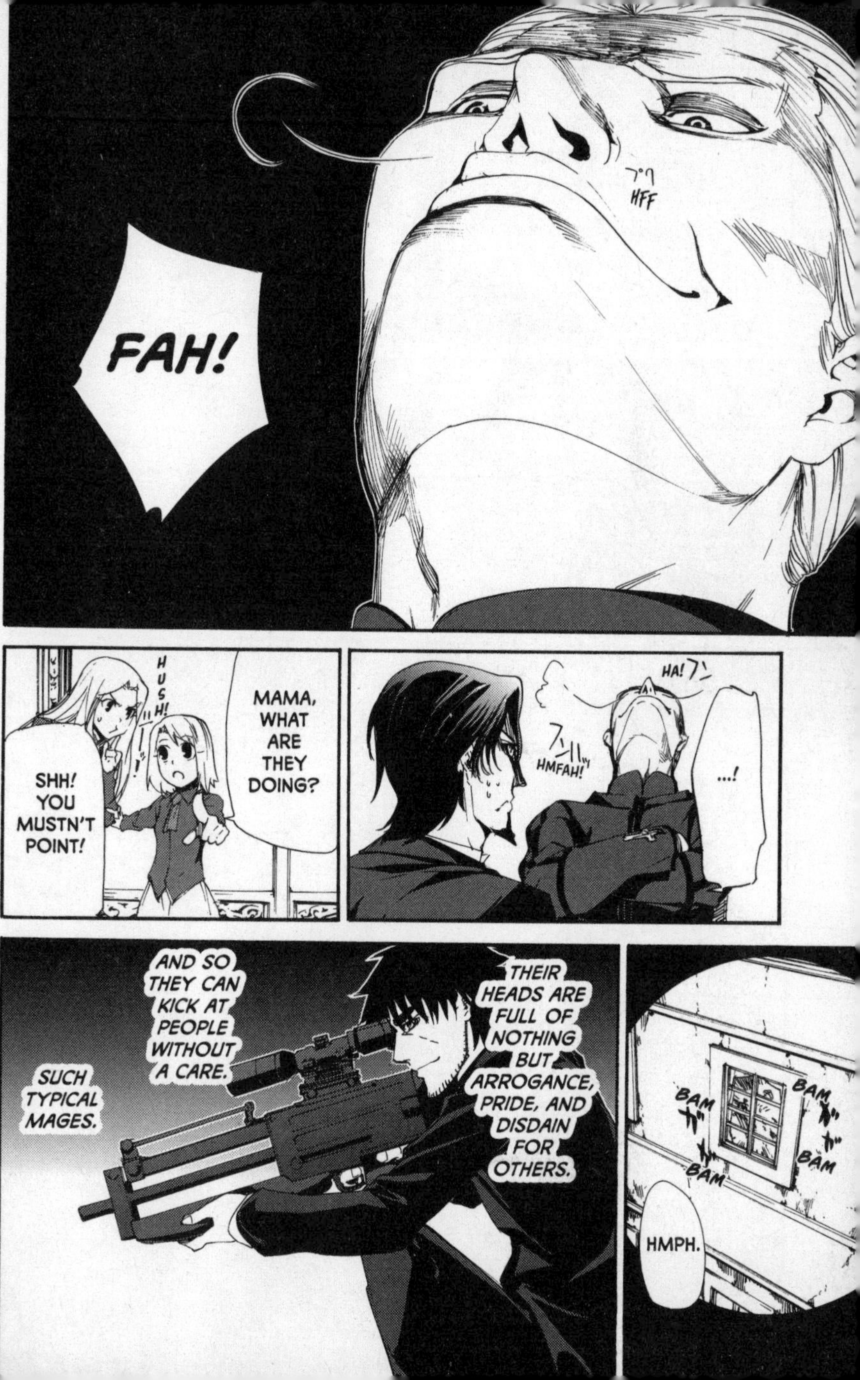
HFF
FAH!
HA!
HMFAH!
...!
MAMA, WHAT ARE THEY DOING?
HUSH!
SHH! YOU MUSTN'T POINT!
BAM
BAM
BAM
BAM
HMPH.
THEIR HEADS ARE FULL OF NOTHING BUT ARROGANCE, PRIDE, AND DISDAIN FOR OTHERS.
AND SO THEY CAN KICK AT PEOPLE WITHOUT A CARE.
SUCH TYPICAL MAGES.

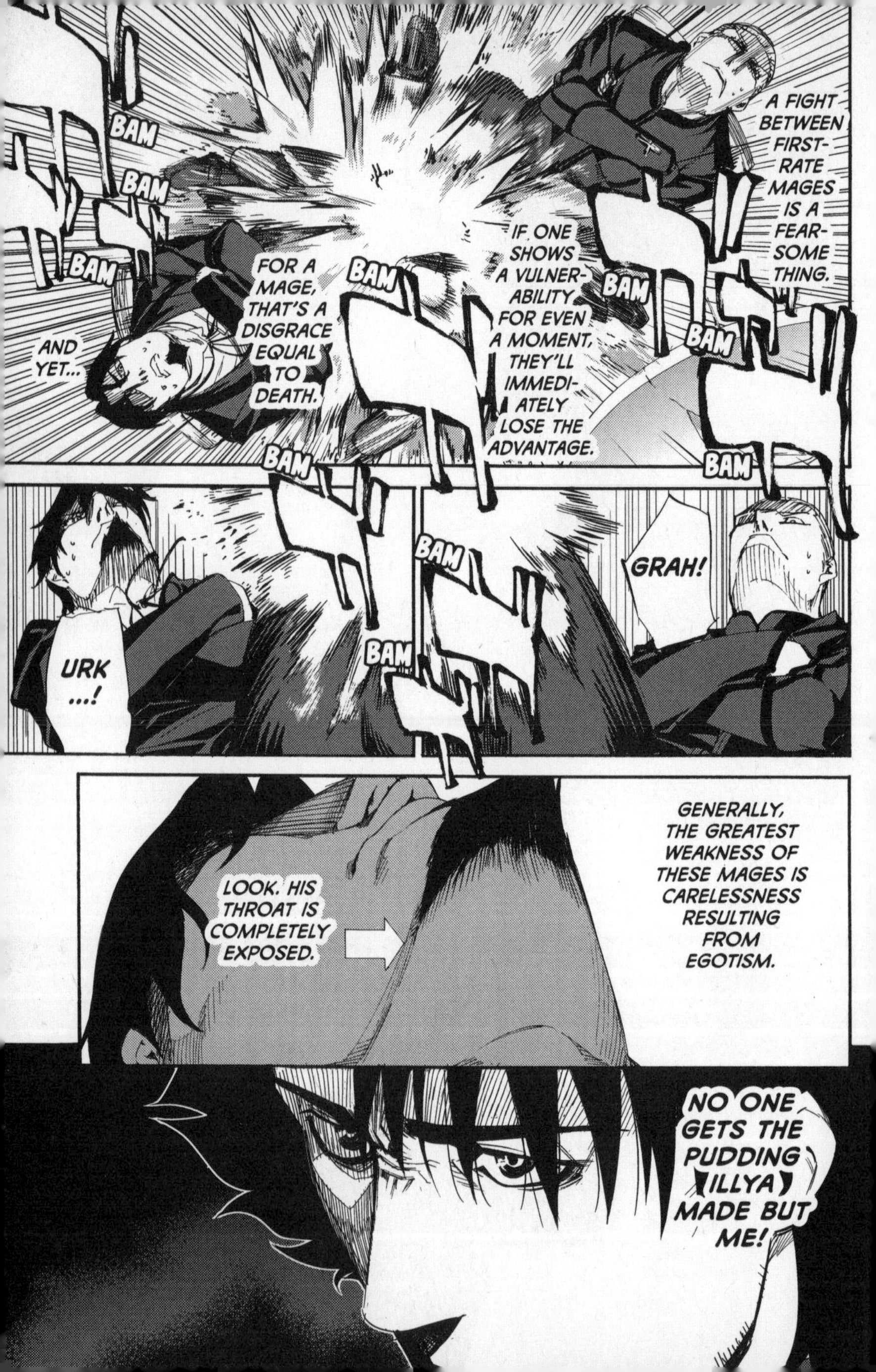
A FIGHT BETWEEN FIRST-RATE MAGES IS A FEARSOME THING.
BAM
BAM
BAM
BAM
IF ONE SHOWS A VULNERABILITY FOR EVEN A MOMENT, THEY'LL IMMEDIATELY LOSE THE ADVANTAGE.
BAM
FOR A MAGE, THAT'S A DISGRACE EQUAL TO DEATH.
BAM
BAM
BAM
AND YET...
BAM
GRAH!
BAM
BAM
URK ...!
GENERALLY, THE GREATEST WEAKNESS OF THESE MAGES IS CARELESSNESS RESULTING FROM EGOTISM.
LOOK. HIS THROAT IS COMPLETELY EXPOSED.
NO ONE GETS THE PUDDING ILLYA MADE BUT ME!

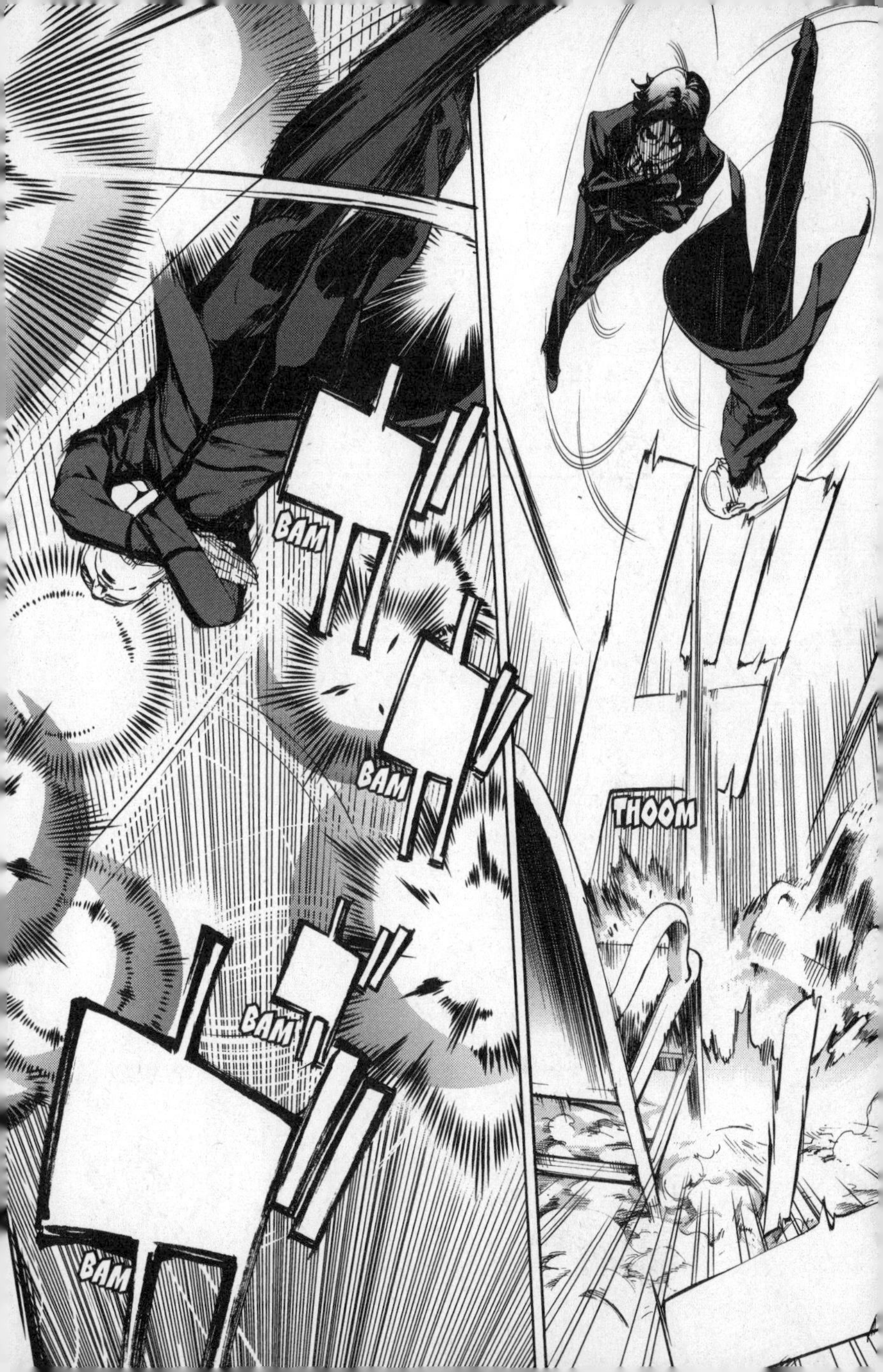
THOOM
BAM
BAM
BAM
BAM

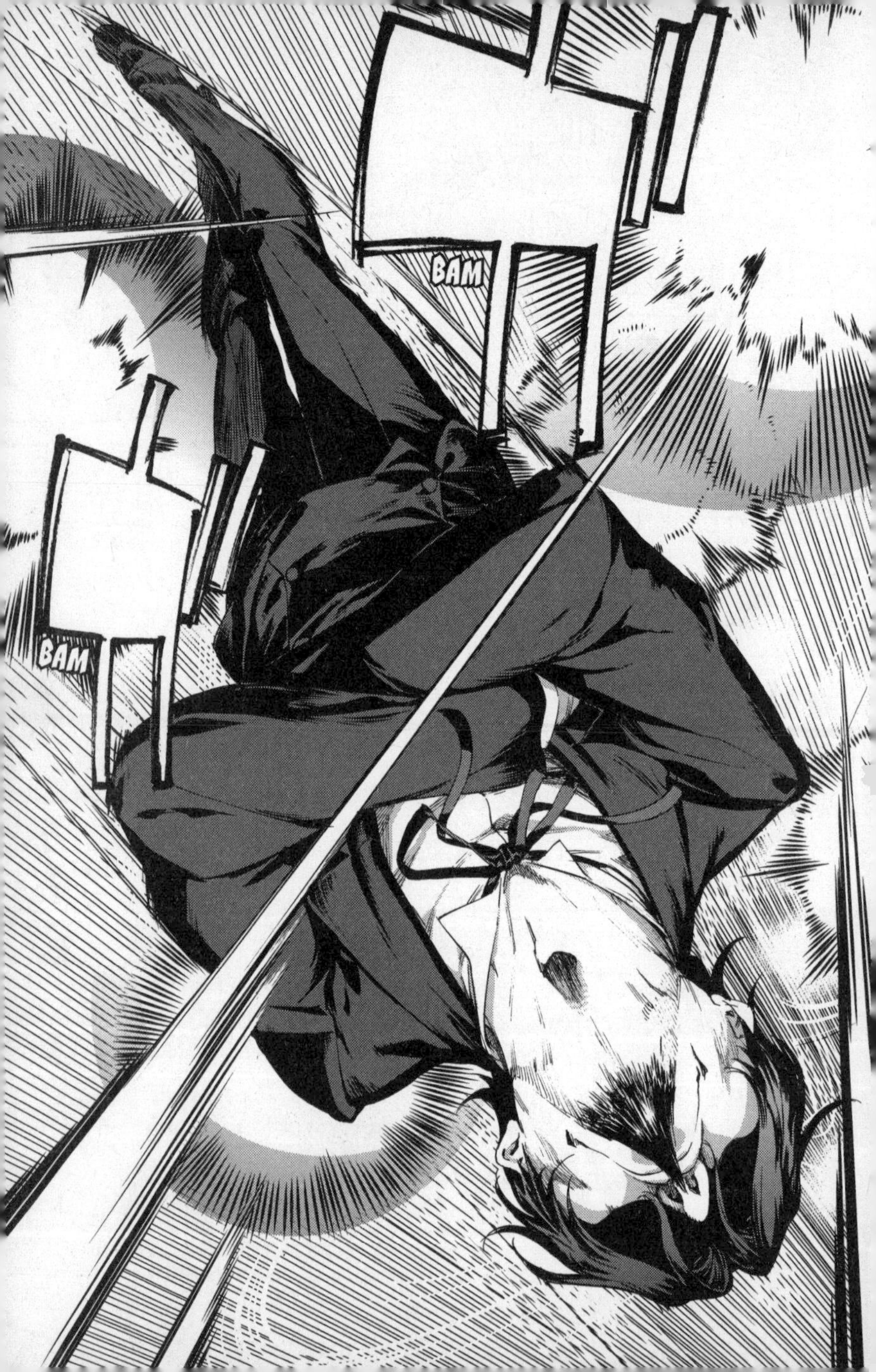
BAM
BAM

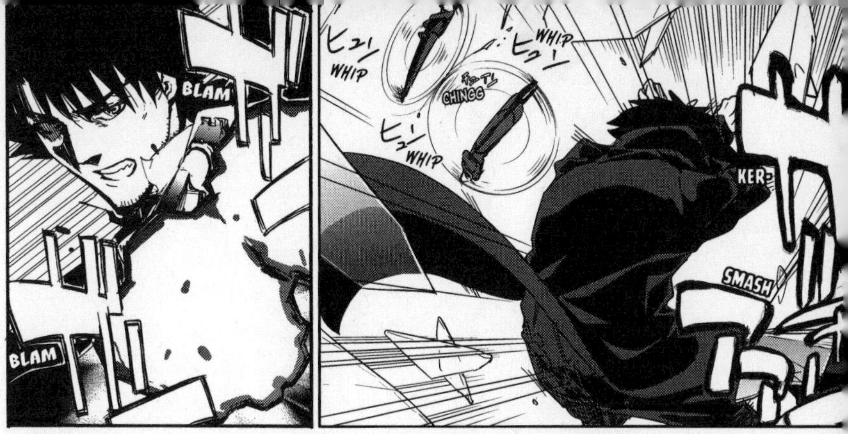
WHIP
WHIP
CHINGG
WHIP
KER-
SMASH
BLAM
BLAM

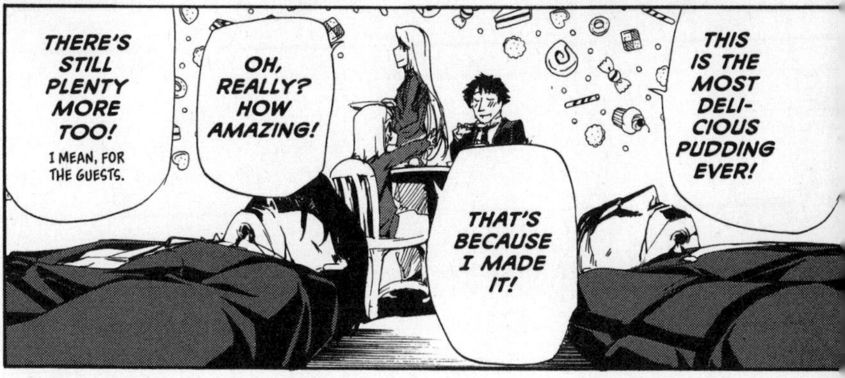
THIS IS THE MOST DELI-CIOUS PUDDING EVER!
THAT'S BECAUSE I MADE IT!
OH, REALLY? HOW AMAZING!
THERE'S STILL PLENTY MORE TOO! I MEAN, FOR THE GUESTS.

TEN YEARS LATER

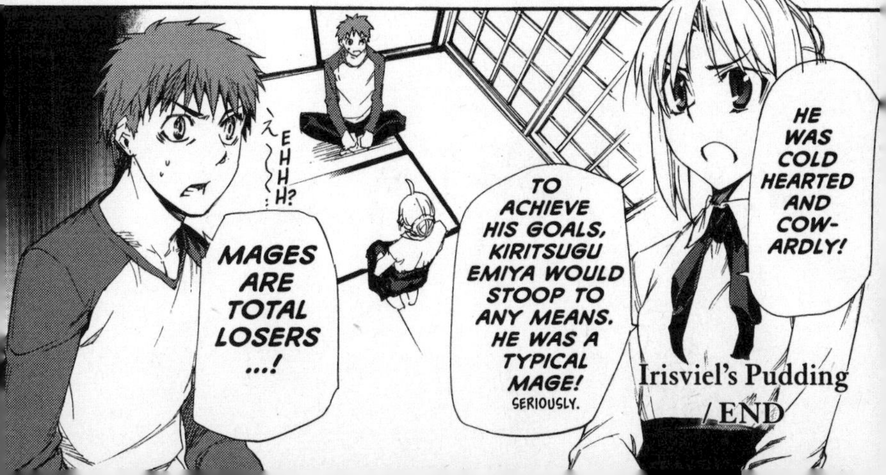
HE WAS COLD HEARTED AND COW-ARDLY!
TO ACHIEVE HIS GOALS, KIRITSUGU EMIYA WOULD STOOP TO ANY MEANS. HE WAS A TYPICAL MAGE! SERIOUSLY.
EHHH?
MAGES ARE TOTAL LOSERS ...!
Irisviel's Pudding
/ END

Special thanks to original-edition staff members Nishikiyama Maru, Haruno Eri, and Ayano Takahiro.

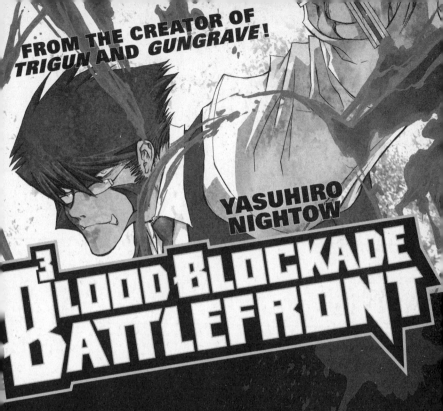

FROM THE CREATOR OF
TRIGUN AND *GUNGRAVE*!

YASUHIRO
NIGHTOW

³LOOD BLOCKADE BATTLEFRONT

Three years ago, a gateway between Earth and the Beyond opened over New York City. In one terrible night, New York was destroyed and rebuilt, trapping New Yorkers and extradimensional creatures alike in an impenetrable bubble. New York is now Jerusalem's Lot, a paranormal melting pot where magic and madness dwell alongside the mundane, where human vermin gather to exploit other-worldly assets for earthly profit. Now someone is threatening to breach the bubble and release New Jerusalem's horrors, but the mysterious superagents of Libra fight to prevent the unthinkable.

Trigun creator Yasuhiro Nightow returns with *Blood Blockade Battlefront*, an action-packed supernatural science-fiction steamroller as only Nightow can conjure.

VOLUME ONE
ISBN 978-1-59582-718-0 | $10.99

VOLUME TWO
ISBN 978-1-59582-912-2 | $10.99

VOLUME THREE
ISBN 978-1-59582-913-9 | $10.99

VOLUME FOUR
ISBN 978-1-61655-223-7 | $12.99

VOLUME FIVE
ISBN 978-1-61655-224-4 | $12.99

VOLUME SIX
ISBN 978-1-61655-557-3 | $12.99

VOLUME SEVEN
ISBN 978-1-61655-568-9 | $12.99

DARK HORSE MANGA

AVAILABLE AT YOUR LOCAL COMICS SHOP OR BOOKSTORE To find a comics shop in your area, call 1-888-266-4226 For more information or to order direct: • On the web: DarkHorse.com
E-mail: mailorder@darkhorse.com • Phone: 1-800-862-0052 Mon.–Fri. 9 AM to 5 PM Pacific Time.

NEON GENESIS EVANGELION

ark Horse Manga is proud to present new riginal series based on the wildly popular *Neon Genesis Evangelion* manga and anime! Continuing the rich story lines and complex characters, these new visions of *Neon Genesis Evangelion* provide extra dimensions for understanding one of the greatest series ever made!

NEON GENESIS EVANGELION
Campus Apocalypse

STORY AND ART BY MINGMING

VOLUME 1
ISBN 978-1-59582-530-8 | $10.99

VOLUME 2
ISBN 978-1-59582-661-9 | $10.99

VOLUME 3
ISBN 978-1-59582-680-0 | $10.99

VOLUME 4
ISBN 978-1-59582-689-3 | $10.99

NEON GENESIS EVANGELION
COMIC TRIBUTE

STORY AND ART BY VARIOUS CREATORS

ISBN 978-1-61655-114-8 | $10.99

NEON GENESIS EVANGELION
The Shinji Ikari Detective Diary

STORY AND ART BY TAKUMI YOSHIMURA

VOLUME 1
ISBN 978-1-61655-225-1 | $9.99

VOLUME 2
ISBN 978-1-61655-418-7 | $9.99

TONY TAKEZAKI'S
NEON GENESIS EVANGELION

STORY AND ART BY TONY TAKEZAKI

ISBN 978-1-61655-736-2 | $12.99

NEON GENESIS EVANGELION
THE SHINJI IKARI RAISING PROJECT

STORY AND ART BY OSAMU TAKAHASHI

VOLUME 1
ISBN 978-1-59582-321-2 | $9.99

VOLUME 2
ISBN 978-1-59582-377-9 | $9.99

VOLUME 3
ISBN 978-1-59582-447-9 | $9.99

VOLUME 4
ISBN 978-1-59582-454-7 | $9.99

VOLUME 5
ISBN 978-1-59582-520-9 | $9.99

VOLUME 6
ISBN 978-1-59582-580-3 | $9.99

VOLUME 7
ISBN 978-1-59582-595-7 | $9.99

VOLUME 8
ISBN 978-1-59582-694-7 | $9.99

VOLUME 9
ISBN 978-1-59582-800-2 | $9.99

VOLUME 10
ISBN 978-1-59582-879-8 | $9.99

VOLUME 11
ISBN 978-1-59582-932-0 | $9.99

VOLUME 12
ISBN 978-1-61655-033-2 | $9.99

VOLUME 13
ISBN 978-1-61655-315-9 | $9.99

VOLUME 14
ISBN 978-1-61655-432-3 | $9.99

VOLUME 15
ISBN 978-1-61655-607-5 | $9.99

VOLUME 16
ISBN 978-1-61655-997-7 | $9.99

VOLUME 17
ISBN 978-1-50670-083-0 | $9.99

Each volume of *Neon Genesis Evangelion* features bonus color pages,
your *Evangelion* fan art and letters, and special reader giveaways!

DARK HORSE MANGA
DarkHorse.com

AVAILABLE AT YOUR LOCAL COMICS SHOP OR BOOKSTORE
To find a comics shop in your area, call 1-888-266-4226 • For more information or to order direct: • On the web: darkhorse.com
E-mail: mailorder@darkhorse.com • Phone: 1-800-862-0052 Mon.–Fri. 9 AM to 5 PM Pacific Time.

publisher
MIKE RICHARDSON

assistant editor
JEMIAH JEFFERSON

collection designer
SARAH TERRY

digital art technician
CHRIS HORN

Special thanks to Roxy Polk, Michael Gombos, Sandy Tanaka,
Annie Gullion, and Carl Gustav Horn.

Dark Horse Manga, a division of Dark Horse Comics, Inc.
10956 SE Main Street, Milwaukie, OR 97222
DarkHorse.com

To find a comics shop in your area, call the Comic Shop Locator Service toll-free at 1-888-266-4226.

First edition: February 2017
ISBN 978-1-50670-139-4

1 3 5 7 9 10 8 6 4 2
Printed in the United States of America

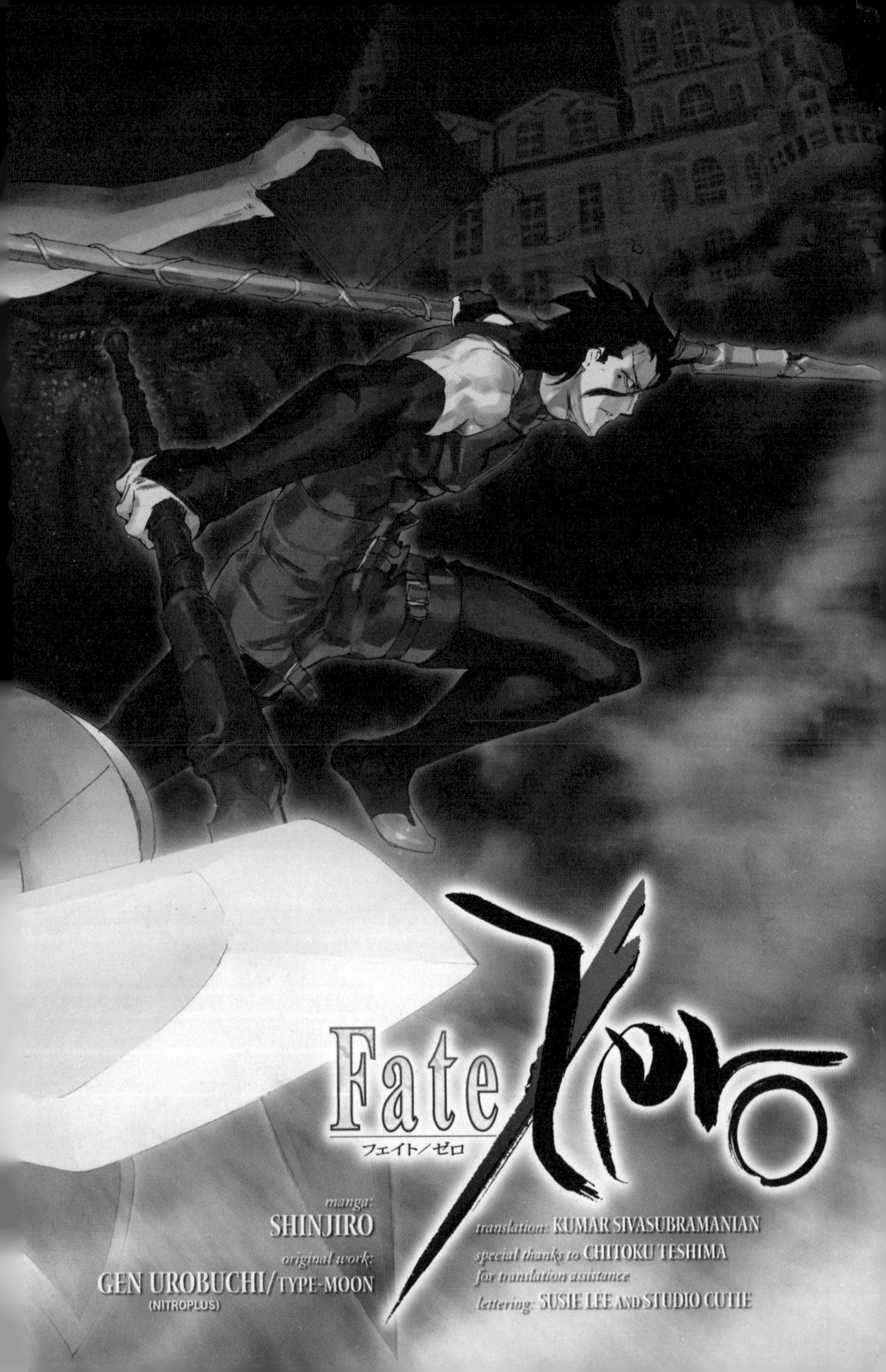
Fate/Zero
フェイト／ゼロ
manga:
SHINJIRO
original work:
GEN UROBUCHI/TYPE-MOON
(NITROPLUS)
translation: KUMAR SIVASUBRAMANIAN
special thanks to CHITOKU TESHIMA
for translation assistance
lettering: SUSIE LEE AND STUDIO CUTIE

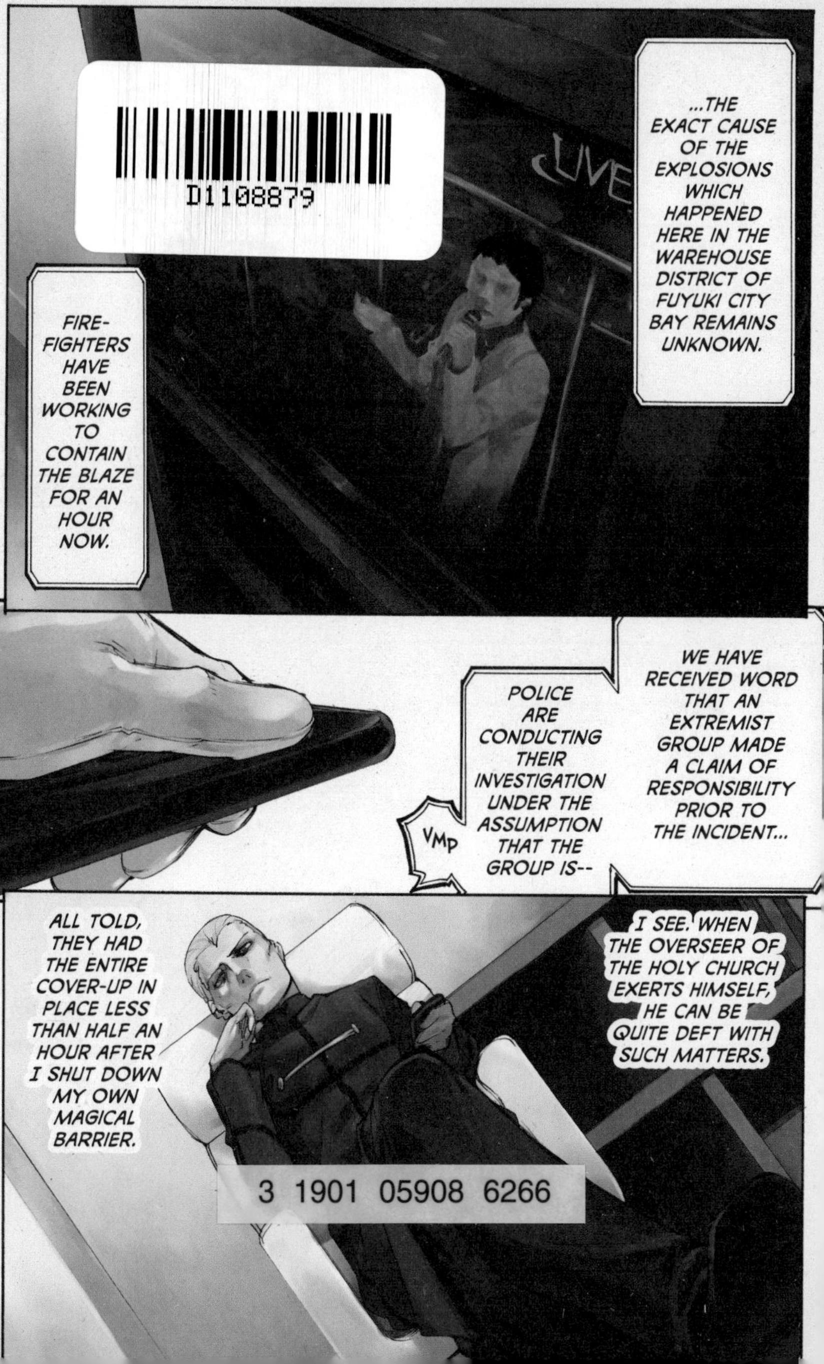
...THE EXACT CAUSE OF THE EXPLOSIONS WHICH HAPPENED HERE IN THE WAREHOUSE DISTRICT OF FUYUKI CITY BAY REMAINS UNKNOWN.
FIRE-FIGHTERS HAVE BEEN WORKING TO CONTAIN THE BLAZE FOR AN HOUR NOW.
WE HAVE RECEIVED WORD THAT AN EXTREMIST GROUP MADE A CLAIM OF RESPONSIBILITY PRIOR TO THE INCIDENT...
POLICE ARE CONDUCTING THEIR INVESTIGATION UNDER THE ASSUMPTION THAT THE GROUP IS--
VMP
I SEE. WHEN THE OVERSEER OF THE HOLY CHURCH EXERTS HIMSELF, HE CAN BE QUITE DEFT WITH SUCH MATTERS.
ALL TOLD, THEY HAD THE ENTIRE COVER-UP IN PLACE LESS THAN HALF AN HOUR AFTER I SHUT DOWN MY OWN MAGICAL BARRIER.